C4

Lost Tribes and
Promised Lands

CU00797898

BOOKS BY RONALD SANDERS

Socialist Thought (Co-edited with Albert Fried)
Israel: The View from Masada
The Downtown Jews
Reflections on a Teapot
Lost Tribes and Promised Lands

LOST TRIBES AND PROMISED LANDS

The Origins of American Racism

BY RONALD SANDERS

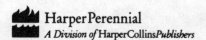
HarperPerennial
A Division of HarperCollins*Publishers*

The author is grateful to the following publishers for permission to reprint selected material as noted below:

Extracts from *Hispano-Arabic Strophic Poetry: Studies by Samuel Miklos Stern*, L. P. Harvey, editor. Copyright © Oxford University Press, 1974. Reprinted by permission of the Oxford University Press.

Extracts from *Esmeraldo De Situ Orbis* by Duarte Pacheco Pereira, edited by George H. T. Kimble, from Hakluyt Society Second Series, Number 79, London, 1937.

Extracts from *De Orbe Novo* by Peter Martyr d'Anghera, translated by F. A. MacNutt. Reprinted by permission of Burt Franklin Publishers, New York, N.Y.

Passages from *Spanish Explorers in the Southern United States 1528–1543*. 1907; reprinted 1959 (Original Narratives) by Frederick W. Hodge, with Theodore H. Lewis, editors. Reprinted by permission of Barnes & Noble Books, division of Harper & Row Publishers, Inc.

Extracts from *The Enlightened*, translated by Seymour B. Liebman. Copyright © 1967 by University of Miami Press. Reprinted by permission of the University of Miami Press.

Extracts from *The Spanish Inquisition* by Henry Kamen. Copyright © 1965 by Henry Kamen. Reprinted by arrangement with The New American Library, Inc., New York.

Date Tree poem by Abd-er-Rahman in R. A. Nicholson: *A Literary History of the Arabs*. Reprinted by permission of the Cambridge University Press.

The poem "When Thy Father Went A-Hunting," translated by Nora Chadwick, from Nora Chadwick: *The Celts* (1970) p. 123. Copyright © The Estate of Nora Chadwick, 1970. Reprinted by permission of Penguin Books Ltd.

A hardcover edition of this book was published in 1978 by Little, Brown and Company. It is here reprinted by arrangement with Little, Brown and Company.

LOST TRIBES AND PROMISED LANDS. Copyright © 1978 by Ronald Sanders. Foreword copyright © 1992 by Michael Dorris. All rights reserved. Printed in the United States of America. No part of this book may be used or reproduced in any manner whatsoever without written permission except in the case of brief quotations embodied in critical articles and reviews. For information address HarperCollins Publishers, Inc., 10 East 53rd Street, New York, NY 10022.

HarperCollins books may be purchased for educational, business, or sales promotional use. For information, please call or write: Special Markets Department, HarperCollins Publishers, Inc., 10 East 53rd Street, New York, NY 10022. Telephone: (212) 207-7528; Fax: (212) 207-7222.

First HarperPerennial edition published 1992.

Designed by Christine Benders

LIBRARY OF CONGRESS CATALOG CARD NUMBER 91-50535

ISBN 0-06-097449-4

92 93 94 95 96 MB 10 9 8 7 6 5 4 3 2

Once again, for Beverly

Table of Contents

Foreword to the
HarperPerennial Edition
by Michael Dorris

LOST TRIBES AND PROMISED LANDS is a tidal wave of fresh ideas. It invites us to forget all the simplistic formulae we thought we knew about "The Age of Discovery," and in the process, it revolutionizes the way we understand the mechanics of cultural interaction. Sweeping across three centuries—the fifteenth through the seventeenth—it leaves the landscape of the past cleaner, brighter in the sun, less obscured by clutter. A book that combines meticulous scholarship with bold speculation, it is, first and foremost, an extended discourse on the origins and consequences of ethnocentrism. Unencumbered by footnotes or pedantic jargon, Ronald Sanders makes of history a vibrant symphony, full of melody and subtlety, a synthesis woven together into a marvelous, plausible whole.

Sanders argues that in culture-contact situations expectation has been at least as important as reality in shaping a perception of "the other." The Eurocentric cosmology of the Middle Ages already presumed to know everything of importance. There was one God, one creation, one chain of linked events that led from the Garden of Eden to the present. The world was a circus with a single center ring, and that was firmly and permanently occupied by Caucasian Christians. Those who were defined as "outsiders,"

Copyright © Michael Dorris 1992

be they Iberian Moors or Jews or sub-Saharan Africans, were infinitely more comprehensible if they were squeezed into preexisting categories: the children of Ham, infidels, the enemies of Christ. Emerging countries on the European frontier, such as Spain after the reconquest, achieved legitimacy by purging their populations of diversity, thus affirming the fiction of social and religious homogeneity. The unexpected appearance of America was a further complication: Native Americans, not forecast by revelation, *couldn't* be simply themselves, but must either be "lost tribes" or, even easier, not human at all. If the latter were the case, after all, the lands they occupied were technically empty, "promised" to Europeans.

The issue of discovery was—and, five hundred years later, continues to be—a complex and identity-threatening debate on all sides. The predominant currency, forged initially in fifteenth-century Europe and subsequently exported to all parts of the globe, was the "modern" notion of race: the self-serving belief that skin pigmentation signifies relative entitlement or subjugation, that societies can be ranked and ordered according to the physical characteristics of their inhabitants, and that there is an absolute and immutable scale on which people and institutions originating in Europe and Europe's colonies will always by definition outdistance the competition.

Lost Tribes and Promised Lands carefully chronicles the origin and evolution of this view, but Ronald Sanders is never strident, never polemical. In the best tradition of even-handed presentation, he trusts that the facts will speak for themselves. An accomplished writer, he vividly portrays the personalities of such principal actors as Christopher Columbus and Bartolomé de las Casas, Hernán Cortes, John Smith, and Squanto. We come away with a sense of having heard their explanations for behavior and attitude, having listened to their justifications and rationalizations, having observed them within the context of their time and circumstance. We better understand why they did what they did, and why they didn't see what they didn't see.

Even more fascinating is Sanders's demonstration of the impact of chance, coincidence, and accident on eventual outcome. Cortés arrived in Mexico on a day and from a direction that conformed to a long-standing and favorably anticipated Meso-American prediction; by happenstance, the populations of the Western Hemisphere were widely susceptible to Old World diseases, and occasional misunderstandings of apparent etymological similarities encouraged self-fulfilling prophesies: *Carib*, the name of a West Indian language group, sounded to some Spaniards like *canis*, the Latin word for dog, which seemed to confirm the lower, "savage" status so convenient for guiltless extermination. And, when treated like dogs, the Caribs quite logically responded in kind.

The history of contact is punctuated by constant confusion, mistaken identity, and erroneous impulse. Even a minor event, if it occurs early enough, can initiate a pattern, create ripples of interaction that are nearly impossible to unlearn or undo. The only real inevitability in the clash of Europeans with the rest of the world's inhabitants, Sanders implies, was a period of chaos leading inexorably toward oppression. The particulars grew out of individual psychology, precedent or imagined precedent, fear, and competition.

Lost Tribes is a book of heroes and lost souls. Each chapter is crammed with information, insight, and speculation, yet this is a text that reads like a magnificent novel, full of episode and drama, the absurd and the violent. In its clear and persuasive interpretation of how spurious and inflexible theories of race came to shape national and international policy, it is an especially seminal—and explosive—work.

In retrospect, it seems impossible that fifteenth-century Western Europe could have maintained its grandiose self-image as the center of the universe. How could a small corner of the Eastern Hemisphere resolutely assert that *it* was all that mattered, just as navigators and overland explorers began to bring back stunning reports of places and civilizations never before imagined? This paradox, this juxtaposition of a blind insistence on the smallness of the world despite the wonder of growing, spectacular refutation, demanded one of two philosophical responses: either Europe must amend its mental geography by incorporating new data and view itself as part of a marvelously heterogeneous planet, or it must somehow devise a way for knowledge to expand while the boundaries of possibility remained the same. The second choice was the easiest, the safest. The status quo endured, to the short-term benefit of a few seafaring nations. It is now our difficult challenge to deal with the ongoing and dangerous consequences—and the first step is to acknowledge the past.

Preface

T͟H͟E͟ ͟P͟E͟R͟S͟P͟E͟C͟T͟I͟V͟E͟ ͟T͟H͟I͟S͟ ͟B͟O͟O͟K͟ provides on the genesis of American racial history down to about 1700 may turn out to be both longer and wider than the reader anticipates. In the end it is centered upon the future United States, but its point of departure is in the Mediterranean more than a hundred years before the New World was discovered, and it includes a good look at the Portuguese and Spanish conquests along the African coast and in America, with even a side glance at the French overseas adventures, before falling at last upon the fledgling English colonies. The ethnic history is multiple, taking in Blacks, Indians, Jews, and the white Christian dominators themselves, as well as some others, because it is the book's underlying premise that the questions it deals with can best be understood as elements in a broad social drama in which all these groups come together as the principals. But the drama also ranges through a perhaps startling variety of subject matters, including aspects of the history of geographical thought and of religion in the age of the Renaissance and the Reformation. The various strands keep coming together in the end, however, and though I hope the reader's patience may each time be appeased along the way by the interest each of them yields for its own sake, their final significance will always prove to be in the formation of the story as a whole. The book is a complex fabric, but it is a unified work that should, in its entirety, yield some fresh insights into problems of race relations and ethnic identity that are still with us today.

Although the text should largely account for itself, some additional explanation may be in order here for my having brought in the Jew as one of the protagonists in a racial history. It will be asked: are the Jews a race? As a preliminary reply, I must point out that to this day we do not even know precisely what is meant by the word *race*, which came into being only in the era taken in by this book. Indeed, it is one of the book's aims to show that, essentially, a race is whatever a wide consensus takes to be such in a given time and place. In the nineteenth century, the Jews often were referred to as a "race" by Jew and gentile alike, with no unfavorable connotation intended. To be sure, the word was sometimes so widely applied as to be all but meaningless. But at other times it has narrowed down to a deadly precision, and in two of the most notorious of such instances — in Nazi Germany, and in Spain and Portugal during the era that concerns us — the Jews have been victims of a violent and destructive racism. The question about the Jews as a race is therefore answerable only in terms of the most qualified historical relativism: occasionally people have thought them such. But the point, in connection with this book, is that just as any study dealing with racism in the twentieth century would have to examine the case of the Jews in Germany among others, so also must this study take in the case of the Jews and the *conversos* in Spain and Portugal.

This having been said, however, it must be added that the role played by the Jew in this book is not just that of one among several actors in a comparative racial history. For though he disappears from view for long stretches, he is in a sense the main protagonist. This is so not on any grounds of ethnic prejudice or favoritism, but out of artistic and philosophical necessity. I have attempted in this work to penetrate beneath the surfaces of data upon which so many learned works settle, and to achieve an understanding that I will dare to call poetic. There is a constant effort here to perceive realities as much as possible from within, an effort that is facilitated, of course, whenever I can make use of literary records left by the actors themselves. Now, in the case of two of our main characters — the Black and the Indian* — such firsthand written material does not really exist from this period. We are forced, for the most part, to adopt the viewpoint of the oppressive but highly articulate white man. But this does not mean we are entirely lacking in literary testimony from the view-

---

* The exception provided by the accounts written in the sixteenth and seventeenth centuries by Mexican Indian scribes and historians under Spanish tutelage, discussed in Chapter 16, is much too qualified by the Spanish influence to alter the point being made here.

point of the racial outsider; for in the Jew we have a special case. He is at once one of the dominators and one of the victims. As a European, he has left records as rich as those of the general culture he represents — indeed, he has done more, for we shall find him taking a central place among the bearers of a vision out of which the American experience first emerged. But as an outcast, he has given a voice to the otherwise silent sufferers from racial oppression in that epoch. Moreover — what is perhaps the most important point — he represents the sole vehicle whereby the author, a Jew himself, can legitimately place his own intuition into the midst of the things described here.

A few words should be said on technical matters. Many writers using English sources from the sixteenth and seventeenth centuries are fond of reproducing quotations in their original spelling, but I have not shared in this inclination. There is no point to it here, either on grounds of quaintness, which would merely be distracting, or of a scholarly exactitude that would be appropriate to a source book, which this is not. (It is appropriate to reference notes, however, and in those I have used the original spelling.) But, on the other hand, I have tried to be pedantic on a less conventional issue. The nuances of this book have made it seem necessary to me that I capitalize the word *Black*, contrary to the prevailing usage, when it refers to a specific people, and to put it in lowercase when I am referring to persons of that color no matter what their origin or habitat. In other words, I have written it as "Black" whenever it has seemed to me an exact synonym for what is meant by the less current term "Negro." As a matter of fact, there are numerous places where, to avoid ambiguity, or for other reasons — such as the fact that it was the very term being used by the authors discussed in some passages — I have used the latter word. Some readers may find it objectionable, but it was, after all, legitimate for many years, and it remains a difficult word to avoid in a history of this sort.

— Ronald Sanders

New York and Putney, Vermont
June, 1977

LOST TRIBES AND
PROMISED LANDS

Prologue
The Catalan Atlas

Hast thou perceived the breadth of the earth?
Declare if thou knowest it all.

Job 38:18

OUR STORY CAN find its beginning with the coronation of Charles VI of
France in the fall of 1381. This, as it happened, was a fairly dismal
moment in French history. Charles at thirteen was king in name only,
under the sway of ambitious uncles; the French popes at Avignon, after
having enjoyed predominance for the better part of the century, had
recently been challenged by a restored papacy in Rome; and hostilities
had just been resumed with England in a new phase of what we now call
the Hundred Years War. The future was to be worse. Charles would go
mad and, as all readers of Shakespeare know, suffer defeat at Agincourt
and the loss of his crown to Henry Plantagenet.

But it is not this larger history that concerns us here; rather, we shall
focus our attention narrowly on one of the gifts received by the young
king in honor of his elevation to the throne. It was the Infante Juan of
Aragon who presented to Charles the remarkable object that can provide
us with a backdrop, as it were, to the opening scenes of our own particular history. A gift to dazzle the eye, it was neither gold, nor precious
gem, nor fine fabric, nor even a work of art in any conventional sense,
though art it certainly was among other things. Aragon, at this moment
in the ascendant as a commercial and shipping power on the Mediterranean, had become a preeminent breeding ground for many of the skills

that went with this status, and one of these was map-making. What Juan had given Charles, then, in evident eagerness to show off some of the unique capacities of his realm, was a map.

This may seem rather common coin for a king, until we realize that in the fourteenth century, long before the world's physiognomy had become as firmly established in men's eyes as the shape of a wheel, cartography was still a fledgling science buried in a creative art, and every map was an original effort of craftsmanship and of the imagination. It can even justly be said that map-making was nothing less than an art form in the best traditions of the Renaissance, a simultaneous quest for beauty and for scientific truth that explored the mysteries of geography — and, often enough, of anthropology — as Florentine painting did those of anatomy and perspective. There were maps that ranked among the most beautiful creations of the age. But all this having been said, a special place must still be accorded to the creation sent to Charles by Juan of Aragon on this occasion; a French national treasure to this day, it is surely the most splendid map of all time.

Made in about 1375 on the island of Majorca, an Aragonese possession, by the Jewish cartographer Abraham Cresques, the map is actually an enormous atlas of the world as then known. It is painted and inscribed on twelve vellum leaves — four of which are given over to a cosmographical text with tables, the rest to the world map — and mounted on boards in such a way that it could be closed or opened out like a folding screen, nearly twenty feet long and more than two feet wide. Covered with illustrations often reminiscent of the miniatures in the celebrated books of the Duke of Berry, one of Charles's domineering uncles, and with inscriptions written triumphantly in the native language of Aragon and Majorca — which is why the map is now generally known as the Catalan Atlas — it is a synthesis for the age, of information and gorgeous display. In one sense, it is an extended miniature in the French manner, providing a decorative glimpse of the wide world through pageantry appropriate to a fourteenth-century coronation; in another sense, it is a *summa geographica,* giving in microcosm a definitive picture of the universe as of 1381.

That universe still hardly comprised anything more on earth than what the Greeks had called the *oikumene,* the "inhabited world" as they understood it. Essentially, this was Europe, Asia, and North Africa, surrounded by an ambiguous assortment of islands; any hints of Africa south of the Sahara, of the Americas, or of the rest of the world as we know it belonged to the realm of myth and conjecture rather than that of reasonably exact science. Not that tradition was wholly lacking in inklings gathered from actual experiences of the outer regions, but these, such as they were — some recorded, though inadequately, others forgotten for all time — had been too few and scattered, and above all too vague, to add up to a solid body of accumulated knowledge. There were maps enough in the Middle Ages, and written narratives as well, that dealt abundantly with marvels, monsters, and unverified landmasses hovering beyond the *oikumene*, but things of this sort were not the business of the Catalan Atlas, which was a scientific work. Of course, science still also meant the astrology that forms a large part of its four leaves of cosmographical text, as well as touches of theology and eschatological speculation, as we shall see. But the fantastic was largely eschewed by the Catalan map-maker.

This caution does not, however, extend to the exotic; on the contrary, the burden of the illustrations and inscriptions on the Catalan map lies toward the outer reaches of the *oikumene*, where the cartographer can show off his special knowledge, gleaned from the most venerable as well as from the most up-to-date reports, with the greatest possible impact and color. He has covered Asia and Africa with pictures of camels, giraffes, elephants, exotic birds, and precious gems of various sorts, and with appropriate inscriptions that mingle wonderment with a good sense for commercial possibilities. "There are animals here which have the name 'Lemp,' from whose leather shields of good quality are made," we read at one place in the northern Sahara, or, way off to the East: "In the Indian Ocean there are 7,548 islands, containing marvelous riches that we cannot enumerate here, as well as gold and silver, spices and precious stones."

But the interest is above all human, one can say anthropological, and the map abounds in figures representing mankind outside of Christendom in a breathtaking variety of his estates and activities. In the western Sahara, not far from a cluster of tents, a veiled Tuareg rides his camel over the desert sands; farther east, a naked pygmy prods a giraffe; in the Arabian desert, outside Mecca, a Muslim pilgrim kneels in prayer; in the Indian Ocean, two nude men fish by hand; somewhere in Persia, the three Magi ride on horseback in the direction of Bethlehem; and north of them, on the steppes of Central Asia, is a splendid caravan — camels, horses, and men marching toward the fabled Cambaluc, ancient capital of Cathay. This represents the expedition led by the family of Marco Polo, out of which came the classic of medieval travel literature that, among its other glories, served as a major source for the newer information embodied in the Catalan Atlas.

Yet, for all this variety, the main human emphasis on the map is royal. The foremost recurring figure is that characteristic motif of late Gothic art, the monarch enthroned. Appearing in more than a dozen places in Asia and Africa, with few variations in their conventionalized pose but many in their physical appearance and dress, these figures alone constitute a subtle essay in fourteenth-century anthropology. There are two queens, one in "Arabia Sabba," the Biblical Sheba, the other on an island "realm of women" in the Indian Ocean. Some of the kings wear turbans and burnooses, while others are dressed more like European kings, with three-pointed crowns on their heads. Some rulers in the Far East have yellowish complexions and almond eyes. And there are two black kings, one in Africa and the other beyond India, on the semimythical island of Taprobana. These are of special interest for the story that is to follow, so we shall spend a further moment or two examining them here.

The black king in West Africa, bearded and draped in an austere, un-decorated robe, is one of the most regal figures on the map. He carries a scepter in one hand and a large gold nugget in the other, and wears a sizable three-pointed crown. He alone of all the kings is shown in profile, a view which tends to emphasize his stateliness, and which also clearly outlines the Negroid conformation of his nose and lips. These, along with his hair and complexion, are treated with striking care and fidelity to type. The inscription next to him reads:

> This Negro lord is called Musa Mali, lord of the Negroes of Guinea. This king is the richest, the most noble lord in all this region on account of the abundance of gold that is gathered in his land.

We are seeing, then, an imaginary portrait of Mansa Musa, who reigned from 1307 to about 1332 as king of Mali, the ruling empire of that region as Ghana had been before it. In 1324 Mansa Musa had gone on a pil-grimage to Mecca, which made him into a legendary figure in the Chris-tian as well as in the Muslim world; riding through North Africa in a procession that included some five hundred slaves, each one carrying a staff of pure gold, he had bestowed glittering gifts wherever he went. During his lifetime, he made some effort at turning Timbuktu into a capital of world renown, hiring a celebrated architect from Moorish Spain to design buildings for it, and inviting scholars from all over the Muslim world to reside there. It was said that he personally possessed the largest gold nugget mankind had ever seen, and it is to this that the Catalan Atlas pays tribute in its portrait of him. In general, what is being honored here is the trans-Saharan trade, then flourishing, which brought gold and other commodities to the Moorish cities of North Africa and thence into European markets. It brought Black slaves as well, but not yet in such quantities as to darken the glitter of gold showing forth from that region.

The second figure of black complexion on the map, whose features do not seem to be Negroid at all, is far more perplexing and ambiguous. This is true even of his domain, which is an island placed beneath Asia at the southeasternmost corner of the *oikumene* and reaching beyond the edge of the map into unknown parts of the Ocean Sea. The medieval inexactitude of this area, which characterizes the whole easternmost section of the map, stands in striking contrast to the precision of the western sections, especially the Mediterranean region. We are out at the frontiers of discovery and of European knowledge, where supposition and rumor must necessarily come to the fore. The second black king's island domain is called "Trapobana" here on the Catalan map, but the more widely used form of the name was "Taprobana," which recurred frequently through ancient and medieval literature, and may often have referred either to Ceylon or to Java. It is clear, however, that the Catalan mapmaker — and other learned men before him — meant by the name something larger and farther east than either of these two islands: the possibility that they had some dim vision of Australia or even of South America cannot be excluded.

The Catalan inscription on "Trapobana" describes it as "the last island of the Indies" and goes on to say that its inhabitants are "a people different from any other. On some of the mountains of this island there are men of great stature, that is, some sixteen feet tall, like giants, who are very black, and without rational faculties. They eat white strangers whenever they can." Oddly enough, this description — even including the exaggerated height of the inhabitants — is not at all unlike accounts brought back by explorers of the southern seas some one hundred and fifty years later, especially by those who had been along the southeastern coastline of South America. Are we getting here some glimpse of the New World, however vague and tentative?

The two black kings of the Catalan Atlas tell us something about the European vision of the darker races of mankind in that era. In one case, the vision takes in an Old World relationship, with an African race that has been known to Europeans since antiquity, and achieves a certain clarity; in the other case, it makes out only the dimmest outlines of a relationship yet to come. There are misperceptions on both sides: the brilliant golden light in which the African is seen softens the dark shadows of servitude that will soon become predominant, and the haze that obscures the man of the New World allows only the terrifying to come through and not enough of the idyllic elements that will also form part of his myth. To some extent, the two figures will even change places with one another in generations to come, as we shall see. But the essential thing here is a sense of the passage from an Old World to some new one still barely understood, and from a waning era into one that is newly dawning. Indeed, this is the essence of the entire Catalan Atlas, which is as decisive a single work as can be found to dramatize the closing of the Middle Ages and the beginning of the modern era.

To understand this point more clearly, we must glance briefly at the traditions of cartography out of which this work came. Broadly speaking, there are two traditions that produced it, one of medieval origin and divinely oriented, the other of more ancient lineage and purely empirical in character. True to our own notion of the Renaissance, the "modern" elements in the Catalan Atlas stem largely from the latter, but this, it should be pointed out, was not the celebrated Ptolemaic tradition at all. The geographical teachings (as distinguished from the astronomical ones) of the second-century Alexandrian Greek Claudius Ptolemaeus, known to posterity as Ptolemy, were not to have a revival in Europe until the following century, but this was not entirely to the disadvantage of the Catalan map-maker. Ptolemy's most important contribution to cartography was the concept of latitude and longitude, but these could not have been applied with any reasonable accuracy by a fourteenth-century map-maker even had he wanted to use them. Skilled navigators were making roughly correct latitudinal readings, at least within the confines of the Mediterranean, but an exact approach to latitude in wider oceans and lesser-known regions would not be achieved until the invention of the astrolabe at the end of the fifteenth century. As for longitude, this remained the merest guesswork until well into the eighteenth century. And without the element of latitude and longitude, Ptolemy's geography tended to be a reactionary force, positing an enclosed Indian Ocean and an unbroken landmass stretching roughly — to use our own anachronistic frame of reference — from South Africa to Australia, and thence to the Malay Peninsula.

Rather, the cartographical tradition which descends from antiquity into the Catalan Atlas is that of the so-called portolan charts. Actually, at their earliest origins in unknowable Mediterranean antiquity, these were not charts at all, but detailed handbooks of sailing directions. Such a handbook was called a *periplus* by the Greeks, and we have some specimens of these, but there undoubtedly were earlier counterparts among the Phoenicians and probably their predecessors as well. By the time of the *portolani*, the equivalent handbooks of medieval Italy — none of which have survived — the accumulated data of untold centuries must have been so detailed that one could probably have drawn from them fairly good maps of various segments of coast. But it was not until the introduction of the magnetic compass into Europe at around the end of the eleventh century that it was possible to render all the data into useful maps of the entire Mediterranean region. Our earliest surviving specimen of a portolan chart dates from 1300 — though they certainly were being made long before then — and its profile, not only of the Mediterranean, but also of the Black Sea at one end and the adjacent Atlantic coast at the other, looks almost as if it could have been copied from an atlas of today. This was scientific achievement for the best of reasons: practical use.

Though he did not apply the concept of latitude and longitude, the portolan chart-maker was not without a system of coordinates; indeed, the one he used was better suited than the Ptolemaic for the relatively limited portion of the earth's surface that he dealt with — for the classic portolan took in only the Mediterranean and its environs. The portolan system was essentially a network of overlapping compass faces, centered at various significant points and usually extending beyond the limits of the chart. From each center, the rhumb or directional lines radiated out over the map to form crisscrossing patterns with lines from other centers, establishing numerous points that could thus be exactly triangulated, and also incidentally creating rhythmic patterns that remain part of the aesthetic enchantment of the surviving portolans.

This was really too unwieldy a system to be applied on a world scale; but when the Majorcan school arose in the middle of the fourteenth century as an offspring of the migration of skilled Italians to the new Aragonese centers of Mediterranean commercial preponderance, its cartographers set out to do precisely that. The Catalan Atlas was not the first Majorcan map to try applying portolan principles to the entire known world, covering the *oikumene* and beyond with crisscrossing compass lines, but it was the most ambitious in the attempt. In this way, a scientific aim becomes a spiritual assertion: the Catalan map-maker sees the whole world, known and yet to be known, as a Greater Mediterranean. We should recognize this as the viewpoint of generations to come, and understand their attitudes accordingly.

But to talk about spiritual assertion is to enter the domain of the second of the two main cartographical traditions that flow into the Catalan Atlas, the purely medieval one of the *mappamundi*. The term, of course, simply means "map of the world," but the tradition designated by it is not so prosaic as this modern translation sounds. Prior to the advent of the Majorcan school, map-makers of empirical bent were not even inclined to try doing the whole world, so far as we know. The whole world, unlike the domain of the portolan chart-makers, was a mystery; and this means that for the Middle Ages it was the domain of theologians. The medieval *mappamundi* was usually the work of a man of religion, and wrought for divine purposes.

As a matter of fact, before the Majorcan school, the basic pattern around which the *mappaemundi* — from the smallest schematic drawings to the largest and most elaborate paintings — were built was not a scientific grid system but a Christian symbol: the cross. It was convenient for this scheme that all *mappaemundi* were drawn freehand and usually quite imaginatively, but nevertheless the cross pattern was not entirely without grounds in geographical reality. We must remember that medieval maps were oriented from top to bottom in an east-west, rather than in our north-south, direction. Now, picture an *oikumene* oriented in this way, framed somewhat more tightly than the one on the Catalan Atlas, and in such a way that Jerusalem stands at its very center, in accordance with pious convention. The Mediterranean thus begins just below the center and flows westward to the bottom of the map, approximating its true shape in the most sophisticated of these maps but often seeming to be hardly more than a river and, in the most naïve versions, a straight line or very close to it. On the earliest and crudest *mappaemundi* still extant, a thus simplified Mediterranean can be quite clearly perceived as the vertical bar of a large letter T, the horizontal of which is formed by the two longest rivers of the known world, the Nile and the Don, going off respectively southward to the right and northward to the left. On the more complex *mappaemundi* of the later Middle Ages, this scheme is less vividly apparent, but it is nonetheless always there.

In the pious scheme as described thus far, only the upper vertical has been missing to complete the image of a fully defined cross. But we must view this part of the picture in slightly different terms. On the original cross, that upper vertical was dominated by the head of Christ, and on the *mappaemundi* it is the domain of conformations that are of a character more spiritual than earthly. The terrestrial paradise was located there, for example, and most of the maps depict this in one way or another, sometimes quite elaborately, with Adam and Eve, walls, gardens, and the four rivers that flow out of Eden according to the second chapter of Genesis. On some maps, the head of Christ is placed in this area instead, making the symbolism more explicit; a few maps have both Christ and the terrestrial paradise. One of the most beautiful and ambitious of all the *mappaemundi,* the Ebstorf map, which was done in about 1235 and was in the shape of a circle more than ten feet in diameter, had in its uppermost, eastern sector both the terrestrial paradise and the head of Christ, and elaborated on the latter with a remarkable decorative device. The head was at the topmost curve of the circumference, and, corresponding to it, drawn disembodied at the other three directional extremes of the map, were the left hand, the right hand, and the two feet. This was indeed the great world cross made manifest.

The *mappamundi,* then, turns out to be a striking example of the medieval passion for totality, of the unique ability possessed by serious minds in that era to find spiritual universes in the world of objects, or at any rate to demand of that world that it assemble itself according to the highest truths. In this respect, there are interesting parallels between the *mappamundi* and that most majestic of all products of pious medieval craftsmanship, the cathedral. For the interior layout of the Romanesque and Gothic cathedrals is similar to the Christian cartographical scheme of the world not only in also being patterned on the cross but in other respects as well. One enters through the western portals as if through the Pillars of Hercules (or Strait of Gibraltar), passing from a world as wide and turbulent as the Ocean Sea into the secure enclosure of the *oikumene*. A serenely flowing nave leads like the Mediterranean to the Jerusalem of the structure, the altar, which is accessible to all pilgrims, while beyond, suffused with a light worthy of a terrestrial paradise, is the apse, which only a few may enter. The entire length of the journey is adorned with configurations of stained glass, sculpture, painting, and other forms of ornamentation, all akin to the illustrations and decorations on the most ambitious *mappaemundi*. For this is a characteristic formula of the Middle Ages: an underlying simple system made complex by meaningful byways and ramifications, like the world, the universe, itself. In literary terms, the formula is essentially that of the *catalogue raisonné*, one of the basic models of medieval literature, from the Herbals and Bestiaries to the Encyclopedia of Isidore of Seville and reaching its sublime pinnacle in the *Divine Comedy* and the *Summa Theologica*.

The parallel in the respective schemes of the cathedral and the *mappamundi* also suggests a significant one in the histories of their development. For the transition from Romanesque to Gothic, which began between the First and Second Crusades, is in one respect a transformation in the geographical spirit, from one of pilgrimage to one of crusade, from the relative repose of the Romanesque nave to the dynamism, the headlong rush toward the altar, of the Gothic. Similarly, in the *mappaemundi*, the earliest stark and simple T-shaped drawings give way to such huge, complex, and, as it were, Gothic works as the Ebstorf map. And in the late Gothic of the Catalan Atlas we can see the forms of yet another stage in the evolving geographical spirit, that of commercial expansion, which has superseded that of crusade. A relative secularization, or at any rate de-Christianization, has set in and has not merely abandoned the pious symbolism of the traditional *mappamundi* but, more significantly, transmuted it.

This change is most dramatically evident at the two extremes of the *oikumene*, the east and the west, now at the right and left instead of the top and bottom. For at the farthermost east of the inhabited world the Catalan map gives us, not the terrestrial paradise, but Cambaluc, a Garden of Eden for worldly entrepreneurs like the Polos, presided over by the enthroned figure of the Great Khan rather than of Christ. And at the westernmost extreme, out on the Atlantic just beyond and above the

Strait of Gibraltar, we see a figure, at once decorative and useful, that nowadays seems common enough on maps but is making here its first known appearance on a world map: a compass rose. Now, if we consider for another moment the world model of the Gothic cathedral, this figure appears to be standing more or less in the position of the rose window. The change of content seems genuinely prophetic.

Not that the religious component has vanished from the Catalan map; far from it, as we shall see. But, not surprisingly in the light of its author's Jewishness, there is a noticeable detachment in it concerning Christian traditions. No more than one or two crosses appear on it, atop as many churches — this in contrast to the vast array of crosses and churches covering the typical *mappamundi*. Of the pious references that do turn up, a large number turn out to be not exclusively Christian but neutrally Judaeo-Christian in import, such as one in Anatolia showing and describing Noah's Ark. There are only two mentions of Jesus on the map, one of them quite perfunctory, the other appearing in a context that is highly ambiguous and suggestive of other than Christian meanings.

The perfunctory mention occurs in the inscription that accompanies the aforementioned drawing of the three Magi, which reads:

> This province is called Tarsia. The three wise kings went out from here, and they arrived in Bethlehem in Judea with their gifts, and adored Jesus Christ. They are buried in the city of Cologne, two days' journey from Bruges.

This turns with such startling rapidity into an advertisement for two western commercial towns (what are said to be the bones of the three Magi are still buried in Cologne Cathedral), that the mention of Jesus Christ in the context has a look of flagrant impiety. Indeed, there are other hints of impiety, and even of irony, in the scene. The star that the three kings are following, while pointing in the general direction of Bethlehem, is on closer examination oddly distant from it and much closer to Shiraz just ahead of them. Alongside this ancient Persian city, celebrated as a seat of philosophy, Cresques has written mistakenly that "here the great savant Ptolemy first invented astronomy," and the figure he uses to represent it is quite unlike any of the others used for cities on the map: it is geometrical, the walls and towers forming virtually a perfect sphere. The effect is of a citadel of classical science and reason. Is all this a sly attempt to say that the wise men of Persia may really have been more interested — or ought to have been — in stargazing of another sort than that which tradition favors, and that the first birth they honored — or ought to have honored — was that of science rather than that of Christianity?

The other mention of Jesus is in a unique sector of the map, which we have not hitherto examined. The only sector given over to material of a mythological character, it is located in the northeasternmost part of the *oikumene*, along a quite imaginary coastline that curves from northwest to southeast in a semicircle, unlike the vast peninsular extension of Siberia which actually comprises that region. On the land enclosed by this curve, we find several picturesque and elaborately drawn scenes based on apocalyptic material in the Bible and on some legends concerning Alexander the Great.

Alexander was one of the preeminent heroes of medieval tradition, and a large body of mythology came to surround him, particularly with regard to his travels and conquests at the outer limits of the known world, beyond the Indus and the Caspian. It is above all in the far northeast that he becomes a figure of Christian apocalyptic import. Here he is said to have had dealings with Satan (some traditions *identify* Alexander with Satan), and to have built an enormous wall within which he enclosed certain peoples. The traditions of the wall seem to have been founded in dim realizations of the Great Wall of China and of the Caspian Gates. The peoples enclosed, according to the predominant Christian versions, were Gog and Magog, the apocalyptic hordes from the north mentioned in both the Old and the New Testaments. "Gog and Magog" are somewhat ambiguous: in Chapter 20 of the Book of Revelation, they seem to be two nations, but Chapters 38 and 39 of Ezekiel describe a ruler named Gog of the land of Magog. Legend thrives on ambiguity, however, and the possibility of conceiving Gog as an individual commanding these barbarian armies enabled tradition to identify him with the Antichrist of the New Testament. It was therefore to be Antichrist who, at the end of days, would lead the hordes of Gog and Magog when they broke through the wall in which Alexander had enclosed them, to overrun the earth as a prelude to the Second Coming. History even provided candidates for this role from time to time, such as the Tartars in the thirteenth century.

The Catalan map presents the essential imagery and lore of this tradition. The wall is depicted, as well as Alexander himself, Satan, Gog and Magog (who are identified here as Tartars), and Antichrist. But there are peculiarities in the presentation. For one thing, the iconography is, as elsewhere on the map, rather free of explicitly Christian symbols. For another, there is an odd serenity about it all, with nothing of the terror normally to be found in Christian visions of apocalypse and Antichrist. The depiction of Antichrist is especially startling. In what is the largest and most elaborate scene on the map, we see a benevolent medieval monarch in a three-pointed crown — the only king, by the way, who is *standing*, on the whole map — holding out two branches of a golden fruit toward his followers, nobles, clergy, peasants, bourgeois, who are gathered around him in various postures of obeisance. They are surrounded by trees, flowers, and more of the golden fruit, all suggesting a domain of abundance and tranquillity.

How can this man be anything but a saviour? But there is nothing of the traditional imagery of Jesus about him; on the contrary, the inscription below the scene reads:

> Antichrist. He will be reared at Chorazin in the Galilee, and when he is thirty years old he will begin to preach in Jerusalem. And contrary to all truth he will say that he is Jesus Christ son of the living God; and it is said that he will rebuild the temple.

This second mention of Jesus on the Catalan map, then, is in a context that hardly seems Christian at all. The language is ambiguous. Only the words "contrary to all truth" suggest criticism of the Antichrist, but even these lose much of their bite in the light of their Jewish authorship. Perhaps, as a conscious ruse or out of a providential delusion, the man who is to rebuild the temple of Jerusalem will have to make some assertions "contrary to all truth" in order to be allowed to proceed, but what pious Jew of the fourteenth century would hold against him this means of achieving such an end? After all, from the Jewish point of view, even the claim for Jesus himself that he was the "son of the living God" was contrary to truth, so what did it matter if the untruth were turned as a weapon against its makers for the sake of Jewish redemption? And in any case, Jewish tradition allows for some violation of conventional morality in the time of the Messiah. For it is clearly a Jewish Messiah that Cresques has given us here, skillfully disguised.

But we must consider another relevant tradition. Many Jews, and some Christians as well, believed that the peoples walled in by Alexander the Great were not Gog and Magog, but the Lost Tribes of Israel. (Some resolved the matter by considering the Lost Tribes and Gog and Magog to be one and the same, and a few went on to conclude that the Tartars were the Lost Tribes.) The legend of the Lost Tribes goes back to the divided kingdom of Hebrew antiquity. Of the traditional twelve tribes, ten were in the northern kingdom of Israel and two, Judah and Benjamin, were in the southern kingdom of Judah. When the Assyrians conquered the northern kingdom in 722 B.C.E., they removed virtually its entire population and "placed them in Halah and in Habor by the river of Gozan, and in the cities of the Medes" (II Kings 17:6). These places are not readily identifiable, and in fact the ten tribes of the kingdom of Israel vanished from history. The fate of the two tribes of the southern kingdom, when it was finally conquered by the Babylonians in 586 B.C.E., was quite different. The people of Judah who were removed into Babylonian captivity did not lose their identity, and Jews and Judaism are to this day descended from them.

The Ten Lost Tribes were not forgotten, however. Starting almost immediately after their disappearance, with Isaiah and Jeremiah, and reaching apocalyptic heights in Ezekiel and the apocryphal Esdras, a tradition developed that the recovery of the Lost Tribes would be part of the general redemption, a central component of the messianic age. In the Middle Ages this became part of Christian tradition as well, with respect to the Second Coming. And just as there often was speculation about the date and the character of final events, so were there theories about where the Lost Tribes might be, most of these assuming that they had continued wandering eastward from their original exile to the remotest corners of the *oikumene*.

Or perhaps even beyond: on the Catalan map, near the inscription about Antichrist but farther out, on the unknown Ocean Sea beyond Asia, is yet another inscription. It reads:

> Isaiah the prophet, LXVI. "I will send those that escape of them unto the nations in the sea, into Africa and to Lydia. And to the islands far off, that have not heard of me and have not seen my glory; and they will announce my glory to the nations."*

With its vision of redemption in far-off lands, of lost tribes — perhaps the Ten Lost Tribes, perhaps some other wandering remnant of the elect — settling in new Canaans that Europeans had yet to discover, this inscription seems to be prophesying an age of discovery and of the Messiah all at once. This certainly would be in keeping with the strain of worldly messianism that has often been noted in the Jewish spirit, but it would also be more: for it comes at one of those junctures when, as with the ideas of Spinoza and of Karl Marx, that strain finds a particular resonance in the history surrounding it. The age of discovery and of racial encounters upon which we are about to embark was more secular in many of its emphases than the corresponding age of the Crusades before it, and was quite different in its religiosity, but it was scarcely less

---

* There are discrepancies between this quotation of Isaiah 66:19 and both the Hebrew and the English versions because it skips a couple of phrases for brevity, and because it is based on the Vulgate, which renders "Tarshish" as "the sea" and "Pul" as "Africa." The result, in geographical terms, is even a bit richer than the original.

religious for all that; indeed, being also the age of the Protestant and Catholic Reformations, it was perhaps the most religious epoch in European history. What we are going to see is a current running through the whole era in which the revived religiosity and the passion for discovery flow together, forming a virtual religious tradition unto itself — a tradition that, among its Protestant, Catholic, and Jewish wanderers in common, is ever in search of the promised lands of its redemption, and ever ready to determine whether the peoples found in them are themselves lost tribes or only Canaanites, to be treated accordingly. This does not begin with the celebrated case of the New England Puritans, but culminates in them, and is to be found at work, consciously or unconsciously as the case may be, from the very beginning. This is the age and the tradition for which Abraham Cresques can be perceived as a prophet.

Not without honor in his own country, however, Cresques was amply rewarded for his achievement. The king of Aragon accorded him the title of *magister mappamundorum et bruxolarum* ("master of world maps and compasses"), granted him a living from the Jewish public baths in his home city, placed him directly under royal protection instead of the normal civil jurisdiction of the Jewish community, and exempted him from the wearing of the round yellow badge that was the Aragonese form of the outward distinguishing mark that the Jews of western Europe had been required, in principle at least, to wear for well over a hundred years. Thus enjoying special prosperity and distinction amidst a Majorcan Jewish community that was already outstanding for both, Cresques lived out the remaining years until his death in 1387 in apparent peace and comfort. He even left behind him a kind of royal succession: for his son Yehuda — or Jafuda, in the Catalan form of the name — who had been his apprentice and probably helped him do the Catalan Atlas, was already on his way to becoming as great and as celebrated a cartographer as his father had been.

But Jafuda's life was to be very different; in more ways than the Catalan Atlas bespoke, a new era was indeed about to begin and an old one come violently to an end. Just four years after his father's death, Jafuda Cresques was to experience his own part in the greatest disaster that the Jews of Spain had ever known. Indeed, Spanish Jewry itself was about to become the first of the lost tribes of our narrative.

I

Master Jacome of Majorca

T HE IDEA OF RACE WAS, for better or for worse, only a dim and sporadic one to most Europeans during the Middle Ages; its outlines did not begin growing distinct until the fourteenth and fifteenth centuries. But when the dawning finally occurred, it shone with particular fury upon the Iberian Peninsula, which discovered itself in that light to contain the most racially varied society in western Europe. The results were soon to be revolutionary: "Antagonism which had before been almost purely religious," writes the historian Henry Charles Lea, "became racial, while religious antagonism became heightened, and Spain, which through the earlier Middle Ages had been the most tolerant land in Christendom, became, as the fifteenth century advanced, the most fanatically intolerant." For some two or three hundred years thereafter a large part of the history of the Iberian peoples was to be dominated by this development, in the Old World and then in the New, where they opened the way to a still more varied racial experience than they hitherto had known. They thus became the pioneers of our modern racial history in the West just as surely as they became the pioneers of European overseas colonization; indeed, after a brief prelude of racism in the Old World alone, the two roles often went hand in hand.

Until that dubious dawning Spain had traditionally been, from the cultural standpoint, not so much a part of Europe as a separate subcontinent, hanging midway between civilizations that had swept into it, now from the north, now from the south, to form a unique ingathering of peoples and religions. Even the primordial encounter between Celts and Iberians from which was distilled the first Spanish population to enter the light of history had been a meeting of Europe and Africa. So also was the fully historic encounter that took place in the third century B.C.E. between the Carthaginians, who had succeeded to the hegemony established in the south of the peninsula centuries before by their Phoenician forebears, and the Romans, who had similarly succeeded to the earlier Greek preponderance in the north. Like the First Punic War, which had pitted these two Mediterranean imperial powers against one another in Sicily — in some ways a smaller, insular counterpart to Iberia — the Second in effect sought a decision as to whether the contested region was thenceforth to be European or African.

This struggle and its outcome established a pattern that was to be repeated in the Middle Ages with the Arabs in the role of the Carthaginians. The Roman victory in the Second Punic War brought Spain into the orbit of Latin Europe, but not necessarily to the complete effacement of that other cultural strain that had come up from Africa and ultimately traced its origins to the Semitic East — not, at least, if we may judge from the persistence of place-names like Cadiz, Cartagena, and Barcelona. May we not assume that at least a few of its deposits lingered in the collective memory as they did on the map? We know that elements of the medieval Arab cultural legacy have persisted in Spain to this day, so it is quite possible that something similar happened with the ancient Carthaginian one. An ambivalence born of history, geography, and blood may well have continued to repose beneath the Romanized surface. But on that surface, at any rate, Spain was primarily and often zealously Latin for the next nine hundred years, even after the Roman hegemony there yielded to the Germanic in the fifth century C.E.; one of the greatest Latin authors of the early Middle Ages, Isidore of Seville, flourished in the seventh century under the Visigothic monarchy.

Finally, in 711, this apparent Roman-Christian idyll was violated by another tidal wave from Africa, carrying another legacy from the Semitic East — this time a militant Islam — which swept up through most of the peninsula and pushed back the remains of Visigothic rule nearly into the Bay of Biscay. There in the rough Cantabrian northwest the forces of the future *Reconquista* gathered strength for what would ultimately be another Latin triumph over this revival of the ancient onslaught from the south. But it was to take time. The Spanish Christians, desultory crusaders at best for the next three hundred years, were not to be aroused to systematic reconquest until, in the eleventh and twelfth centuries, a new wave of invasions from Africa threatened to upset the balance of civilizations that had by then become well established in Iberia. Even then, the eruption of *Reconquista* that was thereby provoked had run its course by the middle of the thirteenth century with part of the peninsula still in Moorish hands: the kingdom of Granada was not to be eliminated until 1492, in a final resurgence of *Reconquista* that had been stimulated, in part, by the new racial consciousness, and that soon showed its imperialist undertones.

Before and between these epochs of militancy, however, we can catch sight of a very different picture, which, in contrast with the simple myth of *Reconquista,* shows a quantity of friendly interchange between Christian and Muslim, and now and then a thorough cultural as well as biological mingling. Indeed, there were moments when Spain seemed ready to produce an unprecedented Latin-Arabic synthesis, a rich and unique Andalusian civilization. One can perceive this potentiality in various sectors of Spanish life in the early Middle Ages.

It manifests itself, for example, in the person of the great tenth-century caliph of Cordova, Abd-er-Rahman III. Unlike most of his Muslim subjects, who were primarily of North African Berber stock, Abd-er-Rahman III could look back upon family origins that were purely Arab as well as royal; but his blood was three-quarters European as well. Christian captive women from the north were favorites in the harems of Cordova, and not only the caliph's mother but his father's mother as well had been of this stock of "Gothic" slaves. The caliph also was European in culture to some extent, above all in speech — for though Arabic was his language of formal occasions, he spoke a Romance dialect in everyday conversation.

Another example of the potential Andalusian cultural synthesis, the dialect spoken by Abd-er-Rahman III, or variants of it, was widespread in Moorish Spain, not only among Mozarabs — Spanish Christians living under Moorish rule — but also among Muslims, many of whom were at least partly of Christian descent, and among Jews. This situation had its literary manifestations. Though Arabic poetry usually was written in the classical language, there were verse forms in Moorish Spain by the twelfth century that employed not only the Arabic vernacular, but the Romance one as well, generally written down in Arabic characters. The latter were used mainly in the refrains of certain types of Moorish troubadour poetry — whose clearly intimate relationship with the emerging Provençal poetry of the day, incidentally, is a mystery yet to be fully understood by modern scholars. These refrains, or *kharjas,* are vivid moments in the Latin-Arabic synthesis; here is an example:

Vais meu corazón de mib —
Ya Rabb, si se mi tornerad?
Tan mal meu doler li-l'habib!
Enfermo yed, cuándo sanarad?

("You are going from me, my heart — / O Lord, will he return to me? / My pain is so harsh for my beloved's sake! / He is sick, when will he get well?") The language here is clearly akin to modern Spanish, which also contains its Arabic components; but the two purely Arabic expressions — *Ya Rabb* and *li-l'habib* — are much more assertive of a Semitic penetration than anything to be seen since the completion of the *Reconquista.* Indeed, there also are other dimensions to the significance of this particular *kharja* as an example of the interpenetration of the Semitic and Latin cultures of the peninsula: for it was written by a Jewish poet, and in Hebrew characters.

It is largely owing to a set of historical accidents that we have today only one, highly ambiguous, text of a *kharja* in Arabic characters, and that the more than twenty others that survive were composed in Hebrew letters by Jews. Yet this fact does seem to symbolize the peculiarly sensitive role that Jews played at the very heart of the Andalusian cultural synthesis we are examining here. For no other group flocked so eagerly as the Jews did to the passageways between the two civilizations, providing, for example, a great many of the leading translators between the Latin and the Arabic literatures. No other group seems so representative, or symptomatic, of the ambivalent and cosmopolitan character of medieval Spain or, for that matter, of Spanish history from its earliest beginnings. It is no wonder that, when the time came for Christian Spain to rise up in anger against her own legacy of cultural and racial complexity, the Jews were the first to feel the sting.

The Jewish presence in Spain has been traced authoritatively as far back as the fourth century C.E., but it is probably more ancient than that. Spanish Jews often reached back a good deal farther to find their origins, not only to show the depth of their roots in the land but also, when occasion seemed to demand it, to absolve their line of any possible implication in the death of Jesus in faraway Palestine. Some of them identified the mysterious Tarshish of the Old Testament with the Hispano-Roman town of Tartessus, implying that King Solomon's ships could have established a colony of Israelite merchants there: this would have made the Jewish presence in Spain as ancient as that other Semitic one, the Phoenician. A more modest tradition reached back to King Nebuchadnez-

zar, and maintained that he brought some of his Jewish captives to Spain
to help establish Babylonian settlements there.[*]

But the Semitic incursion with which the Jews were most deeply
identified in Spain was the Islamic one that had burst forth in 711. Many
believed that the Jews of the peninsula had acted as a fifth column for it;
there can be no doubt that, once it had occurred, they rallied enthusiastically to its banner. This was natural, for though the Visigothic kings of
Spain had once, while they were still Arian Christians, been tolerant of
Judaism, their conversion to Roman orthodoxy in the sixth century had
turned them into the worst persecutors of Jews in all of western Christendom. Islam, on the other hand, after an initial outburst of intolerance
from the founder himself, had then developed a relationship with Judaism
that passed beyond mere tolerance to a fruitful symbiosis in some countries. This was to be particularly the case in Moorish Spain, which produced not only some of the finest works of medieval Islamic literature
but also the greatest flowering of Jewish culture since ancient times. The
instincts of those Spanish Jews who welcomed the Muslim invasion had
been entirely in their own best interest.

In the long run, a newly intolerant Christian Spain would hold this
decision severely against them, but this was far from the mood during
the period when our *kharja* was written, even though the first *Reconquista* had by that time already begun. In that period, the most severe
persecutions of Jews in Spain came not from Christians but, unwontedly,
from Muslims — from those new waves of fanatical Berber invaders, the
Almoravides and the Almohades, who had finally provoked a Christian
reconquest in earnest. El Cid, the exemplary knight of Christian Spain in
that era, welcomed Jews into his entourage, and though literature shows
him engaging in trickery in his dealings with Jewish merchants, this is
merely the sportsmanship of survival, clearly untinged by any racial or
theological vindictiveness. Indeed, he ought to have been struck by the
resemblance between himself and these wily negotiators, not only in
making deals but in larger matters as well. The Cid fought Christians as

---

[*] As with the resemblance between Tarshish and Tartessus, an etymological argument was used for this Babylonian theory: certain Castilian towns bore names, such
as Escalona, which resembled Palestinian counterparts, in this case Ascalon. Furthermore, Verse 20 of Obadiah, speaking of the Babylonian conquest, refers to "the captivity of Jerusalem, which is in Sepharad," and subsequent rabbinical writings had
identified "Sepharad" as a Mesopotamian city called "Ispamia." Spanish Jews took
this word to be a variant of "Hispania," with the result that "Sepharad" — from which
we still have the adjectives "Sephardi" and "Sephardic" for Jews of Spanish descent —
became the standard word for Spain in Hebrew writings. This passion for etymological proofs reached in other directions as well: for example, some Spanish Jews
held that "Toledo" was of Hebrew origin, derived from *toledoth*, which means "generations" and hence "history."

well as Muslims when he was not engaged in *Reconquista,* and for the
realization of his often highly personal ambitions was as ready to ally
himself with Moorish princes as with Alfonso VI; in other words, he
moved between the two civilizations of the peninsula with a facility that
was well-nigh Jewish. Perhaps it was in despair at a prevailing *cidismo*
of this sort that the more fanatical reconquerors from the north — mainly
from France, which was long the major source of Christian militance
in Spain — finally turned their sights away from the southwestern frontier
and upon the Middle East as the target for anti-Muslim crusade.

In some ways, the Cid was no more characteristic a Spaniard of his
time than was the author of our *kharja,* who was, in fact, not just an
ordinary troubadour: he was Judah Ha-Levi, the composer of some of the
greatest Hebrew poetry since Biblical times. Ha-Levi, who grew up in
Toledo in the immediate wake of its reconquest by Alfonso VI in 1085,
well knew the cultural ambiguities of the era. Living and practicing
medicine in both Christian north and Muslim south, he had three mother
tongues — Arabic, Hebrew, and the Romance dialect. Of the three, it
probably was Hebrew that came the least naturally to him and took the
greatest effort of will for him to master; but it was precisely through the
exercise of will that he ultimately sought to rise out of what he apparently considered to be an overcivilized and meaningless existence. The
vision of Zion, of a return to the historic Jewish homeland, steadily
emerged in his Hebrew poetry, and he finally set out on a journey eastward from which he never returned. It is known that he got at least as
far as Egypt, and legend has it that he reached Jerusalem and was killed
there by a Muslim sword.

Ha-Levi is considered by Jewish tradition to be one of its early
"Zionists," but his thoughts and actions can be seen to emerge from a
background that is as much medieval Spanish as it is Jewish. Spanish
history had come from the eastern Mediterranean in two directions — in
the north, from a civilization that had begun in Greece and then been
passed on to Rome, and in the south, from the Semitic cultures of the
Levant and North Africa — and by Ha-Levi's time there had arisen in
Spain a complex, twofold longing for return to the ancient sources. The
yearning to go specifically back to Zion — to Jerusalem — is a phenomenon
of the Christian culture in the age of the First and Second Crusades, into
which Ha-Levi had been brought as a child. But this culture sought to
return by the northern route, by means of, in defense of, and as a
replacement for the ancient Greek power, now represented by the decay-
ing Byzantine Empire, that had once guarded the Holy City for Christianity but had then failed in the task. On the other hand, a more generalized longing for redemption, or at least for rejuvenation, somewhere
in the east is an older Spanish tradition, which comes mainly out of the

Moorish cultural heritage into which Ha-Levi had been born; this tradition seeks the southern route.

For Muslims and Jews, Spain had been a kind of America of the Middle Ages, a frontier land at "the end of the West" (a phrase used by Ha-Levi among others) for seekers of new opportunities and refugees from persecution. But there always were Spanish Muslims and Jews, as there always have been Americans of Old World ancestry, who went on yearning for the "old country" to the east. Abd-er-Rahman I, the eighth-century founder of the dynasty that became the caliphate of Cordova — and, in a sense, as scion of the overthrown Omayyad dynasty of Damascus, Muslim Spain's original political refugee — is said to be the author of the Arabic original of these lines addressed to a date tree transplanted into Spanish soil:

> *O Palm, thou art a stranger in the West,*
> *Far from thy Orient home, like me unblest.*
> *Weep! But thou canst not. Dumb, dejected tree,*
> *Thou art not made to sympathize with me.*
> *Ah, thou wouldst weep, if thou hadst tears to pour,*
> *For thy companions on Euphrates' shore;*
> *But yonder tall groves thou rememberest not,*
> *As I, in hating foes, have my old friends forgot.*

Abd-er-Rahman's highly personal feelings later became more generalized ones in a culture that always recognized the Middle East as its source.

For Jews, these feelings were even more poignant and complex. The East was the region not only of the ancient homeland and of the more recent Babylonian centers of learning but also, in unknown regions beyond, of the Lost Tribes of Israel. During the reign of Abd-er-Rahman III, word reached the court of Cordova about the existence of a nomadic people of the Central Asian steppes called the Khazars, whose king and upper class had been converted to Judaism some two hundred years before, under circumstances that remain obscure. The caliph's first minister, Hasdai ibn Shaprut, a Jew, responded to the news by writing an excited letter to the Khazar king. Since the first reports on the Jewish Khazars had not mentioned the fact that they were converts, Hasdai thought that they might be descended from the Lost Tribes. In writing of the complex diplomatic measures he planned to take in order to get his letter conveyed across the world, he explained that he was doing all this in order to

> know the truth, whether the Israelitish exiles anywhere form
> one independent kingdom and are not subject to any foreign

ruler. If, indeed, I could learn that this was the case, then, despising all my glory, abandoning my high estate, leaving my family, I would go over mountains and hills, through seas and lands, till I should arrive at the place where my Lord the [Khazar] king resides, that I might see not only his glory and his magnificence, and that of his servants and ministers, but also the tranquillity of the Israelites. On beholding this my eyes would brighten, my reins would exult, my lips would pour forth praises to God, Who has not withdrawn His favor from His afflicted ones.

Hasdai later learned the truth about the origin of the Jewish Khazars, but they continued to be a source of excitement among Spanish Jews right down to the time of Judah Ha-Levi, whose great Arabic prose work *al-Kuzari* ("The Khazar") was inspired by them.

This common longing for the East in both Muslim and Christian Spain is another example of the Andalusian cultural synthesis, but it was also to be an area in which the ultimate breakdown of that harmony would manifest itself with the greatest fury. The Christian longing, northward in orientation, implied in the end the Crusaders' program of destroying and displacing Muslim power; it was founded, at one and the same time, upon an awe of the East and a loathing for the south. In later generations, Christian Spain's view of its Moorish past would be a frequent alternation between these two attitudes, sometimes with the most violent results.

But initially, the shift from Muslim to Christian preponderance on the peninsula that occurred from the eleventh to the thirteenth centuries brought only a renewed equilibrium in its wake, and a revival of the old tolerance. Of the four Christian kingdoms there by the end of this period — Aragon, Castile, Navarre, and Portugal — Aragon had the largest Muslim population, but it was the illustrious Castilian king Alfonso X, "the Wise" (1252–1284), who proudly styled himself a monarch of "two religions" and brought to his court statesmen and artists representing all three. The spirit of those times is well demonstrated by an illustration in the manuscript of the *Cantigas*, the sacred songs partially composed by Alfonso himself, which shows a dark-skinned troubadour in Moorish dress singing side by side with a Christian. The different spirit of a not much later time also is represented here, however; for in the miniature as we now have it, part of the Moor's face has been rubbed out.

The first manifestations of a new birth of intolerance in Spain, however, were directed not so much against the Moors as against the Jews. Nor was its racial component immediately evident; rather, the anti-Judaism which accumulated force in Spain through the course of the fourteenth century and burst out violently at the beginning of its final decade was, on the surface of it, part of a general European wave that professed no other motive than the ideal of religious purity. With the notable exception of the Catholic Visigoths of Spain, western Europe had not shown much inclination to anti-Judaism during the first millennium of Christianity. It was not until the eleventh and twelfth centuries, when western civilization came militantly to life, that Jews began to feel its wrath. One of the side effects of the First Crusade was a wave of pogroms in the Rhineland that left the Jewish communities there in a state of devastation. From then on until the close of the Middle Ages, riots, forced conversions, and wholesale expulsions were often recurring afflictions in the Jewish life of western Europe.

The anti-Jewish actions of the epoch were mainly the work of prince and populace; the Church, a conservative force in this as in other respects, usually preferred to leave the Jews alone. Even the notorious decree of the Fourth Lateran Council in 1215 requiring Jews to wear a distinguishing mark on their clothing was not directed against Jewish existence as such. It was a product of the fear that the presence of Jews among unwitting Christians was causing heretical ideas to spread among the latter; in many communities, Jews had become outwardly indistinguishable from Christians, and now the badge would serve as a warning. This was the generation that established the Albigensian Crusade and the papal Inquisition, and its heresy-hunting zeal was reflected in this decree. The traditional attitude remained in force that Jews were not heretics — only Christians could be — but nevertheless, one can perceive an ominous new undercurrent arising. A papacy that now regarded heresy as a veritable disease, so vile that its carriers had to be reduced to ashes like leprous rags, had announced that the Jews were a major potential source of infection. In this notion that a certain group within society is unclean and should be quarantined we can perceive an incipient racism — still only incipient, however, since the idea remains that the uncleanness resides in doctrine, not in blood.

The kings of the emerging nation-states were less ambivalent than the princes of the Church about the Jewish presence in their midst. Many of them came to regard Judaism and heresy in the same light, as entities that were simply not to be tolerated within the body politic — a body as susceptible to infection as the Christian community at large. The idea of imposing religious uniformity as a method of extending royal power was given its most dramatic launching in the Albigensian Crusade, begun in 1208, and this principle of a royal crusade against heresy was finally applied to the Jews by Edward I of England in 1290: in that year, all Jewish subjects who had not submitted to conversion were expelled from the realm. The French crown then followed suit, making several half-hearted gestures of expulsion of the Jews throughout the fourteenth century, until the definitive one was made by Charles VI in 1394. The Iberian monarchs, still deeply involved with their Jews, were to wait another century before doing the same.

The mobs of the peninsula were less forbearing than their rulers, however. At least from the Rhineland pogroms of 1096, it had been the masses of western Europe who provided the chief energies of medieval anti-Judaism. On the popular level, Jews were objects of superstition as well as of social and religious resentment. Jewish doctors, for example, were often thought to be in league with the Devil, and this was taken to be the reason for the seemingly special curative powers which often brought people to them in spite of everything, as well as for their purported inclination to poison Christian patients. The ritual-murder charge, which made its first appearance in twelfth-century England, extended the myth of deadly Jewish vindictiveness to include a recapitulation of the Christ-killing in every generation. The desecration-of-the-Host charge, which came soon thereafter, struck new veins of superstition; for by reducing the Christ-killing to the merest symbolic act, it made uncleanness as evil as murder. One legend told of a holy wafer stolen and buried by a Jew which, when dug up, was found to have turned into a dead, bleeding Christ. The perpetrators of such uncleanness were naturally thought by some to have brought the Black Plague when it struck Europe in 1348, and the result was some of the worst pogroms of the entire epoch. One anti-Semitic rumor in Germany brought together all the components of the myth during the era of the Black Plague: the wells had been poisoned by lepers hired by Jews who were in league with the Moorish king of Granada.

The fourteenth century was in general a period of mass uprisings, and the Iberian Peninsula was not exempt from the social conditions that had brought them on. But to the extent that the rioting had sometimes contained an anti-Jewish component, the situation in Spain, where there were more Jews than in any other Christian country, and where their presence carried special implications from a unique and ambiguous past, was potentially more explosive than any other. At the end of the century, the Spanish Christian masses suddenly rallied to the banner of the general European anti-Semitism of the epoch; but beneath the slogans of the common cause was a quarrel all their own. The sudden fury of intolerance was part of a general western European development; but the undying vehemence of it and its increasingly racial coloration through the course of the succeeding century were something particularly Spanish. The Jews were a vital part of the national organism that now seemed infected, and Spaniards who saw it that way were from then on never certain whether they wanted to treat or to amputate; either way, however, their methods usually were violent.

We do not know the immediate causes of the anti-Jewish riots that broke out in Seville on June 4, 1391. Seville was the home of the largest and most prosperous Jewish community in Castile; it also was located midway along a relatively narrow stretch of territory between the kingdoms of Granada and Portugal, allied in war against Castile at this very time and both ruled by kings notoriously favorable toward their Jewish subjects. Perhaps, then, there were rumors of Jewish collaboration with the two enemies. In any case, on that day, according to one leader of Castilian Jewry, "the Lord bent his bow like an enemy against the community of Seville." The rioters set fire to the gates of the Jewish quarter, killed many of its inhabitants, forced many more to the baptismal font, and sold some of the women and children into slavery in North Africa. A few days later a similar riot broke out in nearby Cordova.

This was the beginning of a tidal wave that overran Castile and Aragon through the summer. In Toledo, Madrid, Cuenca, and Burgos, synagogues were looted and turned into churches, and the historic Jewish communities were virtually destroyed, through death, conversion, and flight. Many Jews found refuge, either in parts of the country untouched by the rioting, or in nearby tolerant kingdoms — Navarre to the north, Morocco to the south, Portugal to the west. Portugal remained immune to the pogrom fever, not only because her Jews were still too few to provoke widespread antagonism, but also because they enjoyed the protection of a popular king, who was at this moment leading a national revolt against Castilian hegemony.

Aragon, however, did not share in this immunity, even though her throne was now occupied by Juan I, who had been Abraham Cresques's patron when he was Infante and was still a good friend to his Jewish subjects. There were simply too many Jews in Aragon, and therefore too much popular feeling against them, for the borders of the kingdom to hold back the wave of rioting when it struck. It penetrated to Valencia on July 9, and the Jewish community there was destroyed. It reached Barcelona, Juan's capital, in the first week of August, and some four hundred members of the largest Jewish community on the Catalonian mainland were killed; only a few escaped, and the remainder were forcibly converted to Christianity.

The rioting began in Majorca, home of Jafuda Cresques, on August 2. On this island, where there was a class of rich Jewish landowners — an unusual phenomenon in this era — the uprising showed more of the earmarks of the kind of peasant revolts that had occurred during the previous decade in France and in England than did any of those on the Spanish mainland. The government in Majorca sought to protect its Jews, evacuating them from the villages into the capital at the first signs of trouble, and sheltering them in the fortresses there when more radical measures seemed necessary. In that maritime community evacuation to North Africa was a readily available recourse, and some resorted to it, but without much help from the government, which was not eager to see the wealthier Jews leave the kingdom. In this first wave of rioting, some three hundred were killed. Then there began a period of negotiations between the peasant leaders and the government, which lasted into the fall. Finally, the peasants won their two chief demands: all debts to Jews were canceled, and those who were still sheltered in the fortresses were to come out and submit to the alternatives of conversion or death.

A vivid picture of what happened on the day of decision is presented by a list, which still survives, of Jewish householders who submitted to baptism, giving their old names and the Christian ones they now assumed. A few of them found continuity with the past by retaining the old family name — Jacob Vidal, for example, became Jaime Vidal, and Salomó Durán became Geraldo Durán; no doubt they could do this because these names were to be found just as much among Christians as among Jews. But in most cases, the transformation was total: Magaluf ben Salem became Pere Cases, Isach Levi became Bernardo Aguilo, and so on. Ancient and once proud identities were shed like ritual fringes falling forlornly and profanely into the dust.

Jafuda Cresques called himself Jaime Ribes, and then went on for a time living in ways superficially similar to the old. He made his home in the large house which had been his father's before him, and in which his mother still lived; he continued making excellent maps for which he was honored by the king. But even if we can only guess at any likely agony in his soul, we can be sure that his personal life had been wrecked by the events of 1391: for his wife — perhaps along with any children they may have had — having somehow escaped the pogrom unscathed and unconverted, was now living in North Africa.

Jaime Ribes finally gave up the ghost of his past in 1394, when he sold his house to the Order of St. John the Hospitaller — as if to confirm its conquest by Christianity — and moved to Barcelona, where his mother eventually joined him. There he presumably basked for a while in the proximity of his royal protector; but Juan I died in 1395. Fifteen years later, his mother now presumably dead, he pulled up stakes again and set out for fresh fields in which to live and work.

For a moment we lose the thread; but now the changing name and destiny of the wandering cartographer reaches out to us through the centuries in a different form, and from another perspective. The new scene is Portugal, the farthermost rim of the West, now seizing the initiative as the foremost Iberian land of refugees and of maritime enterprise.

Duarte Pacheco Pereira, an eminent chronicler of Portuguese maritime achievement, writing about a hundred years after the event, tells us that Prince Henry the Navigator, organizing his historic enterprise of Atlantic exploration just after 1415, "sent to Majorca for Master Jacome, a skilled maker of charts — it was in this island that these charts were first made — and by many gifts and favors brought him to these realms, where he taught his skill to men who in turn taught men who are alive at the present time." Though Pacheco clearly is telling us that this Master Jacome was the founder of Portuguese cartography in its greatest age, he does not mention him again.

Indeed, it was not until our own time that the identity of this mysterious personage was definitely established as being that of our own Jafuda Cresques, alias Jaime Ribes: for "Jacome" — James in English — is simply a Portuguese form of "Jaime," or "Jacme" in Catalan. To be sure, questions remain. Pacheco says that Prince Henry sent to *Majorca* for Master Jacome: was this an error, or had Cresques gone back there after his sojourn in Barcelona? And were the "gifts and favors" with which he was seduced only material ones, or did they include a chance to return to his ancestral faith?

But perhaps Master Jacome had given up caring about such matters. For it also seems possible that, as he took up his new task of helping Prince Henry to chart hitherto unknown regions of the earth, gazing out on the Ocean Sea as his father had — but this time to the west — he began to glimpse entirely fresh possibilities of redemption.

2

The Fortunate Islands

THE COUNTRY IN WHICH Master Jacome had settled was the upstart of the *Reconquista*. A Flemish count, Henry of Burgundy, had married into the Castilian royal family at the end of the eleventh century, and had been given charge of the reconquest in the westernmost part of the peninsula. Henry carved out a large feudal domain for himself, and his son, Afonso Henriques, conquered Lisbon, thereafter laying claim to having created a separate monarchy. His claim received papal confirmation in 1179, but the kings of Castile continued to regard the Portuguese monarchy as a wayward and illegitimate child.

A Mediterranean country that was not on the Mediterranean, cut off from the east by geography and Castilian enmity, Portugal became a virtual island in the western ocean. The majority of her population in fact worked on the land, but her unique identity was above all shaped by sailors and fishermen. Her most natural ally was England, that other country out on the western ocean, and the blood ties of these two monarchies had become close by the beginning of the fifteenth century. King John I of Portugal was married to Philippa of Lancaster, daughter of John of Gaunt, and their sons — one of whom, Duarte, was a future king of Portugal, another, Pedro, a future regent, and a third, Henry, to be the most celebrated of all as the founder of the Portuguese overseas empire — were first cousins to England's Henry V.

For a moment, it could even have seemed that these two countries were joined in an audacious "grand design." The conquest of Ceuta on the Moroccan side of the Strait of Gibraltar by John I and his sons — the first extension of the *Reconquista* beyond the peninsula itself — took place in August, 1415, the same month as that in which Henry Plantagenet invaded France. This could hardly have been a coincidence, though we have no records to prove otherwise. Portugal may then have been planning a flanking movement on the kingdom of Granada, whereby she would snatch it from the underbelly of Castile and achieve control of the strait for herself and her English ally. But Henry V had obtained the French crown by 1420, and so had access to the Mediterranean without any need for the strait. Portugal, left without English support for the conquest of Granada, turned instead to projects of her own that have made the taking of Ceuta look to subsequent generations like the first in a long set of deliberate steps along the coast of Africa to India by the end of the century.

A southeast passage to India may well have been one of Prince Henry's dreams when he organized his enterprise of overseas discovery a few years after Ceuta, but he also had more immediate aims with which to occupy himself — and for which Master Jacome would have been particularly useful. One of these was a project to explore southward along the African coast, above all to find a sea passage to Guinea, the source of the lucrative trans-Saharan trade, which would thereby be outflanked by Portuguese ships. We may assume that Master Jacome knew more about the southward conformations of the West African coast by now than he or his father did when they worked on the Catalan Atlas more than forty years before. On the Catalan map, the southern termination of that coast was at Cape Bojador, on a line only midway down the Sahara. Alongside the cape, in the rough western ocean, the map depicts a frail Mediterranean craft with the flag of Aragon on its prow and a forlorn single sail buffeting in the wind, and four faces gazing out over the bulkhead — in horror, resignation, or grim determination one cannot tell — accompanied by this inscription:

Jaime Ferrer's vessel departed in search of the River of Gold, Saint Lawrence day, which is on the 10th of August, and this was in the year 1346.

Ferrer was a Catalan himself, and his vessel, which had disappeared with everyone aboard, had been the last within memory to try to pass the fearful currents of Bojador.

Yet there were traditions upholding the possibility of a passage beyond them. In about the sixth century B.C.E., the Carthaginian prince Hanno had led down this coast a voyage that seems definitely to have gone far south of the Sahara; indeed, it is possible that Hanno circumnavigated Africa. Herodotus describes an earlier circumnavigation of Africa that had been reported to him in Egypt, made by Phoenician sailors in around 600 B.C.E., and though Herodotus himself seems to doubt the story, it has been accepted as feasible by some scholars. Pliny's *Natural History,* which, though written in the first century C.E., was regarded as a definitive encyclopedia of world geography through all of the Middle Ages, takes it for granted that there were circumnavigations of Africa in antiquity. Nevertheless, this possibility would not be proven to Europeans until Portuguese ships rounded the Cape of Good Hope near the end of the fifteenth century, long after Prince Henry's death. What he would see in his own lifetime, however, was the rounding of Cape Bojador and the discovery of the coast of Guinea.

Another of Prince Henry's more immediate aims — and, in fact, the very first to which he addressed himself — was one for which Master Jacome must have been of the greatest use: the exploration of the western ocean, or the Atlantic as we now call it. The Catalan map shows a rich array of Atlantic islands, with this inviting inscription:

> The Fortunate Islands are in the Great Sea, on the left-hand side, near the end of the west; but they are nearby. Isidore [of Seville] said in his Fifteenth Book: "They are called Fortunate because they are filled with all sorts of good things, grains, fruits and trees; and the pagans believe that Paradise is here on account of the temperateness of the sun and the fertility of the soil."
>
> *Item:* Isidore says that the trees here grow to at least a hundred and fifty feet in height, and are filled with fruits and birds. There is milk and honey here, especially on the island of Caprary, which is so named for the multitude of goats on it.
>
> *Item:* Canary Island is nearby, called Canary on account of the multitude of large, powerful dogs found there.
>
> Pliny, master of geography, said that among the Fortunate Islands there is one on which all the good things of the earth grow, and all kinds of fruits, without being sown or planted. On the heights of the mountains the trees are never without leaves or fruits and have a lovely smell. People eat from them part of the year, then they harvest the grains. This is why the pagans of the Indies maintain that, when they die, their souls go to these islands and live forever in the aroma of these fruits. They believe that this is their Paradise, but in truth, this is only a fable.

This inscription has a formidable classical pedigree. Much of it — though not the passage attributed to him — is to be found in Pliny, but he is far from the only author in antiquity to have written about the *Insulae Fortunatae* (also rendered "Isles of the Blessed"). Plutarch says of them in his life of Sertorius that

> rain falls there seldom, and in moderate showers, but for the most part they have gentle breezes, bringing along with them soft dews, which render the soil not only rich for ploughing and planting, but so abundantly fruitful that it produces spontaneously an abundance of delicate fruits, sufficient to feed the inhabitants, who may here enjoy all things without trouble or labor. . . . The firm belief prevails, even among the barbarians, that this is the seat of the blessed, and that these are the Elysian fields celebrated by Homer.

Some writers associated these islands with the Hesperides, the Ladies of the West, proprietresses of the golden apples. The resemblances to Eden are palpable, except that this is a pagan Eden of the West, not a Judaeo-Christian one of the East. It is yet another distinct direction in our compass card of the human spirit: from antiquity to our own times, the west was always to imply a notion of freshness and purity. Like Eden, the Fortunate Islands were associated with some ideal time in the remote youth of mankind, such as that described in the celebrated "Golden Age" passage of Ovid's *Metamorphoses,* when "the earth itself, without being forced," had given forth "all necessities on its own," and when men lived correspondingly "of their own free will, without judges or laws." But, however ancient this condition, it never grew old; unlike the fading East, the West represented an eternal youthfulness.

But what were the Fortunate Islands in fact? Many of the ancient descriptions are quite detailed, and certainly were not mere products of the imagination. Modern writers have usually identified them with the Canaries, but despite Pliny's own use of this name, he seems to have had something more distant and grandiose in mind. He located the Fortunate Islands more than a thousand miles out on the ocean, and Plutarch put them similarly far away. We cannot look for exactitude in these estimates, but they do give the impression of referring to something closer to the Azores than to the Canaries. The "Fortunate Islands" could even have represented some dim notion of the Americas; there certainly are hints of this in the Catalan map. If so, we have struck a highly suggestive convergence of promised lands in the middle of the vast Ocean Sea, at the point where East meets West. Looking eastward, we have seen it as the "islands far off" of the Catalan map; that was a vision colored by the old oriental perspective, filtered through the Jewish sources of Christianity. Now we are seeing it to the west, in a vision colored by Greco-Roman classicism, containing a touch of the pagan. By Prince Henry's time, in the light of the dawning Renaissance, some Christians even were locating the terrestrial paradise in the Fortunate Islands, though a man still so steeped in Jewish and medieval traditions as Abraham Cresques was made it clear in the inscription just quoted that he regarded such notions as pagan and "only a fable." His son may have come to see the matter differently, however. In general, the transformation of Jafuda Cresques into Master Jacome, his move westward across the peninsula from the more oriental world of his fathers into the spray of waters redolent of a new Golden Age, suggest a vexed and stumbling progress into the Renaissance, and into fresh horizons for that quasireligion of overseas discovery that his father had adumbrated.

But the Fortunate Islands of the Catalan map were by no means a mere literary dream. A few of them, hinting at fragmented and ill-formed premonitions of possible Americas, were ambiguous and to remain so forever, but most of them were solid data for a man like Prince Henry. In particular, the map gives vivid profiles of the Canaries and the Madeiras, both rather accurately drawn, and of the Azores, which are represented erroneously but not unrecognizably. Presumably, by the time he came to Prince Henry in 1418 or earlier, Master Jacome had improved upon the knowledge displayed here. The Canaries had in the meantime become part of European history, and were generally known. The other groups were still "undiscovered," in the language of the time, though knowledgeable Europeans clearly had been to them before. The Catalan map proves that the Madeira Islands were known quite well to Abraham and Jafuda Cresques, and to a handful or so of Italian sailors lost to history: for the names it gives the islands in this group are all Italian, and are otherwise exactly the same as they are to this day. The principal island of the group is called *Legname* ("Wood") on the map, and the Portuguese, when they got there, simply translated this as "Madeira." The group was "discovered" by Prince Henry's ships in 1418, presumably with the expert navigational advice of Master Jacome, and was quickly and profitably colonized.*

The Azores were harder to find, but when they were found, these

---

* North of Madeira and directly west of Portugal on the Catalan map is a group of islands also bearing Italian names. This group is depicted with the same look of authority as that displayed by the Madeiras and the Canaries; it therefore must have been a blow to Master Jacome's pride that Portuguese ships did not begin finding the Azores until 1432, much farther out in the Ocean than where the map had placed them, and in a different set of relative positions. As if in repudiation of a by then outmoded geography, the Portuguese discoverers gave to all but two of the Azores names different from those on the map. Master Jacome probably did not live to see this.

Insulae Fortunatae, like those of the Madeiras, proved to be blessed with good climate, good soil, and a complete lack of any indigenous population: the Portuguese were free to seek out their Golden Age on them without any native interference. This was not the case in the Canaries, however, which had become, even before Prince Henry began taking an interest in them, the scene of a kind of dress rehearsal for the discovery and conquest of America. They enter the clear but still flickering light of history toward the end of the thirteenth century, when a Genoese captain named Lancelote Malocello established a fort on the northeastern-most island of the group, which is called "Lanzarote" in his honor to this day. His colony, if such it was, does not seem to have survived. The islands are not known to have been visited again until 1341, when a major expedition of discovery, trade, and perhaps colonization arrived there, under Portuguese auspices, but including Florentine, Genoese, Castilian, and probably Catalan officers and sailors on its ships. This expedition achieved the first discovery on record of primitive peoples of the West — we might justly say "New World" peoples — by western Europeans, and we are fortunate to have had it commemorated for us in an appropriately remarkable narrative, written by no less an author than Giovanni Boccaccio.

According to the account Boccaccio compiled — he did not himself take part in the expedition — the two ships left Lisbon on July 1, carrying "horses, arms, and warlike engines for storming towns and castles, in search of those islands commonly called the 'Rediscovered.'" On the fifth day out they came to a stony island, covered with goats and other animals, "and inhabited by naked men and women, who were like savages in their appearance and demeanor." At the next island they reached, apparently the Grand Canary, "a great number of natives of both sexes, all nearly naked, came down to the shore to meet them. Some of them, who seemed superior to the rest, were covered with goats' skins colored yellow and red, and, as well as could be seen from a distance, the skins were fine and soft, and tolerably well sewn together with the intestines of animals. . . . The islanders showed a wish to communicate with the people in the ships, but when the boats drew near the shore, the sailors, who did not understand a word they said, did not dare to land. Their language, however, was soft, and their pronunciation rapid and animated like Italian. Some of the islanders then swam to the boats, and four of them were taken on board and afterwards carried away." Such unperturbed collecting of human specimens for examination back home was to be standard behavior in the age of discovery.

The Europeans found a similar state of undress on the other islands, and a similar lack of excuse for the mass of war machinery they had brought with them. To be sure, there was one adversary appropriate to any crusading Christian souls that may have come along, which turned up on one island where the sailors "came upon a chapel or temple, in which there were no pictures or ornaments, but only a stone statue representing a man with a ball in his hand. This idol, otherwise naked, wore an apron of palm-leaves. They took it away and carried it to Lisbon." Nobody knows what became of the statue, and there is, alas, nothing more in the narrative about native religious practices — or about native customs in general, for that matter. This anthropological weakness is evidently due not to any fault of the writer, but to a lack of such interest in the observers who brought him their accounts. They clearly were much better when dealing with the natural rather than the human scene; for they doubtless were looking at these islands with an eye to colonization, and would certainly have preferred to find them as empty of an aboriginal population as the Madeiras and Azores were later found to be.

The humanist back home, however, tended to be more concerned with the natives: this was a pattern to be repeated in generations and dis- coveries to come. Boccaccio's narrative suddenly finds new life toward the end, when it describes the four islanders who had been kidnapped. The vivid description suggests that the author had seen them with his own eyes:

> The four men whom they had carried away were young and beardless, and had handsome faces. They wore nothing but a sort of apron made of cord, from which they hung a number of palm or reed fibers of one and a half or two hairs'-breadth, which formed an effectual covering. They were uncircumcised. Their long, light hair veiled their bodies down to the waist, and they went barefoot. . . .
>
> These men were spoken to in several languages, but they understood none of them. They were not taller than their captors, but were robust of limb, courageous, and very intel- ligent. When spoken to by signs they replied in the same manner, like mutes. . . . They sang very sweetly, and danced almost as well as Frenchmen. They were gay and merry, and much more civilized than many Spaniards. . . .
>
> They absolutely refused wine, and only drank water. Wheat and barley they ate in plenty, as well as cheese and meat, which was abundant in the islands, and of good quality, for although there were no oxen, camels or asses, there were plenty of goats, sheep and wild hogs. They were shown some gold and silver money, but were quite ignorant of the use of it; and they knew as little of any kind of spice. Rings of gold and vases of carved work, swords and sabers, were shown to them; but they seemed never to have seen such things, and did not know how

to use them. They showed remarkable faithfulness and honesty, for if one of them received anything good to eat, before tasting it, he divided it into portions which he shared with the rest. Marriage was observed among them, and the married women wore aprons like the men, but the maidens went quite naked, without consciousness of shame.

This description seems essentially authentic, though colored by a sentiment that foreshadows the "Noble Savage" ideal of later centuries. From virtually this day onward, observers steeped in the Greek and Roman classics, as Boccaccio was beyond most, seem unable to behold primitive men from the West without imparting to them some aura of the Golden Age. The naked maidens walking about with no sense of shame were to be a recurring, even an obsessive, image. And we see here the beginnings of the humanist inclination to use this more natural existence as a stick with which to beat European self-satisfaction: Boccaccio's sly remarks about French dancing and Spanish urbanity reverberate forward to Montesquieu and beyond.

There are not many clues here about the ethnic identity of the Canarians.° Since that primitive culture has now disappeared entirely, one can only guess at its true nature today, but the consensus of modern scholarship is that the population of the islands came from nearby North Africa in pre-Islamic times, and was of either Berber or Iberian stock. Either way, the large portion of those fourteenth-century discoverers who came from the Iberian Peninsula could very well have sensed in these people something of their own primeval ancestry. In any case, it was the Canarians who, in various ways, provided Europeans with a model for future encounters with primitive peoples to the west — a model somewhat different in complexion from that of the encounters that were about to begin to the south.

The next known European incursion into the Canaries took place more than sixty years later, and was the definitive one. In 1402 a Norman knight named Jean de Bethencourt led an expedition there that resulted, a few years later, in the conquest of most of the islands as a feudal domain for his heirs, under the suzerainty of the king of Castile. The story, rather

---

° The long, light hair evidently rules out any Negroid stock, and possibly Moorish stock as well; but later descriptions of the islands do describe men and women of swarthy complexion as constituting at least part of the population. The observation that they are uncircumcised is perhaps meant to indicate that they are not of Arab or Jewish descent. But, on the other hand, later observers do speak of "Saracens" in the Canaries, and rudimentary lexicons made in the sixteenth century of the language of Tenerife — the largest of the islands and the last to be conquered — show Semitic elements. The dislike of wine might also suggest Moorish influence, but this is balanced off by the apparent willingness to eat hog's meat.

confusingly presented in the one account that has come down to us, was recorded by Bethencourt's two missionaries, Pierre Bontier and Jean le Verrier. All the by now traditional elements of European colonial conquest are there: those among the natives who give in to the conqueror and collaborate with him, and those who continue to resist; the conspiracies between rebellious elements in the conquering armies and the resisting natives; recrimination and revenge among the natives, ending in mutual slaughters provoked by the conqueror; enslavement; and, most characteristically for that age, the choice of death or conversion to Christianity.

One passage in the missionaries' account tells how some of the conquerors "had killed many natives, and reduced the others to such extremity that they no longer knew what to do, but came from day to day to throw themselves upon the mercy of the Christians, so that hardly any who remained alive were unbaptized, especially of those who might have given trouble and been too much for the latter." The attitude of the pious narrators is clear. They are not without human, shall we say Christian, sympathy for the Canarians. Time and again, for example, they demonstrate their vehement opposition to any attempts to carry off shiploads of natives and sell them in the slave markets of Europe and North Africa. This attitude, by the way, is shared by their commander and hero Bethencourt; only unruly and mutinous elements try to engage in such traffic, and they usually are reprimanded by Bethencourt as well as by the two clergymen. But as for conversion to Christianity, this is a supreme good so desirable that a little slaughter in the process of achieving it hardly seems to require comment by the missionaries. Such suspension of sentiment where spiritual principles were concerned was characteristic of the age, and the Jews of Spain knew the application of it every bit as well as the Canarians did.

The travails of the Canarians were not ended with this Norman Conquest, for the Portuguese were not ready to relinquish to Castilian control a claim over the islands that they had been making at least since 1341. Prince Henry sent a military expedition there in 1425, and inaugurated what was to be a half-century of intermittent warfare with Castile. In 1479 Portugal was to relinquish her claim at last, and the unified kingdom of Castile and Aragon would then complete its conquest of the Canaries in the same decade in which America was discovered for its monarchs. But by that time the history of overseas discovery and racial encounters had become complicated by a whole new current arising along the coast of Africa, and it is to this that we must now direct our attention.

3

Prester John; or, The Noble Ethiopian

At a place south of Egypt on the Catalan map, a Saracen king is described as being "always at war with the Christians of Nubia who are under the rule of the Emperor of Ethiopia, of the land of Prester John." But Ethiopia is below the southernmost edge of the map and we learn nothing more about this. The narrators of Jean de Bethencourt's Canarian expeditions speak of going to Africa to obtain "news of Prester John," and Prince Henry's chronicler, Gomes Eannes de Zurara, writes of the explorations along the African coast that the Prince "not only desired to have knowledge of that land, but also of the Indies, and of the land of Prester John if he could." Indeed, the search for "Priest John" (for the name, which is *Presbyter Johannes* in Latin and *Prêtre Jean* in French, is simply a variant of this) was considered by Zurara to be one of the main reasons for Prince Henry's whole enterprise. The legend of a Christian prince living at the other flank of the Muslim world had excited Europe for nearly three hundred years, but Henry the Navigator's zeal to find him may seem surprising in the light of the dismal history of race relations that was to ensue as a result; for by this time, most educated Europeans considered Prester John to be black.

This does not mean they had yet specifically identified him with the emperor of Ethiopia as we understand that designation today; the geography of the Middle Ages was too vague for this, and the legend more splendid than that monarch, or any monarch, ever has been. In fact, Prester John had not originally been placed in Africa at all. The legend made its first known appearance in Europe in the twelfth century, when Bishop Hugh of Jabala arrived in Rome to appeal for a Second Crusade on behalf of the beleaguered Christian princes then established in the Near East as a result of the First. Hugh told a heartening story about a Far Eastern king named simply John, a Nestorian Christian, who had invaded Persia not long before and conquered Ecbatana, its capital. John had then taken his army toward Jerusalem, intending to help its Crusader king to defend it against Muslim attack, but had been unable to get his troops across the Tigris. Describing John as a descendant of those Magi who had made obeisance to the infant Jesus and whose land he now ruled, Hugh said that he wielded an emerald scepter.

Hugh's story may have been based on the exploits of an actual Tartar king. The Tartars were often in contact with the far-flung Nestorian Christian communities of Central Asia, and had shown interest in Christianity from time to time. The idea that they might be descended from the Lost Tribes of Israel also helped encourage the dream that they would one day see the light, convert to Christianity en masse, and form the other jaw of a great Christian pincer movement against Islam. And, of course, the example of a mass conversion in the Central Asian steppes had been provided by the Khazars; many Europeans evidently thought this had been a conversion to Christianity. Later on, there was to be a widespread but mistaken belief that Genghis Khan had become a Christian. The Tartar version of the legend was still strong enough in the late thirteenth century for Marco Polo to assume that a neighboring prince he had heard about while in Cathay was Prester John.

But a new and more fantastic version had appeared in the latter part of the twelfth century, some twenty years after the Second Crusade advocated by Bishop Hugh had ended in failure. No doubt the Christian imagination was now in greater need of fantasy concerning the East, and this is what it got in the celebrated "Prester John letter," a work of unknown provenance and authorship, which no longer exists in its original version. We know it today only through a multitude of recapitulations published in the ensuing centuries, in prose and in verse, in Latin and in the vernaculars, many of them embroidered with the fantasies of later generations. The summary that follows is based on an inferential reconstruction, made in the nineteenth century, of the original.

The letter is purportedly addressed to the Christian emperor — in some versions Manuel of Byzantium, in others Frederick Barbarossa — by John the Presbyter, "king of kings and lord of lords," in order to describe himself and his realm "now that knowledge of our greatness has reached you." John claims to have exceeded all men in riches, virtue, and power. When he rides forth into war, he is accompanied by more than one hundred thousand cavalrymen and more than a million foot soldiers, marching behind thirteen enormous crosses made of gold and precious stones. Seventy-two kings pay tribute to him. Thirty thousand men eat at his table every day, and they are served by seven kings, fifty-two dukes, and three hundred and sixty-five counts, as well as by humbler retinue. Roman and Greek clergymen alike eat at John's side. The table itself is made of emerald, supported by legs of amethyst; other tables in the palace are of gold and ivory. The palace, "built after the pattern of the one erected for King Gundaphor by the Apostle Thomas," is a vast structure of shittim wood, ebony, gold, onyx, sardonyx, and crystal. John's bed-chamber is bedecked with gold and precious stones, and his bed is made of sapphire.

But the sapphire represents chastity, and though John has a harem of the most beautiful women in the world, he lies with one or another of them only four times a year altogether, solely for procreation. Nor is this the only demonstration that John's realm is not founded on mere, untrammeled splendor. When he rides forth on ordinary occasions, he is preceded not by martial magnificence but by an unadorned wooden cross and a vase full of earth, to remind him of the Passion of the Saviour and of the dust to which he shall himself return one day. (To be sure, the vase is of gold, and a silver bowl full of gold is also brought along; but this is so that the world may always be reminded of John's greatness.) A bent for self-effacement is above all shown by his simple title of "Presbyter." The reason for it, he explains, is to distinguish his own unique majesty from all the kings and archbishops with whom his palace is regularly overflowing. In this array of high titles, "we choose to be called by a lesser name and to assume an inferior rank, to show our great humility."

An ideal balance of wisdom and wealth also characterizes the realm over which John presides. There is no poverty among his subjects, and no strife; "thieves and robbers are not found here, nor adultery and avarice." There is no flattery, and no lying: "for he who speaks a lie dies forthwith, or is regarded by us as dead. His name is not mentioned, nor is he honored." Pilgrims and visitors are warmly received; indeed, they may find a special reward in store for them, for in a desert place there stands a rock that has incredible curative powers. Two holy men guard it, and ask every arriving pilgrim if he is a Christian or wants to become one; if he answers affirmatively, he is allowed to get into a mussel-shaped cavity in the rock, in which there are four inches of water. If the pilgrim's faith is sincere, the water will rise miraculously above his head three times, and he will be cured of his ailment.

Despite such miracles of nature, the main feature of the landscape in Prester John's realm seems to be desert. It is dominated by a waterless, sandy sea, on which "the sand moves and swells into waves like the sea and is never still." After a desert journey of three days from this sea, one reaches mountains "from which descends a waterless river of stones, which flows through our country to the sandy sea. Three days in the week it flows and casts up stones both great and small, and also carries with it wood to the sandy sea. When the river reaches the sea the stones and wood disappear and are not seen again. While the river is in motion it is impossible to cross. On the other four days it can be crossed." The desert character of the realm is further suggested by John's particular stress upon elephants, dromedaries, and camels among the many animals to be found there. Yet, for all this aridity, there is abundance; the sandy sea, for example, contains all kinds of edible fish.

Where, then, is this remarkable country? "Our magnificence," writes Prester John, "dominates the Three Indias, and extends to farther India, where the body of St. Thomas the Apostle rests. It reaches through the desert towards the place of the rising of the sun, and continues through the valley of deserted Babylon close by the Tower of Babel." Suddenly the vague immensity takes on a Biblical tinge; this is deepened when John informs us that his territories comprise the Pison, which is one of the four rivers that rise up out of the terrestrial paradise according to the second chapter of Genesis. Furthermore, like the land of Havilah around which the Biblical Pison flows, John's country contains gold and onyx; it also flows with milk and honey. A hint at the location of this realm is provided by Genesis 2:13, which tells us that another of the four rivers of Eden, the Gihon, "compasseth the whole land of Ethiopia." John tells us that his palace is in Susa, the ancient capital of Persia, but this also implied proximity to Ethiopia in the vague geographical imagination of medieval Europe.* As the centuries passed, the continental realm of

---

* This confused geography has ancient and honorable roots. The first verse of the Book of Esther describes the realm of the Persian king Ahasuerus, whose palace also was at Susa, as extending "from India even unto Ethiopia." In Greek and Roman authors there is a similar vagueness about a vast region taken in by terms like "India" and "Ethiopia" (the latter even in its narrowest sense comprising a much larger area than present-day Ethiopia, and beginning just south of the First Cataract of the Nile), and about its relationship with the better-known Persia. In the apocryphal *Acts of St. Thomas*, the Apostle moves easily between Persia and "India." Starting roughly with the fifth-century apocryphal writer, the Pseudo-Abdias, who described the exploits of the Apostles Thomas, Bartholomew, and Matthew in each of the "Three Indias," this latter concept became a standard one in the Middle Ages. One of the three "Indias" faced "Ethiopia," according to the Pseudo-Abdias, the second faced Persia, and the third occupied the ends of the earth, between the Ocean and the realm of darkness. The third became especially fruitful for the geographical imagination, the region of untold islands in which the plural term "Indias" — etymologically one and the same as "Indies" — came to rest for once and for all. There also

the Prester John letter, clearly somewhat south of the original Tartar centers of the legend, was to be increasingly identified as Ethiopia.

The Sarastro-like character who thus begins to emerge can be perceived as deeply bound up in the imagery and mythology of the ancient East. In some ways he is another version of the noble non-European whose western counterpart we have come upon in the Fortunate Islands, but there are significant differences. Unlike the Fortunate Islander, this sophisticated oriental knows both the value of money and the necessities of war. The western ideal was founded in a classical simplicity and closeness to a fresh and fertile nature, whereas this oriental one reposes in a natural environment that is harsh, forbidding, and old, and that yields up minerals and miracles more readily than vegetation. The way of life envisioned for the West was essentially democratic; this eastern one is the best of all possible monarchies. The Fortunate Islands beckon to pioneers, Prester John's domains to pilgrims and saints. While the "Noble Savage" sings of a future far from the clutter of decadent civilization, our Noble Ethiopian makes a last plea for the treasures, both material and spiritual, that may still be found among the rubble of a sacred past. He represents a kind of archaeological rediscovery, a digging-up of Hellenistic Christian origins in the East, to which western Europeans have finally been drawn in the age of the Crusades. The Prester John legend thus emerges as a Christian counterpart to those visions of a longed-for and ancient East that we have glimpsed among Muslims and Jews on the Iberian Peninsula. Indeed, it represents an assertion for Europe in general of that tolerant spirit represented above all by medieval Spain, an acceptance of that East in some of its cultural and racial complexity.

In fact, the Prester John letter may, at least in part, have Jewish roots. In the desert that separates the mountains from the sandy sea, the writer tells us, an underground rivulet turns into a large river in which an abundance of precious stones is to be found. "Beyond this river," he goes on, "are ten tribes of Jews, who, though they pretend to have their own kings, are nevertheless our servants and tributaries." Nothing more on the subject is said in the original version of the letter, but it is noteworthy that, in the embroidered versions produced by later generations, this passage is among the ones that underwent the greatest amplification. In an English version of 1507, for example, the weak kings of the above passage become "a great king of Israel" whom Prester John concedes to

---

were less mysterious, more valid definitions of the "Three Indias" among medieval geographers; but for most Europeans, even learned ones, the term covered a vast and distant region of dark-skinned peoples, culminating in a countless array of islands in one direction and in Ethiopia, the Biblical "Cush," in the other.

be "twice as strong as I am." His domains are "twice as great as all Christendom and Turkey," and he "hath under him three hundred kings, four thousand princes, dukes, earls, barons, knights, squires without number." Here he seems to have become an alternate version of Prester John himself.

Indeed, it is very likely that some sort of identification between Prester John and the king of Israel, between this remote realm of Christians and the final refuge of the Ten Lost Tribes, lies buried in the very sources of this legend. This possibility seems very close to the surface in the early, Central Asian version provided by Hugh of Jabala, with its intimations of Tartars and of the king of the Khazars. Only a generation after Bishop Hugh, the celebrated Jewish traveler Benjamin of Tudela described a relationship he had heard about between four of the Lost Tribes and a nomadic people called the Kofar al Turak, on the Central Asian steppes. The Kofar al Turak evidently were not Christians, but their purported relationship with some of the Lost Tribes resembles that of Prester John, and could have had something to do with the making of the latter's legend.

But the most probable Jewish source for the Prester John letter that we know of is the narrative of a curious figure of Jewish history, Eldad the Danite. Making his appearance toward the end of the ninth century, Eldad traveled through Mesopotamia, North Africa, and Spain, sojourning with the Jewish communities in these places and telling them an astounding story that their rabbis and scholars took quite seriously. He said he was a member of the tribe of Dan, which was now living with three of the other Lost Tribes "beyond the rivers of Ethiopia." Dan had left the kingdom of Israel long before the conquest by the Assyrians in 722 B.C.E., for it had refused to participate in Jeroboam's revolt against Solomon's son Rehoboam, and had gone into exile instead. The Danites had thought at first of going to Egypt, but it was forbidden them to return to the scene of their ancient servitude; then

> finally, God gave them good courage and advice, namely, to go up the river Pison . . . until they reached the land of Ethiopia, which they found fertile, with numerous vineyards and gardens. . . .
>
> Thus the Danites dwelled here for many years, multiplying and increasing greatly. They were then followed by three other tribes — Naphtali, Gad and Asher — who crossed the desert and encamped, until they came to the land of the Danites. In their wanderings they slew many Ethiopians in a territory extending four days' journey in each direction, and they have been fighting with seven kingdoms up to this day. And these four tribes, and those who dwelt in the ancient Havilah, where there is gold, trusted in the Lord. . . .

Eldad goes on to describe a way of life that combined nomadic virtues and warlike valor with great wealth. "These tribes possess much gold, silver and precious stones, as well as sheep, oxen, camels and asses," but nevertheless they sow, reap, and dwell in tents. They are splendid when going out to war; then, "the trumpet is blown, and 120,000 horsemen and 100,000 foot soldiers gather round their chief." These are a people even more impressive than the Khazars, though the latter may well have been a source of inspiration for Eldad's story — as also, undoubtedly, were the Falashas, the highly independent and warrior-like Jews of Ethiopia itself. Another source is Zephaniah 3:10: "From beyond the rivers of Ethiopia my suppliants, even the daughter of my dispersed, shall bring mine offering."

Running along one of the borders of Eldad's homeland is a river two hundred yards wide and

> full of sand and stones, but without water; the stones make a great noise like the waves of the sea and a stormy wind, so that in the night the noise is heard at a distance of half a day's journey. . . . And this river of stone and sand rolls during the six working days and rests on the Sabbath day. As soon as the Sabbath begins, fire surrounds the river, and the flames remain until the next evening, when the Sabbath ends. Thus no human being can reach the river for a distance of half a mile on either side; the fire consumes all that grows there.

This river, called the Sambatyon, clearly is an ancestor of the river of stones in the Prester John letter; this is especially evident in the 1507 English version, cited above, where its traits even include that of stopping only on Saturday. Eldad, in accordance with an already ancient Jewish tradition — from which he differs only in locating the river in Ethiopia instead of Syria — has made the legendary Sambatyon a boundary line between the Lost Tribes and their neighbors.*

---

* The first mentions of the Sambatyon on record occurred in the first century C.E. Josephus wrote in his *Jewish War* of a river in Syria that "has an astonishing peculiarity. For, when it flows, it is a copious stream with a current far from sluggish; then all at once its sources fail and for the space of six days it presents the spectacle of a dry bed; again, as though no change has occurred, it pours forth on the seventh day just as before. And it has always been observed to keep strictly to this order; whence they have called it the Sabbatical river [in Josephus' original Greek: *Sabbatikon*], so naming it after the sacred seventh day of the Jews." The Jewish Josephus surprisingly puts his river to work on Saturday, but perhaps this is for him a symbol of spiritual rejuvenation. The gentile Pliny, on the other hand, set the matter aright when he said, only a few years later, that "in Judaea is a stream that dries up every Sabbath." The river flows into rabbinical literature through the Great Midrash, which says that "the Ten Tribes wandered into exile on the other side of the river Sambatyon." The idea of placing it in Ethiopia, which may not have originated with Eldad, probably comes from its having been equated by some with the Biblical Gihon.

We have seen it functioning just this way in the Prester John letter; but the neighbors across the river in Eldad's account are not Prester John and his Christian subjects. Here, rather, is Eldad's description of them:

> There is also the tribe of Moses, our just master, which is called the Tribe of Yanus, because it fled from idol worship and clung to the fear of God. A river flows round their land for a distance of four days' journey on every side. They dwell in beautiful houses provided with handsome towers, which they have built themselves. . . . They sow and reap, and have all sorts of gardens with all kinds of fruit and cereals, namely, beans, melons, gourds, onions, garlic, wheat and barley; and the seed grows a hundredfold. They have faith; they know the Law. . . . Moreover, they see nobody and nobody sees them except the four tribes who dwell on the other side of the rivers of Ethiopia; they see them and speak to them, but the river Sambatyon is between them. . . . They have plenty of gold and silver; they sow flax, and cultivate the crimson worm, and make beautiful garments.

These are Levites, of the tribe of Moses and the priesthood, and though not all of them are necessarily prophets or priests, a whole nation of them implies an exalted religiosity. Indeed, they were too exalted for the possession of territory in Biblical times, and were not one of the Twelve Tribes among whom Joshua divided up the land of Canaan; they are therefore not one of the Ten Lost Tribes. This legend of a gathering of them in a country of their own is not exclusive to Eldad, but its origins are quite obscure, as is the name it gives them. *Yanus* is simply a Hebrew word that means "fleeing," so that it may not be a proper name but part of a designation — "the tribe that flees" (that is, from idol worship). But other texts make *Yanus* a proper name, which can be either that of the tribe or of its Levite founder.

This could be a direct forebear of Prester John. Here is a people of virtually priestly status, living across the Sambatyon from some of the Lost Tribes of Israel in a condition of unique sanctitude, and bearing — either itself or in the person of its leader — the name "Yanus." Could this have been adapted into the Latin form "Johannes"? Isn't "Presbyter" a likely notion to have emerged out of the legend of a tribe of Levites?

If there is indeed a Jewish identity buried in the legendary personality of Prester John, then he is a significant symbol, not only of certain of the more favorable aspects of the Judaeo-Christian relationship in the Middle Ages, but also of the peculiar complexities of the emerging racial consciousness of the Renaissance. For if his remotest Ethiopian origins have a Jewish coloration, his most up-to-date Ethiopian image in the fifteenth century had, as we have seen, a black one. We can thereby see in all its richness the tolerance implied in the vision of Prester John. Although Eldad and his fellow Danites apparently, in their time, did not have to be black to be Ethiopian, an anthropologically more sophisticated fifteenth century tended to take it for granted that a king of Ethiopia could not have been any other color: but, at least for the length of a historical moment, the seekers of Prester John did not seem any more perturbed by his black than by his Jewish aspect.

To the extent that his blackness was that of an Ethiopian, John's emerging coloration had a long and not always unfavorable history in European eyes. It should be pointed out that, like the geographical term "Ethiopia," the anthropological ones "Ethiope" and "Ethiopian" were, in ancient and medieval times, thoroughly ambiguous. When they referred to someone from a specific region they were close to our modern usage, even though that region, which began at the Upper Nile and had its capital at Meroë, sometimes stretched southward and eastward as far as imagination would allow. But "Ethiopian" served to designate color before it came to be applied to a region; the Greek *Aithiops,* from which it is derived, literally meant "Burnt-Face" and referred to any person of black complexion, whatever his place of origin. Homer said of the Ethiopians that they "live at the ends of the earth, some near the sunrise, some near the sunset." In later antiquity the word tended to become restricted to Black Africans, meaning either any Negro or someone specifically from "Ethiopia." The Biblical terms *Cush* and *Cushi,* which may have been specifically geographical designations from the outset, came to be translated "Ethiopia" and "Ethiopian" respectively, and the ambiguity was thereby reinforced.

The attitudes toward the Ethiopians or Cushites on the part of both the ancient Greek and the Old Testament literatures are strikingly free of the color prejudices of later times. True, the implication of the Greek term "Burnt-Face," and of Jeremiah's rhetorical question, "Can the Ethiopian [*Cushi*] change his skin, or the leopard his spots?" is that the Ethiopian complexion is not desirable; but this disapproval is only skin-deep. The *Aithiops* had unfortunately been burned black by the sun, but this had not affected his soul. Indeed, for Herodotus it had not even harmed his appearance, for in one passage in *The Persian Wars* we read that the Ethiopians "are said to be the tallest and handsomest men in the whole world." This admiration of their stature and physical impressiveness is an attitude to be found elsewhere in ancient literature. Nimrod, the son of Cush, is a "mighty hunter before the Lord," and the aspect under which the Cushites most frequently appear in the Old Testament is as a formidable enemy in war.°

We can perceive, then, a clearly defined image of a Noble Ethiopian in the principal literary sources in antiquity. This even is true — indeed, it is especially so — of the one passage in the Old Testament in which the Ethiopian appears as a slave, the story of Ebed-Melech in Jeremiah 38 and 39. The fact that Ebed-Melech (the name means literally "the king's slave") had the misfortune of being "one of the eunuchs which was in the king's house" is in itself no condemnation of him; Nehemiah, the re-builder of Jerusalem, also started out as a slave in a king's house (some scholars think that he, too, may have been a eunuch), and Israel itself had been a slave in Egypt. The rise from slavery is one of the significant moral patterns of the Old Testament, and Ebed-Melech provides another instance of it. It is he alone who is concerned about Jeremiah after the latter has been thrown into a dungeon, and by interceding for him Ebed-Melech obtains the king's permission to move him into the prison's court-yard. For this God rewards the Ethiopian by promising him his freedom.

Nevertheless, a shadow crosses the picture at this point. We have here an image of the Black man as a slave — the image of him that was to become the most typical one in the era launched by Prince Henry the Navigator. To what extent, then, was it becoming typical in Jeremiah's day? This question cannot be answered with any certainty; but it would seem that by this time such Middle Eastern powers as Egypt and Persia were obtaining a significant portion of their slaves from Black Africa. If so, then the slave relationship may well have been replacing the military one as the most characteristic form of contact between whites and "Ethiopians" in the Middle East. By the time of the New Testament this change evidently had gone so far that the only significant appearance of an Ethiopian in it was not as a warrior, but as a slave — though one of high character, as Ebed-Melech had been.†

° Only one passage in the Old Testament has occasionally been cited as a possible instance of color prejudice, though it can also be seen as exactly the opposite. This is the one in Numbers 12 that begins: "And Miriam and Aaron spake against Moses because of the Ethiopian woman whom he had married: for he had married an Ethiopian woman." The rest of the passage is about Miriam and Aaron, so we never learn anything more about this marriage. We are not even told exactly why Miriam and Aaron are angry. But if color prejudice is the reason, then doesn't this story be-come a resounding condemnation of it? For then there would be a horrifyingly apt kind of poetry in God's punishment of Miriam for speaking out against Moses' marriage to the Cushite woman, which is to afflict her temporarily with leprosy; her prejudice against the blackness of another's skin is thus being avenged with the curse of whiteness. Whatever Miriam and Aaron may feel, God and Moses are certainly on the side of the Ethiopian.

† This is in Acts 8, when Philip the Apostle meets "a man of Ethiopia, an eunuch of great authority under Candace queen of the Ethiopians, who had the charge of all her treasure, and had come to Jerusalem for to worship," and who "was returning, and

The Romans, too, had first encountered Ethiopians as warriors, in their African campaigns, and were beginning to see them predominantly as slaves by the first century c.e. At one point in the *Satyricon* of Petronius, the roguish heroes are seeking some means of escape from a ship, and Encolpius proposes that they deceive their captors by dyeing themselves with black ink to look "like Ethiopian slaves." Giton makes this sarcastic, and startling, reply:

> Oh! yes, and please circumcise us too so that we look like Jews, and bore our ears to imitate Arabians, and chalk our faces till Gaul takes us for her own sons; as if this color alone could alter our shapes, and it were not needed that many things act in unison to make a good lie on all accounts. Suppose that the stain of the dye on the face could last for some time; imagine that never a drop of water could make any mark on our skins, nor our clothes stick to the ink, which often clings to us without the use of any cement: but, tell me, can we also make our lips swell to a hideous thickness? Or transform our hair with curling-tongs? Or plough up our foreheads with scars? Or walk bow-legged? Or bend our ankles over to the ground? Or trim our beards in a foreign cut? Artificial colors dirty one's body without altering it.

In more ancient times, all Roman slaves, like all Greek ones, had been white, and even by Petronius' day the great majority of them were chalky-faced Gauls and other European types. But clearly, the increasing number of Black Africans coming into the Roman slave markets was making a strong impression on the imagination and threatening to efface the Noble Ethiopian image of earlier times. We shall see something similar take place in the fifteenth and sixteenth centuries.

Furthermore, there are signs that a conscious effort to defend the virtues of the Negro against detractors arose in late antiquity among men of good will. Among Romans or Greeks of philosophical bent, for example, black men were not necessarily to be scorned as slaves or feared as warriors, but could be admired as gymnosophists. Primarily a phenomenon of India — which, as we have seen, often was confused with Ethiopia — the gymnosophist seems to have been an early type of guru, who practiced nudity as part of a physical regimen that brought him close to nature and to the mysteries of the universe. Pliny could therefore write this way about Ethiopia:

sitting in his chariot read Esaias [Isaiah] the prophet"; Philip converts him to Christianity. (This Queen Candace is not to be confused with the one supposedly encountered by Alexander the Great more than three centuries earlier in the story to be dealt with below, although there was perhaps some confusion between them on the part of the ancient authors.)

> It is known that many of the inhabitants are more than seven feet six inches high, never spit, do not suffer from headache or toothache or pain in the eyes, and very rarely have a pain in any other part of the body — so hardy are they made by the temperate heat of the sun; and that the sages of their race, whom they call gymnosophists, stay standing from sunrise to sunset, gazing at the sun with eyes unmoving, and continue all day long standing first on one foot, then on the other in the glowing sand.

But the warmest tribute in all antiquity to the gymnosophists, and to the Ethiopians, came in the form of a novel written in Greek in the second or third century C.E. by a man who possibly was both. Unfortunately we shall never know for sure, since all we have on the author of the *Ethiopica* is what he tells us in a postscript, that he is "a Phoenician of Emesa, of the race of the sun — the son of Theodosius, Heliodorus." Despite his Levantine home and national designation, his reference to a solar lineage — even his name Heliodorus, probably a pseudonym, means "child of the sun" — suggests blackness of skin and an allegiance to gymnosophy.

Like that more celebrated Hellenistic romance, *Daphnis and Chloe,* the *Ethiopica* describes the endless trials of a pair of beautiful young lovers, but unlike that book, which contains a noticeable bias in favor of what today might be called the Nordic ideal of beauty, it is also a treatise on the virtues of a more southern type. Indeed, in a sense, the book is a defense of the south itself, of the mysterious, sun-scorched regions from which black men and women come. In the story, Theagenes, the young hero, is a pure Greek and a descendant of Achilles, but his beloved Chariclea turns out to be something else again. At first, she and the reader both believe her to be Greek, as do Theagenes and almost everyone else; she enters as a votary of Artemis who carries a quiver of arrows on her back and wears a laurel on her head. But slowly, as the two lovers follow a vexed odyssey from the Thessalian north, through the heartlands of Greece and then of Egypt across the water, southward to Ethiopia itself, the truth about Chariclea emerges: she is an Ethiopian princess. This proves to be no problem, however. Rather, it is the wisdom of Ethiopia, represented by the gymnosophists, that enables the couple to cut through a final set of moral difficulties and have a royal wedding. The south emerges as a shrine of wisdom, nobility, and beauty equal to any in the Hellenic north.

But what about color? The author handles it gingerly and, in the end, evades the issue. Chariclea, who is "of such inexpressible beauty as to be supposed divine," apparently has a somewhat exotic appearance, but she is white. On the other hand, her royal parents, King Hydaspes and

Queen Persinna, turn out to be the normal color of Ethiopians. How had all this come about? Here is Queen Persinna's explanation to her daughter:

> When I brought you to birth I found you white, a complexion alien to the native Ethiopian tint. I knew the reason for this: when I consorted with my husband I was looking at the picture which represented Andromeda just as Perseus had brought her down from the rock, and my offspring unhappily took on the complexion of that body.

Perhaps in that moment Persinna had been wondering why so white a heroine of Greek mythology as Andromeda had become associated with Ethiopia in the first place. In any case, the Greek power of whiteness had triumphed once again, and Queen Persinna had known she would have a hard time explaining the situation to her husband. "How could we two, both Ethiopians, produce a white child?" he asks at the end, when he has been presented with his long-lost daughter. Queen Persinna had dealt with the problem by turning over her infant daughter to a Delphic priest and telling her husband that the child had died.

For the rest, there are occasional, somewhat furtive mentions of the color of individual Ethiopians in the book, but in the final scene of reconciliation the blinding glow of the sun covers all complexions with the same radiance. For, as the Delphic priest tells the Ethiopians, who worship the very orb that has burned them black, "Apollo is your own ancestral deity, being identical with the sun." What better symbol could be offered for the ultimate kinship of blond and black?

A similarly blanched vision of the Noble Ethiopian is presented in another Greek novel of a century or two later, *The Romance of Alexander the Great*, by the Pseudo-Callisthenes. Among the adventures attributed to its hero in this major source book for the Alexander legends of the Middle Ages are a philosophical encounter with the gymnosophists of India and a vaguely erotic encounter with Queen Candace of Ethiopia. The dialogue with the gymnosophists ends in a victory for the Indian wisdom over the Greek. The encounter with Queen Candace, a small novel in itself, is as much a brief for the virtues of Ethiopia as Heliodorus' novel was. When Alexander travels through its countryside to meet the queen, he sees marvels suggestive of the later realms of Prester John — "crystal-bearing mountains . . . which reached as high as the clouds of heaven," and "deep caves with rocky descents," which an Ethiopian prince describes as "the dwelling place of the gods." When Candace first appears to Alexander, she is dazzling "in her royal crown, revealing her very great height and her godly face." The great height is a standard element in the descriptions of the Ethiopian in antiquity; the godly face is also not new, but here the author stops short of color with a Heliodorian evasiveness. In fact, color is mentioned only once in the entire story. In a letter written to the Macedonian before he and she have met, the queen warns: "And do not be mistaken about our color. For in our souls we are lighter than the white men amongst you." The implication is that whiteness is the best color for the soul, at least; as for the skin, one can have a burned face and still be beautiful, but it seems preferable to try not to notice the complexion at all.

With this the line of Prester John's early Ethiopian ancestry fades away in a haze of Hellenistic imagery and romance. Little more is to be seen of the Noble Ethiopian until his revival in the twelfth century, but except for the addition of medieval Jewish and Christian elements providing new dimensions of exaltation, his essential outlines were to be barely altered from antiquity. The pallid portraits painted by Heliodorus and the Pseudo-Callisthenes were a long way from the handsome black warriors of Herodotus, but they were perhaps the best that could be expected from an age in which color probably was becoming a serious problem. These Hellenistic romancers preserved the ideal of the Noble Ethiopian against an advancing wave of color prejudice by emphasizing every one of his traits but blackness. The result was a view of him that was to be revived in the era of Prester John: he was black, to be sure, but somehow his color was invisible. As in the Catalan Atlas, his features were off the edge of the map of the Christian consciousness.

So also was his Jewish ancestry invisible, buried deep in legend. Prester John was a symbol of racial and religious toleration within Christianity's complex heritage, but ultimately he would not be able to withstand the assault of a new outburst of prejudice directed against both the eastern and the southern components of his identity. Even in his simpler Hellenistic form, the Noble Ethiopian had proved unable to withstand the challenge of a demonic black image coming up from farther south. So much the more vulnerable, then, would the complex figure of Prester John be, in an era when Christian fanaticism against the Jew came together with a loathing for the waves of black captives that began rolling off those very Portuguese ships that had gone searching for Prester John in the first place. The ancient image of the Noble Ethiopian was to leave its traces upon the memory, but, for the moment at least, it is Petronius, and worse, who become our authors once again.

4

The Guinea Trade

IF THE PORTUGUESE sea route to Prester John and the treasures of the Indies proved to be long, the consolations of the Guinea trade were meanwhile to be found on the way. This was something well known to Portugal's Carthaginian forebears, of whom Herodotus wrote:

> There is a country in Libya [that is, Africa], and a nation, beyond the Pillars of Heracles, which they are wont to visit, where they no sooner arrive but forthwith they unlade their wares, and, having disposed them after an orderly fashion along the beach, leave them, and, returning aboard their ships, raise a great smoke. The natives, when they see the smoke, come down to the shore and, laying out to view so much gold as they think the worth of the wares, withdraw to a distance. The Carthaginians upon this come ashore and look. If they think the gold enough, they take it and go their way; but if it does not seem to them sufficient, they go aboard ship once more, and wait patiently. Then the others approach and add to their gold, till the Carthaginians are content. Neither party deals unfairly with the other: for they themselves never touch the gold till it comes up to the worth of their goods, nor do the natives carry off the goods till the gold is taken away.

This seems almost idyllic at first sight; but the lack of personal contact between the natives and the foreign traders is strange, even ominous. We have a sense here of the ages-long impenetrability of sub-Saharan Africa, and of a fear on the part of the Carthaginians that could in the end, beneath the pleasant glitter of gold, prove as destructive as the unabashed will to conquer.

We get a much more explicit picture of the fear in another Greek narrative from the same period, translated or adapted from a Carthaginian original, which describes the voyage of King Hanno far down the western coast of Africa. Sailing into hitherto unknown regions, Hanno and his men began encountering "barbarous Ethiopians in a country full of savage beasts," who threw stones at them or simply ran away at their arrival. Crossing the mouth of a great river full of hippopotamuses and crocodiles, they came to a place where at night they could see "fires flaring up on all sides at irregular intervals." Farther on, they came to an island where they "saw nothing but forest and at night many fires being kindled," and "heard the noise of pipes, cymbals, and drums, and the shouts of a great crowd. We were seized with fear, and the interpreters advised us to leave the island." Sailing away quickly, they "coasted along a region with a fragrant smell of burning timber, from which streams of fire plunged into the sea. We could not approach the land because of the heat." Once again they departed hastily, and "in some fear." They continued seeing fires all about, and eventually one that "towered above the others and appeared to touch the stars; this was the highest mountain which we saw and was called the Chariot of the Gods."

At length they seemed to have reached the nethermost circle of this Inferno. "Following rivers of fire for three days we came to a gulf called the Southern Horn. In this gulf was an island like the one last mentioned, with a lake in which was another island. This was full of savages; by far the greater number were women with hairy bodies, called by our interpreters 'gorillas.' We gave chase to the men but could not catch any for they climbed up steep rocks and pelted us with stones. However we captured three women who bit and scratched their captors. We killed and flayed them and brought their skins back to Carthage." The geographical mysteries of this narrative are insoluble, but the descent into bestiality — more so on the part of the intruders than on that of the natives — is as clearly plotted as on any map.

In the Middle Ages, the Sahara served the Arabs of North Africa as the western ocean had served the Carthaginians, and the tradition of a flourishing trade with Guinea from the north was thereby continued. The main channel for the overland route was through the Atlas Mountains at Sijilmassa, alongside which the inscription on the Catalan map reads: "Through this pass go the merchants who enter into the land of the

Blacks of Guinea." The trade was a source of prosperity for Muslim merchants on the Barbary coast, for Jewish merchants at Sijilmassa, and even for the Christian merchants on the Iberian Peninsula who were the eventual recipients of some of its benefits, which included not only gold, but ivory, malagueta pepper, and slaves.

Slaves may not yet have been part of the Guinea trade when the Carthaginians passed it on to their successors; we do not know. But it is certain that slaves were among the commodities being obtained by the Arabs in Guinea by the time Portuguese ships began to outflank them there in the fifteenth century. Indeed, it is possible to say that Negro slavery in the modern western world is an Arab legacy. For though chattel slavery had continued to exist in the Christian countries of the Mediterranean, as in the Arab countries there, right down to Prince Henry's time and long after it had vanished in northern Europe, Black slavery had declined in them after the Roman period and was to be found only in the Muslim world until about the thirteenth century. From then on, small numbers of Black slaves began appearing in Christian Iberia as a direct result of the Moorish presence on the peninsula.

This does not mean that the slaves of medieval Islam had only been black; they were of many complexions and from a wide variety of countries, as in Greco-Roman antiquity. But since the days of the Persian Empire at least, the Middle East had always had an especially large number of Blacks among its slaves, and the Arabs had inherited this tradition. By the eighth century, the image of the Negro in the Arab imagination was mainly that of a slave. Jahiz of Basra, an Arab writer of that epoch who was perhaps partly Negro himself, defended Blacks against accusations of low intelligence by saying that since most Arabs knew them only as slaves, proper conditions for making such a judgment did not exist. His native Basra, in Iraq, became the scene of the greatest slave revolt of the Middle Ages in 869, and virtually all of the hundreds of rebels were Black. One of the Arabic words for "slave," 'abd, eventually became fixed as a specific term for a Black slave, and in some dialects it came to be used as the term for Blacks in general. Some Arab authors found sanction for the advancement of Black slavery in Noah's outburst against his son Ham, when he said: "Cursed be Canaan; a servant of servants shall he be unto his brethren." This only singles out one of Ham's sons, but many Arabs — and later, many Christians, too — held that it condemned all of them to slavery. Indeed, one Arab tradition maintained that blackness itself had been inflicted upon Ham's descendants by a curse from Noah — either this one, or another to be found between the lines.

With the gradual emergence of the notion that the slave status typified the Negro, there also developed among Arabs a vehement anti-Black prejudice. Not that all Arab color prejudice was directed against Blacks; pale-skinned northerners — like Petronius' chalky-faced Gauls — also were considered to have fallen short, in flesh and spirit, of the Mediterranean olive ideal of beauty. Sa'id al-Andalusi ("the Spaniard"), an eleventh-century writer of Toledo, observed that the cold northern climate was what made peoples like the Slavs and the Bulgars — two other prominent sources of chattel slaves in both Christendom and Islam (hence the derivation of our word "slave") — pale of color, lank-haired, fat, coarse-humored, and stupid. But on the other hand, according to Sa'id, it was the excessive heat of the sun that had blackened the skin of the southern peoples, made their hair woolly, and so roasted their spirits that they "lack self-control and steadiness of mind and are overcome by fickleness, foolishness and ignorance." In the long run, this latter prejudice was the stronger, no doubt partly because light skins more easily became invisible in Arab society after a generation or two than black skins.

Arab literature has many examples of an anti-Negro prejudice that apparently was taken for granted, but none are more vivid than those found in the *Arabian Nights,* which abounds with images of boorish and lustful Blacks that could have come out of an American slaveholder's nightmares. In the story of "King Shahryar and His Brother," the king spies on his wife having a secret liaison that is described (in Richard Burton's English) like this:

> . . . the Queen, who was left alone, presently cried out in a loud voice, "Here to me, O my lord Sa'id!" and then sprang with a drop-leap from one of the trees a big slobbering Blackamoor with rolling eyes which showed the whites, a truly hideous sight. He walked boldly up to her and threw his arms round her neck while she embraced him as warmly; then he bussed her and winding his legs round hers, as a button-loop clasps a button, he threw her and enjoyed her.

The very long frontier between the Muslim world and Black Africa was surely one of the reasons why so many of the Arabs' slaves came from there; but, on the other hand, this did not seem to lead to much acquaintance with Blacks in their own habitat. Only a few hardy Arab travelers made their way across desert and grassland into the hot, obnoxious tropics. The celebrated tenth-century traveler from Baghdad, Ibn Haukal, visited the Negro empire of Ghana, and manifested what seems to be a typical attitude when he wrote:

> I have not described the country of the African blacks and other peoples of the torrid zone: because naturally loving wisdom, ingenuity, religion, justice and regular government, how

could I notice such people as these, or magnify them by inserting an account of their countries?

But he ought to have opened his eyes more to what perhaps would have been a wholly different experience of Negroes from the one he was familiar with. This, at any rate, was what was discovered some four hundred years later by the greatest of Arab travelers, Ibn Battuta, when he went to West Africa. At first he was disgusted at the sight of a people he had known only as slaves behaving as masters in their own country; but in time, this was precisely what he learned to respect. Then he could write:

> The Negroes possess some admirable qualities. They are seldom unjust, and have a greater abhorrence of injustice than any other people. . . . There is complete security in their country. Neither traveller nor inhabitant in it has anything to fear from robbers or men of violence. They do not confiscate the property of any white man who dies in their country, even if it be untold wealth. On the contrary, they give it into the charge of some trustworthy person among the whites, until the rightful heir takes possession of it.

Ibn Battuta also admired the punctilious observance of the Koran that he saw among them — for he was in Muslim country. Indeed, his visit had taken place not long after the reign of the great Black Muslim king, Mansa Musa of Mali. The whole atmosphere seems redolent of a western, Muslim version of the realm of Prester John.

But Guinea never was to be a promised land, either for Arab or for European. For the outsider it was always rather a vast circumference, rimmed by desert and by sea, out of which highly valued commodities came, but within which was a darkness that was either unappealing, forbidding, or terrifying. Nor was there ever any need to penetrate it, since the Blacks of West Africa were always the most cooperative of traders, whether with Arabs from across the desert or with Carthaginians — and, later, Portuguese — from across the sea. These factors, along with the formidable military prowess of the Blacks, and the relative indifference of the early Portuguese to the conquest of continents, were what spared Black Africa the fate of the Canaries and of the Americas until the nineteenth century. But they also helped to seal the fate of the slaves brought out of Guinea, first by Arab caravans and then by Portuguese ships. For even the Canarians, whom Jean de Bethencourt had sometimes slaughtered but refused to sell into slavery, were a people in its land to be treated as such for better or for worse; but the Guinea slaves were mere commodities.

Making men into commodities was, among other things, a convenient way of dealing with one's fear of them, of reducing and containing the awesome primitive powers of the wild men and women encountered by Hanno's men, or of the potent Blackamoor described by the *Arabian Nights* narrator. A good picture of the beginning of the Portuguese historic encounter with the frightening black men of the south is provided by Prince Henry's chronicler, Gomes Eannes de Zurara, in his description of a significant moment in the Portuguese conquest of Ceuta. Standing among the defenders of the city gate, he writes, was one Moor who was

> very tall and of a most threatening complexion, all naked, who used no other weapons than stones, but each of the stones that he threw seemed to be hurled by a catapult or a cannon, such was the strength of his arm. And when the Moors were thrust back . . . against the gate of the city, he turned back to the Christians, stooped himself and threw a stone which struck Vasco Martins d'Albergaria and carried away the vizor of his casque.

What sort of "Moor" was this rude giant, so different from the ordinary run of Berbers and Arabs at Ceuta? We learn more in the next sentence:

> The aspect of this Moor was such as to inspire terror, since all his body was black as a crow, and he had very long and white teeth, and his lips, which were fleshy, were turned back.

As it turned out, terror could not daunt the sturdy Vasco Martins, who,

> despite the violence of the blow received, did not lose countenance and did not fail to pay the Moor for his labor; the latter had had barely time to turn around when the lance of the Portuguese pierced him through. So soon as the Moor fell lifeless all the others were taken with panic and rushed towards the gate to take refuge in the city, and the Christians with them.

The first invasion of Africa by the Portuguese emerges here as their first assault on Black Africa as well.* But not all of them were to be so hardy

---

* In a sense, this Black's appearance at the entrance to Ceuta was like a revelation of the more southern aspect that had always been present in the identity of the Moor. The very name by which Spanish Christians had always designated the Muslims of the peninsula — *moros*, meaning "men of Mauretania," which was the Roman name for the region corresponding to present-day Morocco — came from an old Greek word meaning "black." The Iberians were now to specify *moros negros* for the black men farther south, or just *negros*, thereby providing the English language with yet another racial term; although, right down through Shakespeare's time, the word

as Vasco Martins d'Albergaria; in the end, it was easier to slip chains onto the giant than to do battle with him.

The assault on the Blacks now being begun by Portugal and Spain was, in one sense, just a part of the burgeoning vengefulness upon the entire legacy of those civilizations that had once overrun the peninsula from the south and ultimately the east, but in another, the outcome of attitudes inherited from it. Whatever had been feared or loathed in medieval Spain, by Christian and Muslim alike, had come up from the deep south, such as the harsh, uncivilized religious fanaticism of the Almoravide and Almohade Berber invaders in the eleventh and twelfth centuries. The southward thrust that the Portuguese were now undertaking was the beginning of a voyage into the terrifying dark recesses of the Iberian collective unconscious. The farther south their ships took them in the search for an eastward passage, the more the benign black image of Prester John became obscured under the frightening and then contemptible ones of the Moor at Ceuta and the Guinea slave. But there was substantial compensation for this in the gold and other worthy products obtained, and in the glory of the unique, southward-directed Crusade that Portugal could claim as her own God-given mission.

Prince Henry's ships finally rounded the dreaded Cape Bojador in 1434. It is conceivable that Master Jacome of Majorca was still alive to witness this triumph of the old spirit of geographical adventure for virtually its own sake; but his was a dying generation, and a new mood of rapaciousness and cruelty now went along on those bold ships as well. By the next decade, the Portuguese captains were coming back from their voyages south of Bojador carrying not only gold, but slaves, acquired either by trade with coastal chieftains or by direct forays on the part of the sailors, who kidnapped any innocent people they could find along the shores where they landed. Oddly enough, it was the slave trade that the Portuguese proudly proclaimed to the world; gold was something about which they preferred to keep quiet. Portugal was still struggling with the ghost of illegitimacy, and an open quest for gold on her part would have raised it again; slaving expeditions, on the other hand, could be depicted as campaigns against the Moors, a continuation of the glories of Ceuta. The captives were being brought out from pagan darkness into the light of Christianity. The chronicler Zurara writes in his history of the discovery of Guinea how his patron Prince Henry at one point, watching yet

---

"Moor" was to serve often enough by itself as a synonym for "Blackamoor" or "Negro." It is significant, however, that none of these terms produced by the southern thrust of Portuguese conquest and slaving ever achieved the lofty status in English of the word "Ethiopian," which has always tended to be a genteel designation, rather abstract and sometimes faintly absurd in the American democratic vocabulary, much like "Hebrew" or "Israelite" for a Jew.

another consignment of slaves from Africa, "reflected with great pleasure upon the salvation of those souls that before were lost." Zurara then enthusiastically adds these observations of his own:

> And certainly his expectation was not in vain; for, as we have said before, as soon as they understood our language they turned Christians with very little ado; and I who put together this history into this volume, saw in the town of Lagos [in Portugal] boys and girls — the children and grandchildren of those first captives, born in this land — as good and true Christians as if they had directly descended, from the beginnings of the dispensation of Christ, from those who were first baptized.

Zurara tells us nothing of the juridical condition of these fortunate off-spring, but he makes clear enough his view that, at least as far as Africans are concerned, the condition of the body is as nothing to that of the soul.

This view evidently was good enough for the Church. In 1442, Prince Henry received from Pope Eugenius IV a letter that was to be the first in a series of commendations from Rome for his campaigns against the "Moors" — that is, for his slaving expeditions. In a series of papal bulls in the 1450s, Portugal was given full license not only to make war against the infidel and capture slaves in the newly discovered regions of Africa, but to enter fully into trade relations there. This really meant gold for the Portuguese, of course; the slave trade was not to be truly profitable until the colonization of the New World in the next century. In the mean-time, Portugal's fateful entry into the Black slave trade — hitherto virtually a Muslim monopoly — was merely a stratagem that had worked; the West African was in truth being crucified on a cross of gold.

For, if this was Crusade, as it pretended to be, then how the mighty had fallen! Zurara rarely describes a conquest of which a man, not to mention a holy warrior, could really be proud. When the victims are obtained by capture rather than trade, they seem usually to be unsuspecting villagers sitting at home or around their campfires, women and children carrying jugs down to wells, the aged and the infirm left behind when the other inhabitants have fled, or the like. At times our historian even seems a bit embarrassed when telling some of the tales of conquest his doughty Crusaders have brought home for him to transcribe.

A vivid example of such dubious valor is given when one Stevam Affonso, stalking woods near the coast with several companions, comes upon a "Guinea" (as the Blacks were then being called by the Portuguese) chopping wood outside his home and unaware of the danger behind him:

> Stevam Affonso began to move forward; and what with the careful guard that he kept in stepping quietly, and the intent-

ness with which the Guinea labored at his work, the Guinea
never perceived the approach of his enemy until the latter
leaped upon him. And I say leaped, since Stevam Affonso was
of small frame and slender, while the Guinea was of quite
different build; and so the Portuguese seized him lustily by
the hair, so that when the Guinea raised himself erect, Stevam
Affonso remained hanging in the air with his feet off the
ground. The Guinea was a brave and powerful man, and he
thought it a reproach that he should thus be subjected by so
small a thing. Also he wondered within himself what this thing
could be; but though he struggled very hard, he was never able
to free himself, and so strongly had his enemy entwined himself
in his hair, that the efforts of those two men could be compared
to nothing else than a rash and fearless hound who has fixed on
the ear of some mighty bull.

In the ensuing action, the "Guinea" goes on behaving in the noble way
that has clearly appealed to the touch of poetry in Zurara's imagination.
The two other Portuguese who had been with Stevam Affonso at this
encounter come forth to help him at last, but the Negro shakes them off
and runs into the woods. Rather than fleeing, however, he picks up a
spear and attacks the lone Portuguese who had remained back at the
small boat in which all four had landed. The latter is saved only by the
arrival of the three original assailants, who fight off the Negro and a
companion who then comes to his aid. The two Blacks are forced back
into the woods, and the four Portuguese waste no time about pushing off
in the boat and heading back to their ship.

There are glimmers of conscience in Zurara, who is otherwise a kept
historian, in moments such as these; but conscience was not rife among
the Portuguese in relation to Black Africa, where they were to remain
Stevam Affonsos in that epoch, leaping onto the backs of men or onto
women on their backs, paying virtually no price in responsibility at all.
Perhaps a man like Zurara would have achieved a better moral insight
if he had just once gone along in the ships to Africa and seen a people in
its land. Instead, all that he saw with his own eyes was the wretched
refuse of a ravaged African shore, about which he could ruminate only
with the utmost moral indecisiveness:

> On the next day, which was the 8th of the month of August
> [1443], very early in the morning, by reason of the heat, the
> seamen began to make ready their boats, and to take out those
> captives, and carry them on shore, as they were commanded.
> And these, placed all together in that field, were a marvelous
> sight; for amongst them were some white enough, fair to look
> upon, and well proportioned; others were less white like mulat-

toes; others again were as black as Ethiopes, and so ugly, both
in features and in body, as almost to appear (to those who saw
them) the images of a lower hemisphere. But what heart could
be so hard as not to be pierced with piteous feeling to see that
company? For some kept their heads low and their faces bathed
in tears, looking one upon the other; others stood groaning
very dolorously, looking up to the height of heaven, fixing their
eyes upon it, crying out loudly, as if asking help of the Father
of Nature; others struck their faces with the palms of their
hands, throwing themselves at full length upon the ground;
others made their lamentations in the manner of a dirge, after
the custom of their country. And though we could not understand the words of their language, the sound of it right well
accorded with the measure of their sadness. But to increase
their sufferings still more, there now arrived those who had
charge of the division of the captives, and who began to separate one from another, in order to make an equal partition of
the fifths; and then it was needful to part fathers from sons,
husbands from wives, brothers from brothers. No respect was
shown either to friends or relations, but each fell where his
lot took him.

Though the ambivalent Zurara never questions the rightness of this
traffic, he does often interrupt his narrative with prayers for the well-
being of the unfortunate captives, protesting that "they too are of the
generation of the sons of Adam." Not all his contemporaries were to
agree even with this claim, and certainly one can see, beyond the limits
of Zurara's protestations of human sympathy, something like true modern
racism — the notion of a tainted people — beginning to assert itself. At one
point in his narrative, he has to find justification for the fact that the
Portuguese have ransomed a light-skinned Muslim nobleman they had
captured for "five or six Black Moors," a patent violation of the theory
that slaving was part of an anti-Muslim Crusade, and he writes:

. . . you must note that these Blacks were Moors like the
others, but were their slaves, in accordance with ancient custom, which I believe to have been because of the curse which,
after the Deluge, Noah laid upon his son Cain [sic], cursing
him in this way: that his race should be subject to all the other
races of the world.

In other words, the Portuguese are honoring Muslim custom when they
choose to enslave Blacks and not whites. But this unwonted show of
respect for the customs of the Infidel cannot be taken seriously, and is an
obvious disguise for something else. From the wars of the *Reconquista*

right down through the slave consignment of August 8, 1443, that Zurara has described above, Iberian Christians had been as willing to enslave white Moors as the latter had been to enslave them. But by the time Zurara was writing his narrative in the 1460s, Portuguese slavers evidently had decided, as Arab slavers had before them, that they preferred trading in Blacks. This was better for the good relations Portugal often sought with the Moorish kingdoms of North Africa, and it was also an easier trade, since Black chieftains often were notoriously willing to trade off their prisoners of war to foreign slavers. An even more compelling reason, no doubt, was the fact that a Black was a commodity that could not be lost in a crowd; wherever he went, he was betrayed as a slave by his indelible trademark, his mark of Cain — and Zurara was not the only Christian writer to confuse or identify Canaan with Adam's accursed son. For the religious justification of Black slavery that is here attributed to the Muslims by Zurara is really being sanctioned by him, as is the practice itself. From now on, Noah's curse will serve as a standard excuse for Black slavery among Europeans as well.

Yet as an apparently conscienceless Portugal thus stumbles into a new and doleful epoch of man's inhumanity to man, we do hear one voice emanating from Prince Henry's ships to urge the view that Ibn Battuta had presented in the preceding century — that of the dignity of Black men and women living as a people in their land. But it was, significantly, the voice of an Italian, not a Portuguese. Alvise da Cadamosto's° accounts of his experiences with the Blacks of coastal West Africa while voyaging under Prince Henry's banner, written in a spirit of Florentine humanism and wit, display the attitudes of a later, more liberal era. For example, there is a long dialogue between himself and a Black Muslim ruler in the Senegal named Budomel, about the comparative virtues of Christianity and Islam. This provides an opportunity for some ironies about European civilization of the sort that Boccaccio had found in his view of the Canarians. Budomel concedes that Christianity must be good since God had given its adherents so many worldly advantages. His people, on the other hand, had been given nothing but just laws; "and

° Unfortunately, Cadamosto's general veracity has often been questioned, in his own time as well as by scholars of subsequent generations. His story certainly is a remarkable one. A young man in his twenties with little experience as a navigator, he visited Prince Henry while traveling in Portugal — he tells us, in a narrative published after Prince Henry's death — and persuaded the latter to give him permission to command a ship on a voyage to Africa. He also claims to have discovered the Cape Verde Islands on this voyage, and this has been found to be patently untrue. Furthermore, even if we grant that there is a core of personal experience in his account, much of it has clearly been fleshed out by information coming from more than one source besides himself. Yet all this is largely beside the point; for Cadamosto clearly has seen Blacks on their home soil, and the important thing for us is not so much the details he gives in his account of them as the attitudes he expresses.

he considered it reasonable," Cadamosto writes, "that they would be better able to gain salvation than we Christians, for God was a just lord, who had granted us in this world many benefits, but to the Negroes, in comparison with us, almost nothing. Since he had not given them paradise here, he would give it to them hereafter."

Even more than in matters of religion, Cadamosto in matters of race is always ready to stand conventional attitudes on their head. He shows the Black king of Mali speaking of Blacks farther south with a contempt strikingly like that of Europeans speaking of *him*. To the people of Mali, the appearance of the people south of the Senegal is "terrifying." But Cadamosto sees the matter quite differently. "It appears to me a marvelous thing," he writes, "that beyond the river [Senegal] all men are very black, tall and big, their bodies well formed; and the whole country green, full of trees, and fertile; while on this side, the men are brownish, small, lean, ill-nourished, and small in stature; the country sterile and arid." Black is beautiful for Cadamosto, who also perceives that white can be as mystifying to some as black is to others. At a marketplace in a Senegalese village, he observes:

> These Negroes, men and women, crowded to see me as though I were a marvel. It seemed to be a new experience to them to see Christians, whom they had not previously seen. They marvelled no less at my clothing than at my white skin. . . . Some touched my hands and limbs, and rubbed me with their spittle to discover whether my whiteness was dye or flesh. Finding that it was flesh they were astounded.

This white-stained flesh not only was strange, it also could be terrifying. Farther south, the Negroes of Gambia tell Cadamosto "they firmly believed that we Christians ate human flesh, and that we only bought Negroes to eat them."

In a sense, of course, the Gambians were quite right. Could any of the white men's horror stories of Black anthropophagi in remote corners of the world match the Black man's grim experience of being devoured alive by Christian ships? These were ironies worthy of being reflected upon by humane men in that epoch; but Cadamosto's writings did not achieve much popularity outside of Italy.

5

Jews and New Christians

ZURARA'S OBSERVATIONS on the Negro have brought us into the presence of a true racist outlook; but they are not the first on record to display it in fifteenth-century Iberia, nor was the Negro the first to feel its scorn. There can be no doubt that the growing Black presence contributed to the racial tinge that group attitudes now were beginning to assume; but racism, in its most characteristic form, is an attitude generated not at a distance but within a given social framework, which ripens in the relationship between one group and another living side by side. Black Africans were only relative newcomers to such a relationship with Christians on the Iberian Peninsula. The growing revulsion on the part of the latter from the southern component of their own identity found its first racist manifestations toward the Moors and the Jews in their midst, who had come up from Africa centuries before and had steadily infiltrated the life of the peninsula. In particular, as the notion of taint that had hitherto attached to religious doctrines considered unclean began to attach to whole peoples and their bloodlines, the new racism was above all directed at that group whose religion had provoked the most superstitious fear in the past and who had achieved the greatest degree of infiltration into the general society. Its first victims were the Jews — or rather, those most insidious of all infiltrators and bearers of tainted doctrines, the peculiar offspring of Jewish history in Spain known as the New Christians.

There had always been isolated converts from Judaism to Christianity in Spain, of course, but the sudden appearance of a large class of such *conversos* dates only from the riots of 1391. The mass conversions had, by and large, only replaced a religious problem with a social one, leaving behind them whole communities that were now Christian in name but still Jewish in ethnic identity. The situation was highly ambiguous for the New Christians, suspended in a moral space between the rump of Spanish Judaism that had survived the riots on the one hand, and the Church into which they had been thrust and from which any relapse would be heresy on the other. It is well known to posterity that a substantial portion of them went on practicing Judaism in secret, holding Sabbath services and Jewish weddings in their shuttered homes, while carrying on a public display of participation in Sunday mass, church weddings, and baptisms all their lives. These people in particular provoked the opprobrious epithet that often was used against all New Christians: *Marranos,* apparently an ironic application of a Spanish word meaning "swine." Many of the converts who thus remained secretly loyal to the ancestral faith no doubt believed that a time might soon arrive when they could openly return to it with impunity; there were precedents for this in Christian Europe, and in Spain in particular, provided by tolerant monarchs ready to allow it and to protect the recidivists from the wrath of the Church. Besides, the Church itself had mixed feelings about conversions achieved by force rather than persuasion. As time wore on, however, and generation succeeded generation, the Marrano hope of reconversion took on a more messianic character — indeed, became a new metaphor of the Jewish condition in general — or else finally rested upon the will and the strength to emigrate to some country in which the long-awaited fulfillment would at last be possible; this, too, became a search for promised lands.

But such a secret Judaism was by no means a trait of the entire class of *conversos.* On the contrary, many of them meant to be perfectly sincere in their new faith. The Judaism of Spain had not been so firmly shored up in its orthodoxy as that of northern Europe. In one respect it had simply become overcivilized, and unable to withstand the lure of the comfort that comes with submission to the majority; but it also had never been particularly well equipped to deal with the challenge of Christianity. The Talmud, that mighty fortress of Jewish traditionalism, never achieved in Spain the kind of overwhelming authority it had readily found among Ashkenazic Jewry. Spanish rabbis relied as much upon philosophical argument as upon Talmudic exegesis for validation of the faith. In the philosophy-drenched culture of Muslim Spain, this approach had posed few problems of religious identity; it was a situation in which a conservative majority faith and a conservative minority one went from strength to strength in a perennial, often mutually respectful, exchange over the eternal truths of grammar, metaphysics, and law.

But the dynamic Christianity of the late Middle Ages was an entirely different matter. It not only mounted an unrelenting assault upon Jewish resistance to the message of universal salvation, but also challenged Judaism on its most susceptible front — that of the messianic question. The messianic component of Judaism has been less prominent in recent times, but for most Jews in the Middle Ages, it was the main issue; the redemption that had been anticipated from almost the very moment of destruction and dispersion in antiquity, and that was the prinicipal justification for having kept the faith since then, was the object of an excitement that was never far beneath the surface. In Spain in particular, messianic excitement had reached new heights since the beginning of the *Reconquista,* and calculations were rife foretelling the imminent date of the Redeemer's arrival. Messianic inebriation made resistance difficult to a proselytizing Christianity that proclaimed the Redeemer to have arrived already, and medieval Spain saw some dramatic Jewish conversions to Christianity. By 1391, many Spanish Jews found Christianity at least as attractive a creed as the one into which they had been born, and needed nothing more than the external shove the riots provided to send them through the barriers of blood loyalty into an embrace with the religion of European civilization.

Even for many of those whose confessional loyalty had survived the riots, the ambivalence remained. Disaster had served only to raise messianic excitement to a pitch of hysteria, and the impulse spread to give up the ghost of millennial Jewish resistance. The situation was recognized by a newly zealous Spanish Christianity, and a whole class of preachers had arisen even before 1391 to dedicate themselves to the conversion of the Jews. Fray Vicente Ferrer, the foremost of these, became a legendary figure about whom stories of miraculous feats of proselytization were told. One such story tells of how he walked boldly into a synagogue in Salamanca on a Saturday in 1411, holding a cross aloft before the astonished congregation, and began to preach. In a few moments, according to a pious seventeenth-century chronicler, crosses began to appear on the garments of the congregants, and "the Jews, perceiving such a great marvel . . . sought out the baptismal font and, wanting to become Christians, were converted, many of them taking the name Vicente in honor of the Saint." We need not take the story literally to perceive that some kind of genuine mass phenomenon was involved. There were many conversions at this time, although persuasion was abetted by legal coercion: in 1412, a new set of discriminatory laws against Jews was promulgated in both Aragon and Castile, at Vicente Ferrer's instigation.

Another significant turning point was reached the very next year, 1413, when Pope Benedict XIII, an Aragonese by birth, decided to see if he could settle religious scores in his homeland by calling for a public disputation there between rabbis and priests. An important element in Benedict's strategy was a convert from Judaism named Joshua Halorki, who, "after his apostasy," wrote the sixteenth-century Sephardic historian Solomon ibn Verga, "went among the gentiles calling himself Geronimo de Santa Fe and speaking insultingly of his origins. The pope asked him to bring together the wise men of Israel, so he could prove to them that the Messiah had already come, and that it was Jesus, and that this was proven by the Talmud." Halorki was well versed in rabbinical literature, and during the disputation, which was held at the Catalonian city of Tortosa, he was able to score some telling points. For example, he invoked a Talmudic tradition to the effect that the Messiah had been born at around the time of the destruction of the Second Temple, which is to say, roughly in the era of Jesus. The Jewish disputants could not deny this tradition, but in order to avoid the implication here in favor of Jesus, they argued for the possibility that the Messiah, though he had not yet found the right moment to make his appearance, could by now be some fourteen hundred years old.

Many a Jew of Spain must have pondered that reply and wondered whether such grounds for denying Christian claims were adequate to sustain him against all the woes he was suffering in the name of such a denial. In the months following the close of the disputation, according to the leading modern historian of Spanish Jewry, "Jews appeared in Tortosa, singly at first and then in groups, and declared that after listening to the feeble arguments of their rabbis they had decided to become Christians. Others — among them communal leaders — were baptized in their own localities." In 1414 there was another wave of pogroms and forced conversions, but perhaps many of the victims by now shared the feelings of a prominent apostate of Toledo, Master Juan the Elder, who had written of the events of 1391 that: "In that year the Messiah came to us by force, and we were brought into the fold of the Holy Catholic Church; for on the day when a man's understanding comes to full maturity, on the selfsame day, the Messiah comes to him."

But in that generation of mass conversions, and even more so in the subsequent generations of the fifteenth century, the portrait of the New Christians does not resolve itself simplistically into a division between the sincere, sometimes zealous, Catholic on the one hand and the unrelenting secret Jew on the other. The picture is above all characterized by ambiguity: by a Christianity that often remained confused and instinctually unorthodox even amidst conscientious strivings for conformity, and a residual Judaism — in some respects a racial feeling, in the spirit of the times — that became more and more tenuous even in the face of strong efforts to maintain it. Many New Christians probably did not know exactly what they were, at least so far as conventional doctrines were concerned. In some cases, this complexity was to resolve itself into a highly unconventional kind of religiosity, a messianic Christianity as zealous as it was unorthodox, which came to form a strain in the emerging quasi-Protestant spirit of Europe by the end of the century. But in mid-century, a more world-weary spirit, characteristic of the Renaissance, seems to prevail among the middle-of-the-road New Christians.

A good example of the latter can be found in the personality of one Pedro de la Cavalleria, who was converted by his father as a boy in reaction to the Disputation of Tortosa, and who rose to a high position in the Aragonese judiciary. During his lifetime he wrote a Latin brochure defending Christianity against Judaism and Islam, and he took steps, as many New Christians did, to have all evidence of his Jewish origin effaced from his personal and family documents. But his writing shows considerable evidence of Jewish learning and, according to Inquisition testimony — which must always be taken with a grain of salt, but out of which a few valid outlines of the lives involved can sometimes be extrapolated — he was not immune to participating in some of the traditional Hebrew blessings when visiting the homes of unconverted Jewish friends. One such friend told the Inquisition after his death that, when asked why he preferred Christianity to Judaism, Cavalleria had replied:

> Could I, as a Jew, ever have risen higher than a rabbinical post? But now, see, I am one of the chief councillors of the city. . . . Who hinders me from fasting on Yom Kippur, if I choose, and keeping your festivals and all the rest? When I was a Jew I dared not walk as far as this [on a Saturday]; but now I do as I please.

This is as ambivalent a Judaism as it is cynical a Christianity. The rabbis may well have been just as offended by a Jew who became a Christian so he could walk as far as he wanted on Saturday as the priests were by a New Christian who still occasionally fasted on Yom Kippur; for the moment, the kings and nobles who filled their courts with such men did not care one way or the other. But the time was swiftly coming when priestly wrath would have the last word.

The signs of a reaction to the possibility of the taint of heresy in every Christian of Jewish blood had come as far back as 1414, when the university college of San Bartolomé in Salamanca banned membership to anyone who was not "of pure blood." This was a weather vane for the more severe blast of racism that came in the 1440s. In 1446, the town of Villena banned all *conversos* from residence there, and in 1449, the municipal government of Toledo responded to an outburst of rioting against *converso* tax-gatherers by forbidding anyone of Jewish descent to hold official posts within the city. Pope Nicholas V denounced the statute of Toledo, and King Juan II of Castile, whose court was a well-known gathering place of powerful *conversos*, resisted it for a time. But the king soon gave in; the incipient racism of the Old Christian population was beginning to have its way.

The clamor for *limpieza de sangre* — "purity of blood" — came largely from the rising classes in society, and was concentrated mainly in that most democratic of medieval institutions, the Church. But there has survived into our own time a piece of evidence vividly suggesting that something like a courtly version of the emergent anti-Jewish racism also was making an appearance in mid-fifteenth century. This is a short satirical work written anonymously in about 1450. Something of a Swiftian "modest proposal," the work purports to be a letter written by King Juan II to an Old Christian nobleman granting him the "privileges" of a Marrano. The bearer is given royal license to "be like a Marrano, and is empowered to use the subtleties, arts, dealings and deceptions which the said Marranos, without fear of God or shame before their fellow men, use and profit by." These include giving wicked counsel in ruling circles, charging high interest rates on loans, and even entering the priesthood — mainly for the purpose, it would seem, of listening to the confessions of Old Christians and getting to "know their secret sins." The utmost religious duplicity is allowed. "You may go deceitfully into churches and other sacred places without any devotion, carrying your account-book instead of a prayer-book or psalter, and pretending to recite the penitential psalms, as so many of the said race of Marranos are in the habit of doing." The bearer may also go about presenting views contrary to those of the Church, saying, for example, "that there is no other world but the one in which we are born and die, as the said Marranos maintain and affirm contrary to truth." Meanwhile he may, as the Marranos do, maintain his household in accordance with the Torah, observe Saturday as a day of rest while working on Sundays and Church holidays, "drink the wine of the *Baracha*," learn "Hebrew science" in the synagogue, and have a Jewish burial.

One can see readily enough the social reality underlying this vehemently spiteful portrait; but then there comes a sudden departure into pure myth, an ominous fabrication that at once harks back to medi-

eval superstition about murderous Jewish doctors and echoes forward to
Nazi cant about *Rassenschande*. Our satirical letter gives

> license to you and your descendants to become apothecaries,
> physicians and surgeons and, under the pretext of curing and
> seeking to restore the body of any Old Christian from illness
> to health, to endeavor to kill and disgrace him as the said race
> of Marranos do, as much out of enmity and hatred as in order
> to marry the wives of the Old Christians they kill, swallowing
> up their goods and property and polluting and staining the
> pure blood.

"Polluting and staining the pure blood" — what more vivid example could
there be of a spiritual and social revilement turning into a biological one?
At its beginning point, the notion is a metaphor, an image of a blot on the
escutcheon; but at the deepest and most terrified levels of the consciousness, metaphor swiftly translates into reality, as reality does into metaphor. One wonders to what extent that image of poison that Jewish
doctors had used, or that had been infiltrated into Christian wells, had
been a vision of blood all along.

The emerging pattern of anti-*converso* racism in the fifteenth century
was completed by the establishment of the Spanish Inquisition in 1478.
By this time, the papal Inquisition of the Middle Ages had lost considerable energy; it had, in fact, never been strong on Iberian soil. But when the
institution was revived by the kingdoms of Aragon and Castile, united
through the marriage of their respective sovereigns Ferdinand and
Isabella in 1469, it was to take on not only new relentlessness but also a
new character of national exclusiveness. For though papal sanction was
obtained for it, the Spanish Inquisition, unlike the older one, was placed
directly under the authority of the sovereigns and not of the papacy. This
was not the only way in which it became quite Spanish, however; for
whereas the medieval Inquisition had been aimed at heresy in general,
the Spanish one came into being primarily to ferret out what was called
the "Judaizing heresy" — the kind of dual doctrinal existence that Pedro
de la Cavalleria had lived, to be flaunted no more.

According to tradition, the decision to establish the Inquisition in Spain
had come out of an incident involving Marranos in Seville — that old
hotbed of Jewish activity and of violent reaction against it, where the
pogroms of 1391 had first broken out. A Spanish nobleman, pursuing an
intrigue with a Jewish woman, had entered her home uninvited on an
evening near Eastertime and come upon a Passover seder, among whose
celebrants were some of the city's most prominent New Christians. Word

of this reached Fray Alonso de Hojeda, prior of a chapter of the Dominican Order in Seville, who was already a prominent enemy of both Judaizers and Jews. Hojeda brought the story to Queen Isabella, whose court was then temporarily residing in nearby Cordova, and appealed for action. The matter was a sensitive one, because a number of high positions in the courts of both the king and the queen were held by New Christians and by Jews. This did not necessarily mean a court that was exclusively riddled with heresy; the queen's zealously Catholic confessor, Fray Tomás de Torquemada, was also probably of New Christian descent, and he was a strong influence at court. But the time had come for a point to be proven; the newly united and militant Spain was on the brink of a new surge of *Reconquista* that would wipe out the last traces of Moorish political sovereignty on the peninsula, and the presence of a pervasive heresy was no more tolerable than that of the kingdom of Granada. The Inquisition was established on November 1, 1478, and the dreadful tribunal celebrated its first *auto de fe* on February 6, 1481, when a sermon was preached by Hojeda, and six men and women were burned publicly at the stake.

A few years later, the Inquisition issued the following specifications concerning the Judaizing heresy to all associates, neighbors, and servants of New Christians:

> If you know or have heard of anyone who keeps the Sabbath according to the law of Moses, putting on clean sheets and other new garments, and putting clean cloths on the table and clean sheets on the bed in feast-days in honor of the Sabbath, and using no lights from Friday evening onwards; or if they have purified the meat they are to eat by bleeding it in water; or have cut the throats of cattle or birds they are eating, uttering certain words and covering the blood with earth; or have eaten meat in Lent and on other days forbidden by Holy Mother Church; or have fasted the great fast, going barefooted that day; or if they say Jewish prayers, at night begging forgiveness of each other, the parents placing their hands on the heads of their children without making the sign of the cross or saying anything but, "Be blessed by God and by me"; or if they bless the table in the Jewish way; or if they recite the psalms without the *Gloria Patri;* or if any woman keeps forty days after childbirth without entering a church; or if they circumcise their children or give them Jewish names; or if after baptism they wash the place where the oil and chrism was put; or if anyone on his deathbed turns to the wall to die, and when he is dead they wash him with hot water, shaving the hair off all parts of his body. . . .

It goes without saying that there was a good deal for an attentive Old Christian to be on the lookout for, especially an Old Christian servant. Indeed, it was very often servants who turned in names to the Inquisition, in a sensitivity to the smallest suspicious detail that was heightened by the smallest knowable whiff of Judaic blood in the air. For in some ways the Inquisition turned out to be a servants' revolution, since in the long run absolute unimpeachability could reside only with those who could boast, like Sancho Panza, that not a drop of Jewish blood ran in their veins. By the beginning of the next century, even the best Christian will in the world was not always enough to wipe out a taint that was becoming more and more indelibly racial in character.

6

Enter Columbus

THROUGH THE HISTORY of the first, and worst, years of the Spanish Inquisition, the story of Christopher Columbus's rise to fame moves like a counterpoint. At various moments, the relationships seem too resonant to be accidental.

But few conclusions can be arrived at with finality about Columbus's life, which is shrouded in mystery made more complex by nearly five hundred years of controversy. The mystery begins with his birth and origins. The very date of his birth seems to vary in his own and other contemporary writings; 1451 is the likeliest year, but we do not know the month or the day. Genoa is widely accepted to have been his native city, though serious doubts have been expressed about its claims. Why, its detractors ask, if Columbus was born and bred in Italy, do his existing writings show no inclination to use Italian, and possibly little or no knowledge of it? Why, even though he does not seem to have settled in Spain until he was in his thirties, was he apparently so much more at home in Spanish? The most astute scholarship even has ascertained that the Latin in which he wrote many of his letters and annotations contains Hispanicisms, but no Italianisms. For these reasons, the theory has been offered that the Genoese origin was a fabrication, and that Columbus was in fact a Spaniard, perhaps a Catalan, by birth.

Yet the archives of the city of Genoa contain considerable documenta-
tion about the fifteenth-century weaver Domenico Colombo and his sons,
Cristoforo, Bartolommeo, and Giacomo — evidently the future discoverer
and his two brothers, Bartolomé and Diego, who will also be prominent
in the first years of New World colonization. The import of this material
is undeniable to all but the most fervent mongers of forgery theories; yet
it only further complicates the mystery of Columbus's origins. How did
this weaver's son, an apprentice weaver himself, become one of the
most astute navigators of his time, and learned in Latin as well as in
mathematics? Ferdinand Columbus, the discoverer's adoring son and
biographer, endows his father with an education at the University of
Pavia, but no other records support this; Bartolomé de las Casas, another
of Columbus's earliest biographers, also mentions the city of Pavia as the
place where the latter obtained "the basic rudiments of letters, mainly
grammar," but this hardly seems to describe a university education. Diligent self-study may be the answer, but the bootstraps theory becomes all
the more remarkable when we learn that at the age of twenty-eight
Columbus, an ambitious navigator newly settled in Lisbon, married Dona
Felipa Perestrello e Moniz, daughter of an old Portuguese noble family
on her mother's side, and of a prominent landholder on Porto Santo in
the Madeiras who was himself of Italian noble descent. How was this
humble artisan's son, still only starting out in the world, able to contract
such a marriage? Ferdinand and Las Casas both come to the rescue by
attributing a noble and ancient lineage, going back to the Roman Repub-
lic, to the Colombo family, which had fallen upon hard times owing to
"the wars and factions of Lombardy." But nothing in the Genoese
archives supports this claim, and most historians have rejected it.

What is especially noteworthy about all this mystery surrounding the
origins and early life of Columbus is that he himself was the most ardent
contributor to it, making in later years a round of ambiguous and contradictory statements on his youth that bespeaks nothing so consistently as
a desire to be confusing and evasive. No doubt this is to some extent the
mark of a man who has risen in the world and does not care to offer, or
be offered, reminders of his humble birth. But there may be more to it
than that.

The great Spanish statesman and historian Salvador de Madariaga has
offered an audacious theory that, if correct, would not only resolve many
of the contradictions in the story of Columbus's origins and early life, but
also explain a number of mysteries surrounding his later career. According to Madariaga's hypothesis, Domenico Colombo of Genoa, his wife,
and their children were a family of New Christians, most likely descended
from Catalan Jews converted by the pogroms of 1391 who had subsequently migrated to Italy. This would resolve the apparent contradictions

between the "Italian" and the "Spanish" Columbus, for a family of *converso* descent could very well have gone on speaking a form of Spanish at home through the generations — as some do to this day — and it could thereby have been Columbus's mother tongue. Positing a New Christian milieu for the Columbus family also would make it more comprehensible how an offspring of weavers and tailors could make the necessary early contacts to learn cartography and navigation; it is not unlikely that some mute, inglorious Master Jacome could have established himself in Genoa, the old capital of Mediterranean map-making and commerce, and sired a line of teachers ever ready to be of service to fellow descendants of *conversos*. The possibility of New Christian contacts in Spain and Portugal could furthermore help to explain young Columbus's startling ability to rise rapidly, reflected in his career as well as in his marriage.

But before we proceed to find other possible ramifications of a New Christian identity in Columbus, it should be pointed out that all arguments in favor of this hypothesis are purely circumstantial. Yet this is not proof against it, since a good deal of the crucial evidence is either missing or ambiguous, and since even less audacious conclusions about Columbus's life still require circumstantial argument. New Christian biography in general is highly speculative during this epoch. We have seen how a man of high expectations like Pedro de la Cavalleria tried to make the evidence of his Jewish descent disappear from the record — and that was in a more tolerant era than the one of Inquisition and *limpieza de sangre* into which we have entered. From now on, when we encounter persons of strangely obscure and ambiguous origins in Spain, we can often legitimately search for possible Jewish ancestry, especially if they show hints of any of several distinct traits of New Christian personality.

This personality is often characterized by a special Christian ardor and creativity that — as in the case of St. Teresa of Ávila — will form a vital part of the advance guard of Spanish Catholicism in its greatest epoch. But this ardor is often heterodox, and easily veers over into heresy, as is shown by the New Christian presence in considerable numbers among the various Protestant and quasi-Protestant movements about to arise in Spain. Most significantly characteristic of the New Christian religiosity in the moment we are now considering, however, is a worldly messianism concerned not so much with inner questions as with the promises of redemption being raised by the practical achievements of man, above all in the realm of geographical discovery. Even without positing *converso* ancestry for them, one could perceive Christopher Columbus and his two hagiographers, Ferdinand Columbus and Bartolomé de las Casas, as new prophets of the quasireligion adumbrated by the Catalan Atlas. But if they are indeed New Christians — and we shall eventually consider this question in connection with Las Casas as well — then they are in a sense direct descendants of Abraham and Jafuda Cresques, catapulted along with Master Jacome of Majorca into a century of disasters and, ultimately, into a new and dynamic kind of Christianity.

All his life, Columbus's ideas about geography were permeated with a peculiar religious mysticism. He kept a "Book of Prophecies" in which he collected quotations — mostly from the Bible, often those dealing with "isles far off' — that seemed to prophesy his own discoveries. His personal copy, still in existence today, of Pierre d'Ailly's *Imago Mundi* — a kind of Christian-Plinian synthesis of world geography — contains numerous notes handwritten in the margins that are of a similar religious import. D'Ailly was one of the writers who convinced the young Columbus that the western route to the Indies must be fairly short, but the strength of his influence on the latter seems — judging from the notes — to be largely due to the pious factor. Although his geography was for the most part scientific, d'Ailly does not hesitate to try to establish the location of the terrestrial paradise, and the marginal notes in Columbus's copy show consistent interest in this quest. At one point, the notes even leap ahead of the text in their enthusiasm for this discovery. D'Ailly, after describing the blissful climate said to exist in certain regions of the West, goes on to say cautiously: "and most likely terrestrial paradise is like this and perhaps even the place which authors call the Fortunate Islands is like this"; but the marginal note more rashly concludes: "Terrestrial paradise perhaps is the place which authors call the Fortunate Islands." Later on, the notes are more willing to be skeptical about this location for Eden; but Columbus never ceased searching for it, and went to his grave believing that his discoveries had brought him close to it.

A striking element in Columbus's geographical religiosity is his intense and abiding interest in the fourth (or second) book of Esdras. The two apocryphal books of "Esdras" purport to be additional writings by and about the Old Testament Ezra.* But the second or fourth book is a piece of full-fledged Hellenistic apocalyptic writing that was often regarded with suspicion by the Church and just as often embraced by the heterodox. Augustine had given guarded approval to Esdras' prophetic claims, and much was always to be made of this by the latter's defenders, including Columbus. In the marginal notes to Columbus's copy of d'Ailly is a relatively lengthy discourse on II Esdras 6:42, which reads:

---

* "Esdras" is the Greek form of the name, and it is the form used instead of "Ezra" in the Vulgate, where Nehemiah is the second book of Esdras; this is why Esdras I and II of the English Apocrypha are often referred to in Romance countries as the third and fourth books of Esdras. We shall use the English enumeration.

> Upon the third day thou didst command that the waters
> should be gathered up in the seventh part of the earth: six
> parts thou hast dried up, and kept them, to the intent that of
> these some being planted of God and tilled might serve thee.

This was often to be cited by Columbus, who argued that since only one-seventh of the world was water, a good deal more dry land than yet was known remained to be discovered overseas.

But Columbus seems to have found more in Esdras than just this geographical argument. Here is one of the things he writes about this verse in his marginal notes:

> But this prophecy is not accepted by the reprobate Jews, yet
> it has been accepted by the innumerable ones amongst them
> who have believed in the Gospels. Israel has thus been split
> into two branches — a division predicted as inevitable by the
> Prophet Samuel to King Saul. The reprobate Jews themselves
> hold . . . Esdras [that is, the Old Testament Ezra] as a
> canonical authority.

This sudden display of interest in Jewish matters is startling, and weighs considerably in favor of the argument that Columbus was a New Christian. What it clearly does, at any rate, is establish a racial viewpoint on the Judaeo-Christian tradition that is rather unprecedented, though certainly in keeping with the spirit of the times. For the assertion is that there are now two kinds of Jews in the world, those who have seen the light of Christian revelation and those who have not — but that even the former, baptized though they may be, still are Jews. Indeed, the reference to Samuel's prophecy establishes a parallel with the divided kingdom of the Old Testament, and thereby gives to the New Christians the role of the southern kingdom of Judah as the keeper of the great tradition. But if that is the case, then what is the role of the rest of the Christian world, non-Jewish in descent? The ethnocentrism here is extreme.

Along with this racial Christianity is an idea of revelation that places the mystical Esdras right at the center. For the note is saying that the acceptance of the apocryphal Esdras as valid prophecy is what distinguishes the New Christians from the "reprobate Jews," who reject him even though they regard the Old Testament Ezra — the same person, in Columbus's eyes — as canonical authority. In other words, to repudiate the vision of the apocryphal Esdras is as if to repudiate the Jehovah of the prophets, and presumably the result will be the same: the rabbinical Jews of Spain, the note seems to imply, are to be the Lost Tribes of modern times. One wonders whether this note was written before or after the expulsion of the Jews in 1492.

But meanwhile, the apocryphal Esdras — which was, by the way, a
book of special importance to many New Christians — has a good deal
to say about the original Lost Tribes, and this could not have passed
lightly under Columbus's somewhat mystical gaze. Surely he saw special
meanings for his own times, and for himself, in this passage in II Esdras
(13:2–5):

> And, lo, there arose a wind from the sea, that it moved all
> the waves thereof.
>
> And I beheld, and, lo, that man waxed strong with the
> thousands of heaven: and when he turned his countenance to
> look, all the things trembled that were seen under him.
>
> And whensoever the voice went out of his mouth, all they
> burned that heard his voice, like as the earth faileth when it
> feeleth the fire.
>
> And after this I beheld, and, lo, there was gathered together
> a multitude of men, out of number, from the four winds of the
> heaven, to subdue the man that came out of the sea.

But this warlike multitude is subdued by the man from the sea; and then
another multitude, a peaceable one, comes to him, "whereof some were
glad, some were sorry, some of them were bound, and other some brought
of them that were offered" — that is, brought him slaves from their midst.
How could the exaltedly visionary Columbus not have seen an image of
himself in this, certainly after his voyages of American discovery, but
perhaps even earlier, after making some voyages to the Guinea coast
during his young years in Portugal?

If Columbus did indeed glimpse himself in the role of the man from
the sea, then Esdras' identification of the peaceable multitude takes on
special significance (13:40–42):

> Those are the ten tribes, which were carried away prisoners
> out of their own land in the time of Osea the king, whom
> Salmanasar the king of Assyria led away captive, and he
> carried them over the waters, and so came they into another
> land.
>
> But they took this counsel among themselves, that they
> would leave the multitude of the heathen, and go forth into a
> further country, where never mankind dwelt,
>
> That they might there keep their statutes, which they never
> kept in their own land.

Esdras' interpretation of the peaceable multitude then goes on to say that
the lost tribes "entered into Euphrates by the narrow passages of the
river," which they were able to ford because God stopped the flow of

waters for them, and then traveled another year and a half to a region called Arsareth (evidently a Greek corruption of the Hebrew *aretz ahereth*, "another country"). There they were to remain until "the latter time: and now when they shall begin to come,/ The Highest shall stay the springs of the stream again, that they may go through: therefore sawest thou the multitude with peace." We are already familiar with much of this terrain. As for the man from the sea, Esdras identifies him (13:26) as "he whom God the Highest hath kept a great season, which by his own self shall deliver his creature" — in other words, the Messiah.

Did Columbus have any messianic pretensions? There is a decidedly messianic element in Las Casas's literary treatment of him years after his death, but that could be more Las Casas than Columbus. The discoverer himself clearly was a man of enormous ambition, lofty conviction, and unshakable confidence in his own destiny, and though these traits alone hardly make for a messianic pretender, they are — given his mystical streak and the messianic ardor of the age — a step in that direction. It is well known that he developed in his writings and correspondence certain symbolic flourishes of virtually mystical — one is tempted to say Cabbalistic — import, such as his remarkable signature:

·S·
·S·A·S·
X M Y

underneath which usually came the formula "Xro FERENS," a rendition of his first name which stresses its meaning as "Christ-bearer."*

In 1484, after a sojourn of some ten years in Portugal and in Porto Santo, Columbus, an experienced seaman thirty-three years of age, presented to King John II of Portugal a plan for the discovery of a western route to the Indies. So far as we know, the king's ships were not to round the southern tip of Africa for another four years, nor to reach India that way for ten more after that, but perhaps the Portuguese were already too committed to this route to entertain any other possibility. John II ap-

---

* The meaning of all this — including the careful distribution of the dots — has been anyone's guess for centuries, though it seems likely that the X that begins the bottom line is the Greek initial for Christ, just as it is in the first-name signature right below it. A possible reading for that line, then, is *Christus Messias Israel*, the initial Y for the I in that context being a common form in Spain at that time, and Latin being a language frequently employed by Columbus. This, coupled with the "Xro FERENS," certainly would suggest messianic pretensions. The upper triangle of letters with dots is beyond reasonable speculation, although it is highly suggestive to anyone who would want to think of Columbus as something of a Cabbalist and be willing to posit a small knowledge of Hebrew on his part. Could the middle A stand for *Adonai* ("Lord")? Might the uppermost S be a *Shaddai* ("Almighty")? Can we see in the two lateral S's the Wings of the *Shekhina* (roughly, the Jewish counterpart to the Holy Ghost)?

pointed a committee of scientists to hear out Columbus's plan, and they at length decided against acceptance of it.

By 1485 Columbus's Portuguese wife was dead, and John II had definitively rejected his proposal. The young widower then moved to Spain and placed his small son Diego in the care of a monastery. In 1486 he again secured a royal audience, this time with the Spanish sovereigns Ferdinand and Isabella, and was again given a hearing by a royal commission, which was composed of some of the learned men of the university city of Salamanca and was presided over by that outstanding clergyman of New Christian descent, Fray Hernando de Talavera. The upshot is not clear. Columbus was not given a go-ahead, but he was not rejected outright and was granted a royal salary. This clearly was not entirely to his satisfaction, for he went on to present his project successively to the kings of England and of France, both of whom rejected it. But he made Spain his home, and settled down with a Spanish woman named Beatriz Enríquez (Madariaga thinks that she, too, may have been a New Christian), who became the mother of his second son and future biographer, Ferdinand, in 1488, but whom he never married. There presumably were other audiences and hearings in Spain, but the decisive confrontation between Columbus and the Spanish sovereigns did not occur until January of 1492, outside the city of Granada, which had been conquered for Christianity at last at the beginning of that month.

7

The Other 1492

A<small>N INSANE MOOR</small> wandered through the streets of the city, calling upon the people to remain," wrote the Spanish royal chronicler Hernando del Pulgar of the last days of Moorish Granada, "and so many joined in with him that the Moorish king did not dare to leave. So the next day he called together his councillors along with the people who had taken part in the demonstration, and . . . said that this was not the moment for resistance because they had not the wherewithal to sustain it. . . . When he had finished, he returned to the Alhambra, which was already so besieged it could not have held out any longer, and wrote to King Ferdinand that he could now take the fortress without any fear of public disturbance, and that he should do so as soon as possible.

"The king and queen responded by setting out for Granada on the second of January, accompanied by all the royal host. The queen and the prince [Philip the Handsome of Burgundy] and the Infanta Doña Juana stationed themselves on a hill near Granada, and the king met its people near the Genil River, where the Moorish king came out and handed him the keys of the city. He wanted to dismount and kiss King Ferdinand's hands, but the latter would not consent to this, and gave his hand to be kissed directly from horseback instead. King Ferdinand then gave the keys to the Count of Tendilla, whom he had appointed mayor of Granada, and to Don Gutierre de Cardenas, commander-in-chief of León. These men entered the Alhambra and set up the cross and the royal banner atop the tower of Comares. And then the cry was raised: 'Granada, Granada for their majesties Don Ferdinand and Doña Isabella.' When the queen and her party saw the cross, the strains of the Te Deum rose up from among them. The joy was so great that everyone wept. Then all the grandees went up to the queen and kissed her hand as Queen of Granada. And the pennant of Santiago de Compostela was raised alongside the royal banner atop the Alhambra."

Don Diego Hurtado de Mendoza, a knight who took part in the conquest, adds to this in his own history of the event: "Of the Moors who remained alive, some became peaceable and others went to North Africa. As for the remaining rebels, they were finished off by patrols, by the cold of the mountains, and by misfortune; and thus ended the war and the uprising." Of the houses and lands that had been vacated by Moors who fled, the great ones were granted, in recognition of their services, to Spanish noblemen who had taken part in the conquest and the small ones were allotted at modest annual rents to any Christian subjects who wanted to resettle in them. The Moors who remained in Granada, like those in Valencia, were reduced under the Spanish system of *encomienda* to a kind of serfdom, and were allowed to continue practicing their ancestral religion, for the time being, at least.

Not so the Jews of the realm, however. For one of the first acts performed by the Catholic sovereigns after the conquest of Granada was to sign a decree expelling all the professing Jews in their domains. The last of the large states of western Europe to come into being, Spain was now also the last of them, with the exception of Portugal, to have an organized Judaism openly existing on its soil. This obviously had seemed problem enough to other kings, but to the rulers of a Spain militant with the resurgence of Catholic *Reconquista,* the problem was made especially grievous by the fact that their professing Jewish community was an unusually large one, and that its presence was having a particularly complicating effect upon the vast New Christian population of the realm. This aspect of the matter was made quite clear by the Expulsion order signed on March 31, which said that "there were some bad Christians who Judaized and apostasized from our holy Catholic faith, the chief cause of which was the communication of Jews with Christians." The Jews of Castile, Aragon, and their overseas possessions were given exactly four months, until July 31, either to convert or to leave.

Can the Conquest of Granada and the Expulsion of the Jews, both occurring in the same year, be seen, then, as simply two arms of the same resurgence of *Reconquista?* This certainly was the view of one man who should have known, the Jewish scientist and historian Abraham Zacuto, who lived through the Expulsion, as well as through many of the other disasters and triumphs of the era. Born at around the same time as Columbus, Zacuto grew up in Salamanca, a city great not only for its learning but for the tolerance prevailing in the relations between its Jews and Christians. Some historians even have thought, though without adequate evidence, that Zacuto held a chair at the university there; but what is true, and not much less remarkable, is that he enjoyed the patronage of the Bishop of Salamanca for a time, and then of a devoutly Christian nobleman whom he instructed in astrology. It is also likely that he sat as a member of the Talavera commission that heard Columbus defend his project in Salamanca in 1486. Columbus certainly knew Zacuto's work in astronomy and made use of it; indeed, it was to save the discoverer's life one night in 1504, when he pacified a group of hostile Indians in Jamaica by using Zacuto's *Almanach Perpetuum* to predict successfully an eclipse of the moon. An ironic aspect of this story is the fact that the *Almanach Perpetuum*, finished by Zacuto in 1478 — the year the Inquisition began — was originally written in Hebrew, and intended mainly for such pious purposes as the calculation of the new moon for the Jewish calendar, which is lunar. As a matter of fact, it was a Jew who translated the book into Latin only about ten years before Columbus's exploit with it — Joseph Vizinho of Lisbon, who had sat on the Portuguese royal commission that rejected Columbus's project in 1484. The spiritual descendants of Abraham Cresques, converted and unconverted alike, were still engaged hand-in-hand in the ancestral pursuit of geographical and astronomical knowledge.

Zacuto's historical work, the *Sefer Yuhasin* ("Book of Genealogies"), begun immediately after the completion of the *Almanach Perpetuum*, was also meant at first to be an astronomical treatise of sorts. "Israel is exemplified by stars," he wrote of the great men of the Jewish past in his preface, "who shine like the splendor of the firmament."* And what follows at first is a veritable description of the heavens, a series of brief biographies, from Adam, Noah, and the Patriarchs all the way through to Judah Ha-Levi, Moses Maimonides, and the great rabbis of medieval northern Europe. But this book was written through a period of some twenty-five years, during which its author experienced disasters that were bound to shake up the serene vault of his spirit and transform his sense of history. An abrupt change in its character occurs in a passage dealing with the expulsion of the Jews from France in 1306, which breaks into the following digression:

---

* See Daniel 12:3. "And they that be wise shall shine as the brightness of the firmament; and they that turn many to righteousness as the stars forever and ever."

And so, too, because of our sins, we saw with our own eyes the expulsions from Spain, Sicily and Sardinia in 1492, and in 1497 from Portugal. For, from France we had come to Spain, where we had our enemies on one side and the sea on the other; but flight was possible from France, from which my great-grandfather came, so that the descendants of [my grand-father] Abraham Zacuto were in Spain and I was born there into that good name. And all of them withstood the Castilian persecutions [of 1391] and remained steadfast in the faith of the Holy One, Blessed Be He, and His Torah. I too was given the privilege of sanctifying the Holy Name along with my son Samuel, and we came to Africa after having been prisoners twice.

The rest of the book is often angry and passionate, even poetic, but the scientist remains as well; now, however, he is more the astrologer than the astronomer, less interested in the stars themselves than in meaning-ful configurations. In a passage on the persecutions of 1412, "instigated by the priest Fray Vicente [Ferrer], supported by Don Ferdinand, King of Aragon, grandfather of the King Ferdinand who ordered the expulsion of the Jews of Spain in our time," Zacuto fills out the picture with this cosmic digression:

And in the same year, a great storm broke out on the sea, during which many ships were wrecked, and there were epi-demics and plagues — although not like those of around 1348 when two thirds of the world's inhabitants died, and when people killed all the lepers for fear that they had perhaps poisoned the atmosphere. At the same time, people in many countries rose up against the Jews and killed them as never before. They burned the Jews in Germany, saying they had polluted the waters with deadly poison. But the learned men of the day attributed these fateful events to the configurations of the planets, caused by celestial forces.

Similarly, when he comes to the capture of Málaga — until then part of the kingdom of Granada — by the Christians in 1486, he begins with de-scriptions of a rainfall that inundated the city for sixty days, and of a six-month-long famine that followed it. The atmosphere is virtually Biblical, and the inevitable doom is appropriately related with pregnant simplic-ity:

The city fell on the Sabbath, the 29th of Ab, which was August 18th. Twelve thousand were taken captive, among them four hundred Jews, who were ransomed by the Jewish communities of Castile.

And here we come upon what is for Zacuto the most significant configuration of all: the intertwining destinies of Jew and Moor. This theme
is first sounded dimly, in tones that are richly resonant but scattered.
Dealing with the middle years of the fifteenth century, he refers to the
Portuguese capture of a North African town called Sabata, which, he says,
was founded by Noah's son Shem, and which the Portuguese attacked
because it had been overly hospitable toward Jewish refugees from the
Iberian Peninsula. He describes the Turkish conquest of Constantinople
in 1453 in terms that hint at the angry Christian reaction which is to come
against all infidels and heretics. Other such soundings of the theme move
on with increasing swiftness to this culmination:

> And in 1482, Alhama was conquered by the Marquis of
> Cadiz because the Ishmaelites had taken the Spanish city
> called Zara. This was loathsome for Ishmael — and, in our sin-
> fulness, for the children of Israel as well — because with the
> conquest of Alhama the war against the Ishmaelites began
> and in another ten years the whole Kingdom of Granada was
> to be taken.

This passage contains two word-plays, a literary device more meaningful
in Hebrew than in English. The emphatic one is in "loathsome," which is
zara in Hebrew, and thus a play on the name of the city taken by the
Moors. A subtler one is in "Alhama," for this is the Arabic word that was
used in both Moorish and Christian Spain for the Jewish community of
a city. Zacuto thus uses this literary device to reinforce his point that the
war begun against the Moors was also one against the Jews, a point made
more explicit in the next sentence, in which Zacuto dates the Inquisition
from 1482:

> And in that same year an Inquisition was begun among the
> *conversos* over their religion and they were sentenced to death
> at the stake and their property was confiscated by the king.
> And in that year they separated Jewish homes and neighbor-
> hoods from Christian ones.

All of this leads inexorably, through the conquest of Málaga described
above, to Spain's final solution:

> In 1492, right after the Christian New Year, Granada was
> taken, and the expulsion of the Jews from Spain was then de-
> creed.

The configuration is so emphatic here that one could almost think
Zacuto is dating the Expulsion decree immediately after the taking of

Granada rather than three months later. But, curiously enough, we get
the same impression in an important text by Columbus: the preamble,
addressed to Ferdinand and Isabella, of the journal of his first voyage to
America. Indeed, Columbus goes a step beyond Zacuto in presenting the
fateful configurations of the year 1492, for he places his own historic
enterprise in significant juxtaposition with the closing of Moorish and
Jewish history in Spain. The preamble goes like this:

> Most Christian, most high, excellent and mighty princes,
> King and Queen of the Spains and of the islands of the sea,
> our Lords: In this present year of 1492, after Your Highnesses
> had brought to an end the war with those Moors who had been
> reigning in Europe — finishing that war in the very great city
> of Granada, where, in this present year, on the second day of
> January I saw the royal banners of Your Highnesses placed by
> force of arms on the towers of the Alhambra, which is the
> fortress of the said city, and saw the Moorish king come out
> of the gates of the city and kiss the royal hands of Your High-
> nesses and of my Lord the Prince — later in that same month,
> on the basis of the information I had given Your Highnesses
> concerning the lands of India and a prince called the Great
> Khan (which means "King of Kings" in our language), and
> how he and his predecessors had often sent to Rome for doc-
> tors who could instruct them in our holy faith, and how the
> Holy Father had never provided any, so that so many peoples
> believing in idolatries and proliferating perditious sects among
> themselves have been lost, Your Highnesses, like true Catholic
> Christians and princes who love and seek the increase of the
> holy Christian faith, and enemies of the sect of Mahomet and
> of all idolatries and heresies, thought to send me, Christopher
> Columbus, to the said parts, the Indies, to see the said princes,
> peoples and countries, and everything concerning them and
> their disposition, and the way in which their conversion to
> our holy faith might be brought about, and ordered that I not
> go eastward by land, which was the customary route, but by
> the westward route, which we do not know with certainty to
> this day whether anyone has ever taken.
> Therefore, after having expelled all the Jews from all your
> realms and possessions, in the same month of January, Your
> Highnesses commanded me to go with a sufficient fleet to the
> said Indian parts. . . .

Here we see with great emphasis Columbus the holy crusader, possibly
the would-be Messiah — though, to be sure, there also are good practical
reasons for depicting his enterprise to the king and queen as an extension

of their most Christian victory at Granada. But is the mention of the Expulsion of the Jews in this context simply an overflow of *Reconquista* exuberance, or does it have particular significance for the author? In any event, it is curious that he places the Expulsion or the Expulsion decree — in either case, erroneously — in the same month of January as that in which the Conquest of Granada and the sovereigns' consent to his plan took place. What a penchant for fateful configurations this bespeaks!

But the story is in several respects more complicated than Columbus makes it sound here, and one element he has left out in his depiction of the sudden royal consent to his project is a New Christian one. For, as both Ferdinand Columbus and Bartolomé de las Casas relate, when Columbus once again obtained an audience from the king and the queen — this time in the royal camp at Santa Fe just after the victory over Granada — his plan was at first rejected by them, apparently for once and for all. Columbus thereupon set out for his home in Cordova, intending to go from there to France, where he would begin trying out his luck all over again. But then the story takes a remarkable turn; for on the very day of Columbus's departure from Santa Fe, King Ferdinand's Secretary of the Exchequer, Luis de Santángel, appeared before the queen and argued eloquently in favor of Columbus's proposal. The queen wavered, and Santángel then clinched the matter by offering to lend whatever money the project would require. A messenger was sent after Columbus, who was on the road back to Cordova when he thus received news that his plan had been accepted after all.

Another mystery enters the Columbus story, then, in the form of Luis de Santángel: how many discussions went on, how many understandings were exchanged, between him and Columbus of which we can have no inkling? What was the relationship between these two men? For one fact about Santángel stands out with perhaps special significance: he was a New Christian, scion of an Aragonese family that had been wealthy and prominent as Jews before 1391 and still were so as Christians. But it was also a family whose name was scattered all over the records of the Inquisition. One of Luis's cousins, bearing the exact same name as his, had been burned at the stake in 1487, and only six months before his intercession with the queen on Columbus's behalf, Luis himself had been made to do penance. Nor was he an unusual phenomenon at court, especially Ferdinand's, which was filled with New Christians. Gabriel Sánchez, Ferdinand's Treasurer-General, belonged to a New Christian family closely related to the Santángels through frequent intermarriages, that had also suffered greatly at the hands of the Inquisition. Sánchez and two other Aragonese New Christians at court with similar family histories also were ardent supporters of the Columbus project.

There also were a number of unconverted Jews at court, mainly in Isabella's entourage, but they do not seem to have been interested in Columbus's "Enterprise of the Indies." Abraham Senior, the foremost among them, had been influential in arranging the marriage of Ferdinand and Isabella back in 1469, and Isaac Abravanel, a Portuguese Jew who had fled to Castile from political embarrassments back home, had provided considerable funds for the campaign against Granada; yet despite this propensity to be at the center of things, neither of them gave any support we know of to Columbus. We catch glimmers, then, of a divergence of opinion about Columbus between Isabella's Jews and Ferdinand's New Christians. Was this simply a matter of conflicting regional interests? If so, then both groups of advisors were shortsighted, for Castile in particular was bound to profit from the possible westward crossing to which its Jewish councillors were indifferent, just as Aragon, a Mediterranean power, was bound to lose preponderance if this project endorsed by its New Christian courtiers were to be successful.

The possibility does present itself, then, that the divergence was ideological, and that the "Enterprise of the Indies" was dear to the hearts of New Christians — especially those whose religion or religious status was in some way marginal — for reasons other than statesman-like. Did Columbus's powerful and mystical personality inspire them with messianic hopes? On a more prosaic level, he also could have talked to them about finding, on some hitherto unknown island, a place of refuge for them.

If there is any validity to these conjectures, then it is ironic and significant that unconverted Jews did not seem interested in the project. On the practical level of search for a refuge, Jewish needs in 1492 were even more urgent than New Christian ones. But it is not characteristic of orthodox Jews in any era to look for homes in wildernesses, at least if any alternatives are available. And there still were alternatives, countries in North Africa, the Middle East, and even Europe, where the Jewish community structures absolutely essential for a daily life in conformity to Mosaic law were in existence. As for the possible spiritual, even messianic, aspects of the Columbus enterprise, these in particular would have been highly suspect to rabbinical Jews, who were no less sensitive to intimations of heresy in this era than orthodox Christians were, and who were certainly not going to be led anywhere pointed out as a place of their redemption by someone born and baptized a Christian.

The last of the fateful configurations of the year 1492 occurred at the end of July and the beginning of August, when the final departure of the Jews from Spain and Columbus's departure for what turned out to be a New World took place within three days of each other. The Jews had begun leaving Castile "in the first week of the month of July, in the 1,492nd year of the Nativity of our Redeemer Jesus Christ," wrote the pious chronicler Andrés Bernáldez, curate of the village of Los Palacios. "And blindly giving themselves over to their vain hopes, they submitted to the hardships of the road and left their native regions, great and small, old and young, on foot and mounted on donkeys and other beasts, and in carriages, and made their way to the various points of departure to which each of them had to go. And on the roads and terrains over which they passed they encountered much hardship and misfortune, some of them falling down, to be picked up by their companions, others dying, others being born, others getting sick, so that no Christian could look upon them without anguish, and many along the way tried to persuade them to accept baptism. And some in their grief converted and remained, but very few, for their rabbis were ever by their side giving them courage, getting the women and children to sing, and playing tambourines to cheer everyone up. And thus they left Castile, some going to the ports from which they then embarked, others going to Portugal."

"Some of the Jews emigrated to Turkey," Abraham Zacuto wrote in the *Sefer Yuhasin*, "others to Africa, to the cities of Fez and Oran whither they were pursued by hunger and pestilence, so that almost all perished. But the bulk of Castilian Jewry, unable to reach the sea quickly, emigrated to Portugal after giving up a tithe of all their possessions. In addition, every person paid one ducat besides a fee of one ducat for a transit permit. They also surrendered one quarter to one third of all the possessions they brought into Portugal with them. Eight ducats at the very least had to be paid even by those who had no money, or else they were taken as slaves." Portugal was to be the scene of still more misfortune, and the Jews who escaped from there a few years later with their religion still intact, like Zacuto himself, were mainly to follow the established refugee route to the south and to the east. This flight back to the ancient and traditional lands was to be repeated by the Moors of Spain when their turn came to suffer full-fledged religious and racial persecution, beginning in the ensuing decade with the forcible conversions of the Muslims of Granada and of Castile. The grip maintained by both these groups on their ancestral religions implied a steadfastness in the old geographical ideals as well.

At Isabella's court, Abraham Senior finally accepted baptism, perhaps hoping that a day for Judaism could yet come again in Spain. Isaac Abravanel made no such bet, and departed for Italy on July 31, the last day allotted by the Expulsion decree.* By nightfall, not a single out-

---

* There has been a persistent Jewish tradition that the Expulsion deadline was extended two days at the last minute, causing the final departure to occur on August 2. Tradition has favored this date because in 1492 it corresponded to the Jewish Ninth

wardly professing Jew was left in Aragon or Castile. Only New Christians remained, bearing a faith ever heretical in terms of their Jewish past and often so in terms of their Catholic present as well, and marked by a racial taint that was to grow more virulent in the years to come.

The final scene of the drama of 1492 takes place just before dawn on August 3, as the sails are unfurled on Columbus's three ships at the port of Palos in the mouth of the Guadalquivir, from which some of the last shiploads of Jewish refugees had departed three days before. There are other New Christians aboard besides the possibly New Christian Columbus himself. Among the troubled races who flee the crumbling edifice of medieval Spain, then, it is the New Christians alone — at least those among them who are the true spiritual descendants of Master Jacome of Majorca — who can be seen turning away from the ancient promised lands and looking for a new one westward across the ocean. How much this enterprise of discovery owes to New Christian initiative we can only guess; but it may well be that America began its history as a promised land of Spanish heresy.

---

of Ab (*Tisha b'Av*, in Hebrew), on which the destruction of both the First and the Second Temples of Jerusalem is said to have taken place, more than six and a half centuries apart. Modern scholarship has denied this remarkable configuration to August 2, 1492, but it has given us another that is perhaps more interesting. Columbus had apparently been quite ready to sail on August 2, but he waited another day. Pondering the question of Columbus's possible New Christian identity, the eminent Jewish historian Cecil Roth has wondered whether there is any significance to the fact that the discoverer deferred his departure to the next day after this one on which "no Jew would begin an enterprise." Perhaps some racial instinct still alive in Columbus had impelled him to commemorate in his own way the destruction of yet another Jerusalem; in this way, through him at least, Jewish history in Spain would have reached its Ninth of Ab.

8

Columbus's Golden World

"THIS HIGH SEA was most necessary for me," Columbus wrote in his journal for September 23, 1492, seventeen days out at sea after a month-long stopover in the Canaries. By now the crew were becoming restless, and there was loud grumbling among them that they would never get back to Spain. They had encountered few winds blowing back eastward, and on this day the waters were so becalmed that the sailors claimed the sea simply was not high enough to bring them home again. But then the waves rose dramatically without even a wind, so that everyone was astonished and silenced for the time being. This is when Columbus made the entry just quoted, adding that "nothing like this had ever been seen, save in the time when the Jews went out of Egypt and complained against Moses, who had brought them out of captivity."

We do not know much concerning Columbus's crew of about ninety men aboard the three ships, but at least one of them was an Israelite whose presence as such was not merely accidental. This was Luis de Torres, a convert of possibly only that year, who had once held a position with the governor of Murcia. He was said to have known Hebrew, Aramaic, and some Arabic, and had been brought along by Columbus specifically as an interpreter. One of the purposes of the voyage, as we have seen, was to find the Great Khan, and Torres was to be the mouthpiece for this encounter, presumably on the basis of his Hebrew. Perhaps Columbus and his supporters had decided that the Great Khan reported on by Marco Polo and others might be the Israelite king who dwelt across the river from Prester John.

Land was sighted at last on the night of October 11, and on the next morning, which was a Friday, the Spaniards reached the island that they subsequently called San Salvador, in the Bahamas. There they saw nude men, and some of them set out for shore in armed boats. The boat bearing Columbus and two of his captains, holding the banners of Spain, preceded the rest. When they landed, they stepped ashore and, staying close to the boats, solemnly proclaimed possession of the island in the name of the king and the queen. The no doubt astonished islanders gathered round, and, as Columbus writes of this historic encounter: "I, in order that they might regard us with great friendship — because I perceived that they were a people who would be better delivered and converted to our holy faith by love than by force — gave some of them a few red caps and glass beads which they hung around their necks, and many other things of little value, which gave them a great deal of pleasure and so won them over to us that it was a marvel." The act here may hardly seem a worthy offspring to the thought, but Columbus had shipped to Guinea a few times and knew the value that small trinkets could have. Against the background of the usual treatment of primitive peoples by Europeans in this epoch, Columbus's trifles shine forth like jewels.

Columbus was in the latitude of the Canaries, and it was clearly the aboriginal peoples of those islands who were now providing his mind with a worldly model by which to perceive the islanders in front of him. There is a touch of Boccaccio's Canarians in his ensuing description:

> Then they came swimming to the ships' boats, where we now were, bringing us parrots and clews of cotton thread, as well as spears and many other things, and we took them in exchange for other things we gave them, like small glass beads and hawk-bells. In short, they gave as they received, all with the utmost pleasure.
>
> But they seemed to me a people very poor in every respect. They all go about naked as when their mothers bore them — the women, too, apparently, although all I saw of them was one very young girl. I only saw young men, none of whom seemed more than thirty years old. They were very well formed, with very handsome bodies and very fine faces. Their hair was slick and rough, almost like that of a horse's tail, and they wore it down to the tops of the eyebrows, except for a little in back which they let grow long and never cut. Some of them paint themselves a sooty color, though they are in fact

the color of the Canarians, neither black nor white. Some paint themselves white, some red, some whatever color they can find; some paint their faces, some the whole body, some only the eyes, and some only the nose.

They do not carry arms or even know what they are; we showed them swords and they grabbed them by the blades and cut themselves in their ignorance. They do not have any iron; their spears are wooden sticks without iron, some of them having a fish's tooth at the tip, or other things of that sort.

As he contemplated these people, was Columbus perhaps recalling the peaceable multitude who greeted Esdras' man from the sea?

His idyllic view of life on this and other islands he was to encounter during the fall and winter of 1492–1493 is even more strongly emphasized in the letter he dispatched on returning home to his patrons, Luis de Santángel and Gabriel Sánchez. "They manifest great love towards all others in preference to themselves," he writes; "they also give objects of great value for trifles, and content themselves with very little or nothing in return." In fact, he claims, he had to intervene when his sailors went in for unfair bartering. At all times, he strove to set a good example to the natives, he says, because he regarded them as excellent candidates to become Christians by persuasion. "They practise no kind of idolatry, but have a firm belief that all strength and power, and indeed all good things, are in heaven, and that I had descended from there with these ships and sailors, and it was under this impression that I was received after they had cast aside their fears." There had been rumors and indications among the peoples encountered of other natives of the islands who were fierce and warlike and who ate human flesh, but none of them appeared in person on this first voyage. "I did not find," Columbus writes, "any bestial men among them, as some of us had expected, but on the contrary men of great deference and kindness." The onset of the warlike multitudes was for another day. "Neither are they black, like the Ethiopians," he goes on; "their hair is smooth and straight, for they do not dwell where the rays of the sun strike most vividly." This clearly was meant as reassurance to anyone who felt, as he did, that black men tended to be more barbarous than whites of any condition. Columbus returned home in 1493 thinking that Cuba was part of the Asian mainland — while there, he had even sent Luis de Torres on an expedition to find the Great Khan — but he nevertheless clearly felt himself to be closer to the region that Ailly and some others had gone on referring to as the Fortunate Islands, in spite of the Canaries, than to Ethiopia in any sense of the term. He had come to the part of the world where East meets West, but his approach to it was westward, and so was his vision of it. We can see in Columbus's outlook the first glimmers of an unfavorable comparison, to be made often

by him and by his successors, between the black men of the Old World
and most of the tawny men of the New.

This attitude was taken up by the first chronicler of Columbus's expeditions, Peter Martyr of Anghera, who wrote only a few years later concerning the natives of what he was the first to call the "New World" that "the
inhabitants of these islands have been ever so used to live at liberty, in
play and pastime, that they can hardly away with the yoke of servitude,
which they attempt to shake off by all means they may." This surely is
an implied comparison with the peoples of Guinea, who did submit to the
yoke of servitude from Peter's point of view, and of whom he occasionally
manifests a firm dislike. Indeed, Peter, a Renaissance humanist at heart,
was palpably a man who looked westward rather than eastward for
images of the ideal life. Liking neither "Ethiopians" nor orthodox Jews —
though he was always a good friend to New Christians — he was on the
other hand so inspired by what he learned of the New World natives that
he, even more than Boccaccio, was able to find in the West for Ovid's
airy nothings a local habitation and a name. "And surely if they had received our religion," he writes,

> I would think their life most happy of all men, if they might
> therewith enjoy their ancient liberty. A few things content
> them, having no delight in such superfluities, for the which in
> other places men take infinite pains and commit many unlaw-
> ful acts, and yet are never satisfied, whereas many have too
> much, and none enough. But among these simple souls, a few
> clothes serve the naked: weights and measures are not needful
> to such as can not skill of craft and deceit and have not the use
> of pestiferous money, the seed of innumerable mischiefs. So
> that if we shall not be ashamed to confess the truth, they seem
> to live in that golden world of the which old writers speak so
> much: wherein men lived simply and innocently without
> enforcement of laws, without quarreling judges and libels,
> content only to satisfy nature, without further vexation for
> knowledge of things to come.

Here, then, is another milestone in the early history of the Noble Savage.

Columbus, who gave to the peaceable multitude of the islands the
name *indios* — because he considered their habitat to be "the Indies," of
course, but perhaps also because he thought of them as living "in God" —
maintained a vision like Peter's, but it was also more alive with religious
and mystical implications than that of the rationalist clergyman. For the
next few dramatic and ultimately disastrous years of Columbus's life,
there was a constant pull between the visionary and perhaps messianic
streak in him on the one hand, and the man of affairs he had now become

on the other. Only seven months after his triumphal return home in March, 1493, he was at sea again, this time leading to the newly discovered "Indies" a fleet of seventeen ships, filled with seedlings and livestock, as well as with some twelve to fifteen hundred colonists for the island of Hispaniola. It naturally fell upon the Admiral to be in charge of the establishment of this colony, and though subsequently its administration was placed in the hands of a governor, the charge remained close to Columbus himself: the first governor was his brother Bartolomé. The affairs of a colony, however, with a largely roughneck population from home seeking to grab advantages wherever they could be found, and pitted against a stunned, fearful, and increasingly hostile native population, proved to be more than the relatively unworldly Columbus brothers could handle. Other domineering interests arrived in the colony during the three years following its establishment, rivaling the Columbus hegemony and inciting new waves of discontent. By the time the Admiral returned home in June of 1496, his reputation had fallen under a cloud. As if doing penance, he wore the brown habit of a Franciscan friar almost from the moment of his return.

His third voyage to the New World, on which he finally embarked in May, 1498, was permeated with the old visionary spirit once again. The letter he wrote to Ferdinand and Isabella reporting on this voyage is largely taken up with his search for the terrestrial paradise. A sense of awesome expectation fills his description of every stage of the journey. "When I sailed from Spain to the Indies," he wrote, "I found that as soon as I had passed a hundred leagues westward of the Azores, there was a very great change in the sky and the stars, in the temperature of the air, and in the water of the sea; and I have been very diligent in observing these things." This striking, and to him portentous, climatic change is mentioned not once but three times in the course of the letter. "When I reached the parallel of Sierra Leone, in Guinea," he says in a more graphic repetition of the point, beginning with the unusually long southward course he followed this time before heading out into the ocean, "I found the heat so intense, and the rays of the sun so fierce, that I thought we should have been been burned." This is of course the sun that, in Columbus's view as in that of most of his contemporaries, has burned the Guinea Negro black. "And although it rained and the sky was heavy with clouds, I still suffered the same oppression, until our Lord was pleased to grant me a favorable wind, giving me an opportunity of sailing to the west, so that I reached a line where I experienced, as I have already said, a change of temperature. Immediately upon my reaching this line, the temperature of the sky became very mild, and the more I advanced, the more this mildness increased; but I did not find the positions of the stars to correspond with these effects." According to the positions of the stars, this was the latitude of Guinea, the farthest south Columbus ever was to travel in the New World — we now know that what he came to was the island of Trinidad and the adjacent Venezuelan coast — and the climate simply was not hot enough to satisfy any of the established notions of world geography. "I look upon this as something new," he goes on, "and I think my opinion will be supported by that of others, that it is a short distance for so great a change to take place in the temperature."

Columbus has come upon a mystery for which he is determined to propose a dramatic solution, and he does so with disregard for all those mythmakers of future generations who would make him the most ardent advocate of his time for the view that the earth is a sphere. "I have always read," he proceeds, "that the world comprising the land and the water was spherical, as is testified by the investigations of Ptolemy and others. . . . But I have now seen so much irregularity, as I have already described, that I have come to another conclusion respecting the earth, namely, that it is not round as they describe, but of the form of a pear, which is very round except where the stalk grows, at which part it protrudes much higher; or like a round ball, in one part of which is a prominence like a woman's nipple, this being the part that is highest and nearest to the sky. This part is situated under the Equator, in this Ocean Sea at the end of the East (I call 'the end of the East' that place where all the lands and islands terminate)."

In other words, this wondrous region is so cool because of its height, on the same principle whereby there are snow-capped mountains in tropical Africa. This, in turn, affects the color of the inhabitants. "When I was off the island of Arguim," on the west coast of Africa, he explains, "which is twenty degrees north of the Equator, I found the people black and the land very much burnt; and when after that I went to the Cape Verde Islands, I found the people there blacker still, and the further south we went the more they approached the extreme of blackness; so that when I reached the parallel of Sierra Leone, where, as night came on, the north star rose five degrees, the people were the blackest of all; and as I sailed westward, the heat became extreme." But then, across the ocean beyond the miraculous climate line, at a point where the north star also rose five degrees, where the temperature was "exceedingly mild" and "the fields and foliage . . . remarkably fresh and green, and as beautiful as the gardens of Valencia in April," the people were "very graceful in form, whiter than any others I had seen in the Indies, with long, smooth hair." Clearly, Columbus thinks it fitting that the complexion of the Negro is not to be found in a part of the world to which he is about to accord a very lofty status.

"The Holy Scriptures record," he goes on, now approaching the crucial point, "that our Lord made the earthly paradise, and planted in it the tree of life, and from it springs a fountain which flows and divides into the four principal rivers of the world: the Ganges in India, the Tigris and Euphrates in [here there is a gap in the manuscript], which divide a chain of mountains and form Mesopotamia, flowing from there into Persia, and the Nile, which rises in Ethiopia and goes down to the sea at Alexandria. I do not find, nor have ever found, any account by the Romans or Greeks which definitively fixes the site of the terrestrial paradise, nor have I seen it laid down from authentic sources in any *mappamundi*. Some placed it in Ethiopia, at the sources of the Nile, but others, traversing all these countries, found neither the temperature nor the altitude of the sun to correspond to their ideas respecting it; nor did it appear that the overwhelming waters of the Deluge had been there. Some pagans pretended to adduce arguments to the effect that it was in the Fortunate Islands, which are the Canaries." Columbus evidently has rejected this latter view, which he had entertained in days when it had still been possible for him to think of the Fortunate Islands as something far more wonderful and remote than the Canaries.

"I have already described my ideas concerning this hemisphere and its form," he reminds his readers as he approaches his dramatic conclusion, "and I have no doubt that if I could pass below the Equator, after reaching the highest point of which I have spoken, I would find a much milder temperature, and a variation in the stars and in the water. Not that I suppose that place of utmost altitude to be navigable, or even to have water — or that one can even get up there, for that matter, since I am convinced that it is the terrestrial paradise, to which no one may attain without the will of God."

Since this startling opinion was to win criticism for Columbus even from so stout a supporter as Peter Martyr, he was ever eager to bolster his visionary conclusions — and with them, his credibility — with a display of sound geographical argumentation. Having discovered on this voyage the mouth of what we now know to be the Orinoco, for example, he argues for this river as proof that the terrestrial paradise must be nearby because "I have never read or heard of such quantities of fresh water coming out and mingling with the salty waters of the sea." His idea is that the river must be a branch of one of the four that flow out of paradise, for it must descend from an abnormally high place to achieve such a volume. The true explanation — that these abundant fresh waters are the discharge of a vast continent — even occurred to him in passing, but this overwhelming reality, to be proclaimed only a year later by Amerigo Vespucci, clearly was less attractive to him than his own grandiose spiritual theory. "The more I reason on it, however, the more convinced I become that the place of which I have spoken is the terrestrial paradise."

Going on to proclaim how he has raised the cross and announced the glories of the king and queen in every land that he has discovered in this precious part of the world, Columbus concludes the letter with its most important immediate aim: a paean of self-justification. For his record was still tainted by the disasters of his regime in Hispaniola, and his troubles were by no means at an end; indeed, the next two years were to be all downhill from the terrestrial paradise. At the end of this third voyage of discovery, Columbus had put in at Hispaniola and found the affairs of the island — under his brothers Bartolomé, still governor, and Diego, mayor of the newly founded city of Santo Domingo — in utter disarray. Factional strife had reached the point of open armed rebellion. Finally, in the summer of 1500, the Spanish sovereigns had sent as their plenipotentiary to the colony one Francisco de Bobadilla to settle all disputes. Bobadilla ended by sending all three Columbus brothers back to Spain as prisoners. The man from the sea, the discoverer who had begun a transformation of the world while harboring visions of terrestrial paradise and possible messianic pretensions, returned home eight years to the month after his initial historic landing in the New World, wearing not a crown of thorns but manacles and chains.

9

Black Devils

COLUMBUS MUST HAVE been especially relieved to have found gentle, well-formed *indios* living near the Equator, because his first encounter to the southward of the islands explored in his first voyage had been with men of a very different sort. This had occurred in the very first landfalls of his second voyage to the New World, in the autumn of 1493. By this time, of course, he had been thoroughly prepared for meeting a warlike multitude in the Indies, not only by Esdras and by the Indians he met on his first voyage, but also by d'Ailly, who wrote that in the frigid north and the tropical south of the westernmost parts of the northern hemisphere

> are savage men who eat human flesh and have depraved and frightening faces; and the cause of this . . . is the heat and the cold, on account of which their bodies are of abnormal complexion and poor and repulsive of physique. Therefore, they are base in manner and savage in speech, and there are men or beasts in these places who present such a dreadful aspect, that one can tell only with difficulty whether they are men or beasts, according to what the blessed Augustine says. And . . . in these two extremities live evil spirits, devils, and malignant beasts harmful to man.

It was no surprise for Columbus, then, that four or five bones of human arms and legs were found when a reconnaissance boat landed at what is now believed to have been the island of Guadeloupe, on November 4, 1493. "On seeing these," wrote Dr. Álvarez Chanca of Seville, who had come along as one of the physicians of the expedition, "we suspected that these were the islands of Carib, which," as was known from the first voyage, "are inhabited by people who eat human flesh." On other islands, the evidence became yet more vivid. In one place, a group of women who had been held captive by the Caribs and used as concubines said that

> the Caribs used them with a cruelty that seems incredible; that they eat the children they have by them, bringing up only those they have had by their regular wives. They bring the men taken alive by them to their houses to eat, and those who are dead they eat on the spot. They say that human flesh is so good there is nothing like it in the world; and this seems so, because the bones we found in their houses had been so gnawed at that nothing remained of them but the parts that were too tough to be eaten. In one house we found a man's neck being cooked. When they capture boys they emasculate them, and make use of them until they are fully grown, and then kill them and eat them when they want to have a feast, for they say that the flesh of boys and of women is not good to eat. Three such boys came fleeing to us, all of them emasculated.

As far as Columbus was concerned, these people, along with any other natives who made war against the Spaniards and were taken captive, were eligible to be sold into slavery — a treatment he did not consider proper for peaceable islanders, even though many of his shipmates and fellow countrymen saw the matter differently. This is what he wrote in January, 1494, to a representative of the king and queen on the subject of the man-eating Caribs, whom he was now beginning to call "Cannibals" in a significant dialectal variant of their name:

> Tell their Highnesses that because we do not have an interpreter through whom these people can be made to understand our holy faith, as their Highnesses wish — and as we do, too, intending to bring this about whenever possible — we are sending with these ships some of these Cannibals [*caníbales*, in Spanish], men, women, boys and girls. Their Highnesses can command that they be placed under the power of persons with whom they can best learn our language, as well as the tasks of service, little by little getting more attention than other slaves do . . . so that they will become better interpreters. . . . And because among all the islands those of the Cannibals are the

largest and most populous, it seemed that taking some of them
and sending them to Spain would be of some benefit, for they
might then be made one day to give up their inhuman practise
of eating men. Furthermore, there in Spain they will learn the
language and thereby more quickly receive baptism, to the
benefit of their souls. And among those peoples who do not
engage in such practises, it will be much to our credit when
they see taken captive those who inflict so much injury upon
them and whom they fear so much that even a single one
terrifies them.

The "peoples who do not engage in such practises" are *indios,* of
course, and Columbus himself never was to use this word for the
caníbales, who were a separate breed. A new word was thus beginning
to make its way into the European vocabulary. Some of Columbus's
men had heard the Indians use the term "Carib" for the main island of
the man-eaters — evidently Puerto Rico — and from this was obtained
not only Dr. Chanca's *caribes* but also our word "Caribbean." The variant
name of the island presumably heard from other Indians, which Columbus came to prefer, was "Caniba"; hence, in Spanish, *caníbales* for its
natives.*

---

* One apparent reason for Columbus's partiality to this form of the island's name
was its suggestion of the presence of the Great Khan (*Gran Can,* as Columbus always
wrote it in Spanish). But perhaps there were other reasons, grounded in the discoverer's mystical nature. Is there something special to be noted in the opposition between the word *caníbal* and his own name in Spanish, Cristóbal? If he is the Christ-
bearer, then these people who form the warlike multitude against him surely are the
bearers of the mark and — in terms of the confusion expressed by Zurara and others —
the curse of Cain, who, incidentally, had been the object of worship of a heretical
cult in the Middle Ages. It is noteworthy in this context that, in subsequent Latin
writings on the New World, "cannibals" often was written *cambali:* here, the component "cam" is close in spelling and identical in pronunciation to *Cham,* the Vulgate
form of the name of Noah's accursed son, Ham.
   The great popularity that the word achieved in general — so that in some languages it all but replaced the traditional "anthropophagi" — can perhaps be explained
on less mysterious grounds. The Oxford English Dictionary points out that the first
two syllables of *caníbales* suggests "dogs" to Romance ears — a highly suggestive
point, since the Spanish colonists often used the word *perro* ("dog") as a term of
opprobrium for Indians, since the notion of dog-faced men was a traditional part of
the imagery of exotic climes, and since few things seem more truly "cannibal" than
the sight of dogs tearing at flesh. Furthermore, the notion of "flesh" — *carne* in
Spanish — also echoes in those first two syllables of this word that describes supremely
carnal men. There is yet one more point at which the word *cannibal* resonates richly
in the culture of that day: its resemblance to the name Hannibal, the bearer of wild
beasts and the culture of human sacrifice from the south. At this very time, North
Africa was being fought off again by Christian Europe, in grim bombastic reality by
the Spaniards, and in literature by the Italians — from Petrarch's *Africa,* which
revived a learned debate as to whether Hannibal or Scipio Africanus had been the
greater general, to Ariosto's *Orlando Furioso,* which transforms Charlemagne's war
against the Saracens into an elegant Renaissance tapestry.

It is in the writings of yet another Italian adventurer sailing in Spanish ships, Amerigo Vespucci, that we find some of the most vivid prose of the day about the European encounters with this "fierce and cruel people, eaters of human flesh, called cannibals." By 1499, when Vespucci was making his observations in a voyage along the coast of Brazil under the captaincy of Alonso de Hojeda, "cannibals" had already become a generic term referring to man-eaters wherever they were found and not just those of a particular area. In terms echoing Columbus's very different spirit, Vespucci even says of them, "We have found such a multitude in these countries that no one could enumerate them, as we read in the Apocalypse."

But Vespucci had literary talent enough, and presumably experience enough not to have to resort to sacred texts for doomsday imagery, as we can see in the following passage from his pen, which begins by describing what seems to be only a group of particularly shy natives at one place along the Brazilian coast:

Nearly every day the people of the locality came down to the beach, but they would not speak with us. On the seventh day we headed ashore, and as we did so we noticed that the men had all brought their women with them. When we landed, many of them sent women to speak with us. But, seeing that they remained unsure of us, we agreed to send them one of our young men, who was very brave and agile. And we went back to our boats so that the women would be less fearful.

This young man went among the women, and they all began to touch and feel him, marvelling at him extraordinarily. But meanwhile a woman with a great stick in her hand was coming down the hill, and when she arrived where the boy was standing, she gave him such a blow on the back with her stick that he fell dead immediately.

In an instant, the other women grabbed him and brought him up the hill, dragging him by the feet, and the men who had been on the hill came down to the water's edge armed with bows and arrows and, shooting at us, so terrorized our men that none of them even thought of taking up his arms because the boats had run aground and it was hard to get away quickly.

They were thus able to discharge a great many arrows at us, until finally the ship got off four cannon shots against them. And, though none of them was hit, they had scarcely heard the report when they all fled precipitously to the hill. There the women still were, tearing the murdered young man to pieces before our eyes. And, holding up the pieces one by one for us to see, they roasted them in a great fire they had made, and ate them.

In this remarkable account, a new dimension is added to the emerging myth of the cannibal — that of carnal women, descendants of the "gorillas" of Hanno's narrative. These creatures of an all-consuming sexuality are the dark, southern opposites to the unblushing nude maidens of Golden Age visions of the West, such as those of Boccaccio's narrative who "went quite naked, without consciousness of shame."* They are also, in this region of the earth where East meets West, probable offspring of the Amazons of Greek mythology, as is suggested by Columbus in one passage of his journals. Writing about the cannibals, he says he has heard that they

> form unions with certain women, who dwell alone on the island of Matenino [Martinique?], which lies next to Hispaniola on the side towards India. These women employ themselves in ways wholly inappropriate to their sex. They use bows and javelins just as I have described their paramours doing, and wear as armour plates of brass, having this metal in great abundance.

Here we can see the elements of manly bellicosity and ferociously immured sexuality that seem only to have added a perverse attractiveness to the Amazon legend, which is by this time fully established in medieval folklore and located often enough in the vicinities of remote promised lands. It is now a regular component, for example, of the Prester John letter, which in the 1507 English version already quoted says of the women living in a part of the realm called the "Grand Feminie" that they "be very manly in fighting and hardy. And in this same land may come no men but nine days in the year and no longer, and then they have conversation and fellowship with the men and no more of the whole year. For if the men there would abide the women should flee them all."

This vision of overpowering, carnal women located in dark and remote corners of the world cannot but have been related in the minds of Europeans with a significant phenomenon of that day: witchcraft. It was

---

* A more complex image of the savage women of the West, blending the qualities of the Golden Age north and the bestial south, is to be found in a narrative of the Portuguese discovery of Brazil in 1500, written by Pedro Vaz de Caminha. Describing the natives of a certain locality, Caminha writes: "There were also among them four or five young women just as naked, who were not displeasing to the eye, among whom was one with her thigh from the knee to the hip and buttock all painted with . . . black paint and all the rest in her own color; another had both knees and calves and ankles so painted, and her privy parts so nude and exposed with such innocence that there was not there any shame." The black makeup on the thighs seems nevertheless to bespeak a deep sensuality underlying her otherwise innocent aspect.

precisely in this era that Europe saw a revival of the phenomenon, or at any rate a revival of witch-hunting, signaled by Pope Innocent VIII's bull against witchcraft in 1484 and the appearance, about a year later, of the most exhaustive diatribe ever written on the subject, the *Malleus Maleficarum* ("Hammer of Witches"). A cannibalism said to have been practiced as often in a final gesture of passion for a dead lover as out of ferocity was part of the tradition and mythology of witchcraft, as attested to by its most sympathetic historian, Jules Michelet, who speaks of the tragedy of "ces monstrueux sacrements de l'amour anthropophage." Witches were said to have been especially fond of children, a trait that gives significance to the youth of the sailor who was eaten by the Brazilian women in Vespucci's account. A mysterious sexuality is ever present in the legends surrounding witches, above all in one of the essential functions attributed to them through the ages, that of providing or restoring sexual potency; the fact that their detractors often accused them of causing sexual impotence in their victims is simply the other side of the vision of a carnality that was capable of eating men whole.

It is not hard to discern connections between the emerging racism of the epoch and the new outburst of antagonism against these shadowed creatures of the night. The enchanting uncleanness of witches seems often to have had affinities in the Christian mind with that of the Jews, another group considered to have entered into league with the Devil. The parallels between the two reach into the very vocabulary of witchcraft. Another word for a witches' "coven" was "synagogue," no doubt partly inspired by the "synagogue of Satan" in the Revelation of John. And, as is well known, the night when witches flew from all directions on broomsticks for their gloomy congregation under the Devil's pastorate was the "sabbath." In general, there were always occult associations suggested by the presence of Jews to the Christian mind, owing, among other things, to their oriental origin, to the impact of the Cabbalah, and to the fact that the Jews were Europe's most astute practitioners of astrology. Such associations had occasionally seemed attractive in the past, but now they were coming to represent more ominously than ever an unknown that terrified the newly zealous Christianity as much when appearing in its own midst as when encountered in remote parts of the world.

Even though there probably were indigenous roots to the phenomenon of witchcraft reaching back to pagan Europe, for western Europeans it seemed to be something primarily southern and eastern in origin, like the Jews and the Moors. The Old Testament itself tends to confirm this orientation. Egypt in particular was seen as a homeland of unholy magic, a viewpoint given sanction by such a Biblical passage as this one (Exodus 7:11–12) showing that magic being undone by a priest of the true religious tradition:

> Then Pharaoh also called the wise men and the sorcerers:
> now the magicians of Egypt, they also did in like manner with
> their enchantments.
>
> For they cast down every man his rod, and they became
> serpents: but Aaron's rod swallowed up their rods.

A Midrashic tradition supplied two of the Egyptian sorcerers in this
passage with names, Jannes and Jambres, and medieval Christian tradition then gave them a prominent role in the establishment of witchcraft.
Egyptian magic and an implied component of sensuality figure in one of
the medieval legends of Alexander the Great, which holds that he was
the illegitimate son of a sorcerer from the land of the Nile named Nectanebos, who used his sorcery to seduce the conqueror's mother Olympias.
An element yet more eastern, and, to the mind of medieval Europeans,
no less southern, enters the picture here as well, in that Nectanebos was
said to have carried a magical tablet that bore on it a representation of
Ahura-Mazda, the Persian god of gods. Persia is, of course, the very
homeland of "magic" in the literal sense, and the story of the three Magi
paying homage to the infant Jesus is a recapitulation of that of Aaron's
rod, showing how the true religion conquers the magical arts of the
ancient East.

Now, there is a hint of darkness of complexion in all this. To medieval
Europeans, Egyptians, living just north of Ethiopia, seemed dark-skinned
enough, but Persians — coming as they did from a country virtually
identified with India and Ethiopia — probably seemed more so. In this
connection, the *Malleus Maleficarum* offers a startling theory about the
origins of witchcraft. The magic arts in general, it tells us, originated in
Persia, and were introduced there by Zoroaster — and Zoroaster, it goes on
to say, may have been Noah's son Ham! This is certainly a fateful remark
to be made at the very moment when the children of Ham were becoming
in their divinely ordained role as slaves, a noticeable presence in some
parts of Europe. Is it perhaps their presence that has provoked it? We
can only perceive the fateful conjunctions here, and must remain helpless
before a chicken-or-the-egg question of causality. A dark notion in the
minds of men for centuries is now, like an aforementioned golden one,
finding a local habitation and a name, an unfortunate flesh with which to
invest it.

Even more to the point than the dim image of witchcraft is the vivid
one of the Devil, who for centuries now had been black. This may seem a
truism, until we realize that Satan has no color in any of his appearances
in the Old and New Testaments, except for Chapter 12 of the Revelation
of John, where he appears as a serpent that is quite *red*. On the other
hand, his blackness emerges distinctly in a most significant text of the

sixth century c.e., the apocryphal *Acts of Thomas*. For example, a woman who has been resurrected from the dead by Thomas describes her descent into Hell this way:

> A man took me who was hateful to look upon, altogether black, and his raiment exceedingly foul, and took me away to a place wherein were many pits, and a great stench and hateful odor issued thence.

In another place, the wife of one of Thomas's disciples is raped by devils whom she describes thus:

> I saw a black man standing over against me nodding at me with his head, and a boy like unto him standing by him; and I said to my daughter: Look at those two hideous men, whose teeth are like milk and their lips like soot.

It is noteworthy that this last scene has taken place in Persia. One wonders whether this country, the true homeland of early myths about warfare between light and darkness, was not the soil on which not only Thomas's pronounced Manichaean tendencies but also their peculiar coloration were engendered. And if so, then were any of the attitudes toward black devils that arose in Persia a response in some way to the presence of black men, whom we know to have been there as slaves since ancient times?

Some of the images of black men in the *Acts of Thomas* do suggest the possibility of concrete experience, although a description of a devil in a roughly contemporary account of the acts of Saint Bartholomew, another of the apostles to the Three Indias, seems to come exclusively out of the imaginative chiaroscuro of the Manichaean mind. Bartholomew exorcises a devil from a temple of Ashtaroth, who is described as "black, sharp-faced, with a long beard, hair to the feet, fiery eyes, breathing flame, spiky wings like a hedgehog, bound with fiery chains. . . ." This hardly resembles anything human; and yet by the thirteenth century, in Jacobus de Voragine's retelling of the story in his enormously popular compendium of the lives of the saints, *The Golden Legend,* this very devil is described as an "Ethiope." Whatever the intentions of the sixth-century authors, by the late Middle Ages the trend toward some kind of concrete anthropological identification of these black men seems inexorable. In the witchcraft proceedings of 1324 against Dame Alice Kyteler in Ireland, the Devil is described as one who appeared to her "sometimes in the form of a cat, sometimes in that of a shaggy black dog, and sometimes in that of a kind of Ethiope. . . ." Was there even another unconscious sign of the trend in the inclination of English and other European languages, prevailing until well into the modern era, to render "necromancy" as "nigromancy"?

But the fact remains that, until well into the generation that gathered the first European impressions of the New World, images of devilish black men of the south were not necessarily based only on Africans. The terrifying black giants of Taprobana on the Catalan Atlas, who eat white strangers and are without rational faculties, were a pointed contrast with the noble Black king of Guinea. And one can perhaps find no better account of these Taprobanans in the flesh than in the description of the Patagonians written by Antonio Pigafetta — another Italian free-lance adventurer on the tides of Iberian discovery — as part of his narrative of the celebrated voyage of circumnavigation of the world, in which he participated, made by Ferdinand Magellan's fleet from 1519 to 1522.

On the first leg of the journey after their Atlantic crossing, Magellan's ships sailed down the eastern coast of present-day Argentina, which the commander named "Patagonia" ("Land of the Clodhoppers") in honor of the gigantic black-skinned savages they encountered there. Pigafetta, a true Renaissance spirit, clearly enjoyed the opportunity these natives presented for vivid description, including the women. One naked savage girl, he says, sneaked aboard the moored ship one day looking for something to steal, and found a nail in the captain's cabin; she "grabbed it immediately, stuck it deftly into her snatch [la leure de sa nature, in the French version of 1525], then jumped overboard and got away." He also speaks of women with breasts half an arm's length long. These are the Amazons and carnal women of the distant East and south, rather than the demure naked maidens of the West.

Pigafetta has a good deal more to say about the gigantic, cannibalistic men of the country. One of them was so tall, he says, that an average-sized European did not even reach his waist. Naked and black, they looked to Pigafetta like "those who sail upon the infernal marshes." As for their hellish appetites, "they eat the human flesh of their enemies, not because this seems good to them, but on account of custom." He describes one of them thus:

> He was of good corporature and well made in all parts of his body, with a large visage painted of divers colors, but for the most part yellow. On his cheeks were painted two hearts, and red circles about his eyes. The hair of his head was colored white, and his apparel was the skin of a beast sewed together. This beast . . . had a large head and great ears like unto a mule, with the body of a camel and tail of a horse. The feet of the giant were folded in the skin after the manner of shoes. He

had in his hand a big and short bow, the string whereof was
made of a sinew of that beast. He had also a bundle of long
arrows made of reeds feathered after the manner of ours,
tipped with sharp stones in the stead of iron heads. The Captain caused him to eat and drink, and gave him many things,
and among other a great looking glass: In the which as soon
as he saw his own likeness, was suddenly afraid and started
back with such violence that he overthrew two that stood
nearest about him.

Captain Magellan gave him some hawk-bells and sent him off. This game
of taming the wild man of Patagonia with trivializing ridicule became a
favorite one for Magellan and his men during their stay there, for like
enslaving them, turning devils into minstrels was a way of neutralizing
the terror they aroused. Another Patagonian, a "giant of somewhat
greater stature," was induced by them to sing and dance and taught to
say "*Jesus, Ave Maria, Johannes,* even as we do, but with a bigger voice.
The Captain gave him a shirt of linen cloth, and a coat of white woolen
cloth: also a cap, a comb, a looking glass, with divers such other things,
and so sent him to his company."

Relations were not always so jolly as this, and indeed grew gravely
hostile when Magellan at last decided to make the traditional roundup of
some specimens to bring home. Picking out two of the "youngest and
best made," he filled their hands with trinkets until they were, in effect,
defenseless. "Then he caused two pair of shackles of iron to be put on
their legs, making signs that he would also give them those chains: which
they liked very well because they were made of bright shining metal."
When they began growing suspicious, Magellan tried to convince them
that nothing was wrong, but finally, "when they saw how they were
deceived they roared like bulls and cried upon their great devil *Setebos*
to help them."

One result, as it happens, of this ominous scene was literary immortality
for the "devil" called upon by the victims; for Shakespeare read this translation by Richard Eden, and no doubt had this very scene in mind when
he caused Caliban — another play on *Carib–Cannibal* — to say of
Prospero:

> *His art is of such power*
> *It would control my dam's god, Setebos,*
> *And make a vassal of him.*

Setebos reappears in the Pigafetta narrative, as an adversary to efforts to
make a Christian of one of the captive giants:

> On a time, as one [of our men] made a cross before him and kissed it, showing it unto him, he suddenly cried *Setebos*, and declared by signs that if they made any more crosses, *Setebos* would enter into his body and make him bruised. But when in fine he saw no hurt come thereof, he took the cross and embraced it and kissed it oftentimes, desiring that he might be a Christian before his death. He was therefore baptized and named Paul.

An appropriate name for a convert from the Devil's faith! Elsewhere we learn more about Setebos and some of the beliefs surrounding him:

> They say that when any of them die, there appear ten or twelve devils leaping and dancing about the body of the dead, and seem to have their bodies painted with divers colors. And that among other, there is one seen bigger than the residue, who maketh great mirth and rejoicing. This great devil they call *Setebos*, and call the less *Cheleule*. One of these giants which they took, declared by signs that he had seen devils with two horns above their heads, with long hair down to their feet: and that they cast forth fire at their throats both before and behind.

This becomes rather complex communication for sign language, and one begins to wonder how much of the imagery is really being supplied by the imagination of the Christians. Particularly in the more Hebraic-looking version — "Settaboth" — used by Sir Francis Drake during the Patagonian part of *his* voyage of circumnavigation in 1578, this devil's name suggests another piece of demonology that is at least partially inspired by Jewish sources.*

For one ambiguous moment in history, then, we can see all of the mythic imagery of East, West, and south, of noble non-Europeans and of black devils, converging on the geography of the newly discovered parts of the world, still only dimly organized on the map of the European imagination. With Columbus still believing until his death in 1506 that Cuba was part of the Asian mainland, and with North America to remain an unknown entity until well into the 1520s, South America and Africa, along with all the islands of the "Indies" east and west, seemed to comprise in that moment a vast undifferentiated region, or at least one of more or less exact counterparts. South America and Africa, on their east-

---

* The hint of "Sabbath," the seventh day ("seven" is *sette* in Italian, *sete* in Portuguese, and *siete* in Spanish), in this word becomes particularly strong when we recall that a standard dialectal variation in Hebrew of the pronunciation of "Sabbath" is *Shabbos*. No doubt the echoes of "Satan" in *Setebos* are another source of its appeal to Christian ears.

ern sides, loomed up in the darkness as either identical or, at any rate, fraternal twins, through which the various exotic races were scattered from north to south in the same way. If westward-leaning spirits were inclined to place their visions of paradise in or near northeastern South America, eastward-leaning ones could still bestow such qualities on the land of Prester John somewhere in northeastern Africa, and the two ideals could virtually converge. The Noble Ethiopian was still a worthy alongside the Noble Savage. The crucial distinctions still lay, in that moment, between north and south, not East and West. Men like Columbus, admirers of the "Indians," tended to want to enslave "Cannibals" just as they accepted the enslavement of Black Africans. And if some of the Negro slaves could look to Zurara like "the images of a lower hemisphere," this hardly seems different from what men way down in Patagonia looked like to Magellan's sailors.

But this moment was already passing in the brightening sunlight of geographical knowledge. And once again, we find the initiative to move on taken by those hardy pioneers of overseas discovery, the Portuguese.

10

The End of Prester John

TIME WITHOUT LIMIT, wrote Abraham Zacuto, "would not suffice to relate the happenings in Portugal, into which over one hundred and twenty thousand Jews entered from Spain and only a small remnant survived the ravages of the plague. Of these some were taken captive, their children seized and carried off to distant islands; others, overwhelmed by suffering, changed their religion."

The long Portuguese tradition of tolerance toward Jews had come to an end even before 1492. In 1481, the Cortes of Evora had given King John II official notice of a groundswell of popular anti-Semitism that he could no longer ignore. Members' complaints about Jews ranged from ostentation in dress, to tax-farming, and to Jewish artisans — tailors, shoemakers, and the like — who, they said, entered rural Christian homes under the pretext of doing their work but then tried to seduce the women while the men were out in the fields. The king agreed to legislation curbing Jewish sumptuary habits and reviving the ancient and hitherto long-forgotten requirement that Jews wear an identifying badge on their clothing.

The arrival of a huge Jewish refugee population in 1492 was therefore more than the king could put up with, although he could not resist the opportunity to fill his coffers by charging the new arrivals a large entrance fee. But he would not allow them to stay, and made March 31, 1493, the deadline for their departure. When the time came, many of the Jewish refugees pushed on to North Africa and elsewhere, but others stayed to put this unwonted Portuguese severity to the test; the threatened penalty was enslavement to the Portuguese crown, an ambiguous status that may even have seemed to promise advantages in the eyes of some Jews.

But the king dashed any such sanguine expectations, commanding, according to the royal chronicler Ruy de Pina, "that all who were minors, youths and girls alike, were to be taken captive from among those Castilian Jews in his kingdom who did not betake themselves away within the appointed time according to the conditions of their entrance." All these children were forcibly converted to Christianity and sent to the island of São Thomé (Saint Thomas) in the Gulf of Guinea, which had been discovered by Portuguese ships a little over twenty years earlier, "insomuch that, being separated, they would reasonably be better Christians; and it was as a result of this that the island came to be more densely populated, and on account of this it began to thrive exceedingly." Indeed, it was to thrive so well that, by the middle of the next century, it would be the most important entrepôt between the African mainland and the New World for the transatlantic slave trade. This is not the only instance of the persecuted being turned into persecutors during the course of that cruel age.

John II died toward the end of 1495, and the accession of his cousin Manuel I seemed at first to promise a better fate for the Jewish refugees who had remained in Portugal. He granted them free status shortly after his accession, and no doubt it was hoped that he would soon bring the converted children back from their São Thomé exile. But then the situation was completely changed once again the following year by his betrothal to one of the daughters of Ferdinand and Isabella. Manuel attached great importance to this alliance, hoping that a descendant of his might one day sit on the throne of Spain as well as that of Portugal, and he therefore was willing to make significant concessions to his prospective royal in-laws. One of their demands was that their work of expulsion be completed and the entire Iberian Peninsula be made, to use a most appropriate word from another time and culture, *Judenrein*. Manuel agreed not only to expel the refugees, but to eliminate Judaism from Portugal altogether. The decree that he accordingly published in December, 1496, commanded that all the Jews of his realm either convert to Christianity or go into exile by the following March 31.

Manuel was still a true Portuguese king at heart, however, and was not so ready as the Spanish sovereigns had been to renounce an economically valuable segment of the population merely for the sake of principle. "It caused Manuel great uneasiness," wrote a chronicler, "to think of so many thousands of men leaving his kingdom, and being driven into banishment; and he was desirous of at least converting their sons." The cruel precedent of stealing away Jewish children had already been established by his cousin, so Manuel decided to try it. "He ordered all the sons of Jews under fourteen years of age to be forcibly taken from their parents, that they might be instructed and initiated in the Christian faith. This could not be executed without causing the most affecting and heart-rending scenes." Then, in the last moment before the deadline went into effect, Manuel turned away from such head-on confrontations and resorted to quiet bargaining with Jewish community leaders. He agreed that, in exchange for a token conversion on their part, he would allow them to go on practicing Judaism in private, and would keep the Inquisition away from their doorsteps. The result was that, for generations to come, Portugal was to be the homeland of a secret Judaism more rampant than any that Spain had ever known. But even this arrangement was of course unacceptable to Jews uncompromising in their faith, and a significant portion of Portuguese Jewry went into exile on March 31, 1497. "In that year," Abraham Zacuto adds, "there was an expulsion of Jews from the Kingdom of Navarre, so that no Jew [as such] was left in the whole Iberian Peninsula."

The fact that Vasco da Gama was to leave on his historic first voyage to India later that year calls to mind the striking confluence of similar destinies, involving Jews and the Columbus voyage, in Spain five years earlier. Indeed, from the days of Master Jacome right down to the Expulsion, men of Jewish descent had been playing as important a role in the Portuguese enterprise of discovery as in the Spanish one. We have already noted the presence of Joseph Vizinho of Lisbon, Abraham Zacuto's disciple and translator, in the Portuguese royal commission that reviewed and rejected Columbus's plan in 1484. Later that year, Vizinho and one Master Rodrigo, another Jewish savant who had sat on that commission, were sent on a voyage down the African coast to gather astronomical and geographical information. Having rejected the western route, they clearly were part of the project that was then under way to open an eastern one to the Indies.

Indeed, three years later, at around the time of Bartolomeu Dias's departure on the voyage that would take him around the Cape of Good Hope at last, Vizinho and Master Rodrigo were among those called upon to give instruction to two men who were about to leave on an important geographical mission in the Middle East. Its purpose was twofold: to try to ascertain from that side whether Africa was indeed circumnavigable, and to obtain information about Prester John. The two men, Pero da Covilhan and Alfonso de Paiva, traveled together in the Mediterranean to Egypt, and thence to Aden, where they separated. Paiva headed for

Ethiopia in the company of a Jewish merchant of Cairo who knew the way. Covilhan went to India, where he spent a few years making voyages with Arab merchants down the East African coast. Returning to Cairo, he learned that Paiva was dead and had left no account of his discoveries: this information was brought to him by two Jews from Portugal, one a "Rabbi" Abraham of Beja, the other a "shoemaker" named Joseph of Lamego, according to existing accounts — surely none other than Abraham Zacuto, who lived in Beja after the Expulsion from Spain, and Joseph Vizinho, assuming the guise of a humble occupation to protect the secrecy of his mission. Covilhan sent Vizinho back to Portugal with a report on his travels and observations, and set out with Zacuto to Ormuz, apparently in an effort to determine for once and for all whether Prester John's realm was in Persia or not. At last satisfied that it was not, Zacuto headed home, while Covilhan resumed his travels, going on the *hajj* to Mecca disguised as a Muslim, and finally reaching Ethiopia. There he ceased to be heard from, at least for the time being.

Possibly some of the information relayed to Portugal by Vizinho and Zacuto, from Covilhan and from a wide network of largely Jewish sources, had been discouraging, for although Dias had brought back his good news in 1488, it was not for another nine years that a voyage to India by the route around Africa would be attempted. Apparently the prolonged illness from which John II finally died in 1495 also had something to do with the delay. In any case, Manuel wasted no time about resuming the project after he succeeded to the throne; but, like his predecessor, he decided that a little Jewish advice might be useful before going on. "Because it was fitting in this matter," writes the chronicler Gaspar Correa, "and also because he was some little inclined to astronomical matters, [the king] sent to Beja to summon a Jew with whom he was very well acquainted, who was a great astrologer named Zacuto." Speaking to him in great secrecy, the king asked Zacuto to use his "good science" to ascertain whether it was advisable for him "to engage himself in the discovery of India." The Jewish savant thereupon returned to Beja, presumably to consult both his astrological and his geographical charts, and after a while came back to the king with his reply.

"Sire," he said, "with the great care which I have taken in the matter which your highness so much enjoined upon me, and with the great pleasure of Our Lord, that which I have found out and learned is that the province of India is very far off from this our region, far removed by wide seas and lands, all inhabited by dark people, in which there are great riches and merchandise, which go forth to many parts of the world, and there is much risk before they can come to this our region. That which I have looked at, and by the will of Our Lord have attained to is, that your highness will discover it, and will subjugate a large part of

India in a very short time — because, Sire, your planet is great, under the sphere, the device of your royal person, in which are contained the heavens and the earth. For God will be pleased to bring all this into your power, which power will never end for the king who fears God, even though he spend his whole kingdom in this; because God kept this enterprise reserved for your highness."

According to Correa, these words were all the king needed to make him go ahead and call for the outfitting of the expedition that was to be led by Vasco da Gama. But Zacuto's services were not to be confined to such astrological pep talk, for he had a good deal of practical knowledge as well. Correa tells us that da Gama, just before his final departure from Lisbon, held a private and apparently very secret meeting with Zacuto in a monastery, in which he "received from him much information as to what he should do during his voyage, and especially recommendations of great watchfulness never to let the ships part company, because if they separated it would be the certain destruction of all of them." Elsewhere, Correa suggests that one of the things Zacuto gave da Gama was exact information about the southern conformations of the African coast. No doubt he also gave him some pointers on the use of the astrolabe, an instrument that had become a trademark of the Jewish cosmographers in Portugal.

It is no surprise that da Gama's meeting with Zacuto was so secretive, since the latter should have been out of the country by then; this was already some three months after the deadline for the Jewish departure from Portugal. For a man so useful as Zacuto, an exception evidently had to be made; indeed, Correa suggests that he did not leave Portugal for good until 1502. How had he managed to stay on all that time? Perhaps he had even undergone a token conversion to Christianity, as we know Joseph Vizinho to have done. But whatever temporary course he may have taken in religious matters, he at any rate, according to Correa, "died in the error in which the Enemy had blinded him, having acquired such knowledge of the stars, and remaining blind in such a bright day as is our holy Catholic faith." We last hear of him wandering in the Middle East, perhaps hoping for a final resting place in the Holy Land, perhaps lifting his cosmographer's eyes to some yet more distant oriental horizon.

The great interest shown by Correa and other Portuguese chroniclers of that time in Jewish participation in the discovery of India does not quite stop with da Gama's departure. A significant bit of Jewish history makes its way, often confusingly but without fail, into all the narratives of his return trip. After leaving Calicut, da Gama's fleet put in for a refit at the island of Anjediva below Goa, where, according to the anonymous diarist of the voyage, "there arrived a man, about forty years of age, who spoke Venetian well. He was dressed in linen, wore a fine *touca* on his head, and a sword in his belt. He had no sooner landed than he embraced the captain-major and the captains, and said that he was a Christian from the west, who had come to this country in early youth; that he was now in the service of a Moorish lord, who could muster 40,000 horsemen; that he, too, had become a Moor, although at heart still a Christian." Correa corrects the anonymous diarist on this point, telling us that this interesting stranger was a Jew from Granada who, upon the taking of his city by the Spanish Christians, had wandered to the East. Other writers of the period, agreeing that he was a Jew, alternately give his place of origin as Egypt and Poland. At any rate, all agree that his strongest desire was to return with da Gama's fleet to Portugal — and to become a Christian. Da Gama, finding him to be in the possession of extensive knowledge about the Indian Ocean and its trade routes, complied with his wishes on both counts, baptizing him on the voyage home and giving him — with no excess modesty — the Christian name of Gaspar da Gama! Gaspar shipped out as a pilot on the next Portuguese voyage to India, under Pedro Álvares Cabral, and continued playing a prominent role in this enterprise during the succeeding years.

But the enthusiasm shown by chroniclers over Gaspar's arrival on the scene seems to go beyond his mere practical value; rather, one can perceive beneath the surface of their accounts a sense of the symbolic importance of this episode, which tends to read like a ritual summing up the Portuguese conquest of the Orient. It represents a final settling of *Reconquista* scores for the Portuguese, who have reached, both physically and spiritually, the outermost goal in that drive to exorcise and then take under control the southern and eastern components of the Iberian civilization. Our view of this history has been primarily from the Castilian perspective, whereby we have seen the final expulsion and conversion of the Jews of the realm take place within the framework of the final act of *Reconquista* on Iberian soil. To a certain extent, the Spanish history of the ensuing century would continue in just this way, in the New World as well as the Old, as a series of Quixotic, head-on efforts to stampede and then swallow up the enemy; the Spanish Inquisition would have this character, too. But this was not the way of the small people who, in the generation that saw the author of *Don Quixote* grow to maturity, was to produce as its own great national literary work an elegant pastiche of Latin and Italian epic styles telling the story of Vasco da Gama's historic voyage — Luis de Camoens's *Os Lusíadas*. The deft Portuguese did not charge into problems and continents, but outflanked them. By the time of da Gama's voyage, Portuguese Africa was simply a chain of coastal trading posts on the way to India, and the technique of control-by-en-

clave would now be extended in the next few years to the entire northeastern circumference of the Indian Ocean. In a sense, this approach was
transforming vast areas of the world into networks of Portugals, of islands
and coastal enclaves with one foot in the sea, ever ready to maneuver.

The approach taken by the Portuguese to the Jewish question was another version of this; they outflanked it, instead of attempting to stampede
it and swallow it up in the Castilian manner. They imposed a mass conversion upon their Jews, but allowed them to go on practicing Judaism in
open secret. They expelled those who refused to convert, but seem to
have held on to a few among them who were useful, like Abraham Zacuto, at least for a while. The Jews were, after all, preeminent instructors
in the kind of knowledge the Portuguese most needed for their own particular brand of *Reconquista* – in a sense they were the very model for
it, the most Portuguese of all peoples, scattering their enclaves into the
farthermost Orient, gathering knowledge from all the corners of the
earth. But bringing it back to where? In every age, there are always some
one or two countries whose Jewish communities are the central reposi-
tories for Jewish learning and aspirations throughout the world, and Portugal evidently went on thinking of herself as one of these even after the
mass conversion and expulsion, quite typically wanting to have it both
ways. She saw herself above all as the homeland of the great tradition of
Jewish cosmography brought to her by Master Jacome of Majorca, and if
a man like Abraham Zacuto finally left her bosom even this was no disaster, because the success of his own services had in the end rendered his
services obsolete. The ideal Jewish geographer of Portugal's new era was
one who knew the Orient at first hand, and who was furthermore happy to
accept the new religious dispensation; Gaspar da Gama was the ideal,
and this is one reason why he looms so large in the chronicles as a symbol and not just as a man.

Gaspar's advent and conversion did not stand merely for the conquest
of the Orient, however; he also represented its demystification. When
Vasco da Gama's ships at last led the way through the southeastern corner of the *oikumene,* penetrating through the ancient imaginative haze
into the clear light of scientific geography, they found on the other side
not the Lost Tribes of Israel but a wandering Jew, apparently of European and perhaps Iberian origin at that. Gaspar's return on board was,
like the Black captives coming back from the Guinea voyages, a symbol
of the reducing and taking in hand of the awesome south and East.

The most dramatic of such demystifications, however, took place a
few years later, in 1520, when a Portuguese diplomatic mission arrived
in Ethiopia, and the blurred and dreamlike vision of centuries hardened
into focus at last. What the guests found was not the jewel-studded realm
of the Prester John of legend, but the thatched roofs and hewn rock of the

kingdom of Lebna Dengel. The mission's priest and chronicler, Francisco Álvares, was no doubt thinking of the fabulous processions of the former when he described the character of those made by the real-life monarch whom he and the Portuguese continued to refer to as "Prester John" in spite of everything:

> It is unbelievable how many people always travel with the Court; for certainly for a distance of three or four leagues from each place at which they break camp the people are so numerous and so close together that they look like a procession of Corpus Domini in a great city. . . . The tenth part of them may be well-dressed people, and nine parts common people, both men and women, young people, and poor, some of them in skins, others in poor cloths, and all these common people carry with them their property, which all consists of pots for making wine, and porringers for drinking. If they move short distances, these poor people carry with them their poor dwellings, made and thatched as they had them; and if they go further they carry the wood, that is, some poles. Rich men bring very fine tents. I do not speak of the great lords and great gentlemen, because each of these moves a city or a good town of tents, and loads, and people on mules, a matter without number or reckoning. I do not know what to say of those on foot. We Portuguese . . . often talked of these mules, because in the winter . . . the Court does not move with less than 50,000 mules, and from that upwards, they might reach 100,000.

One hundred thousand mules are most impressive, but not in the way of the same number of cavalrymen, such as the legendary Prester John brought in his train.

It was this mission that finally learned the whereabouts of Pero da Covilhan, who had not been heard from since his parting with Rabbi Abraham at Ormuz nearly thirty years before: he was living in Ethiopia as a courtier to the king, a kind of Marco Polo of the south, but with one important difference — he was not permitted to leave. He told his whole story to Álvares, how in 1493 he "travelled by land until he reached the Prester John . . . and he came to the Court, and gave his letters to the King Alexander, who was then reigning, and he said that he received them with much pleasure and joy, and said that he would send him to his country with much honor. About this time he died, and his brother Nahum reigned, who also received him with much favor, and when he asked leave to go he would not give it. And Nahum died, and his son David [Lebna Dengel] reigned, who now reigns; and he says he also asked him for leave and he would not give it, saying that he had not come in his time, and his predecessors had given him lands and lordships to rule and enjoy, and that leave he would not give him, and so he remained." Álvares adds his own observations, saying that Covilhan "was given a wife with very great riches and possessions. He had sons by her and we saw them. In our time, when he saw that we wanted to leave, a passionate desire to return to his country came upon him. He went to ask leave of the Prester and we went with him and we urged it with great insistence and begged it of him. Yet no order for it was ever given." So far as is known, Covilhan ended his days in Ethiopia. He, too, was a living symbol of the demystification of the East, ending like the legend of Prester John in the Abyssinian dust.

With that legend went, for the time being, all hope of a noble image of the Negro to counter the one that was coming with growing force out of West Africa. One of the most vivid depictions of the West African image now taking shape in the minds of many Portuguese can be found in the *Esmeraldo de Situ Orbis,* a geographical and historical handbook of the African coast written in about 1508 by Duarte Pacheco Pereira, from which we have already quoted with reference to Master Jacome of Majorca. Pacheco had worked for years as a civil servant in various parts of the growing Portuguese empire, and had had intimate experience of the African slave trade in all its ugliness. The result in this apparently somewhat sensitive man is a bitterness turned, not against the exploiters from among his own people as might have been the case in a later era, but against the abject African participants in the trade. "For a poor horse you can receive here six or seven slaves," he writes typically of one place on the coast, and with equal contempt for those who hand in human beings for horses and those who are thus handed in, goes on to warn that "the captain who is engaged in this barter should guard against these Negroes for they are bad people." The loathing that permeates his descriptions begins gradually to extend to physical characteristics, some of which are wholly imaginary as he describes them; for example: "The inhabitants of this region have the faces and teeth of dogs and tails like dogs; they are black and shun conversation, not liking to see other men." But Pacheco only rarely indulges in such departures into medievalism from sound if contemptuous observation, and when he refers elsewhere to "a great multitude of new peoples and black men" in Africa, "whose color and shape and way of life none who had not seen them could believe," calling them in yet another place "almost beasts in human form," he makes it clear to his readers that he is speaking of men and women any one of them may have seen coming off the slave ships. It is a doomsday vision — evil, repulsive men sending out cargoes of other men who seem hardly more than beasts in exchange for trivia — and it is colored black.

A true child of that callous and coldly theological age, Pacheco saw suffering in other men as the outward sign of God's contempt for them, and like many other Europeans, he considered blackness to be another such sign. In one particularly striking passage, he joins the growing chorus of those who, in his day, were rejecting the old and relatively humane climate theory of color:

> Many of the ancients said that two lands lying east and west of one another would both have the same degrees of the sun and would be in all things alike; as to their equal share of sun this is true, but such is the variety employed by the majesty of great Nature in her creative work that we find from experience that the inhabitants of . . . Guinea are very black, whereas the inhabitants of the same latitudes beyond the Ocean to the west are brown, almost white. These are the inhabitants of Brazil. . . . If any should aver that they are white because of the many forests which protect them from the sun, I would answer that there are as many and as dense forests in this eastern side . . . ; and if they should say that the inhabitants of Guinea are black because they are naked and the inhabitants of Brazil white because they wear clothes, I answer that Nature has given them an equal privilege in this, for they are all naked as when they were born; so that we may say that the sun affects them equally. And now it only remains to know if they are both descended from Adam.

The theory of differing racial lineage is, in principle, good modern anthropology, but it is characteristic of Pacheco's time that the step cannot be taken into it without one's including the notion that the "different" race must be outside of the family of the elect — or, as in this case, outside the human family altogether.

With these examples we can see the dehumanization of the West African proceeding hand in hand with the demystification of the East and the concomitant dissolution of the ideal of the Noble Ethiopian. It is significant, moreover, that we see Pacheco speak of the Negro this way in the context of a comparison between him and the New World Indian. Although we have seen the concept of an undifferentiated southerly world of "black devils" appearing as late as the 1520s in Pigafetta's account of the Magellan voyage, it is Pacheco's view — the unfavorable comparison hinted at by both Columbus and Peter Martyr — that will come to the fore and prevail in the ensuing epoch. Whatever the Indian is to suffer, he is to emerge gradually as a full-fledged member of the human family, even when feared and despised: the legacy and the experience of the fresh western horizons will work in his favor in this respect. But the human condition of the Negro, circumscribed with chains of the body and spirit as Africa itself was by the trade routes of European ships, was with only occasional and fleeting exceptions not to be thought about for some two hundred years.

II

Isles Far Off

Bᴜᴛ ᴛʜᴇ ʜᴜᴍᴀɴɪᴛʏ of the Indian was not decided upon without a long struggle between his friends and his enemies, and the impulse of many Europeans to destroy him was never completely suppressed. If the Black African, known to most whites only as a slave, was for the most part contemptuously ignored, the Indian more often provoked paroxysms of admiration or of rage, for he was the true native of the New World that the colonists wanted to make their own, either through him or in spite of him as the case may be.

The divergence in attitude originates in Columbus's own Manichaean distinction between *indios* and *caníbales*, which we may well perceive as the first formulation of that enduring moral expedient for dealing with the question, the concept of the "good Indian" and the "bad Indian." History has tended to stress Columbus's effort to enslave the "bad Indian," and so has featured him as the first in the long line of wielders of the European scourge in the Americas. But the fact remains that, by the standards of his own generation, and above all by the standards of his own rapacious colonists, he was a model of sweet reasonableness in Indian relations; he is, furthermore, the first in a long line of men from Spain who felt a special, and historically significant, admiration for the New World native — a group that might justly be called, if the anachronism be permitted, the pro-Indian intelligentsia of the sixteenth century.

One of the outstanding traits of this intelligentsia was a passion for — to use another anachronism — the anthropology of the New World. Columbus was not only intrigued by the culture of Indians but was also the patron of the first ambitious effort to study it. On his second voyage in 1493 he brought along a Hieronymite friar named Ramón Pané, "a poor hermit," in the friar's own words, about whom little is known except that he went to live among the Tainos — the natives of Hispaniola — for two years. No doubt the friar hoped to convert them, but he does not seem to have been in the great hurry to do so that many of his ecclesiastical colleagues were soon to be in, and his first impulse clearly was just to observe, with a calm objectivity that is especially admirable in the age of the Spanish Inquisition. There are occasional displays of righteous impatience in his *Relation Concerning the Antiquities of the Indians*, such as when, in describing the powers attributed to the various *cemíes*, or idols, of the Tainos, he remarks that "these ignorant people hold this to be the most certain truth"; there is overeagerness to find the threads that might lead to salvation when he talks in one place about what seems to be a concept held by the natives of a supreme being in heaven. But for the most part he is satisfied just to record what he has seen and heard, and the result is a remarkable little treatise on the customs and beliefs of the Tainos, the first such study ever written on the New World native.

But the ominous shadow of another Spanish presence appears in a passage dealing with a prophecy that Fray Ramón records, told to him by a *cacique*, or chieftain, who claimed to have heard it long ago from one of his *cemíes*. It said that

> there would come to this country a people wearing clothes, who would establish dominion over them and kill them, and cause them to die of hunger.

At first, Fray Ramón says, the Tainos thought that this was a reference to the cannibals,

> but then, when they recalled that the cannibals came only to rob and then always fled, they realized that the *cemí* must have been speaking of another people. And now they believe that the prophecy dealt with the Admiral [Columbus] and the people he brought with him.

Did Fray Ramón actually hear such a prophecy, or did something he heard merely reach his understanding this way through an inadequate grasp of the Taino language and the filter of his own imagination? Or, if this was in fact what he heard, then was it perhaps a creation, conscious or instinctual, of the Indian imagination in response to events then occurring? These questions cannot be merely passing ones, for we are dealing here with a phenomenon — the imputed prophecy of the European arrival — that was destined to recur dramatically in Spanish-American history during this epoch. Indeed, it had already occurred — if we are to believe a Spanish narrative written on the basis of folk accounts more than a hundred years after the event — at that first frontier of Spanish conquest in the Atlantic, the Canary Islands. From 1493 to 1496, the Spaniards were engaged in a violent campaign to subjugate the Guanches of Tenerife, the last of the islands to hold out against Spanish domination; yet, we are told, many of these fierce and freedom-loving people had lost their will to resist because an ancient prophecy foretold the coming of a conqueror from the east. The tradition of such a prophecy was even to extend itself beyond the Americas, farther along the Spanish westward route into the East Indies themselves; for when Magellan's ships reached the island of Tidore in the Moluccas on their voyage around the world late in 1521, "the king of the island," according to Peter Martyr of Anghera, "told the Spaniards that he gladly received them as guests, because a few months earlier he had read in the circle of the moon that strangers, bearing an absolute resemblance to the Spaniards, would arrive by sea." A people that hears, or thinks it hears, this story often enough can easily become satisfied that even its cruelties are the work of a higher will; such touches of the miraculous and the supernatural were the trademark of the Spanish version of manifest destiny.

Peter Martyr seems to acquiesce in such a view of destiny's will when, in the passage in his *De Orbe Novo* ("Of the New World") that deals with the prophecy recorded by Fray Ramón, he writes:

> And in this they were not wrong, for they are all under the dominion of the Christians, and those who resisted have been killed; all the *cemíes* having been removed to Spain, to teach us the foolishness of those images and the deceits of devils, nothing remaining of them but a memory.

The outlook expressed here hardly seems in keeping with the spirit of the "golden world" passage we have already cited from elsewhere in Peter Martyr's book; it is as if this important writer, the first historian of the New World enterprise, is in one place the first of the literary apologists for the wielders of the scourge, and in another, the first fully articulate spokesman for the viewpoint of what we have called the pro-Indian intelligentsia.

Yet another of the many Italians we have seen wandering into the Iberian age of discovery, Peter Martyr was a true son of the Renaissance.

Born in 1457 near Anghera on the shores of Lake Maggiore, which straddles the border between Italy and Switzerland, he received an aristocratic education, and studied in one of the celebrated humanist academies of the day, in Rome. It was while he was living there in 1486 that he formed a friendship with the Count of Tendilla, who had arrived as an ambassador to the pope from Ferdinand and Isabella. Eventually, he was invited by Tendilla to return with him to Spain to pursue an official career there, and he accepted. At first he considered the military profession, and took part in the siege of Granada. But then, like Julien Sorel rejecting the red in favor of the black, he laid down his arms and took minor orders. He obtained a canon's post at the newly consecrated Cathedral of Granada, formerly a mosque, under the celebrated Bishop Hernando de Talavera, whose ancestors had been Jews. Peter was ever to be closely associated with a number of prominent New Christians. He remained even through the worst days a stout supporter of Columbus, whom he probably met through Bishop Talavera, and when the latter was, in his eighties and at the end of a distinguished career in public service, brought before the Inquisition on charges of Judaizing, Peter rallied passionately to his defense. This friendliness did not extend to unbaptized Jews, however.

Peter's espousal of unorthodox causes can be seen as the spirit of the Renaissance humanist asserting itself amidst the stark excesses of Iberian religiosity, but there might also be another element underlying his behavior. This is suggested by the ecclesiastical name he chose for himself, which he remains known by, and which has obscured his own family name for all time to come. The choice is a startling one for a man of his inclinations: the original Peter Martyr was a saint of the medieval Inquisition, who had been murdered not far from Anghera by Waldensian assassins in the thirteenth century. In fact, from that day down to the one that now concerns us, the region around Lake Maggiore was a hotbed of the Waldensian heresy, brought there early in the thirteenth century by fugitives from the Albigensian Crusade. Had our own Peter perhaps been tainted with it? This would certainly help account for the pointed choice of a name representing a spirit so unlike his own; he would be concealing his identity by labeling himself its exact opposite. It would also help to account for Peter's entry into the tradition of the pro-Indian intelligentsia, which seems above all to have been founded on an innate sense of the affinities between religious and racial outsiderness: if he was indeed a Waldensian by origin, then his sense of the Indian plight was subjectively grounded, as that of some New Christians was, and as that of the Quakers would be in a later day.

In any case, Peter Martyr must surely have known that when he described the brutalities of settlers and the sufferings of natives he was presenting scenes that echoed racial and religious persecutions closer to home. It is, in fact, between the lines of the protests against mistreatment of the Indians written by Peter and his successors in this tradition of pro-Indian humanism that we must look to find the otherwise silent Spanish history of the denunciation of pogroms, of laws of *limpieza de sangre,* and of the Inquisition. If the Spanish relationship with the Indian had begun in a Manichaean vision of warlike and peaceable multitudes among the latter, of *caníbales* and *indios,* it was now resolving itself into a similar division among the men from the sea — between those who had come to exploit and persecute, and those who had come to tolerate, understand, even to love. Peter seems to be delivering the opening salvo in the emerging war between these two forces when he summarizes in his *De Orbe Novo* the behavior of those who brought about Columbus's overthrow in Hispaniola — a faction of "debauchees, profligates, thieves, seducers, ravishers, vagabonds . . . given over to violence and rapine; lazy, gluttonous, caring only to sleep and carouse" — as follows:

> They spared nobody; and having been brought to the island of Hispaniola originally to do the work of miners or of camp servants, they now never moved a step from their houses on foot, but insisted upon being carried about the island on the shoulders of the unfortunate natives, as though they were dignitaries of the State. Not to lose practise in the shedding of blood, and to exercise the strength of their arms, they invented a game in which they drew their swords, and amused themselves in cutting off the heads of innocent victims with one sole blow. Whoever succeeded in more quickly landing the head of an unfortunate islander on the ground with one stroke, was proclaimed the bravest, and as such was honored.

Unfortunate islanders, indeed; these were the victims of the pogromists of colonization.

As a defender of the Indians, Peter is at his best in moments like this, when the moral issues are clear; writing in an earnest, if flawed, Renaissance Latin, he can easily make his sentences roll when they have to into the thunder of outraged humanism denouncing the behavior of brutes. He is more ambivalent when he gets to matters lying closer to the very essence of the Spanish manifest destiny — we have seen an example of this. But this ambivalence was partly because the Spanish colonial enterprise was not yet fully defined. Peter, like the man whose discoveries he was the first to proclaim to the world at large, was really one of the last of the seekers of the Fortunate Islands in the west. The oriental complexity of an empire that included Mexico and Peru was still in the future when he wrote the above lines not long after the death of Columbus in

1506; indeed, the very existence of North America was not yet known, and the immensity of the South American continent was no more than dimly suspected. To cultivated men of Peter's generation, the New World was simply a more western, more exciting version of the Canaries, alive with classical associations.

To be sure, the image of this golden world had become a bit tarnished from the outset as a result of the discovery, made by Columbus himself during his first voyage there, that it contained real gold. This was the condition that had brought hundreds of colonizers, including some rabble, onto the Admiral's ships for his second voyage. Quite typically, Columbus had given even this element of hard gain the coloration of an exalted religious enterprise. Noting that the Indians had a custom of refraining from all sexual intercourse while they searched for gold, which they seemed miraculously able to find at a glance in rivers and streams that Spaniards had to scour, he tried to make his colonists not only do the same (there were no women among them at first, but they freely enjoyed the favors of Indian women), but also fast, pray, and say confession whenever they were going for gold. Needless to say, this regimen did not last, and the search for gold became yet more unholy instead when veins were discovered in the earth. Then the settlers renounced the rigors of personal effort along with those of piety and sexual abstinence, and put the Indians to work in the mines. Suddenly the easygoing natives of Hispaniola were being subjected to a regime of back-breaking toil such as they had never known; this was yet another crucifixion of simpler men on a cross of gold.

"It is gold alone of all the products of Hispaniola to which the Spaniards give all their attention," Peter Martyr wrote, but when he proceeded at first to discuss the system whereby the colonists exploited Indian labor to obtain it, the edge of his moral fury became dulled; for he was touching upon what was widely assumed to be the foundation stone of the incipient Spanish colonial system, the *encomienda*. From the earliest days of the *Reconquista* — especially in Valencia and the Balearic Islands, where oranges and sugar grew — down through the occupation of Granada and the Canaries, Spanish conquerors and colonists had customarily been rewarded for their services with grants of *encomienda* (also sometimes called *repartimiento*), of parcels of the newly conquered lands along with the right to use the labor of the indigenous peoples living on them. Although the laborers under this system had fewer rights than medieval serfs, the Spanish overlords nevertheless considered it to be a form of serfdom and not chattel slavery — this latter also being in existence, but used primarily for domestic service rather than for large-scale agricultural labor. Theoretically, the *encomendero* was under an obligation to instruct his charges — who had been Moors and pagans until destiny struck them — in the principles of Christianity and the laws of civil society, while he was to honor their own social organization to the extent of delegating to their leaders the task of choosing and sending out the various labor gangs required each day. Above all, he could not buy and sell the laborers of his *encomienda* the way he could chattel slaves.

These qualifications were meaningful, although they became far less so in the New World than they had been in the Old. The system was more stable in the Old World, in the first place because the peoples conquered there were genuine peasantries with solid agrarian traditions, and in the second place because its conquerors usually came from the established ruling classes and were held to patterns of responsible behavior by social and political, as well as geographical, continuity with the society from which they had come. In the New World, on the other hand, the naked and relaxed inhabitants of Eden hardly were peasants, nor was there much responsibility among colonists who had come from all walks of life in search of quick fortunes far from the normal restraints of civil society. It was gold in particular that led to abuse, not only because of the unwontedly heavy labor it entailed for the Taino, but also because it meant often transporting the labor gangs to distant places, far off the lands owned by their *encomendero* and on which they lived, to mines in which he was a shareholder along with other settlers; this was not a traditional practice of the *encomienda,* and it produced a condition approaching that of chattel slavery.

But when Peter Martyr wrote his first description of the system as it worked in Hispaniola, he was not sure whether his disapproval was merely of its abuses, which he could dislike openly, or of the system itself, which he could criticize only with caution. His words show this ambivalence:

> Each industrious Spaniard, who enjoys some credit, has assigned to him one or more *caciques* (that is to say chiefs) and his subjects, who, at certain seasons in the year established by agreement, is obliged to come with his people to the mine belonging to that Spaniard, where the necessary tools for extracting the gold are distributed to them. The *cacique* and his men receive a salary, and when they return to the labor of their fields, which cannot be neglected for fear of famine, one brings away a jacket, one a shirt, one a cloak, and another a hat. Such articles of apparel please them very much, and they now no longer go naked. Their labor is thus divided between the mines and their own fields as though they were slaves. Although they submit to this restraint with impatience, they do put up with it. . . . The King does not allow them to be treated as slaves, and they are granted and withdrawn as he pleases.

A system which once, however oppressive, had fit into a controlled and legitimate framework of medieval traditions was now turning into a method of pirating bodies and their labor as if before Peter's very eyes; but for a moment he seems unable to know what to do or say.

Things were changing rapidly by now, however, among the peaceable men from the sea as among the warlike ones. A company of Dominican missionaries reached Hispaniola in 1510 and, shocked by the abuses that they saw being committed against the Indian population, immediately began waging a campaign to prevent them, on the island and through their correspondents back in Spain. Among some ecclesiastics, apologists for the excesses of the colonists, a philosophical argument began gaining currency: purportedly based on Aristotle, it claimed that Indians were a people eligible for slavery because they were not fully endowed with rational faculties. In 1511, a Dominican friar named Antonio de Montesinos preached a sermon in a church on Hispaniola denouncing this "Aristotelian" doctrine and calling upon his congregants to mend their ways. Montesinos returned to Spain to plead his cause with the crown, and was given the opportunity to hold a public debate at Burgos with a Franciscan friar who represented the opposite position. If the Indians were natural slaves, then all pretenses at *encomienda* could be dropped; if they were not, then the system as practiced in the West Indies – which by that time also included Spanish settlements on Jamaica, Cuba, and Puerto Rico, as well as at Panama – had to be reformed. The widowed King Ferdinand preferred, as his wife had done, to think of the Indians as his "vassals," who therefore could not be enslaved, and Montesinos's position won the day. On paper at least, the excesses of the *encomienda* in the New World were made illegal by the Laws of Burgos, passed in 1512. Colonists were forbidden to beat Indians or call them "dogs"; they had to provide minimally decent working and living conditions for the natives that they held in *encomienda*, and to watch over their Christian education and salvation; they could not force Indians to carry heavy loads at the mines, and a woman more than four months pregnant could not be made to work in the mines at all – she could be used only in light household chores.

But this little gesture at improvement was largely ignored, and the abuse continued to such a degree that it was beginning to cause death among the native populations of the islands in large numbers. Peter Martyr, whose *De Orbe Novo* was written in a series of installments that provide a changing image of the Indies – and a dramatic testimony to the steady decline and downfall of Peter's dream – through the years, was no longer able to maintain the classical restraint of old by 1516. In that year's installment, during a lengthy description of the natural beauty and productivity of the Hispaniolan landscape, he suddenly pauses and writes:

Yet amidst all these marvels and fertility, there is one point which causes me small satisfaction; these simple, naked natives were little accustomed to labor, and the immense fatigues they now suffer, laboring in the mines, is killing them in great numbers and reducing the others to such a state of despair that many kill themselves, or refuse to procreate their kind. It is alleged that the pregnant women take drugs to produce abortion, knowing that the children they bear will become the slaves of the Christians. Although a royal decree has declared all the islanders to be free, they are forced to work more than is fit for free men. The number of these unfortunate people diminishes in an extraordinary fashion. Many people claim that they formerly numbered more than twelve millions; how many there are today I will not venture to say, so much am I horrified.

Although Peter's estimate of the original size of the population — of Hispaniola or even of all the West Indian islands colonized by then — is exaggerated, he has placed his finger quite accurately upon the process that Bartolomé de las Casas later would call "the destruction of the Indies." In some places, the indigenous population was to disappear entirely.

But the rape of Peter's Noble Savage did not stop with the mere abuse of *encomienda;* there also were Indians whom the more rapacious colonists could treat unqualifiedly as slaves, and against them anything was permitted. These came from islands that, not having yet been colonized, were therefore not yet subject to the fiction that their inhabitants were free under Spanish law. Slave-raiding, which became increasingly popular as the Indians of the colonized islands died off under the abuses of the *encomienda,* seemed to find its most fertile source of supply in the Bahamas, which were known to the early Spanish colonists as the Lucayos. Peter Martyr wrote of this scene of Columbus's first encounters with a "golden world":

It is stated that these islands formerly abounded in various products, which constituted their riches; I say formerly, for they are now deserted. . . . The reason for this is that large numbers of the wretched islanders were transported to the gold mines of Hispaniola and Fernandina [Cuba], when the native inhabitants there were exterminated, exhausted by disease and famine, as well as by excessive labor. Twelve hundred thousand of them disappeared.

Most of them died like the natives of Cuba and Hispaniola before them, many not even surviving the dreadful conditions of the slave ships onto which they were crammed unmercifully. Las Casas later wrote that a ship could easily have sailed from the Lucayos to Hispaniola "without compass or chart, guiding itself solely by the trail of dead Indians who had been thrown from the ships."

This was a final blow to Peter, who seemed to be composing an epitaph to his own vision of the world as well as to the victims when he wrote these words in 1525:

> Thus perished the unfortunate Lucayans, and there only remains today a very small number of them, either in the Spanish colonies or in the archipelago itself. Nevertheless I think that the sighs and groans of those wretched innocents have provoked the Divine wrath, and that many massacres and disorders among these peoples have been punished, the more so because the Spaniards pretended they labored to propagate religion while influenced by cupidity and avarice. Some of them are dead, killed by the natives or pierced with poison arrows or drowned or stricken with different maladies. Such has been the fate of those first aggressors, all of whom followed other ways than those laid down in the royal instructions.

More than this genteel protest against the violation of royal instructions, or this literary invocation of divine wrath, was needed to deal with the problem, of course; but the time for Peter's brand of humanism had passed. Columbus was long gone, and the discovery and conquest of Mexico had by this time replaced the old vision of a new realm of Fortunate Islands with something Peter could no longer comprehend. Insular abuse had given way to something more grandiose; and furthermore, tougher spirits than his own were taking up the crusade for justice toward the Indian that he had softly but decisively helped to awaken. In another year he was dead, never having even set foot in that New World to which he had given a name and a portion of its mythology. Elements of his idyllic vision were not to pass readily from the collective consciousness, but the fullness of his moment had been superseded rather quickly. From him we shall move on to continents, to the full enormity that henceforth would constitute the America of fact and of the spirit; but only after a brief, romantic interlude.

12

Interlude: In a Garden

Entering a garden in pursuit of one of his falcons, Calisto comes upon Melibea, and begins to speak of his love for her. . . .
Calisto: In this, Melibea, I see the grandeur of God.
Melibea: In what, Calisto?
Calisto: In that he has given nature the power to endow you with such perfect beauty, and has granted to my unworthy self the boon of getting to see you — and in a place so suitable for the confession of my secret longings. . . .
Melibea: . . . Away, you lout, get away! It is beyond my patience to endure being an object of illicit love for any human heart.

The Comedy of Calisto and Melibea, a satirical romance published anonymously at Burgos in 1499, continues to its last page to be as bizarre and mystifying as these opening lines. The atmosphere is permeated with ambiguity; we are never told where the story takes place, nor do we learn if these two young people had ever met before. Calisto with his falcons is of course a nobleman, but Melibea turns out to be only of bourgeois stock despite her haughty contempt for him, and the reason for her attitude is never provided. Neither of them is married, nor are there any other visible obstacles to a marriage between them — Melibea's family clearly is wealthy enough for it — but Calisto's love seems doomed and illicit from the start. They are star-crossed like Romeo and Juliet, but without anything like the manifest reasons for being so that Shakespeare gave his two lovers in a play that may have been partially inspired by this romance in dialogues. Indeed, we must make our way through more than half of the work before we can perceive without a doubt that it is not a comedy at all.

Calisto, who in the opening scenes is a parody of the swain of troubadour poetry, hires the services of a wily old crone named Celestina to intercede for him with the haughty Melibea. A part-time witch as well as a procuress, Celestina uses a combination of magic and shrewd psychology

— we never are sure precisely which is the element that turns the trick — to win the girl's heart. The two lovers arrange a secret tryst in the garden of Melibea's house.

At this point, the satire begins to collapse in a succession of disasters. Celestina, who has secured the aid of two of Calisto's servants in her schemes, is accused by them of withholding their share of the promised reward, and in a sudden outburst of violence they kill her. The two culprits are quickly captured and brutally done away with by the police. Meanwhile, that same night, the two young lovers have had their assignation, and as Calisto departs over the high garden wall — the seeming absence of this obstacle in the opening scene is just another of the story's many mysteries — he misses his footing on the ladder he has set up and falls to his death on the street. Melibea summons her father, Pleberio, from his bed and climbs atop a high turret of their house; from there she confesses to him the story of her love and dishonor, then leaps to her death. The "comedy" ends with a long diatribe against life and love delivered by Pleberio over his daughter's battered corpse.

The book was popular, and it went through two new editions in 1501 and 1502; but by this time, especially with the addition of some new scenes that only added to the atmosphere of gloom and violence toward the end, there could be no more pretenses about its character, and it was reentitled *The Tragicomedy of Calisto and Melibea*. Furthermore, the author, undoubtedly pleased by his success and perhaps reassured in other ways as well, decided this time to reveal his identity — though coyly. From an acrostic formed by the first letter of each line in a poem placed at the beginning, we learn that: "The Bachelor [of Arts] Fernando de Rojas finished the comedy of Calisto and Melibea, and was born in La Puebla de Montalbán." Furthermore, a preface tells us that he composed the work in his student quarters during a fifteen-day university vacation, but that — as if to restore something of the mystery he has now otherwise taken away — he did not write the opening section, but found it in manuscript and then elaborated upon it.

A few other things also are known about Fernando de Rojas. We know that he attended the University of Salamanca, that he was a lawyer, and that he went on after his literary escapade to enjoy a quiet and distinguished career in public service, spending a number of years as lord mayor of the town of Talavera de la Reina. We also know that he was a New Christian, whose father apparently was burned by the Inquisition and whose father-in-law was brought before it on charges of Judaizing in 1525. Álvaro de Montalbán was even defended before the Inquisitors by his son-in-law, "who composed the Melibea," as he informed them, and he was subsequently cleared of the charges; Rojas himself seems never to have been accused of heresy.

This is remarkable, considering the questionable religious orthodoxy that runs through his book. There are very few expressions of Christian piety in it. Pleberio's final soliloquy, a cosmic outburst of moral anguish that occasionally resembles the Lamentations of Jeremiah, contains no religious references at all; the name "God" appears only when Pleberio says that some have misguidedly given it to Love, the cause of all his ills. Love seems to be Calisto's only religion; he goes to church, but his scheming servant Sempronio rightly observes that this is only to pray for Melibea's hand. For love's sake, he just as readily pays homage to a witch — who is, incidentally, the only character in the story who consistently pays lip-service to conventional religious piety. Calisto is always invoking heavenly images, but only to praise Melibea, and at one point he actually refers to her as "God." On the other hand, her cruel indifference brings his blasphemies to another extreme when he says: "Surely, if the fires of Purgatory are like this, then I would rather my soul went the way of the dumb animals than that it pursue such a route to the glory of the saints." The ever attentive Sempronio picks this up and the following exchange ensues:

> SEMPRONIO: Just as I thought, matters are going to an extreme. Madness wasn't enough; now we have heresy. . . .
> CALISTO: Why?
> SEMPRONIO: Because you are saying something contrary to the Christian religion.
> CALISTO: What's that to me?
> SEMPRONIO: Then, you're not a Christian?
> CALISTO: Me? I'm a Melibean. I worship Melibea, I believe in Melibea, and I serve Melibea.

Not a Christian, but a Melibean: such a profession of perverse faith could have been atoned for only by Calisto's death in the end; although, perhaps it was because he felt the need for further protection from possible imputations on the basis of these lines that Rojas — whether truthfully or not is a matter of learned controversy to the present day — proclaimed another authorship than his own for the part of the book in which they appear. His initial anonymity and subsequent devious emergence from it also suggest a concern about the public response that perhaps was not just over the book's literary qualities.

Rojas may have had good reason to worry, for a careful reading of *La Celestina* — as tradition has since named the book in honor of its most vivid character — suggests that he may initially have had something more in mind than just a cynical reworking of Renaissance literary conventions about love. There are veiled and uncomplimentary references to the Inquisition in it, and in general the cataclysmic atmosphere suggests a profoundly negative response to the times: Rojas shows us not just a Renaissance convention, but a world, coming to an end, and the conclusion is irresistible that this vision is specifically a product of the author's New Christian identity. The reverberations of pogrom, expulsion, and Inquisition are everywhere. Indeed, some commentators have gone further and believe that they see a New Christian theme right in the foreground of the story: pointing to certain sociological peculiarities in Pleberio and his household, and to Melibea's otherwise inexplicable resistance to the idea of marriage with Calisto, they have suggested that this is a family of *conversos,* clinging to its racial identity and unwilling to intermarry with Old Christians. Since it is widely accepted by scholars that Rojas probably wrote this work at first only to be read among friends — perhaps only New Christian friends at that — one could conceive of such a point as this having been made explicit in the manuscript and then suppressed for publication, leaving only ambiguous traces for the discerning eye to interpret.

But it is possible to go even further and see this strangely surreal work as an allegory, summing up the entire spiritual universe of the day from a New Christian perspective. Calisto seems to be the old, relatively easy-going, tolerant Spain of the Middle Ages, now become the very essence of a Christian chivalry gone to seed — in this respect, he is the palpable precursor of Don Quixote, the creation of another Spanish author in whom some scholars think they can discern the lineaments of the New Christian. His unflagging quasireligious passion for Melibea often comes across as an aspiration for spiritual renewal in the highest sense; as a "Melibean," he seems to want his "God" to provide salvation itself. Of course, he dismally fails in his quest, and the fault is as much in himself as in his stars. There is a significant moment early in the story when Celestina, having begun to make inroads upon Melibea's heart, returns to Calisto with a token she has obtained of her initial triumph: Melibea's girdle. This has brushed against many holy relics, and Celestina has persuaded Melibea to part with it by claiming that Calisto has a toothache — a euphemism for the condition of his heart — and that it will help cure him. When she presents it to the young swain he grabs it, embraces it, and lyricizes over it with such an unseemly ardor that Sempronio is moved to remark: "Sir, you're having such a good time with the girdle, you won't want to enjoy Melibea." This bit of coarseness exemplifies what Gerald Brenan has called "the raciest conversation ever written by a Spaniard," but the implications of it seem to be not only sexual. The talk of holy relics implies a higher fetishism as well, and the racy language seems merely to soften the impact of a traditional sort of Jewish scorn for the pagan appetites of the goyim — now reappearing as the contempt of an austere Hebraic New Christian for the decadent idealism of the

Old. This is the outlook of an incipient Protestantism, looking down upon an object-ridden form of religiosity that seems to it bound to fail.

But in Rojas's pessimistic vision, the purer New Christian ideal to which Calisto vainly aspires is doomed to go down with him. This is Melibea, so high-minded and inscrutable at the beginning, so disdainful of Calisto's hot unreasoning blend of carnal lust and religious ardor, that he takes her for divine; she certainly is a vision of redemption, for Calisto as for Rojas, but she is only an earthly ideal after all, attainable, corruptible, and in the end mortal. Calisto the Catholic embraces the idea of God made manifest, but Rojas the New Christian sees even messianic redemption as a thing of this world. It is Pleberio, rather, who seems to stand for divinity itself; distant and awesome in his upper room, at times only a troubled voice offstage, he does not emerge until the end, to witness his daughter's death. Then thundering curses at the world, he cries despairingly: "For whom did I erect towers? For whom did I acquire honors? For whom did I plant trees? For whom did I build ships?" — surely this is more than just the wealthy New Christian entrepreneur surveying his contracts that some have perceived. As for Celestina, she is evidently Rojas's satirical image of the Church that the precursors of Protestantism already were calling "the Whore of Babylon." She is an unscrupulous seducer and a superstitious old hag, but she is also the shrewdest and saltiest character in the book, an irresistible magnet to those who rail against her as well as to those whom she fools. In the end, it is she who drags everyone down to destruction, including herself, overwhelmed by forces even more relentless and primal than her own, the groundswell of plebeian fury and of Inquisition. It is not Reformation that comes in her wake, however, in Rojas's doomsday vision, but a hellish, forsaken world and a helpless, anguished God to denounce it. This is the End of Days, but without the hope of Redemption, which has been dashed to the ground with Melibea's body.

Running through all this cosmic dejection, there also are hints of an outlook that might be called Columbian. It is known that Rojas was fond of the utopian travel literature of the day, and Pleberio's reference to shipbuilding seems to accord a special place in the author's universe to navigation. But most significantly, there is a moment in a long soliloquy by Melibea confessing the abjectness of her love for Calisto when she says:

> If he wants to cross the sea, I'll do it with him; to go around the world, I'll come along; to sell me in a hostile land, I'll not refuse his wish.

The book has its clear topical references, such as to the conquest of Granada, and the imagery in this passage apparently is right up to the minute. Even more so than meets the eye, in fact; because this speech was not in the first edition of 1499, but was added only in the revised version two years later, which was a year after Columbus had returned from the New World in chains. If Columbus did indeed represent a hope of New Christian Redemption, then his return in chains was bound to present the image of a people betrayed back into slavery; his history would thereby be remarkably similar to the one Melibea has proposed as a possibility for herself. But the reverberations of the passage are even wider than this, for Melibea's words could also serve as a description of the treatment by the Christian of the darker-skinned peoples of the world. The fact that these words are even more appropriate for the Negro than for the Indian suggests that this could not have been a conscious intention on Rojas's part — for nobody was worrying about the Negro at this moment — but it does indicate what a deep chord can be sounded by Rojas's poetic probe into the tragedy of the New Christian: it is one in which all the racial themes of the moment come together and sound their significant relationship to one another.

There is even a Moorish undertone in this, for 1502 is the year in which all the Muslims of Castile — which is to say, primarily those of Granada — were forcibly converted to Christianity, or went into exile. Romantic gardens are primarily a Moorish trademark at this time, and one cannot but hear echoes of the rape of Granada in Calisto's invasions of Melibea's sacred preserve. For Rojas, Granada may have been symbol enough of an Eden violated by an insensitive and irrepressible Spanish Catholicism, but the enchaining of Columbus and the beginning of the destruction of the Indies certainly were final blows against the terrestrial paradise of his spirit. In this sense, La Celestina is, like Peter Martyr's De Orbe Novo, a steadily growing lament for the golden world, the insular idyll, which Columbus had briefly held up before the men of the anti-Inquisition and which was now dying.

But God sends the cure before the disease to those who wish it, and during this very decade another literary tryst in a garden was being arranged, the issue of which would provide spiritual energy for a new, more militant, generation. Perion and Elisena make love in a garden at the beginning of Amadis of Gaul, published in 1508; but unlike Calisto and Melibea they subsequently marry, and the son they have conceived, Amadis, goes on to be a paragon of knight-errantry. Amadis of Gaul was an adaptation into Spanish of an earlier version in some other language, probably Portuguese, and its setting is mainly northwestern France and the British Isles, but the result in this version by Garci Rodríguez de Montalvo is pure Castilian, as much an expression of the crusading spirit of the land as La Celestina was a protest against it. One could almost say that it was the confrontation between these two books in Cervantes's mind that gave rise to *Don Quixote*.* In any case, it is possible to perceive the elements of a conscious reply to Rojas in *Amadis of Gaul* and Montalvo's sequel to it, *The Exploits of Esplandian.*

This connection is suggested not only by the garden scene and its outcome in *Amadis of Gaul,* but by the entire career of Amadis's son Esplandian, who seems to be a subtle hispanicization of the theme of knight-errantry — in his name, so resonant with *España,* in his childhood history of having been nursed by a lion (suggesting the lion of Castile), and in the southern, primarily Mediterranean, location of his activities. Esplandian is also less of a dilettante of chivalry than his father, who, with perhaps a touch of Calisto still in his bones, had always sought out damsels in distress and tilted at giants wherever they appeared, as Don Quixote tried to do. The son, after a few miscellaneous adventures, settles down to a leading role in a more markedly Catholic task, that of defending Constantinople against the besieging Turks — for in Montalvo's never-never land, the disaster of 1453 has not taken place, nor will it, thanks to a more resolute crusading spirit than Christendom had shown in fact. The Turks — depicted as "pagans" who worship Jupiter and other Roman gods — bring together for the battle all the dark-skinned peoples over whom they rule. These include the inhabitants of an island "on the right hand of the Indies, called California, very close to the region of the terrestrial paradise, which was populated by black women, who had no men among them, for their way of life was almost like that of the Amazons." The women of California are great warriors, who fly into battle on the backs of griffins. But in spite of such formidable opposition, the Christians eventually fight off the Turkish hordes. Montalvo fills his narrative with frequent editorial asides, exhorting the Christian kings to stop fighting one another and turn their combined strength against the infidel, like Esplandian and his associates at Constantinople, and like Ferdinand and Isabella at Granada.

Esplandian is amply rewarded, obtaining the daughter of the emperor of Constantinople in marriage and, when his new father-in-law retires to a monastery, the imperial crown itself. His uncle, Amadis's brother, also

---

* Indeed, their relationship could be even more concrete. The author, or adapter, of the Spanish *Amadis of Gaul* lived in Medina del Campo, not far from Salamanca, and when he followed up that book's success two years later with *The Exploits of Esplandian,* about Amadis's equally chivalrous son, this time written out of whole cloth, he had as his proofreader a Salamancan teacher named Alonso de Proaza, who had performed such services for Rojas. Furthermore, his name, Montalvo, or Montalván, suggests that he or his family might have come from La Puebla de Montalbán, or Montalván, Rojas's home town; in fact, but for an insignificant variant of spelling, he has the same family name as Rojas's father-in-law. It is going too far, perhaps, to suggest kinship, but it does not seem out of the question that the authors of *La Celestina* and of *Amadis of Gaul* knew one another.

is rewarded by marriage, to Queen Calafia of California, who gladly accepts conversion to Christianity and to submissive wifehood after her defeat. The news of all this is greeted joyously by Amadis himself, who rules with his wife Oriana over an island in the western ocean, off the English coast, called Insula Firme. From the regions of the Fortunate Islands, it would seem, to those of Prester John, crusading Catholicism has emerged triumphant. There are no wilting Calistos here, and if the Melibeas give in, it is only to their advantage. The imaginative groundwork has been laid for the age of the Conquistadors.

13

Amadis of Mexico

THERE IS REALLY more of Calisto than of Amadis in the early years of Hernán Cortés. Born in 1485 in the town of Medellín in southeastern Estremadura, he was the son of an infantry captain, but was burdened with a weak constitution throughout his childhood. Intended for the legal profession by his father, he entered the University of Salamanca at the age of fourteen — which means he was there at around the time when Rojas composed the first draft of *La Celestina*. The student atmosphere there seems to have remained deliciously free as ever, even after two decades of the Inquisition, but young Cortés gave up his studies at the end of two years, apparently determined to live, as Prescott put it, "in the idle, unprofitable manner of one who, too wilful to be guided by others, proposes no object to himself. His buoyant spirits were continually breaking out in troublesome frolics and capricious humors, quite at variance with the orderly habits of his father's household."

But with the approach of his late teens and the onset of the new century, he apparently felt a sudden need to get a grip on himself, and with the ardor that often accompanies this kind of decision, he nearly enlisted in the army of the "Great Captain," Gonzalo de Córdoba, which was soon to set out onto the traditional battlefields of Europe. But then something made him change his mind and turn his eyes to the New World instead.

This was a more appropriate horizon for the ambitions of a young man whose character was still above all marked by capriciousness — as was amply demonstrated by an incident that occurred in 1502, just as he was about to depart for Hispaniola with the fleet of the new Governor, Don Nicolás de Ovando, appointed in the wake of the Columbus brothers' downfall two years earlier. "One night Cortés was going to a house for a tryst with a woman," according to Francisco López de Gómara, writing years later as the Conquistador's secretary and official biographer, "and was walking along the top of a poorly cemented garden wall, when it collapsed under him. Hearing the crash of the wall and of Cortés's arms and shield, the woman's new husband came out and saw the stranger lying near his door. Suspecting something was going on with his wife, he wanted to kill Cortés, but his old mother-in-law arrived in time to stop him. Cortés was weakened by the fall, and suffered a relapse of an old quartan fever, which stayed with him quite a while; and so he could not go with Governor Ovando."

He did recover, and finally sailed to the New World two years later; but this episode reads like a final farewell to the life of Calisto. Was Cortés aware of it in this way? It is remarkable that, in the course of a highly abbreviated account of his patron's early years, Gómara has told this seemingly trivial story at disproportionate length. He would not have done so had Cortés not wanted him to. Whether he saw the young man on the garden wall specifically as a Calisto, or as the typical Salamancan cavalier of his generation, whom Calisto among others represented, the mature Conquistador obviously thought the story was significant.

Not that the young Cortés promptly gave himself over to the Amadis of his soul when he arrived in the New World in 1504. These were still the days for island idylls, when Hispaniola could be a kind of Salamanca of the tropics. Apparently enjoying some family connection or influence with Governor Ovando, Cortés obtained a post as a notary with a small grant of *encomienda* in an outlying village, where he settled down to a few more years of relative indolence and of amorous adventure. There were plenty of Indian women for him, but there were Spanish ladies as well, now that many of the older settlers were bringing along their wives and daughters; it is said that he bore through life the scars of duels from this period. One can discern the lineaments of a man of burgeoning toughness and daring, but not yet of a man of destiny.

The shape of his personality was rapidly growing and changing, however, along with that of the Indies. In 1509, an expedition sent out from Hispaniola overcame Indian resistance on Jamaica and established a Spanish colony there. A similar one went to Cuba two years later under Diego Velásquez, Governor Ovando's chief lieutenant; Pánfilo de Narváez, one of the conquerors of Jamaica, was its chief military officer. Cortés had

gone along with Velásquez on various campaigns of "pacification" in remote parts of Hispaniola, and now he accompanied him to Cuba as well.
This brought its ample rewards, for when Velásquez established himself
as governor of the newly conquered island, he gave Cortés a large *encomienda* there and a high post on his staff. The momentum of insular
expansion was increasing: in 1512, Juan Ponce de León, a relative of the
Marquis of Cadiz who had initiated the campaign against Granada thirty
years before, took on Puerto Rico, the toughest of the conquests so far
because of its Carib population.

Meanwhile, the continent was entering the picture. The long stretch of
east-west coastline from northern Venezuela to Costa Rica was where the
first contacts with the continental landmass of the New World had been
made, by Columbus himself in his third and fourth voyages, and by
Alonso de Hojeda with Amerigo Vespucci aboard in 1499 or thereabouts.
In 1509, two expeditions went out to establish trading settlements along
this coast, which was known by then to have gold. Hojeda led one of
them to what is now Colombia, and Diego de Nicuesa led the other to
the isthmus, whose character as such was not yet known. Both ended in
disaster. Nicuesa and his company were never heard from again; but
Hojeda, plagued by shipwreck, starvation, disease, and war with the
natives, managed to get back to Hispaniola, leaving behind him a garrison
under the command of a lieutenant named Francisco Pizarro. Wounded
and sick, Hojeda sent reinforcements under the command of Martín Fernández de Enciso, a lawyer and a historian as well as a soldier, who believed that the Spaniards had to deal with the inhabitants of the New
World as Joshua did with those of Jericho. He proved to be no Joshua
as a leader of men, however, and was soon supplanted in this role on the
isthmus by a young man who, fleeing from creditors on Hispaniola, had
stowed away on one of his ships: Vasco Núñez de Balboa.

It is poetically appropriate that the history of the first Spanish assault
on the American continent should feature the names of both Balboa and
Pizarro, for they represent the two opposite poles of the emerging Conquistador personality. Pizarro, an illiterate brute whose capacity for
cruelty seemed only to grow with the advance of his fortunes, regarded
Indians as mere obstacles on the road to plunder. Balboa, though certainly no paragon of gentleness, was of a nature that could be tamed by
adversity and the experience of power, and he quickly developed a special
relationship with the Indians. To be sure, he looked no more kindly upon
"bad" Indians than Columbus had, and advocated that the cannibals of
the isthmus be rounded up and sold into slavery; but among those whom
he befriended, he grew to an apparent recognition that they commanded
a unique access to the core of the New World experience. A man who
made his entry into history on the margins of legitimacy, he found it easy

to "go native," and he settled down at his headquarters in Darien with a local chieftain's daughter, whom he deeply loved. When the elderly civil servant Pedrarias Dávila arrived in 1514 as the new governor of Darien, his advance party came upon the man who had discovered the Pacific the year before, dressed as a laborer and thatching the roof of his house with a group of Indians. Pedrarias made various attempts to harness him, even offering him his daughter in marriage; but the last straw came in 1519 when Balboa, on his own initiative, led a party across the isthmus to the ocean he had discovered, planning to sail in search of the fabled treasures of Peru. The governor sent Pizarro to arrest him. "What is this, Francisco?" Balboa is said to have exclaimed when he encountered Pizarro awaiting him on the road. "It was not your wont to come out and receive me this way." The act was symbolic, for Balboa was brought to Darien, summarily tried for treason, and beheaded, and the way to Peru was thereby opened for Pizarro and his manner of conquest.

A relationship similar to the one between Balboa and Pedrarias Dávila was to develop between Cortés and Diego Velásquez. The tensions between them were merely personal at first,° but more serious matters for contention began arising on the larger stage of history. It was on a slave-raiding expedition in 1517, searching for new sources of supply now that the Lucayos had virtually been emptied of their inhabitants, that Hernández de Córdova came to an island – or so he thought it to be – that seemed to be called Yucatán by the people living there. Hernández recognized immediately that its natives were far different from any that had so far been encountered in the Indies. These descendants of the Maya civilization were a relatively sophisticated people, who went about fully clothed, built structures of masonry, and created elaborate works of art. The expedition sent there under Juan de Grijalva immediately upon Hernández's return even discovered large stone crosses, which gave rise to speculation about a possible Christian prehistory of this region; some thought it may even have been part of the "India" in which Saint Thomas had preached. If so, times had changed, for human sacrifices now were performed there as part of the pagan cult. Grijalva also discovered that Yucatán was not an island, but part of a hitherto unsuspected northern continent – one on which there were said to be fabulous treasures in gold and precious stones. The old image of Fortunate Islands populated by

---

° Trouble between the conqueror of Cuba and his once loyal follower began when Cortés proposed marriage to Catalina Juárez, daughter of a family from Granada that had settled on the island, and then reneged. Governor Velásquez thereupon rose to the defense of the dishonored family, evidently because he was himself interested in another one of its four daughters, and in the ensuing conflict Cortés did not scruple to join into political intrigues against his erstwhile patron. Cortés finally married Catalina – it was a mismatch that would be resolved only by her early and somewhat mysterious death – and this placated Velásquez for the time being.

men and women whose hearts were as pure as their bodies were naked,
already devastated by a quarter of a century of Spanish rapacity, was
now giving way entirely to something more oriental and more complex —
a realm of Granadas and of Prester Johns after all.

And with this change began the final transformation of Cortés. Upon
Grijalva's return, Governor Velásquez, from whose jurisdiction the first
two expeditions to Yucatán had gone out, promptly ordered a third one
and placed it under Cortés's command; but no sooner had he done so than
he repented of this rash appointment and revoked it. This was not fast
enough for Cortés, however, who sailed his fleet out of Santiago harbor
under the governor's nose. It was as though he had learned the lesson of
the mistake made by Balboa that very same year; his bold and ultimately
successful flouting of the governor's authority runs as a counterpoint
through the whole subsequent history of the conquest. From the moment
he sailed out of Santiago, he never looked back to any other authority than
that of the Spanish crown itself, which was safely an ocean's distance away,
and which furthermore was now being worn by that young representative
of a new vision of Empire, Charles V. In a sense, Cortés was the first great
exponent of the imperial ideal of the Counter-Reformation; but for him
this also was an excuse for defying the commands of his immediate
superiors. Like the Crusaders proclaiming their old ideal of universal
Christendom, he would invoke a higher sanction for his unorthodox
political initiatives; but like his true forebear the Cid, he would always
know of the great things the sovereign wanted before the sovereign himself necessarily knew. He took history into his own hands, and it was his
capacity to do so that enabled him, in the end, to succeed where Balboa
had failed and kill the ghost of his own illegitimacy.

In this way the indolent though plucky *encomendero* of the islands
began to emerge at last as the first Castilian knight of the New World,
performing a bewilderingly rapid succession of feats of admirable daring
and revolting cruelty, but acting in his worst moments as in his best on
terms far different from the casual avarice of the early colonists of Hispaniola. We see him summarily overturning stone idols in Indian villages
and setting up images of the Virgin in their place; establishing the Villa
Rica de Vera Cruz on the Mexican coast under no authority but his own
and that of the emperor; sinking his ships behind him; marching boldly
with his small band into the continental wilderness; and passing lordly
judgments upon Indians wherever he encounters them — making the conquered people of Tlaxcala his firm friends and ultimately the foremost
native beneficiaries of the Conquest, wreaking slaughter upon those of
Cholula when he suspects them of planning betrayal. In broad outlines he
emerges as the bearer of that old continental appetite that had recon-
quered the homeland from Toledo to Granada, now so zealously revived

in Mexico that, upon seeing its mountains and plateaus, he could not but be struck by its resemblance to the original and name it New Spain.

Cortés can thus be seen as the link between the Cid and the Conquistadors, a bridge between the era of the *Reconquista* and that of the Spanish manifest destiny in America. Indeed, he is as much the former as the latter, for a time at least, and displays during the march to Mexico some of the familiar ambiguities of the old Castilian knight. This is not so apparent in the official account written by Gómara years later for the aging Conquistador, which is filled with stilted Counter-Reformation pieties and centered worshipfully upon a hero whose boldness and brutality alike seem to be the inexorable unfolding of God's will. But it is quite discernible in Cortés's letters to Charles V – the only account we have of the Conquest written while it was going on – and, above all, in the *True History of the Conquest of New Spain,* written in reaction against Gómara's book by Cortés's old lieutenant, Bernal Díaz del Castillo. The Cortés of this latter work is rather like the Cid, prone to an easygoing comradery with his men and always ready to consult them before making a decision. He is even capable of warm relations with Indians, as long as his fear or his anger has not been aroused – after all, he had always been critical of the abuses of the *encomienda,* and it was on this march to Mexico that Doña Marina, an Aztec woman who had been a slave in the Yucatán when he found her, became his closest companion and perhaps the one true love of his life. He displays a lingering touch of Calisto in this relationship.

Both Cortés's letters and Bernal Díaz's narrative show an appreciation that is not evident in Gómara for the indigenous Mexican civilization, and even, in the case of Bernal Díaz, an obvious admiration for a man like Jerónimo de Aguilar, a shipwrecked former member of the Darien colony whom Cortés's men found living among the Mayans, and who had so successfully "gone native" in language, manner, and dress that the Spaniards had taken him for an Indian when they first saw him. One suspects that a feeling of this sort – despite the moral lapse, provoked by fear, of the massacre at Cholula – was quite characteristic of that hardy band of Spaniards and of their leader as well during their march up to the Aztec capital. This is what comes across in the celebrated passage by Bernal Díaz, describing their first entry into the region of lakes and island cities in which Tenochtitlán reposed:

> The next morning we arrived at the broad causeway on which we made our way from Ixtapalapa. And when we saw the populous towns and cities on the water, with all the towers and temples and buildings of stone masonry rising as if from its surface, and the other great settlements on the shore, and that straight and level causeway heading right into Mexico, we were

filled with wonder, and said to each other that it seemed like those works of enchantment described in the book of Amadis. And some of our soldiers even said that what they were seeing must have been a dream, so it is no wonder I am writing thus, for there was so much in it to admire which I don't even know how to describe, things we saw that had never been seen, or heard of, or even dreamed of before.

Rising out of his own illicit affair in the garden to discover such marvels, Cortés had here indeed become the Amadis of Mexico.

Amadis, but not Esplandian just yet, despite Gómara's portrayal. It is significant that a Moorish atmosphere, depicted more with a romantic fondness than with a zeal to destroy, hangs over both Cortés's and Bernal Díaz's accounts of the march to Tenochtitlán, as if the towers of the Alhambra itself could all but be seen rising in the distance over that shimmering lake. In his first two letters to the emperor, Cortés does not refer to Indian temples but to *mezquitas* — "mosques" — as though he implicitly accepted Montalvo's conception of Muslims as pagans. When he destroys the idols of Cempoala and persuades its people to accept Christianity, he proposes to rename it "Seville"; Tlaxcala, he writes, reminds him of Granada. Bernal Díaz goes a step further in sensing the presence of a familiar old brand of oriental "paganism": he thinks he sees traces of Jewish influence in the idols and temples he had come upon, brought over somehow by refugees from Titus' campaign against Palestine in the first century C.E.

There is even an ironic echo of the surrender of Granada in the scene, described by both Cortés and Bernal Díaz, which occurs when Montezuma arrives to greet the Spaniards at the gate of his city. Here is Cortés's account:

> Montezuma came down the middle of the street with two lords, one at his right and the other at his left . . . all three of them dressed the same way except that Montezuma had sandals on and the other two were barefoot; each of the two lords held him by the arm. When we reached one another I dismounted and was about to embrace him, but the two lords put out their hands and prevented me from touching him; instead, all three of them got down and ceremoniously kissed the ground.

But Bernal Díaz adds that Cortés had first tried to offer his own hand to be kissed, and that Montezuma had refused it. There had been a similar confusion over the protocol of kissing at the Granada gate, but not such uncertainty over who was master of the situation and who its victim. That would take only a little longer to be resolved, however.

The Spaniards had barely been shown to their quarters, when Cortés was led by the Aztec emperor into a large room and told to sit on the throne there. Then, according to Cortés's account, Montezuma proceeded to regale him with gifts and to tell him this story:

> "Long ago in our sacred writings our ancestors informed us that neither I nor any of the other inhabitants of this land are indigenous to it, but are foreigners, come here from a completely different place, and that our race was brought here by a lord whose vassals they all were, who then returned to his native country. After a long time he came here again, and found the men he had left behind now married to the native women of the country, with many children, and living in the villages they had built. He wanted to take them back with him, but they wouldn't go; they wouldn't even accept him as their lord, and so he went home."

The moral drawn from this history is:

> "We have always believed that his descendants had to come and subjugate this land and make us their vassals. Now, since you say that you come from the direction where the sun rises, and because of what you tell us about the great lord or king who sent you here, we believe and hold it for certain that he is our natural lord, particularly since, as you tell us, he has known about us for a long time. Therefore you may be assured that we shall obey you and treat you as our lord in place of the great lord of whom you speak . . . and that you may command at will in all the land over which I rule, for you shall be obeyed. All that we have is completely at your disposal."

Subsequent tradition has made this story into a legend of Quetzalcoatl, the "plumed serpent" of the Aztec pantheon, but this is not necessarily so. The lore of Quetzalcoatl was collected and elaborated after the Conquest, and it is quite likely that tradition was unwittingly bent by the combined consciousness of Spaniard and Aztec to conform to the powerful myth spun here by Cortés. For the story was bound to appeal to the imagination of victor and vanquished alike, since it justifies the most dramatic conquest of all in the inexorable march of a Spanish manifest destiny gratified by similar prophecies going around the world. Indeed, it is too good to be entirely true. Did Cortés make it up out of whole cloth?

One must make allowances for his own sixteenth-century imagination, excited with the wonders of Amadis and with his emerging destiny as a Catholic conqueror of the unknown world, and for the tenuous method whereby he and Montezuma communicated complex ideas to one an-

other.* Doubtless there was a kernel of Cortés's final version in the story
Montezuma must have struggled to convey: it could, for example, be taken
as evidence by those who seek it of possible early arrivals from the Old
World onto American shores, commemorated thus by native tradition.
But there are political and religious overtones that probably could only
have been imparted by a European sensibility. The religious element is
not clearly evident at first glance; the stress, for the emperor's sake no
doubt, is on feudal traditions, and on the reasoning whereby Montezuma
has paid manifest homage — whether he did in fact is another story — to
Cortés as his liege lord, and through him to the emperor. But the whole
account also has a messianic ring to it.

In his letters to Charles V, Cortés rarely departs from the level of
spare, down-to-earth narration into anything like theological speculation,
so that if he thought Montezuma's story had genuine religious significance,
it is just like him not to have said so; he certainly was not going to present
himself to the emperor as the Messiah — it was good enough that the
Aztec leader thought he was. There are, however, noticeable echoes of
Esdras — including his Old Testament incarnation Ezra — in Montezuma's
legend as we have it. When the founding lord returns and discovers that
his vassals have intermarried with the native women, one cannot but
recall Ezra's similar discovery of the Jews and their Canaanite wives, and
his strong disapproval. But it is above all Chapter 13 of the apocryphal
second book of Esdras, the passage about the Man from the Sea, that
reverberates in this homage to a man who has come from the east to
restore a lost tradition among a forsaken people. Cortés seems to be
endorsing Columbus's vision, but on a vaster scale: the isles far off now
turn out to be continents teeming with treasure. The true end of a Messianic tradition is in the muscular practicality of Cortés, reflected in his
prose as in his acts: the doomed breathless hope of Calisto is now surely
being resolved at last into the crusading zeal of Esplandian, Redemption
turns out only to be Empire after all.

And with that emerging realization we perceive the final transition
from the spirit of Balboa to one foreshadowing that of Pizarro. After
some initial vehement persuasion, Montezuma was apparently willing

---

*Since, of course, Cortés did not know Nahuatl nor Montezuma Spanish, they con-
versed through at least one and possibly two interpreters. Cortés's interpreter, Doña
Marina, did not know Spanish at first, so that she started out by working with
Jerónimo de Aguilar. She would translate from Nahuatl into Mayan, being by her
origins and experience familiar with both those languages, and Aguilar, being by his
own experience familiar with Mayan, would render her translation into Spanish for
Cortés; the latter's reply would go back by the same route. Eventually, Marina
learned Spanish well enough that Aguilar could be dispensed with, but it is not
clear whether this was the case at the time of Cortés's first encounters with Montezuma; even if it was, her Spanish could not yet have been wholly reliable.

enough to become Cortés's royal prisoner, though his subjects were not to share this feeling for long. In the spring, Cortés received word of the arrival down on the coast of the army of Pánfilo de Narváez, sent out by Velásquez to subjugate him. Leaving a small garrison in the capital under the command of Pedro de Alvarado, Cortés went down with a coalition of Spaniards and Indians and won a smashing victory over the intruding army, enlisting many of its troops in his own cause. But Alvarado, not a politic man, thought in the meantime that he smelled an impending insurrection and thereupon staged a preventive massacre, which only aggravated or created the mood of rebellion he had wanted to extinguish. Cortés returned to Tenochtitlán to find the Spanish garrison under siege in its quarters. In an attempt to placate the mob, Montezuma was brought to the roof in his imperial robes, and for a moment there was an awed silence; but when he began to speak there was a sudden new outburst of rage and a shower of missiles. Montezuma was struck on the head by a stone and died three days later. The Aztecs quickly appointed a successor and drove the outnumbered Spaniards from the city; their disastrous retreat over the causeways was always to be remembered by them as *la noche triste* — "the Night of Sorrow." The time of enchantment was over.

All of this has been described in Cortés's first two letters to Charles V, but by the time of the third, describing the final assault upon Tenochtitlán, there is a change of tone. The Aztecs are no longer seen in the image of the Moors: their pagan cult is denounced at every opportunity, and their temples are not *mezquitas* any more, but *torres de sus ídolos* — "towers for their idols." This is not Granada, after all — not the repository of a religion and a culture that may have been deceived in the pursuit of the true God, but that were pursuing him all the same, and that had in the process created a heritage. Cortés had once looked admiringly over the towers and pyramids of Mexico, just as Bernal Díaz had done, and had been proud to think of them as jewels now added to the Spanish crown. But something had happened on the causeways of Tenochtitlán as Cortés's men stumbled over them on the *noche triste*. When he returned over those same causeways a year later, leading an army strengthened by the alliance of still more Indian enemies of the Aztecs, by Spanish reinforcements who had come to join Narváez and joined the victor instead, and by a fleet built on the shores of Lake Texcoco to blockade the Aztec capital, he went with a vindictiveness that seems to have been fired by the bitter memories strewn along the route. The Conquest had been begun in earnest. Pushing against the mighty resistance put up by the Aztecs under their latest ruler Guatemozín. Cortés waged the first true colonial war in history, the onslaught of an overpowering European army against a foreign people ready to fight to the last man and with every last inch of their territory. The Spaniards had destroyed Canarians and Indians before this; now they were destroying the monuments of a complex civilization as well as a portion of its people — for by the time the smoke of battle had cleared, they had razed the city to the ground.

"The gold and other things were collected," Cortés wrote to the emperor, "and were melted down in accordance with the advice of Your Majesty's officials. The total was valued at 130,000 castellanos or more, of which a fifth was set aside for Your Majesty's treasury — along with the fifth of the rights to slaves and other things that also belong to Your Majesty — as will be shown further on in accounting of all Your Majesty's acquisitions, confirmed by our signatures. The gold which remained was divided up between myself and the other Spaniards, according to the rank and service of each." Instead of the towers of the Alhambra, there now was only loot; this was the promised land of men like Francisco Pizarro.

Curiously enough, echoes of the old Cortés would remain; he was, for example, to remain critical of the harsh treatment of Indians held in *encomienda*. But, on the other hand, he regarded the wielders of a proud and furious resistance against him as eligible only for chattel slavery. The onetime Salamancan had come a long way from the milieu of his youth. He had perpetrated the final rape and downfall of Melibea, and survived triumphant; but she was not to be without her Spanish mourners.

14

Bartolomé de las Casas

IN HIS *Brief Relation of the Destruction of the Indies*, Bartolomé de las Casas writes of the massacre at Cholula that, "as five or six thousand Indians were being put to the sword," Cortés sang this snatch of an old Spanish song:

> *Mira Nero de Tarpeya,*
> *á Roma como se ardia.*
> *gritos dan niños y viejos,*
> *y él de nada se dolia.*

("Nero looked out from Tarpeia,/ at Rome while it burned./ The young and the old cried out,/ And he was troubled by none of it.") This must be taken as one of Las Casas's frequent embroideries of the truth for the sake of dramatizing the monstrousness of Spaniards in the New World; Prescott observes ironically that it "is the first instance, I suspect, on record, of any person being ambitious of finding a parallel for himself in that emperor." But what is startling about the passage is the particular poem Las Casas has chosen to put into the mouth of the terrible Conquistador; for it appears in *La Celestina*. In one of the early scenes, Sempronio sings it to

Calisto, who is still pining with unrequited love, and who replies upon hearing it: "My fire is greater, and [Melibea's] pity is less." Calisto, the essential Salamancan, sees himself as the burning Rome and Melibea as Nero, but now Las Casas has turned the tables to conform with the true historical outcome: it is the Salamancan, Cortés, who is the cruel tyrant after all.

Was this a settling of old scores? For Las Casas was a student at Salamanca at around the same time as Cortés — which is also roughly the time Fernando de Rojas was there — and perhaps this song was then popular at the university. Nor do the parallels between their early careers stop there. Las Casas sailed to the New World in the Ovando voyage of 1502 that Cortés missed because of his escapade in the garden, and nine years later took part along with his fellow Salamancan in the expedition to Cuba led by Velásquez and Narváez. By that time he was a priest, but he wielded his cross as Cortés did his sword, and was rewarded for his services like the latter with a grant of *encomienda* on the newly conquered island. The two old Calistos knew one another well, and probably saw eye-to-eye in those days on a good many things. Both had set aside the quiet prospects of the Old World *licenciado* for a life of adventure in the New; it was now also becoming a life of militancy as well, but in ways that were soon to be diametrically opposed, though they may not have suspected this yet.

There were, of course, important differences between them from the outset. The bookish Las Casas, who did complete his studies at the university, was neither sensualist nor soldier, and was perhaps as much as eleven years older than Cortés — although his birth date is uncertain, as is much of his early life before his arrival in the New World. He seems to have come from a background that was at once more parvenu and more sophisticated than that of Cortés, for he grew up in the cosmopolitan port city of Seville, the son of a small tradesman who shipped out with Columbus in 1493 and became rich on Hispaniola. Pedro de las Casas returned home with his wealth as soon as he had acquired it, and used it to send his slightly overage son to the university; he even brought him an Indian slave, to serve as his page while he was a student, but young Bartolomé had to relinquish this prize in 1495 when Queen Isabella finally ruled that she would not allow such treatment of her New World "vassals." In other words, the New World had become a vital part of Las Casas's life while Cortés was still a child — and so, it would seem, had the guilt of the Spanish role there.

But the most profound of all the differences in background between these two Salamancans of the Cuban expedition lies in their respective origins — for Las Casas was almost certainly a New Christian. This is another of the many cases of possible New Christian descent that are lacking in hard evidence, but there are good circumstantial arguments for it that have persuaded a number of modern specialists in the field.°

Hints of such an identity can be extrapolated from Las Casas's remarkable career, which we are about to examine, but we might here digress for a moment to one of its final products, his major literary work and an essential source for much of what we know about him and about the early history of Spanish discovery and settlement in the New World, his *History of the Indies*. This book is characterized by a peculiar religious tone, messianic, Biblical, and, one is tempted to say, Hebraic. The burden of its Scriptural citations is from the Old Testament. The very first word of the book, in its prologue, is "Josephus," and Las Casas goes on to explain why the author of the *Jewish Antiquities* is for him a model historical writer. But if Las Casas is indeed a New Christian, the affinities between himself and the first-century historian lie a good deal deeper than in a common spirit of literary craftsmanship: in the Jewish revolt of 66 to 73 C.E. Josephus, a rebel commander in the Galilee, surrendered to the Romans, provided them with intelligence, and ultimately stood among his people's enemy watching the destruction of Jerusalem. This is a very suggestive life history for anyone of *converso* origin who lived through the Expulsion of 1492, and since Josephus then went on to become the historian of the people he had forsaken, he would be an especially appealing figure to someone of that background who had made himself into the historian of sufferers from Spanish oppression. Las Casas even explicitly defended the Jews during the course of his life, arguing that they, as well as the Muslims living in Christian lands, had a right to the protection that the Church had traditionally afforded them, and that had been violated by the Spanish and Portuguese expulsions; he stayed clear of the more dangerous question of New Christian heretics, however, or of any of the manifestations of what the Spanish Catholics of his day sweepingly called "Lutheranism." But the oppressed people who became his major lifelong concern, as if by an act of psychic transference from the Jews, who were no longer in the picture, and from the New Christians, who represented a delicate and complex problem of religious orthodoxy, were the Indians. There is a passage in his *History* in which, after

---

° In particular, recent scholarship has unearthed a list of New Christians of Seville who, in 1510, were given special permission by the king to settle in the Indies — something that persons known to be of "impure" blood were not normally allowed to do — and several of them bear the name Las Casas. None of them has been proven a relative of our Bartolomé, but he, on the other hand, spent a good deal of energy in his earlier years trying to prove that his name was not Las Casas but Las Casaus, and that he was of noble descent: this claim has been rejected even by those scholars who hesitate to attribute New Christian origins to him. Here is a distinct case of that highly suspect zeal to disguise one's background which often was the mark of the New Christian.

describing the destruction of Mexico by Cortés, he enters upon a philo-sophical digression comparing it with the destruction of Jerusalem by Titus, citing Josephus among his sources. That conception seems to pervade all of his mature life and work.

Even more suggestive of some kind of New Christian outlook is Las Casas's treatment of Columbus in his *History of the Indies*. After a first chapter which reads something like a paraphrase of the opening of Genesis, the very next chapter of the book begins thus:

> We now have arrived at the time of God's marvelous mercy, when in those parts of the earth where the seed or the word of life had been sown, the supreme fruit ever granted to the predestined by this Orb was harvested . . . and the Divine and Supreme Master chose from among the sons of Adam in-habiting the earth at this time the great and illustrious Columbus . . . and entrusted him, on account of his virtue, genius, industry, shrewdness, wisdom and accomplishments, with one of the most sublime and glorious tasks to be per-formed in the world in our time.

This fulsome praise takes on a messianic flavor with frequent subsequent references to Columbus as "chosen," with comparisons between him and King David, and with the sense pervading the entire book that the dis-covery of the New World opened up a new era for mankind: all of this is in the character of the quasireligion, the geographical messianism, that we have traced back to the Catalan Atlas and noted to be especially strong among New Christians by this time, especially in Columbus himself. The picture that emerges, moreover, is one of profound identifica-tion on Las Casas's part with a man whose achievements he depicts in an exalted light: he seems almost to be arrogating to himself the role of Paul to the Columbian Jesus, if one may invoke an earlier New Christian parallel.

The fact that the very name of Christ appears in his hero's name is of no small significance to Las Casas, who writes:

> It is the custom of Divine Providence to ordain that those appointed to serve it be given first and last names conforming to the functions determined for them, as is clear in many parts of the Holy Scriptures. . . . [The discoverer] therefore was given the name Cristóbal, that is, *Christum ferens,* which means bearer or carrier of Christ, as he often signed himself. For in truth it was he who was the first to open the gates of the Ocean Sea, through which he entered bringing our Saviour Jesus Christ and his blessed name to remote lands and hitherto unknown realms. . . . And his surname was Colón [the

Spanish form of "Columbus"], meaning new populator, which was fitting because it was through his effort and achievement in discovering these peoples that infinite numbers of souls among them, through the preaching of the Gospel and the administration of the holy sacraments, have gone and continue going each day to populate anew the triumphant city of heaven.

Las Casas, who is fully aware of Columbus's shortcomings in the treatment of the Indians, but forgives him for it as a child of his generation, does not seem aware of the irony of the final lines here, even though he was the foremost among those who condemned Spaniards for being too quick to send the New World peoples to heaven.*

There are signs that he may even have begun to mourn the fate of the Indians as far back as his participation in the Cuban expedition of 1511, but we have no other account for his early years besides that written by Las Casas himself, and it gave the mature writer and reformer a certain pleasure to excoriate the totally conscienceless young man that he took himself to have been. He describes the arrival in Hispaniola of the four Dominican missionary reformers in 1510 — Las Casas was later to become a Dominican himself — and gives us the entire text, undoubtedly embroidered by him, of the epoch-making sermon denouncing the abuses of the *encomienda* that was given by Fray Antonio de Montesinos on Hispaniola in 1511; but he tells us nothing of his own reaction to these things at the time they occurred. It was not until the year after his arrival in Cuba, according to his account, that a disastrous incident occurred which began to change him. The young priest had gone along on an expedition led by Pánfilo de Narváez to "pacify" the Indians of Camagüey province — to enter each village, establish the authority of Spain and the Church by force or peaceful persuasion, as the case might be, and to sprinkle the holy waters of baptism upon the assembled inhabitants. But in one village

---

* But if Las Casas, a man of destiny if ever there was one, felt this way about names, what did he conclude with respect to his own? Surely he recognized that "Bartholomew" was most appropriate for an apostle to the Indies, although with a smattering of Hebrew he might also have noticed that someone with his passion for geographical theory was very fittingly called *Bar-Ptolemaeus*, "son of Ptolemy." As for "Las Casas" — the form of the name that he at last settled for unequivocally — the range for speculation is almost as wide as that opened by Columbus's signature. But there is at least one way that a New Christian significance could be read into it. Cecil Roth, in his speculations about Columbus's possible New Christian identity, noticed that the discoverer once used the word *casa* ("house") with reference to the Temple of Jerusalem, a usage peculiar to Hebrew as a rule. Now, if Las Casas's name in any way suggested "the Temples" to his own ears, he could very well have been reminded by it not only of the two destroyed in antiquity, but also of the two destroyed metaphorically in his own lifetime virtually before his eyes — that of an openly Jewish racial existence in Spain, and that of an autonomous life and culture for the natives of the New World. It could well be that, in his maturity, he mourned all of them at once.

in which the situation seemed peaceful enough at first, something went wrong:

> It was customary among the Spaniards that one man chosen by the captain would take charge of distributing the food and other things given them by the Indians. As this was being done, the captain and the other soldiers on their horses, and the padre [Las Casas] watching the bread and the fish being handed out, suddenly one of the Spaniards drew his sword, saying that he saw the Devil before him. Then a hundred Spaniards all drew their swords and began to cut them down like sheep, killing and disemboweling men and women, children and old people, all of whom had been calmly sitting and watching the Spaniards and their horses in amazement; and in a few moments not a single one of them was still alive. Then the Spaniards entered the large house of the village and likewise commenced to stab and slash to death everyone they found inside, until there was a river of blood, as if a multitude of cows had been slaughtered.

The stunned priest managed to recover his senses in time to prevent a group of the rampaging Spaniards from entering another large house and wreaking a similar slaughter. When it was all over, the not too perturbed Narváez turned to Las Casas and asked, "What does your reverence think of our Spaniards and what they have done?" To which he replied: "You and the rest of them can all go to the Devil."

But it took him another two years, he tells us, to undergo his final conversion. Preparing a sermon for Pentecost in 1514, his eyes fell on Chapter 34 of Ecclesiasticus, and on verses 19 through 22 in particular:

> The most High is not pleased with the offerings of the wicked; neither is he pacified for sin by the multitude of sacrifices.
>
> Whoso bringeth an offering of the goods of the poor doeth as one that killeth the son before his father's eyes.
>
> The bread of the needy is their life: he that defraudeth him thereof is a man of blood.
>
> He that taketh away his neighbor's living slayeth him; and he that defraudeth the laborer of his hire is a bloodshedder.

This seems to have been Las Casas's Pauline moment, and the fact that it was derived from a canonically marginal text is another suggestion of a New Christian background. No doubt as a result of their own marginality, New Christians were drawn to the apocryphal and deuterocanonical writings, and we have noted the power that Esdras had among them. But the fact that Las Casas's text in this instance was a piece of wisdom literature bespeaks a step forward from a medieval mysticism into a modern rationalism, a spirit on the whole more congenial to the formation of a concept of social justice. Such a rationalist spirit was dramatically on the rise at this moment among Christian humanists, stimulated by the figure of Erasmus, whose ideas had taken a special hold among Spaniards discontented with the atmosphere of the Inquisition and had perhaps by now reached Las Casas. Upon reading the above-quoted verses, he writes — still using the third person for himself — the priest

> began to ponder the misery and servitude that those peoples [of the New World] were suffering. His reflections were deepened by what he had seen and heard on Hispaniola, by what the Dominican friars had preached at Santo Domingo, to the effect that one cannot in good conscience hold Indians in servitude, or confess and absolve those who do — none of which the priest had accepted at the time.

He accepted it now, however. His life was changed as he sat in his study, like Martin Luther reading a passage from Paul at around this time. He decided to begin a new course by giving up his *encomienda*.

From the moment he did so, Las Casas rapidly emerged as a reformer far more vigorous than his Dominican mentors had been. Returning to Spain with Antonio de Montesinos at the end of 1515, not merely to agitate against the abuses of the *encomienda* but to demand its abolition, he gained his royal audience just in time to present his petition to the representatives of the newly enthroned Charles V. He thereby became the Cortés of the counter-conquest, presenting to the new emperor the sufferings of a people just as the Conquistador presented its treasures. And there is another respect in which he can be seen as one of the spokesmen of a new era: for the proposal that he presented to Charles for a new social order in the Indies — consisting of model communities in which Spaniards and Indians would work as free men side by side, under the supervision of educated and selfless men of the cloth — has affinities with the *Utopia* of Sir Thomas More, published that same year in Flanders.

It has often been remarked that there is a blot on More's ideal society in the form of slavery; for that era still could not conceive of certain kinds of necessary toil being performed — quite possibly because there were no material means available for doing so — without the use of forced labor. A similar blot disfigures Las Casas's proposal of 1516, one that is even more ominous: for he, too, regarded forced labor as unavoidable, in the mines at any rate, but since he would not have it imposed on the Indians he recommended that Negro slaves be imported instead. This is by no means the first manifestation among the Spanish pro-Indian intelligentsia of an implied comparison between the natives of the New World and those of sub-Saharan Africa that is detrimental to the latter. It was first hinted at by Columbus and then grimly proclaimed in the writing of Duarte Pacheco Pereira. It was furthermore discernible in Peter Martyr, and Las Casas's Dominican predecessors in the war against the *encomienda* also had called for the importation of Negro slaves to alleviate the Indians' plight. But the advocacy of this expedient by a man of the enormous moral stature that Las Casas was to attain — and was already beginning to attain at this time — is particularly fateful in the history of the Western conscience. It was even more than that, for immediately in the wake of a revised form of this proposal, presented to the emperor in 1518, Charles granted the first *asiento de negros* — a monopoly allowing the purchase of large numbers of Blacks from Portuguèse slavers for direct importation into the Indies. Although individual Black slaves had been coming into the New World as personal servants at least since the Ovando voyage of 1502, the true beginning of the dismal history of Black slavery in the Western Hemisphere can be dated from Charles's grant of 1518.

One thing that can be said in mitigation of Las Casas's guilt on this issue is that when the monstrousness of the evil became apparent in the ensuing decades, he was outspoken in repenting of his earlier position on it. In his *History of the Indies* he finally saw fit to state the view, rare for its time, that "the same law applies equally to the Negro as to the Indian," and, attempting to trace the violation back to its source, he condemned the Portuguese for having initiated the nefarious trade among Europeans; he also had some severe words for his fellow historian Zurara, who had graced this historic injustice with an apologetic narrative instead of denouncing it. But why had this realization not yet entered his conscience in 1518?

This question is significant not merely psychologically, but historically: for Las Casas is assuredly a barometer to the conscience of his time, and his indifference to the plight of the Negro in the early decades of the sixteenth century serves only to dramatize a general attitude. It is noteworthy that his first fateful proposal of 1516 calls for the importation of "Negroes or other slaves"; by 1518 it has become simply "Negro slaves." Las Casas had begun, in other words, not so much by condemning a single race as by taking note of the international slave market in general and specifying what had seemed available. After two years back in Spain — his first time since departing from there with Ovando in 1502 — it had evidently been impressed upon him that, for all practical purposes, the one type of slave obtainable on the market was the Negro. The latter's tough constitution and relative capacity for moral survival under the conditions of servitude had already — in southern Iberia, in the

Canaries, and in various Portuguese islands off the African coast, such as
São Thomé — enabled him to pass a dreadful, unasked-for test. Now, the
moral indifference of the Portuguese toward the Blacks under their
hegemony was joining forces with the moral concern of some Spaniards —
including the king — over the Indians under theirs to provide license to
that judgment: the Blacks had become the chosen people, as it were, for
chattel slavery in the Americas. The decision against them had not even
been made out of any attitude so honorific as fear or hatred, which were
accorded to "bad" Indians; it had been produced merely as the residue
of a struggle over the Indians that had resulted in their partial destruction
as well as in a moral decision in their favor. The coin thus minted was
to remain currency for generations to come in the New World, one side
of it consisting of a passionate relationship, alternating between love and
hate, with the Indian, the other of indifference or contempt toward the
Negro.

Having thus stamped the reverse side with appropriate indifference,
Las Casas then went on to shape his own golden mission as "Protector of
the Indians," the title that had been accorded him by the emperor.
Returning to the New World in 1520 armed with permission to establish
one of his model colonies on the coast of what is now Venezuela, he went
about organizing it with characteristic energy; but there were severe
problems. This was the region of the pearl fisheries, and there already
were conventional Spanish settlements nearby; tensions within them
between colonists and natives soon led to the summoning of troops from
Hispaniola. This act inevitably caused antagonism between the European
and Indian members of Las Casas's colony, even though the Spaniards
in it had been carefully chosen as men content to be hardworking, small-
scale agriculturists rather than get-rich-quick *encomenderos*. Fearful of
the tensions, Las Casas's Spanish farmers deserted to the other colonies,
and by 1522 the experiment had ended in failure. The disconsolate
Protector returned to Hispaniola and retired into the Dominican convent
there; joining the order at last, he remained in the cloister for the next
twelve years.

But this air of defeat was only superficial, and can justly be compared
to that which obscured the reality of Karl Marx — another Jewish heretic
who turned social reformer with a fury and moral absolutism inherited
from the Biblical prophets — when he retired into the British Museum
after the failure of the revolutions of 1848. The colony of Cumana on
the Venezuelan coast had really only been a Utopian experiment. But
from now on, Las Casas was to place the main emphasis of his efforts upon
the wholesale transformation of society in the New World; this meant
he had to become a teacher to his generation, and in order to achieve

this he had to study, and to write. It was during his years in the Dominican convent on Hispaniola that he ripened from an agitator into a profound and truly revolutionary thinker, and from a composer of Utopian proposals into a writer of propaganda and partisan history comparable to Marx. In his moral capacity, he proved able to take full measure of the great continental conquests — that of Mexico, which was coeval with the whole cycle from initiation to failure of his Cumana experiment, and that of Peru, which culminated in Pizarro's treacherous murder of Atahualpa only a year before Las Casas finally left his retreat to preach in Nicaragua. As a young man, he had cut his teeth on a colonial world of islands and enclaves, still shaped in the image of the Portuguese era of overseas expansion; but leaving it for a time had enabled his mind to grow with the emerging world of continental empire, the true onset of overseas Spain. He would henceforth be as inexorable with tongue and pen as Pizarro was with garrote and sword.

Not that Las Casas went on to neglect the old field of model social experiments; this, after all, was the one way in which his points could be dramatized to the world. By this time, groups of missionary friars — Franciscans and Hieronymites, as well as Dominicans — had begun arriving in Mexico and establishing the first versions of the type of community that was later to be called a "praying town" by the New England settlers. These communities had no other Spaniards in them than the friars themselves, who sought to make the Indians under their benevolent but paternalistic authority into good farmers and good Christians at the same time. Las Casas organized and watched over a group of these in Guatemala from 1536 to 1538, apparently with outstanding success. But the limitations of this approach were demonstrated in the views of one of the most outstanding of the pious community organizers, Vasco de Quiroga, Bishop of Michoacán. In the era of islands, Quiroga had been as ardent a partisan of the golden-age view of the Indian as Peter Martyr had been; but his views had changed somewhat with the Conquest of Mexico. The decadent barbarism of the Aztecs, with their ritual of human sacrifices and their vast storehouses of treasure, was something that could only be dealt with by force as far as he was concerned; he justified the principle of holy war by the Spaniards, and even came around to seeing civilizing virtues in the *encomienda*. Thus the typical Utopian had arrived at a viewpoint entirely opposite to that of Las Casas, who wrote in 1538:

> The only way in which the peoples [of the New World] can
> be brought to the true religion is the one followed by Christ,
> to wit: the preaching of the Gospel by missionaries who are not

accompanied by soldiers, by unarmed missionaries sent out like lambs amidst the [Spanish] wolves. This method, in spite of the risks involved, is the sole legitimate one. Military conquest is the method not of Christ, but of Mahomet.

Las Casas was equally vehement in his opposition to mass baptism, which was the practice at this time of even the most peaceable missionaries: the Indian had to be won by persuasion, he maintained, and his baptism should not take place a moment sooner. One can hear in this the voice of the New Christian, speaking out against the various ways in which his ancestors had been yoked unreasonably into the fold.

Las Casas was not afraid to pursue these views, highly unorthodox among his contemporaries, to their logical conclusions. In 1550, at the high point of his career, he took part in a debate at Valladolid with Juan Ginés de Sepúlveda, the outstanding Spanish scholastic of his day, on the question of whether or not the Indians were a people condemned by nature to servitude in accordance with the Aristotelian doctrine of barbarians and slavery. By that time, Las Casas was not so rash as to reject the authority of Aristotle altogether, as he once had done, and as Luther did; this was a position that smacked of heresy, and instead of taking it at Valladolid, he embarked there on an ambitious historical and anthropological defense of the various Indian societies as civilizations no less valid than those of Europe. The most difficult challenge arose over the issue of human sacrifices: how could Las Casas justify a religion that performed such a revolting rite, and defend it against the immediate imposition of baptism, by force if necessary? Undaunted, he marshaled all the evidence he could find that human sacrifice was an inevitable and legitimate stage in the evolution of many religious cultures, including those of the Hebrews, the Greeks, the Romans, and all the peoples who make up modern Christendom. Indeed, he argued, this willingness on the part of a society — and, often enough, on the part of the victims themselves — to make the supreme sacrifice shows a highly developed religious conscience; it is only the last stage before the realization comes that Jesus has once and for all submitted to this sacrifice for all mankind. And besides, he added pointedly, was this immolation of a few individuals performed each year by the Indians in the name of their highest ideal any worse than the mass slaughters the Spaniards were constantly committing in the name of theirs? This question, once again, carries echoes of a New Christian indictment of a society of pogromists and Inquisitors. It seems no accident that all the arguments against Sepúlveda were finally summed up in writing by Las Casas in his most Josephus-like work, the *Apologética Historia,* a vast polemical survey of Indian civilizations reminiscent of the *Jewish Antiquities* and the *Apology against Apion.*

But if Las Casas had indeed become a latter-day Hebrew prophet in Christian garb, denouncing Inquisition Spain in the name of the beleaguered Indians, the supreme expression of this was his *Brief Relation of the Destruction of the Indies*. This thunderous outburst, written in 1540 and published in 1552, is the crowning work in the tradition of protest on the Indian's behalf that had been begun in scattered passages of Peter Martyr's *De Orbe Novo*, which served Las Casas as one of his sources. Like Peter, Las Casas has evidently drawn upon both written and oral accounts; but unlike his Italian predecessor, he can above all fill his book with the fruits of his own experience — and of his own imagination. For there clearly is considerable exaggeration in it, especially in its statistics on numbers of Indians killed in various places, and it is a problematic source for historians. This aspect of it, combined with the fact that it has through the ages been the chief instigator of the so-called *leyenda negra*, the "Black Legend" of Spanish cruelty, has aroused paroxysms of anger among Spaniards down to the present day.° But the book should not be judged by scientific criteria alone, for it is the work of a prophet — of a man whose imagination could embrace the entire historic reality of his generation and translate it into moral poetry.

Indeed, on the factual level, the fault with this compendium of persecution and slaughter is not that it says too much but that it says too little; for the largeness of its vision clearly comprehends the Inquisition, which is never mentioned. Yet the Inquisition certainly is there in such passages as this one, describing the murder of the Cuban *cacique* Hatuey:

> After Hatuey was tied to the stake, a Franciscan friar — one of the holy men who were there — began telling him about God and our faith (about which he had never heard anything before), and about the few things that it might suffice for him to do in the little time left him by the executioners if he wanted to go to heaven, where he would have glory and eternal peace, instead of to Hell, where he would suffer perpetual torments. Thinking about it a moment, Hatuey asked the friar if all Christians go to heaven. The friar said yes. Then the *cacique* replied without further hesitation that he would rather go to Hell than have to be among such a cruel people. This is the fame and honor that God and our faith have won by means of the Christians who have gone to the Indies.

One can almost hear a Marrano dying at the stake with the same words upon his lips. There is a sense in which Karl Marx's vision of the pro-

---

° As recently as 1963 one of the greatest of Spanish scholars, Ramón Menéndez Pidal, published a book on Las Casas hotly denouncing him as a paranoiac and a liar.

letariat, of its travails and of its destiny, can be seen as a metaphor for the Jewish condition experienced by his ancestors, which ceased as such to be of interest to him; with him and with others in the nineteenth and twentieth centuries, socialism was a Jewish heresy. The same can be said for the New Christian religion of geographical discovery, the creed that we might call Columbian, which we have seen in various early manifestations, and which has now found its Marx in Bartolomé de las Casas. Among Las Casas's most direct successors in this creed, the vision of the Indian destiny as a Jewish one is far more explicit, for they will see the New World natives as descendants of the Lost Tribes of Israel. Las Casas evidently did not share this view, nor is there any direct evidence that he consciously perceived the Indians in terms of the historic condition of Jews and New Christians. But the age of the Inquisition was characterized by concealed motives and indirect modes of expression, and if Las Casas did not explicitly attack the dreaded tribunal in his *Brief Relation*, the effect upon Europe at large when he published it — to be promptly translated into several languages — was as if he had done precisely that. And the Inquisition knew it, even though it waited a hundred years before finally banning the book with these observations:

> This book contains a narrative of very terrible and savage events, whose like does not exist in the histories of other nations, committed, says the author, by Spanish soldiers, settlers in the Indies, and ministers of the Catholic King. It is advisable to seize these narratives as injurious to the Spanish nation, since even if they were true it would have sufficed to make a representation to His Catholic Majesty and not to publish them throughout the world, so giving the initiative to enemies of Spain and to heretics!

The publication of the book does indeed seem to have been Las Casas's angry offering to the Reformation, for he had in fact written it at first as merely the most fervent in his long line of memorials to Charles V, in order to instigate wholesale reform from the top, and apparently without the intention to publish it at that time. And it had worked. As a direct result of the agitation by Las Casas and others, as well as of his own convictions on the subject, Charles finally promulgated the New Laws for the Indies in 1542, which declared the Indians to be free and vassals of the crown, and abolished the *encomienda*. To a certain extent, the New Laws were to lose their teeth in the next few years as a result of vehement protests by the white settlers in the New World and outright rebellion in Peru — their virtual nonenforcement was probably what provoked Las Casas to publish the *Brief Relation* in 1552 — but nevertheless this placing of a long-cherished principle into law represented the crowning achievement of Las Casas's career as a reformer. It was to take the remainder of the century for the *encomienda* as such to die, and the Spanish upper classes of the New World were eventually to find in its place subtler methods of squeezing labor out of the Indians; but the brutal scourge of the first half-century of Spanish America had decidedly been tamed — at least as far as the Indians were concerned.

15

Estévanico's Revenge

THE COLLECTION of tales written in the fourteenth century by the Infante Don Juan Manuel of Castile, *El Conde Lucanor,* contains an early version of the story known to us as "The Emperor's New Clothes." The king in this version, told nothing by his fearful subjects, finally learns the truth about his state of undress one day when

> a Negro, groom for the king's horse, who had nothing to lose, came up to him and said: "My Lord, since there is no chance of your ever taking me for a gentleman, I can speak frankly and tell you that I'm quite sure you are going around naked."

This can serve as an epigraph to the real-life sixteenth-century history of Estévanico, the first Black to emerge as a full-fledged personality from the pages of American history.

Our story can take its point of departure from another fourteenth-century work of fiction, that popular and influential compendium of geographical folklore written by a man who probably never left home, *The Travels of Sir John Mandeville.* Sir John tells us that in one part of Prester John's realm there is a fair well and a great, that hath odor and savor of all spices. And at every hour of the day he changeth his odor and his savor diversely. And whoso drinketh three times fasting of that water of that well he is whole of all manner sickness that he hath. And they that dwell there and drink often of that well they never have sickness; and they seem always young.

This seems to be a late medieval variation upon the curative rock with a water-filled cavity that we have seen in the original Prester John letter of the twelfth century; but there is a significant new twist in the last phrase, which Sir John develops thus:

Some men clepe it the well of youth. For they that often drink thereof seem always young-like, and live without sickness. And men say, that that well cometh out of Paradise, and therefore it is so virtuous.

Ponce de León, after landing in Puerto Rico in 1512 and finding that its subjugation was not going to be so easy, took some time off from the struggle and sailed northward to search for an "island of Bimini," which, according to stories told him by the Indians, contained a fountain very like the one Sir John had described. During his journey, he came upon a land that he named "La Florida" because he saw it on Easter Sunday — *Pascua Florida* in Spanish. Convinced that this was where he would find the Fountain of Youth, Ponce de León returned there in 1521 to continue his search, but was killed by an Indian arrow. He had not discovered the fountain, although he had discovered a place that would once again, centuries hence, be a haven for those who sought its restorative powers against the passing of youth; he also had been the first to open the way to realization that in the north there was not a passageway to the shores of Cathay, nor islands alone, but another continent.

Islands may still have provoked visions of idylls and magical fountains to Spanish explorers of the early sixteenth century, but continents were coming to mean military expeditions and gold. Even as early as 1519 a captain named Alonso de Pineda, who explored the whole Gulf coast from Key West to the mouth of the Mississippi, had come back with rumors of great quantities of gold farther north. The Spaniards continued hoping that the northward extent of the continent would be far less than it actually is, and that they would find around it both a northwest passage to the Indies and a nearer access to the rumored gold fields. Accordingly, Lucas Vásquez de Ayllón, a colonist who had made his fortune on Hispaniola, sent out ships the year after Pineda's return to explore the eastern coast of Florida. They returned in 1521, having got as far as present-day

South Carolina: this, and much of the coast even farther north, continued to be regarded by the Spaniards as "Florida." In 1526 Ayllón sailed in person with another fleet and established a colony in Chesapeake Bay; but neither gold nor the northwest passage was anywhere in sight, and when he died soon after the landing, his companions wasted no time about returning to Hispaniola.

It was in 1528 that Pánfilo de Narváez, whom we know, set out on what was evidently meant to be the Florida version of the Conquest of Mexico. Landing in Tampa Bay with a band of some four hundred men, including cavalry, he marched northward in pursuit of a fabulous realm of gold called *Cale* by the Indians. (Historians have often noted the understandable readiness of Indians in those days to locate the most delicious objects of the white man's desires over the most distant possible horizons.) With the ineptness that seems to have dogged his career, Narváez had fully prepared himself for Mexico or Peru, with respect not only to treasure but to climate and terrain; but his horses and fully accoutred troops were not much good against the hot disease-ridden swamps of the Gulf coast. By the end of summer, sick, starving, dying, and nowhere near any gold, his men were ready to return home; but they had left their ships far behind, and were forced to build their own craft. In September, the approximately two hundred and fifty survivors of the expedition set out in five boats that they had built, hoping to get across the Gulf to the province of Pánuco in northeastern Mexico, now a Spanish settlement. But they ran into a hurricane and were shipwrecked on a coastal island, probably the site of modern Galveston; the Spaniards called it *Malhado* — "Misfortune." Narváez and a handful of men had survived, but he and most of the others soon were killed, in skirmishes with the Indians and in struggles with the elements. In the long run, only four men survived to tell the tale.

The most eminent member of this group of four, and eventually its leader, was Álvar Núñez Cabeza de Vaca, the offspring of two distinguished families. His paternal grandfather, Francisco de Vera, had been the conqueror of the Grand Canary in 1483. On his mother's side he was descended from a semilegendary figure, a shepherd named Martín Alhaja, who, in the summer of 1212, had guided the Spanish armies through a pass he had marked with the skull of a cow, thereby enabling them to win the historic victory of Las Navas de Tolosa, which decisively put an end to Moorish predominance on the Iberian Peninsula. In honor of his role in this, the shepherd was dubbed *Cabeza de Vaca*, "Cow's Head," and the name remained. The Álvar Núñez of the Narváez expedition to Florida had originally borne his father's family name, but had chosen to carry the rubric of his distinguished maternal ancestor instead.

But Cabeza de Vaca was not the only figure of unusual interest among the four survivors, for of the three others, only two were Christians. The two latter were Alonzo del Castillo of Salamanca and Andrés Dorantes of Béjar del Castañar, a town in Estremadura. The fourth survivor was a Negro known as Estévan or Estévanico, who had been captured by Spanish ships off the coast of Morocco some years before and now was Dorantes's personal slave.

Estévanico was undoubtedly not the only Black slave to have come along on this expedition. Indeed, we know for a fact that when Narváez had gone to Mexico in 1520 intending to bring Cortés to his knees, a number of Black servants had accompanied his army. One of them, Narváez's personal slave, was later said by chroniclers to have been the man who introduced smallpox into Mexico: this can be read either as a racial slander or as a real form of cosmic revenge by the victim against the entire New World scene of his captivity, directed against white men and Indians, alike, a plague on both their houses. Bernal Díaz tells of another Negro in Narváez's Mexican expeditionary force, a jester named Guidela, who went over to Cortés's side along with most of the white troops in it: one doubts whether he was rewarded for this gesture with his freedom. One does not hear of Black slaves in the New World obtaining their freedom within organized society during this period; the only perceptible quantity of free Blacks were runaways, the *cimarrones* — so called because they tended to live in rebel bands in the fastnesses of mountaintops, *cimas* in Spanish. (The English would later transform this name into "Maroons," perhaps grasping at the hint of color that it conveyed to their ears.) These bands often were made up not only of Blacks but also of Indians who had run away from Spanish oppression, and the fusion between them was in many cases producing a new race of men, one that was usually troublesome to Spanish rule. At the very time of Estévanico's appearance to history, a *cimarrón* revolt that had begun in 1519 was still going on in Hispaniola under the leadership of an Indian known as Enriquillo.

Perhaps Estévanico, apparently a man of some sophistication, already had ideas of his own about the possibilities of Afro-Indian relationships; perhaps it even seemed to him that it should be Blacks who lead Indians, the Old World commanding the New, and not the other way around. Indeed, he may already have seen some examples of members of his own race, servants to the whites, assuming positions above Indians in the hierarchy of servitude. Writing only a few years later, the Spanish judge Alonso de Zorita — one of the few lay officials of New Spain to take a sympathetic position toward its natives — described instances of harassment of Indians by the Black slaves of some of the *encomenderos*. Among Black slaves at this time, the temptation may have been strong to find emotional compensation for their own condition by looking upon Indians as greatly inferior to themselves. These, at any rate, are speculations that leap to the mind in the light of Estévanico's subsequent career.

For the moment, the main protagonist of our story continues to be Cabeza de Vaca, for he is the author of the one surviving narrative of Narváez's disastrous Florida expedition and its sequel. Much of his history finds him alone and separated from the other survivors, suffering incredible hardships. A slave to the Indians on the Texas mainland, he at first performed the most menial tasks, but gradually the application of his European knowledge in health matters enabled him to gain the reputation and the status of a healer. This gave him increasing freedom of movement, so that he could seek out and meet with the other survivors, the slaves of neighboring tribes, from time to time; but all this progress was slow. It was not until 1534, some five years after the shipwreck, that the four last survivors got together to make their escape into the wilderness. Taking a route that curved northwestward and then southwestward through present-day New Mexico and Arizona, they eventually got to the west coast of Mexico, down which they walked until at last they reached a Spanish settlement at Culiacán, in Central Sinaloa, two years after their escape and more than eight years after their departure from Cuba with the Narváez expedition.

Cabeza de Vaca's narrative of the long journey to Mexico provides significant glimpses of the unusual relationship between white, Black, and Indian that inevitably arose during its course. Regardless of the social and juridical rules of the society from which they had recently come, the four intruders from the Old World were inevitably reduced to something like equality under the conditions of the wilderness. The imperatives of survival alone will achieve some equalization, but an additional impetus had been provided by the fact that the one Black man and the three whites had all been slaves together. Furthermore, when they joined forces for their escape, Cabeza de Vaca taught the other three his arts of healing, so that they could wield this power together among the Indians they encountered. Everything conspired to make the four survivors into an entity, a "we" as distinguished from the "they" formed by the Indians. To be sure, there are hesitations over this point at first in Cabeza de Vaca's narrative. At one moment, he talks thus about the awe in which he and his companions were held by some Indians they had met:

> We possessed great influence and authority: to preserve both, we seldom talked with them. The Negro was in constant conversation; he informed himself about the ways we wished to take, of the towns there were, and the matters we desired to know.

Here, the "we" seems to be the three white men, eager to maintain an exalted status with relation to the Negro that the Indians, for whom it was intended, may not necessarily have perceived. But in the next paragraph, Cabeza de Vaca writes:

> We passed through many and dissimilar tongues. Our Lord granted us favor with the people who spoke them, for they always understood us, and we them.

He goes on to say that "we" knew six Indian languages: all of this clearly includes Estévanico, who shows signs of having been a more proficient linguist than the three white men. As the four of them moved on through the wilderness, serving as healers from tribe to tribe, each one receiving them more enthusiastically than the last and relaying them with some pomp to the next, they imperceptibly took on a common identity.

But what kind of identity was this? In becoming alike under these extraordinary conditions, the three white men and one Black had to a certain extent become something quite different from what they had respectively been before. Toward the end of their journey, before reaching the main centers of Spanish settlement, the four men came upon an outlying garrison of Spaniards, who were slave-raiding among the local Indians. Cabeza de Vaca's group interceded and settled matters in a manner favorable to the Indians, whom they would not permit to be enslaved by the Spaniards. Cabeza de Vaca was then ready to go off with his own countrymen, but the Indians objected:

> They were willing to do nothing until they had gone with us and delivered us into the hands of other Indians, as had been the custom; for, if they returned without doing so, they were afraid they should die, and, going with us, they feared neither Christians nor lances. Our countrymen became jealous at this, and caused their interpreter to tell the Indians that we were of them, and for a long time we had been lost; that they were the lords of the land who must be obeyed and served, while we were persons of mean condition and small force. The Indians cared little or nothing for what was told them; and conversing among themselves said the Christians lied: that we had come whence the sun rises, and they whence it goes down; we healed the sick, they killed the sound; that we had come naked and barefooted, while they had arrived in clothing and on horses with lances; that we were not covetous of anything, but all that was given to us we directly turned to give, remaining with nothing; that the others had the only purpose to rob whomsoever they found, bestowing nothing on any one.

A few lines later, Cabeza de Vaca emphatically adds:

> Even to the last, I could not convince the Indians that we
> were of the Christians; and only with great effort and solici-
> tation we got them to go back to their residences.

The satisfaction at having successfully "gone native" is in no way concealed here — it becomes gloating in the stress on the need for the other
Spaniards to use interpreters — and the suggestion is clear that a kind of
moral superiority can be achieved through identification with the "Noble
Savage." This identification had been completed long before the reunion
with the other Spaniards; back in the region of present-day New Mexico,
a tribe of Indians had welcomed the four survivors warmly, and

> among other things, two of their physicians gave us two
> gourds, and thenceforth we carried these with us, and added
> to our authority a token highly reverenced by the Indians.

Such a token had obviously come to mean even more than survival to
Cabeza de Vaca; it was a permanent link between himself and the
Indians among whom he had lived. To Estévanico, the slave of white men
and a master among Indians, it must have meant even more; he came
into possession of one of the two gourd-rattles, and never relinquished it.
    All along their route, Cabeza de Vaca and his companions had heard
stories from the Indians about regions of fabulous wealth farther to the
north, with which they aroused considerable excitement among the
Spaniards after their return. In particular, they brought new life to the
old Iberian legend of the "Seven Cities of Cibola," all of them Tenochtitláns, which once had been supposed to be located on an island in the
western ocean; since this was a time when islands were rapidly turning
into continents, the Seven Cities were now eagerly relocated in New
Mexico. Hernando de Soto, a gifted soldier who had served with
Pedrarias Dávila in Darien and with the conquering Pizarro, heard
Cabeza de Vaca's report back in Spain, and decided that the time had
come for his own Mexico and Peru. At the beginning of 1539 he set out
from Cuba with six hundred soldiers and landed on the Gulf coast of
Florida; after following Narváez's route for a time, he headed up into
what is now Georgia, where he enjoyed some friendly encounters with
the Indians, and then marched westward as far as Oklahoma. But in 1542
he succumbed to a fever and was buried in the Mississippi; the following
year, some three hundred survivors of the expedition made their way
down that river and along the coast of Mexico in barges they had built,
until they reached the Spanish settlements at last. In four years they had

covered a vast portion of the future United States, but they had found nothing of the Seven Cities.

At the same time, a search for them was being organized under the auspices of the Viceroy of New Spain, Antonio de Mendoza, who planned to send an expedition overland, retracing the route of Cabeza de Vaca's group and then moving on farther north. The charge of the enterprise was given to a rising young colonial administrator named Francisco Vásquez de Coronado, for neither Cabeza de Vaca nor the two white companions of his journey were now available. Estévanico was available, but the position could not be given to a Black whose status may still have been that of a slave, although he does not seem to have been any longer in Dorantes's service. He could, however, be employed as a guide; indeed, in this role he was indispensable, as he no doubt well knew.

Coronado established himself in Culiacán and decided that, before embarking upon a major expedition, he would send out a scouting party along Cabeza de Vaca's route. To lead this party, he chose a Franciscan friar known only to history as Fray Marcos of Nice. After serving in that Mediterranean city — he may not have been Spanish, but no one knows for sure — Fray Marcos had come to the New World and served in Peru, and had perhaps been with Pizarro at the conquest of Cuzco and the murder of Atahualpa. He had apparently established a reputation as an explorer in Mexico, where he had subsequently become ensconced; at any rate, his mind's eye was certainly filled with images of fabulous realms of gold, and the glitter of it was perhaps sufficient inducement for Coronado to appoint him. Estévanico, whose eye may also have gleamed, but with the image of what was really a different sort of promised land, was sent with him as guide.

"I, Fray Marcos of Nice," begins this unlikely captain's narrative, "of the order of St. Francis, for the execution of the instruction of the right honorable lord Don Antonio de Mendoza, Viceroy and Captain General for the Emperor's Majesty in New Spain, departed from the town of St. Michael in the province of Culiacán on Friday the seventh of March in the year 1539, having for my companion Fray Honoratus, and carrying with me Estévan, a Negro belonging to Andrés Dorantes, and certain of those Indians which the said lord Viceroy had made free, and brought for this purpose." Fray Honoratus soon fell ill and had to be left behind, so that Fray Marcos was the only white member of this expedition as it pushed on northward toward the Seven Cities of Cibola; he was soon under the sway of primitive forces beyond his own control, of which Estévanico inevitably became master.

Estévanico was by this time a truly remarkable figure to behold. We do not know what his dress had been in his early days as a Negro slave, but it was surely nothing like what it had now become: for he went with

Fray Marcos as an Indian healer, with bells jingling on his arms and ankles, and carrying his sacred gourd-rattle, which also was covered, like himself, with bells and feathers. Two spaniels ran by his side. He could only have been an awesome figure to the Indians encountered along the way, whose languages he spoke fluently; and he probably grew more and more awesome to Fray Marcos himself. Indians gathered around the party wherever they went, and though some would reach out to touch Fray Marcos's gray cassock, it usually was Estévanico they wanted to see. In particular the women came to him and often were eager to show him their favors.

Eventually, Fray Marcos, evidently unable to contain Estévanico in his northward rush, decided to send him on ahead to scout out the field. "I commanded," the friar writes, that he "go directly northward fifty or threescore leagues, to see if by that way he might learn any news of any notable thing which we sought to discover, and I agreed with him that if he found any knowledge of any peoples and rich country which were of great importance, he should go no further but should return in person. Or else he should send me certain Indians with that token which we were agreed upon, to wit, that if it were but a mean thing, he should send me a white cross of one handful long; and if it were of any great matter, one of two handfuls long; and if it were a country greater and better than New Spain, he should send me a great cross."

Estévanico had not been gone more than four days when Fray Marcos received from his messengers "a great cross as high as a man." Furthermore, they told the friar that "I should forthwith come away after him, for he had found a people which gave him information of a very mighty province," and that he had sent one of them to the friar. "This Indian told me that it was thirty days' journey from the town where Estévanico was unto the first city of the said province, which is called Cibola. He affirmed also that there are seven great cities in this province, all under one lord. The houses there are made of lime and stone, and are very great, and the least of them with one loft above head, and some of two and three lofts, and the house of the lord of the province of four, and that all of them join one onto the other in good order, and that in the gates of the principal houses there are many turquoise-stones cunningly wrought, whereof he saith they have there great plenty; also that the people of this city go very well appareled; and that beyond this there are other provinces, all which (he saith) are much greater than these seven cities." The outlines of the pueblos of New Mexico begin coming sharply into view before the eyes of the modern reader; indeed, Estévanico and Fray Marcos were finally to locate their fabulous province right in the heart of Zuñi country. But were exaggerated accounts by Indians the only source of the delusion that those humble villages were Cuzcos and Tenochtitláns?

Fray Marcos now assumed that Estévanico would wait for him, so that the two would march together, captain and guide, into the province of Cibola; but he reckoned not with his man. Estévanico was on his own, a Black Conquistador, taking charge in places where men from the Old World had never been before. The situation was so unprecedented that Fray Marcos, like Captain Amasa Delano of Melville's *Benito Cereno*, seems to have been completely unable to perceive that the roles of master and subordinate had been reversed; rather he goes on referring to Estévanico from time to time as "Dorantes's slave" in his account of the strange pursuit that now took place, the white man arriving in village after village to find that the Black healer had been there before him, leaving a trail of wonderment, of fabulous stories, and — as if to stress the ironies of this bizarre Afro-European relationship that had evolved in the American wilderness — of crosses. We can never know what went on in Estévanico's mind during all this. Did he believe the fable of the Seven Cities? Even if he did, he surely knew that the wilderness now held for him a treasure greater than gold. Did he intend to vanish altogether into the unknowable north, or did he intend to maintain relations with Fray Marcos and the world of white men? If the latter, he surely meant it to be only under conditions of a power he had just discovered for himself; but this would have been without a full grasp on his own part of the relentless banality of the white suprematist attitude. At one point, Fray Marcos writes of how he hears that Estévanico was now escorted by a train of three hundred Indian servants, and he is capable of arriving at no other conclusion from this news than to assume that "in like sort many of them would go with me to serve me, because they hoped to return home rich." There is a hopelessness in Estévanico's situation in the light of an outlook such as this but, in the meantime, he may have been able to relish the satisfaction of a kind of moral revenge — not only against the white man, who had enslaved him, but against the Indian, for whose sake he had been enslaved.

The end finally came within the area of present-day New Mexico. "Here met us an Indian," Fray Marcos writes, "the son of the chief man that had accompanied me, which had gone before with Estévan, who came in a great fright, having his face and body all covered with sweat, and showing exceeding sadness in his countenance. And he told me that a day's journey before Estévan came to Cibola he sent his great mace made of a gourd by his messengers, as he was always wont to send them before him . . . in token that he demanded safe conduct, and that he came peaceably. And when they came to Cibola before the magistrate, which the lord of the city had placed there for his lieutenant, they delivered him the said great gourd, who took the same in his hands, and after he spied the bells, in a great rage and fury he cast it to the ground, and willed messengers to get them packing with speed, for he knew well enough what people they were, and that they should will them in no case to enter into the city, for if they did he would put them all to death." Obviously the charismatic power of the rattle that had helped Estévanico to become worshipped by so many Indians could also have the opposite effect; but he would not accept this danger signal. "The messengers returned," Fray Marcos goes on, "and told Estévan how things had passed, who answered them that it made no great matter, and would needs proceed on his voyage till he came to the city of Cibola. There he found men that would not let him enter into the town, but shut him into a great house which stood without the city, and straightway took all things from him which he carried to truck and barter with them, and certain turquoises, and other things which he had received of the Indians by the way, and they kept him there all that night without giving him meat or drink."

Later on, Pedro de Castañeda, the chronicler of the expedition that finally set out the following year under Coronado, added some details to this part of the story, but without giving his source. "For three days," he wrote, the Indian leaders at Cibola "made inquiries about [Estévanico] and held a council. The account which the Negro gave them of two white men who were following him" — Castañeda thought Fray Honoratus was still with the expedition — "sent by a great lord, who knew about the things in the sky, and how these were coming to instruct them in divine matters, made them think that he must be a spy or a guide from some nations who wished to come and conquer them, because it seemed to them unreasonable to say that the people were white in the country from which he came and that he was sent by them, he being black." Castañeda's logic is obscure, since the Indians were quite right in assuming that the whites had come to conquer them, whether they had been preceded by a Black man or not. The suggestion that it was simply Estévanico's black complexion that aroused a hostility among the Indians that they would not have evinced toward a white one may simply be Castañeda's racist fantasy; but what is his source for the whole story? If he got it from Fray Marcos or, as the friar claims he got *his* story, from some of the Indians involved, then it is possible that there were Indians who felt this way about Estévanico's blackness — just as there obviously were Indians who were fascinated by it. We have here, in other words, the possibility of a whole complex of Indian attitudes toward the Negro at the very beginning of the recorded history of North America: to what extent, then, were they spontaneous, on the one hand, or influenced by the white man, on the other? These are very important questions, but we can never know the answers to them; we do not even know how trustworthy the surviving narratives are.

"Besides these other reasons," Castañeda continues, "they thought it was hard of him to ask them for turquoises and women, and so they decided to kill him." Fray Marcos ends his tale of Estévanico with the return to him of two more Indians of the latter's party, "bloody and wounded" and making "great lamentation." They told of how, on the last day of his captivity, "when the sun was a lance high, Estévan went out of the house, and some of the chief men with him. And suddenly came store of people from the city, whom as soon as he saw he began to run away and we likewise, and forthwith they shot at us and wounded us, and certain dead men fell upon us. And so we lay till night and durst not stir, and we heard great rumors in the city, and saw many men and women keeping watch and ward upon the walls thereof. And after this we could not see Estévan any more, and we think they have shot him to death, as they have done all the rest which went with him, so that none are escaped but we only."

This Job-like conclusion is not the final ending of the legend of Estévanico. According to a Zuñi tradition that lasted right down until recent times, Estévanico did not die, but ran off to become a powerful Indian chieftain. This would be the most gratifying outcome, but perhaps Estévanico's shade, in whatever happy hunting ground it may finally have reached, at least enjoyed the ironic satisfaction — and one suspects he had a strong sense of irony — of knowing that the fabulous reports brought back to Mexico by Fray Marcos were enough to induce Coronado to undertake his historic but fruitless march through the future southwestern United States. In this tale there are fitting implications for the nation that would eventually rise on that soil. The land that had entered history preceded by the most fabulous legends of all — of fountains of youth and jewel-encrusted cities — was in the end not a Mexico to be conquered by Spanish knights but a place of more prosaic qualities, to be conquered by men of shrewdness, enterprise, and often of bluster. It is appropriate that this aspect of the American reality was first pointed out to the dreamers — as other grim American realities were eventually to be pointed out to those who had ignored them — by a Black, and one who was, at that, the first known to have lived and flourished on this country's soil. Estévanico knew perfectly well that the king had no clothes on, but in his effort to exploit this secret, he was more like an American of the future than like a medieval slave.

16

Friars and Lost Tribes

T HE SPIRITUAL CONQUEST of Mexico began almost immediately after the
military one. In May of 1524, twelve Franciscan friars of the Observantine
Order — thenceforth to be known widely as the "Twelve Apostles" —
landed at San Juan de Ulúa and, retracing the path of Cortés's march as
well as they knew how, walked up to Mexico City. There they were met
by the Conquistador himself, coming out much as Montezuma had done
four years before, with a retinue of Spanish soldiers as well as Indian
chieftains. Cortés, in a pointed variation on the Aztec emperor's ritual of
welcome to the earlier conquest, got onto his knees and kissed the friars'
hands; he would have kissed their clothing as well, had they let him. The
soldiers and the Indians of his retinue then followed suit. The friars,
ragged and physically exhausted but exalted in spirit, were met with the
awestruck stares of the Indians when they entered the city; "Motolinia,
motolinia!" ("Poor, poor!" in Nahuatl) some of them were said to have
cried at the sight of these true disciples of St. Francis, and Fray Toribio
de Benavente, one of the Twelve, henceforth took this word as his name.
Two years later, a group of twelve Dominicans arrived, likewise to start
a Christian mission in New Spain, but the occasion does not seem to have
made the same vivid impression.

The arrival of the Twelve Apostles in 1524 was actually the most dramatic move in a Franciscan revival that had begun in the very first years of the century under the aegis of Queen Isabella's confessor, the celebrated Cardinal Ximénes de Cisneros. In the insular period prior to the conquest of Mexico, the Franciscans had not on the whole been equal to the dominant moral role of the Dominicans — Montesinos's and eventually Las Casas's order — in fighting against Spanish abuse of the Indians: indeed, their detractors claimed that they had endorsed it. Somehow, the Franciscan sense of a special mission in the New World did not arise until the continent came fully into the picture, and with it a vast and sophisticated Indian civilization that seemed worthy of their concern. The Dominicans, on the other hand, had been aroused primarily by the helpless and pristine condition of the naked savages of the islands; indeed, that supreme Dominican reformer Las Casas was often accused of having really understood only the Indian situation of the islands and not those of Mexico and Peru. The awakening of the Franciscans was, in a sense, the religious counterpart to the transformation in the image and destiny of the New World that had been wrought by the Conquest of Mexico. It was the true beginning of the Catholic Reformation in the Western Hemisphere, the priestly arrival in the wake of the historic march by Cortés, whom Franciscans came to see as a latter-day Moses.

The two old rival mendicant orders, which in earlier days had shared equal responsibility in both the medieval and Spanish histories of the Inquisition, thus represented in their New World manifestations two layers in the recent religious history of Spain. The Dominicans were by and large representative of the Erasmian humanism that had enjoyed a lively following in Spain, as in other parts of western Europe, during the two decades before the outburst of the Protestant Reformation. Lutheranism was something of a stampede against the delicate balance of Erasmus's views, which seem for the most part to have disappeared from the scene by the middle of the sixteenth century. Las Casas, whose own brand of New Christian prophetic zeal had completely absorbed and transmuted the spirit of Spanish Erasmianism, was the outstanding figure who carried the torch for the latter through two-thirds of the century until his death in 1566, at possibly ninety-two years of age. But he represented an outlook that, on the surface of it at any rate, had been superseded by a more militantly orthodox Catholicism, the counterpart to Luther's challenge that is widely known as the Counter-Reformation but is more aptly called the Catholic Reformation. Ultimately, the Jesuits were to be the supreme product of the Spanish form of this movement, but in the meantime the Franciscans were its chief representatives, in the New World at any rate. They were also to be Las Casas's most persistent opponents on Indian questions.

Not that the Franciscans, eager as they were to complete the Chris-

tianization of the New World as soon as possible, were therefore un-
appreciative of the indigenous cultures there — on the contrary, they were
the first Spaniards to learn a great deal about Indian customs and traditions. They were keenly aware of their superiority to Las Casas on this
point, criticizing him as an upstart and a dilettante on the subject of
Indian culture, who was too absorbed in sailing back and forth over the
ocean and making trouble to have time to achieve any real understanding of the peoples he claimed to defend. It has been well established, for
example, that a large part of the anthropological data on the Aztecs in
the *Apologética Historia* comes from two books on that subject written
in the early 1540s by Motolinia — Fray Toribio de Benavente. Las Casas
certainly did not know Nahuatl, which some of the Franciscan missionaries learned so well that they were said to have preached better in it
than in Spanish. Colonial administrators may have been as eager to his-
panicize the Indians as to Christianize them, but the Franciscans did not
care about the former at all; indeed, they felt that the conversion of the
Indians could be better accomplished if the latter remained a people with
their own language and cultural identity, like Spaniards or Frenchmen.
God could be prayed to only in Latin, and he could be explained in any
language.*

But the result was that the friars walked a difficult line between the
sophisticated paganism of the Indian of New Spain and the elements of
Christianity that would naturally be the most appealing to him. It was, in
a sense, very easy to remove a traditional native idol from its perch and
set up an image of the Virgin or a crucifix in its place — this was a very
ancient Christian practice, and the Conquistadors had done it as well —
but was this really replacing superstition with the true religion? We have
entered the age of the Reformations, Catholic as well as Protestant, which
is characterized by a greater austerity of religious standards than had
marked the early centuries of Christianity, at least so far as preachment
to the masses was concerned. Many of the New World missionaries were
quite vehement in their efforts to make it clear to the Indians that the
Christian holy images were not idols like their predecessors in the native
pantheons; but on the other hand, to deny the sacredness of the Christian images too vehemently smacked of heresy in the age of Luther and
Calvin. In the end, touches of the vivid paganism of the Aztecs were

---

* This produced problems to tax the ingenuity of the friars. There was a constant
debate among them as to whether certain key Christian terms were best translated
into Nahuatl or inserted into it directly from the Latin. Translation carried with it
the danger of a loss of the real meaning or, what was far worse, possibly heretical
implications. But insertion had its complications as well: for example, *papa*, the
Latin for "Pope," at first seemed an especially suitable insertion because it was
exactly the same as a Nahuatl word which carried a priestly connotation — but unfortunately, the connotation was pagan.

bound to survive, as can be seen in the imagery of so many of the great religious festivals and processions, the creations of the Franciscan missions, for which Mexico is celebrated to this day. It surely was a keen sense of the vitality of Aztec culture, and of the importance for the success of the Christian mission that it be fully grasped by the missionaries, that led to such pioneering works as those of Motolinia on native history and traditions.

The crucial distinction between the Las Casian and the Motolinian approaches is not so much in the degree of knowledge of the indigenous culture as in the conviction for or against its innate validity. In the major discussions of Indian culture in this epoch there is a prevailing sense of old and new dispensations; in the back of many minds, there seems to be an implicit analogy with the Old and New Testaments. From the more orthodox Catholic Reformation viewpoint, the old dispensation of the Indians is to be treated more or less like the Old Testament, a significant, even a highly respectable, prelude to Christianity, but nevertheless only a prelude which has now been superseded. Las Casas and his true successors, on the other hand, though they certainly welcome the Christian dispensation, nevertheless seem to look back upon the old one with a powerful and more than incidental nostalgia. Las Casas was always perfectly ready to recognize the ways in which old testaments had been superseded: when Martín Fernández de Enciso invoked Joshua in Canaan as a model for treatment of the Indians, it was Las Casas who pointed out that the subsequent historical intervention of Jesus had rendered such tactics unnecessary. But it was the Old Testament that obviously appealed the most to his imagination, because unlike the New it was the sacred history of a people. So also did Indian traditions contain the sacred histories of peoples, and no new dispensation should be so self-righteous as to make itself a Joshua to the Jerichos of folk memory and cultural integrity. This was a most vital and poignant position in a moment when the exhortations of Enciso and the battalions of Cortés were being followed by the censorial fury of Juan de Zumárraga, the first archbishop of Mexico, who was destroying not only precious works of Indian art and architecture in his relentless war on paganism, but writings as well. The Indian Old Testament was steadily being obliterated.

The irony here is that it was not Las Casas, relatively unlearned in Indian matters, but Franciscans like Motolinia and his immediate successors who were the first to salvage some relics of the old cultural memory from utter oblivion. Indeed, there are signs that even Motolinia, in collecting such data for the greater good of Christianity, was suddenly more captivated by it all than he perhaps originally intended to be. In the works written by him and the other friars interested in Indian anti-

quities, there was always the danger that overenthusiasm could provoke
sacerdotal censure. This was particularly true when Las Casas was in
full voice, "polarizing" attitudes toward the Indians.

The result was that Motolinia finally made a violent reversal in order
to avert the danger. It was in January of 1555, a little over two years
after the publication of the *Brief Relation of the Destruction of the Indies,*
that he was moved to write a letter to Charles V, severely denouncing
Las Casas for having so blackened the name of the Spanish Conquest of
the New World that he seemed by implication to be attacking the Christian mission itself. In the shrillness of his rejoinder to the radical Dominican, Motolinia carries his wrath to the Indians themselves, asserting that
they had been an idolatrous people at whom God was justly angry, and
who therefore had deserved their treatment at the hands of the conquerors. Though he does not seem to have had much to say on the subject
before, Motolinia became in this letter an ardent supporter of the *encomienda.* There is something familiar in this to students of political
movements and ideologies: Las Casas's rather abstract and doctrinaire
radicalism had driven a man who had a much longer and more intimate
experience of the Indians into a conservative position. Motolinia's outlook
was undoubtedly marked by an innate paternalism, but one can see the
poignancy of his situation.

An apparently much less troubled spirit was that of Fray Diego de
Landa, also a Franciscan, who was the bishop of Yucatán in the 1560s.
Landa was younger than Motolinia or Las Casas, and for his generation
the Conquest was a given fact. Its corollaries, the *encomienda* and the
destruction of pagan temples and artifacts, also presented themselves to
him as established realities. Landa seems to have been as relentless as
Zumárraga in his carrying out of the latter policy and, according to some
of his detractors, even went so far in his campaign against all traces of
paganism that he waged a kind of Inquisition against Indian recidivism,
torturing "heretics" en masse. Since Landa was convinced that the
Indians were descended from the Lost Tribes of Israel, he no doubt saw
a special challenge in any signs of "Marranism" among them. And for
him, the actual presence of the Indian form of Old Testament was evidently as unclean as heresy itself: it was he who burned huge piles of
Mayan codices, removing them forever from posterity's grasp. Yet, ironically, he is also the single source from which we know the most about
Mayan antiquities, for his *Relación de las Cosas de Yucatán* is an even
more thorough work than Motolinia's on the Aztecs. The book not only
describes the physical character — the clothing, art, and architecture —
of that ancient Mayan way of life whose traces its author had done so
much to destroy, but also gives an account of the celebrated Mayan calendar that is one of the main original sources on that subject to this day.

Landa was thus a paragon of the Catholic Reformation of late sixteenth-century Spain as expressed in the New World. Pre-Catholic documents like the Hebrew Old Testament and the Mayan codices are not valid on their own, according to this point of view; it is only once their elements have been coopted by the only true religion that they become valuable parts of its tradition. The severely censorious treatment of Mayan historical sources was only a more exaggerated version of the sacerdotal disapproval of the reading of the Bible by laymen; all of these contained matters that the masses should be informed about, but through the medium of learned and qualified interpreters.

The appearance of Landa above all signals the fact that a truly Spanish cultural phenomenon had imposed itself upon the history of the New World. This was simply the American manifestation of a major theme in the Spanish history of the preceding centuries: the conquest and absorption of monumental pre-Christian pasts. These pasts were nothing like the insubstantial forest paganism of the European north, or of the West Indies, which had easily been absorbed — if not necessarily extirpated — by Christian conquest: the Moorish and Jewish civilizations of Spain, the Aztec, Mayan, and Incan civilizations of the New World, were each of them so grand that the conquest and absorption of any one of them would have been a remarkable achievement; the sum total is unique in world history.

It is particularly noteworthy that, during the very time when Landa flourished, the metropolitan history of that surge of conquest and absorption was reaching its final chapter. By the 1560s, the laws of *limpieza de sangre* were so thorough and widespread through Spain that it was virtually impossible for anyone of known New Christian ancestry to hold a position based on intellectual qualifications: government, university, and Church were all closed to him. The result was that the New Christian issue had all but disappeared from the surface of life in metropolitan Spain — the New World was another matter — and the Inquisition there was primarily occupied with other heresies than the Judaizing one. As for the relics of Moorish society, they were coming to the kind of violent final solution that the Jews of Spain had faced at the end of the previous century. The Moors of Castile had been forcibly converted en masse in 1502, and those of Aragon in 1526; but the Moriscos — as these formerly Muslim counterparts to the formerly Jewish New Christians were called — had been allowed for another generation to maintain openly their traditional language, customs, and dress, and their continuing adherence in private to the old religion was no secret. The government of Philip II, however, who succeeded his father, Charles V, to the throne of Spain in 1556, was less tolerant of such deviations than its predecessor had been, and ten years later an edict was promulgated requiring of the Moriscos strict conformity to Spanish custom. The result, in 1568, was a Morisco uprising in Granada. It was to fail, of course, and the final upshot was to be a wholesale expulsion of the Moriscos of Spain in 1609.

Spain was thereupon to do the best it could to forget the Moorish and Jewish elements in its background until the nineteenth century. But Spaniards were never as bothered by the physical manifestations of race differences as northern Europeans have tended to be; it was doctrinal divergence, and the possibility of the taint of heresy being carried in the bloodstream, that primarily worked to arouse racism in them. Instinctual anthropologists by dint of their ethnically varied historical experience, Spaniards were foremost among those in the sixteenth century who could find alien racial traditions to be interesting and significant so long as they were not dangerous. Once all the Devil's work had apparently been destroyed in the New World, there was nothing left to do about the Aztecs, Mayas, and Incas but to tell their story. In fact, many of Landa's contemporaries in the New World were so eager for the story to be told that they did not merely settle for transcribing themselves what they heard from the Indians, but taught some of the latter to write and become their own historians. With a regard for native languages typical of the friars, they did not even necessarily require that their literary charges learn Spanish, so that many of the Indian memorialists of the time wrote in their own tongues.*

The greatest work of this kind is the monumental *Historia General de las Cosas de Nueva España,* produced mainly between 1572 and 1585 by and under the supervision of the Franciscan friar Bernardino de Sahagún, who, though not a crusader, was a true heir to the intellectual tradition of Las Casas. This twelve-volume compendium on traditional Aztec gods, festivals, literature, history, customs, arts, sciences, and many other *cosas,* is as characteristic a Spanish work of the epoch as *Don Quixote,* solemn and lanky like that novel's hero, endlessly ramifying like his adventures. Its principal language, however, is not Spanish but Nahuatl. Sahagún seems to have run something like a seminar, teaching letters to his Aztec disciples and assigning them to the various special areas about which they then wrote. The work was never finished, but his plan was to publish it in folio pages of three columns each: the central column would contain the Nahuatl text, which would be flanked on one side by a Spanish translation and on the other by a commentary in Spanish — both these latter the work of the friar himself. Had it been published in that day — it was

---

* One result was the celebrated *Popol Vuh,* the sacred book of the ancient Quiche Maya, which was written down by an unknown native scribe in the 1550s, and shows significant signs of the syncretism that was resulting from the simultaneous destruction of the records and cooptation of traditions by the Spaniards: for the tribal religious history in the *Popol Vuh* displays Christian influences.

not to see print until the nineteenth century — the work would have borne a distinct resemblance to another monumental Spanish publishing effort of the sixteenth century: the Complutensian Polygot.°

But the fact that one of the columns in Sahagún's work was commentary rather than translation also brings to mind another religious text: the Talmud. In a sense his encyclopedic compilation is indeed not only the Old Testament of the Aztecs, but their Mishna and Gemara as well, the most exhaustive rendering of the Mexican old dispensation ever made. To be sure, the Indian New Testament is there too, in the form of "confutations" placed every so often at the end of summaries of old Aztec religious traditions, but these seem mere afterthoughts. The zeal of the Catholic Reformation normally characteristic of the Franciscans at this time is not present. Indeed, the author and compiler does not seem to be an orthodox Spanish Catholic of his day, but something closer to the kind of Erasmian that was still present at the University of Salamanca when he went there from 1512 to 1514 — for, having been born in 1499, he was the child of an earlier epoch who, like Las Casas, happened to have lived a very long time. And like Las Casas, he may very well have been a New Christian.

This, at any rate, is the position toward which some recent scholars have leaned. "Sahagún" was the name not of his family but of the town in which he had been born, and which he assumed upon taking monastic vows in 1518. His family name was Ribeira, which is distinctly Portuguese, and which suggests possible *converso* origin, since it was from this class that most of the emigrants from Portugal to Spain came in that epoch; his eagerness to be rid of the name also is suggestive. But it is above all in his unprecedented ethnographic passion, his admiration — despite the proper displays of shock at various indications of the Devil's work — for the traditional culture of the Aztecs, and his tragic awareness that their character and strength as a people have been destroyed by the Conquest, that one may discern the personality of the New Christian. Like Las Casas, he is an elegiast to the destruction of the Indian. Here is a tradition that cuts across the line that had divided Franciscan from Dominican a few years earlier. Las Casas and Sahagún are simply two

---

° Issued starting in 1513 at Alcalá de Henares (which was *Complutum* in Latin, hence the source of the rubric "Complutensian"), this project dear to the heart of Cardinal Ximénes de Cisneros contained the Vulgate text of the Bible with the Hebrew and Greek versions on either side of it, and the Aramaic one at the bottom. All this was a response to Erasmianism and its call for critical examination of the originals of the sacred texts, but in the characteristic tone of the Spanish Catholic Reformation: for, as one of the prefaces of the Complutensian Polyglot observed about it, the Vulgate text on its pages seemed to hang suspended like Jesus on the cross between two thieves. In the case of Sahagún's *Historia,* it was the Nahuatl text that held this place of exaltation and anguish: does this commemorate the crucifixion of Mexico by the usurping Spanish culture that surrounds it?

offspring of the New Christian religion of Columbus, one the prophet of the destruction, the other its archivist, both Calistos after all, joined in mourning the passing of their New World Melibea.

If this picture is true, then another figure belongs to it, to be in effect the poet of the great trio of sixteenth-century elegiasts for the victims of the Spanish New World conquest. Not that the Dominican friar Diego Durán wrote in verse; his medium was prose, and his intention was, like Sahagún's, to record the antiquities of the Aztecs as best he could. But there is a special poetry in his writing, which is all in his own vibrant Spanish, and which draws upon personal experience and observation — indeed, upon personal feeling — wherever possible. For example, in his *Book of Rites and Ceremonies*, there is a passage in which he describes the ancient Aztec custom of the *tiánguiz*, or marketplace, and of the essentially religious fear on the part of many Indians even after the Conquest of selling their goods anywhere else. He then applies his gift for anecdote:

> I shall now relate something that happened to me: One morning I left my convent to go to Mexico City, and, because it was November, there was a great frost. Upon leaving the village, I ran into a naked Indian carrying a load of firewood, which he was taking to sell at a *tiánguiz*. It broke my heart to see him nearly dead with the cold and, taking pity on him, I asked him how much they would have to pay for that load of wood in the marketplace. He told me one *real*. I took out a *real* and gave it to him, telling him to go back home and warm himself with the fire of that load of wood, which I was hereby giving him. And with that I went on, assuming he had gone home.
>
> A little over an hour later I saw him coming up behind me with his load of wood, and I asked him angrily why he had not done what I told him to do. He replied that when he had left his house his heart had been set on going to the *tiánguiz* with his wood; he said that he still had my *real* if I wanted it back. Waving away the *real*, I proceeded to reprimand him for his outmoded signs and superstitions, and for his want of any proper fear of God. He took all this with great humility, and swore to me that he was not following any outmoded beliefs, but only custom, for he was now a believer in God and in what the Holy Mother Church of Rome believed.

Durán goes on to refer to this particular custom as a bit of "foolishness" (*niñería*) that had been planted in the minds of ordinary Aztecs as a way of bringing income into the marketplace for the benefit of the old ruling classes. His analysis here is probably sound; but it is not nearly so powerful as his poignant human portrait of the unflagging dignity of adherence to tradition.

Another remarkable aspect of this story — and of others like it throughout Durán's writings — is the aptness with which it could serve as a metaphor of the Marrano condition. So also does a certain type of New Christian, like the naked Indian, carry ancient custom on his back against the icy — or fiery — blasts of the Inquisition. Did Durán sense this analogy? It is quite possible that he did, since, as is widely suspected today, he may have had New Christian origins — although his background is as obscure as that of most of the persons in this epoch who are now believed to be of *converso* descent.° In fact, all that can be said with certainty about his cultural identity is that, having learned Nahuatl in childhood and received all his formal education in New Spain, he was really in a sense the first true "Mexican" in Spanish-American literary history. How significant a distillation his spirit would represent, then, if he were also a New Christian! Growing up amidst the ruins of the Aztec civilization as he did, but also with the ruins of Sephardic hopes in his heart, he could have looked both within and without to ponder all the signs of the deadly relentlessness of Spanish conquest.

But even if we set the question of his origins aside, Durán's work suggests that he viewed the Indian destiny from a perspective influenced by the New Christian experience of his time, whether he was conscious of this or not. For with increasing frequency and conviction Durán came to see elements of a Judaic character in the old Aztec religion. At first this tendency appears only as a fervent search for Jewish analogies, provoked by Aztec customs such as the eating of only unleavened bread on certain days of the year, the prohibition of drinking liquids after the eating of certain ritual foods, and the use of baths for purification. In time, this begins to seem to Durán like overwhelming evidence that the Indians are indeed descended from the Lost Tribes of Israel, and he opens his last and most important work, the *History of the Indies of New Spain*, with an unqualified assertion to this effect. In this way, even certain fundamental legends can be explained, such as the one that Montezuma presented to Cortés: the departure of the great lord in antiquity now seems to Durán to be a memory of Moses. As for the abject condition of the Indian, it can now be accounted for in the classic way: this is God's

---

° Durán was born in 1537 in Seville — always a significant New Christian population center — and bears a family name that, before the Expulsion, could be found more often belonging to Jews than to Christians: indeed, it was the name borne by one of the great rabbinical families of medieval Spain. Little is known about his father aside from the fact that he was a merchant, and that he went to New Spain, settling in Texcoco, five years after his son Diego was born. There are only hints of ethnic identity here.

punishment once again wrought upon the Jewish people for their sins. The history that Durán then proceeds to tell after this introduction, which begins with the remotest Aztec past and ends in the Conquest, becomes a tragedy that reverberates with the Jewish destiny. Ever a poet in prose, he has thereby moved from the elegiac lyricism of his earlier works to the vast scale of epic; it is the final and most ambitious of the tributes by sixteenth-century New Christians to peoples who have been crushed under the Spanish onslaught.

Durán lived during a time when apocalyptic hopes flourished in some parts of the New World; but these were the hopes of a militant even if sometimes unorthodox Catholicism. In Peru in the fifteen-sixties and -seventies, a Dominican friar called Francisco de la Cruz had declared himself the Messiah of a New World Christianity which had to fight a war to the death against the Indians in order to bring on the final redemption, because they were the Lost Tribes of Israel; he was finally burned at the stake by the Inquisition in 1578. Gerónimo de Mendieta, born in 1525, was a more truly Franciscan apocalyptist, who believed that the mission among the Indians would produce a perfection of Christianity that would help to usher in the End of Days. Toward the end of the century and of his life — he died in 1604 — Mendieta became disillusioned with Philip II's policies in the Indies, which had produced a disastrous decline in the Indian population; but he finally concluded that this was merely the final time of troubles before the advent of the millennial kingdom.

Such Catholic optimism was not to be found in Diego Durán's probably Jewish soul; there was not even left in him a grain of the millenarian optimism that had accompanied so many New Christian views of the Indies at the beginning of the century — its time was long past. In a sense, Durán's elegiac vision was not only more worldly than those of Mendieta and Francisco de la Cruz, but also more true to what was happening to the Spanish manifest destiny itself. The great surge of conquest and reconquest was over, and a rapid decline of Spanish energies was setting in, both in the Old World and in the New. It seems appropriate that Durán died in 1588, the very year in which England gave notice to Spain that she was now to be the heir to the latter's expansionist energies. The religion of the Catalan Atlas had departed from Spain, and from Portugal, for good, and had made its way northward.

17

The Passion of
Luis de Carvajal

THE DECLINE OF THE New Christian messianic ideal was accompanied, in both the Old World and the New, by a revival of Marrano Judaizing. The oncoming seventeenth century was to see a great number of dramatic histories of Marranos emigrating to more tolerant countries, such as the Netherlands or some of the Italian states, there to declare their Judaism openly at last. Others decided to see if they could live a life closer to their Jewish heritage in the New World, where they had reason to hope for a freer climate of religious expression, but still within their ancestral Hispanic culture. To a large extent, this was a Portuguese phenomenon. For reasons we have already examined, secret Judaizing was always far more widespread and robust in Portugal than in Spain, and revivals of it in the latter country were very often the direct result of influxes from the former. There were two major periods of Marrano emigration from Portugal to Spain in the sixteenth century: the first came in the wake of the long-delayed establishment of the Inquisition in Portugal in 1536, and the second came after the union of the two kingdoms under the Spanish crown in 1580. After the latter date in particular, Judaizing became a matter of greater concern for the Inquisition than it had been for many years, especially in the New World, where,. in the common parlance of some regions, the word "Portuguese" had become a euphemism for "Marrano." From the latter part of the sixteenth century until the middle of the seventeenth, the phenomenon was perhaps nowhere in the world so strong as in Portuguese Brazil. But in general it was widespread throughout colonial America.

No more vivid example of the revival of Judaizing in the New World can be found than in the story of Luis de Carvajal the Younger. Born in the Castilian town of Benavente in 1566, Carvajal was of Portuguese stock on both his mother's and his father's sides, but otherwise there was nothing on the surface of it to compromise the distinction of the family to which he belonged. His maternal uncle and namesake, Luis de Carvajal the Elder, was a man rising rapidly in the service of Spain who went to the New World two years after the nephew's birth; there, in 1579, he became governor of a province newly carved out of the region of Pánuco, the New Kingdom of León. In the following year, the governor invited his sister's family to come and settle in his new province, no doubt on particularly favorable terms; the governor was childless, whereas his sister and her husband, Francisco Rodríguez de Matos, were the parents of eight — a ninth was soon to come — and he regarded these as his heirs. In witness to this, his family name became their own. An illustrious future seemed assured for all of them.

But the entire family on both sides was New Christian. Indeed, the governor's wife, Guiomar, who had refused to accompany him to the New World, apparently was something more extreme; she seems to have been a secret Judaizer. It must be understood that we are now completely within a twilight region of racial and religious identity, in which the forms of human self-consciousness and behavior are extremely hard to discern. There is little reason to doubt that Governor Carvajal was perfectly aware not only of his own New Christian origins but of his wife's when they were married around 1566; there also is good reason to assume that he aspired only to be a good Catholic and Spaniard all his life, even though he was eventually to be persecuted by the Inquisition because of his tainted family associations. His racially endogamous marital choice may therefore have been the merest accident; or it may have been due to a tendency still prevailing among New Christians, even when they were unimpeachable Catholics, to circulate and find spouses primarily in one another's society. There was much to be said for marrying someone who, being burdened with the same guilty secret as you, was therefore as inclined to keep it from the world at large. On the level of racial background at least, the future governor's marriage was not incompatible with his determination to have a perfectly correct sixteenth-century Spanish life and career.

His bride's secret Judaism is another matter. Perhaps he did not know about it at the time of their marriage; perhaps she had not yet become a Judaizer by then. Perhaps he also did not know that his sister had married a Judaizer and, later, that it was among her heretically inclined family that his wife became the foremost agitator for the ancestral faith. We have a picture of a remarkably naïve governor, and of a ferociously active cell led by his wife, unbeknownst to him, at his sister's home. But none of this can really be perceived with clarity, for our only evidence about it comes from Inquisition testimony, which must be read in the same way that the records of the Moscow trials of the 1930s are to be read — with a realization that it all belongs to a special realm of self-fulfilling inquiry, whereby the judges, having driven the witness into some state of psychic extremity, can then make him say with conviction exactly what they want to hear. Much of it is too neat.

If this were all we had, the story of the Carvajals might not — except for the governor's special eminence — have been very different from many other such stories buried in the records of the various New World Inquisition tribunals. But we also have a special record, and the outlines of a special personality, left us by the life and writings of the governor's nephew, the younger Luis de Carvajal. Young Luis's high-strung and mystical nature was one especially in tune with the apocalyptic atmosphere of the times, and what is especially remarkable about the autobiographical memoir and handful of letters he has left to posterity is their affinities with the writings of the great Catholic mystics of the day. The fact that some of them, such as St. Teresa of Ávila and Fray Luis de León, were also of New Christian descent leads one to wonder whether, but for a special set of family circumstances, the younger Luis might not himself have become a saint instead of a victim of the Inquisition. He was in any case a true child of his generation, the final despairing residue of Spanish zeal and of New Christian hopes in the discovery and conquest of America.

According to Luis's autobiography, he received a conventional Christian education until he was thirteen years of age, and only then, at the traditional moment of Bar Mitzvah, was he solemnly apprised by his parents of the truth about their background. This revelation, coming not long before the family's departure for New Spain, seems to have signaled for Luis a season of ambiguous rebirth. He was ill when they landed in Tampico, and was placed in the care of a Portuguese doctor named Manuel de Morales, who had sailed across with them and who proved to be an even more ardent Judaizer than the governor's wife, Guiomar, had been. The Carvajal family went on ahead to its residence inland, leaving Luis and his next older brother, Baltasar, in a shed at the port, where they spent a stormy night described by Luis like this:

The winds were so strong that they tore the trees from their roots and threw down most of the houses in that town. The house in which my brother and I were sleeping threatened to fall down as the fierce wind with terrible fury tore out some beams from the roof. The debris fell all over, causing us to hide under the bedding — a deceptive protection in our great fear. At last, perceiving the imminence of collapse, we arose. It was raining and blowing terribly. The force of the wind was such that we could not open the door. Realizing our danger, we tried, against our better judgment, to push it out, counter to the way it opened. The Lord permitted that, with the help of the wind, it be opened enough to allow us to get out. After we escaped, the house crashed to the ground. The Lord, blessed be His name, freed us on the third attempt.

One has the impression of a rather rough and traumatic birth. That it was also an ambiguous one is suggested by Luis's earlier remark that "it must have been [my father's] moving and coming to this land that was one of the sins for which justice punished his sons."

Luis has sounded some of his central themes here, which are underscored in the very next scene in his autobiography. He and Baltasar ran from the scene of the disaster "to the house of our parents, who were afraid that their sons might have been killed. Hearing someone knock on the door, our loving father opened it and received us with tears in his eyes, thanking and praising the Lord." Loving father? This was the man who had placed them in that desolate womb of a house to suffer the shocks of the storm alone. Actually, the scene is reminiscent of one in a text especially revered by Luis, the deuterocanonical Book of Tobit, in which young Tobias, sent out by his blind father to wander amidst the perils of the Babylonian exile, returns home at last:

Tobit also went forth toward the door, and stumbled: but his son ran unto him,
And took hold of his father: and he strake of the gall on his father's eyes, saying, Be of good hope, my father.
And when his eyes began to smart, he rubbed them;
And the whiteness pilled away from the corners of his eyes: and when he saw his son, he fell upon his neck.

"Blindness" was a word that Luis would ever apply to those who had been born of Jewish descent but had not followed the ancestral religion. The reproach to his father is clear, for Luis wrote this passage long after he had abandoned his forebears' path of craven Marrano concealment. But the sense of moral superiority to the "blind" parent whom he has taught to see is only one side of the picture; the other is the ambivalence and anger at having been sent out on the mission of discovery, at having even been brought into the world, in the first place.

When Luis's father died five years later, the young man immediately sensed his moment to step forward and assume the full burden of a tradition that his family had hitherto only diffidently taken on. He had been journeying through the wilderness, working as a trader in Indian villages, when he heard the news, whereupon he returned to Pánuco and bought a Bible. Then he set out again on his travels, studying his Bible all along the way:

> I came to know many of the divine mysteries. One day I read Chapter 17 of Genesis, in which the Lord ordered our saintly father Abraham to be circumcised, and especially those words which say that the soul of him who is not circumcised will be erased from the book of life. I became so very frightened . . . that I immediately proceeded to carry out . . . the divine command. Prompted by the Almighty and His good angel, I left the corridor of the house where I had been reading; leaving behind the sacred Bible, I took some old worn scissors and went over to the ravine of the Pánuco River. There, with longing and a vivid wish to be inscribed in the book of life — something that could not happen without this holy sacrament — I sealed it by cutting off almost all of the prepuce and leaving very little of it.

The recollection of the example of Abraham is significant, for Luis usually felt a deep identification with Isaac; certainly his own father had willingly enough brought him into the world as a potential sacrificial victim to the ancestral faith. But now Luis had taken on the obligation that the father should have taken on but did not; he alone had performed the covenant of circumcision. From this point on, Luis's relationship to his own family — to his brothers and sisters, even to his mother — becomes quite paternal; he has assumed the role of the father. Only his eldest brother, Gaspar, escapes his influence, by joining the Dominican order. As for his next older brother, Baltasar, the companion of his ordeal in the shed at Tampico, Luis successfully persuades him to circumcise himself as well: the results are described in a bloody scene that seems to stand in as a Carvajal version of a New Testament Passion sequence. The great pains that Baltasar suffers, Luis explains, are in expiation for his past sins.

The time was now coming, however, when the whole family would have to pay for its past sins. The Inquisition had reached the New World at last in 1569, and trouble began for the Carvajals in about 1586, when a soldier named Felipe Núñez tried to court Luis's elder sister, Isabel, by then a widow living in Mexico City. According to the Inquisition records, Isabel was now as zealous a Judaizer as Luis was, and since Núñez was himself a New Christian, she responded to his protestations of love by preaching reconversion to the old faith. Núñez thereupon denounced her to the Inquisition. Isabel, under torture, proceeded to name the other members of the family who had reverted to Judaism, and Luis, their mother, and two other sisters were arrested as a result. Baltasar managed to go into hiding and eventually escape to Europe, as did a younger brother, Miguel. The governor was arrested as well, even though Isabel and the others vehemently denied that he had been implicated in their Judaizing. His New Christian identity had already been revealed during a quarrel with the viceroy of Mexico over a boundary question; it was convenient now to have him arrested on charges of having harbored Judaizers. He was removed from his post, sentenced to a year in prison and to six more years of exile; in sickness and despair, he died in his cell a few months later. His wife, Guiomar, had died back in Spain eight years before.

For Luis, this experience in prison was another occasion for him to undergo a spiritual return to the womb and the trauma of rebirth. A special intensity was added to the situation for him by the fact that his mother was a fellow prisoner in another cell along those dark corridors. She was already in prison at the time of his arrest, and his way of letting her know of his own incarceration was to have a code message sent to her in the form of several of his own shirts wrapped in her undergarments — certainly the work of a powerful, if unconsciously functioning, metaphorical imagination. Later, he was able to watch her interrogation and torture through a small hole he had dug in his cell wall with two lamb bones:

> I watched her being taken in and out. Seeing that she still denied the charges, those tyrants decided to subject her to torture. Thus they led the gentle lamb to the torture chamber, preceded by the wicked judges, the warden, and the guard. The executioner was already in the torture chamber, completely covered from head to foot with a white shroud and hood. They ordered her to undress and directed that the gentle lamb lay down her pure body on the torture rack. Then they tied her arms and legs to it. As they turned the cruel cords in the iron rings, they tightened the flesh, making her cry out with agonizing wails that everyone heard. I knelt in my cell, for this was the most bitter and anguished day that I had ever endured. . . .

— except perhaps for the day of his birth, which this seems for all the world to resemble.

Luis in his prison cell also had visions, like St. Teresa in her conventual one, in which the symbolism of rebirth continued to prevail. As a result of these visions, Luis took a new name for himself as a Jew, calling himself Joseph Lumbroso. The last name, meaning "the Enlightened," suggests affinities with the *alumbrados,* a Spanish pre-Protestant movement of the late fifteenth and early sixteenth centuries in which a significant number of New Christians had participated. The first name was a declaration of another of Luis's deeply felt Biblical affinities, this time with the young man who had been delivered into exile by his family, but was ultimately to stand before his father a prince and a savior of his people. Luis's own father, five years dead, was burned in effigy by the Inquisition during this ordeal of 1590. Luis and his family were all eventually released and allowed to return to society as penitents. He was able to play the role of their savior to some extent by raising enough money to pay a fine that freed them from the obligation of wearing penitential garments.

During the next five years after his release, Luis carried out the orders of the Inquisition by teaching at a school for Indians. Like so many heretical New Christians, he was an ardent reader of the books of Esdras, and one therefore can legitimately wonder whether he saw the Indians as the Lost Tribes of Israel described in that text. Such a view would certainly accord with his own heightened vision of redemption in the wilderness. But we have no words from him on this subject. Indeed, we have few words from him on anything at all but his own personal experience and intense inner existence. His extreme inwardness is typical of the age, a retreat from the New Christian universalism of the beginning of the century, just as the stress on personal and exclusive salvation made by Luther and Calvin was a retreat from the Erasmian humanism that had preceded them.

Luis and his family did not cease to carry on their few, sparse rituals of Jewish observance in secret, and in 1595 he was arrested again, along with his mother, the same three sisters as before, and two younger ones as well, now grown to the age of heresy. This time the charge against the five elder members of the family was more serious than before; whereas they could have been classed earlier as persons inadvertently in error, they now were intransigent Judaizers, recidivists by the standards of the Inquisition. Their doom was sealed. During this final spell in prison, when Luis wrote letters to his mother and sisters in their cells with pen and ink that he had been given in the hope that he would reveal the names of more Judaizers — he did not — he was able to raise his vision of himself to a virtual apotheosis. The letters abound not only in the old themes of rebirth, but also in apocalyptic visions, and images implying his role as substitute father to the family. His attempts at paying tribute to their actual father are constantly mingled with echoes of reproach.

A significant element in the letters is the frequency with which Abraham and Isaac are referred to; twice Luis retells the story of the binding of Isaac at great length, despite the lack of a Bible in his cell. In one of these retellings, a revealing imaginative interpolation suddenly occurs:

> Upon arriving at the top of the mountain, Abraham said to his son: "My son, you have to know that the Lord our God has commanded me to offer you as a holy sacrifice to His Divine Majesty. Blessed and fortunate are you, since it is certain and without doubt that, among the sons of Adam, you die in a royal manner as an offering to God, the almighty Lord of eternal life. I envy you rather than feel sorry for you, my son."
>
> "You are offering me to the Lord," answered the holy Isaac . . . , "Certainly, my father; if the Lord orders it this way, may His will be carried out, as I am here, obedient and prepared. Only, I beg of you, put a band across the eyes of this frail body, so that it may not see the knife when you deliver the blow and flee. . . ."

When you deliver the blow and flee: the reproach cannot be contained; and yet, despite the father's cravenness and the son's nobility, it is the father who wins divine approval in the end. "You have shown me how much you love me," the angel of the Lord says to Abraham, "since you did not hesitate to offer your own son. Since you acted in such a manner, you will be requited handsomely." The whole story becomes an indictment not just of the father, but of Judaism itself, which is ready to offer its children as sacrificial lambs and praise itself for doing so. Ever since his Bar Mitzvah day sixteen years before, it has been Luis's lifelong struggle to reconcile himself to being the Isaac of this history. How has he achieved the reconciliation? By becoming, as he has already signaled in his change of name, Joseph as well: "I asked in my poor manner," he writes in another letter, "in silent prayer before the Lord, how it is that this poor worm is worth His great mercy and how I can have in His kingdom a greater crown than my father. The following answer was unveiled and given to me: This will be as it was when Joseph stood before his father as Prince of Egypt and the holy Jacob took so much pleasure in seeing his son praised and honored." Luis eagerly looked forward to this meeting in heaven.

In December of 1596, Luis, his mother, Isabel, and two other sisters were burned at the stake. Apparently a profession of adherence to the

Catholic faith was extracted from them at the very end, in a bargain for a more merciful death: traditionally, those who remained unrepentant were burned alive, whereas those who made a final avowal of Catholicism were garroted before being dragged to the stake. The gesture made by the five Carvajals was undoubtedly no more sincere than their earlier profession of Catholicism had been, for which they had won five years' respite. Yet it may have been more than just a buffer against physical agony: it was perhaps a final manifestation of their despair, of strivings that seem in the end to have been not so much a Jewish revival as a hopeless and pathetic lunge at an End of Days that had not really arrived. Imagining, in their stark loneliness, that Judaism now resided nowhere else in the world but in themselves, they were prepared for no future for it anywhere but in heaven. This was indeed a vision of the drying-up of their own once abundant line; when they went to the stake in 1596, there was only one member alive of a new Carvajal generation — Leonor, the daughter of one of the sisters burned with Luis, who was later to become an active informer against the Judaizers of her acquaintance. Furthermore, the two youngest sisters of the family, who were allowed to go free in 1596, were also eventually to be burned by the Inquisition. This was the impending atmosphere within which Luis, his mother, and his three sisters could tell the confessor they were Catholic as they went to their execution: for them, what happened in the world simply did not matter any more.

Yet the Carvajal line did survive elsewhere. We have seen that the two brothers, Baltasar and Miguel, escaped to Europe; there, they settled in countries tolerant of Judaism, openly embraced the ancestral faith, and took the name Lumbroso that their brother Luis had chosen. One of them called himself David and the other Jacob, though it is not clear which was which. David Lumbroso became a surgeon and settled somewhere in Italy; Jacob Lumbroso, also a physician, for a time served the Sephardic Jewish community of Salonica, and wrote an important religious tract in Hebrew, which was published in Venice in 1617. Some forty years later, another Dr. Jacob Lumbroso appears to history in a very different place, on the records of the English North American colony of Maryland. Since this Lumbroso apparently was a Jew, and the name was an unusual one, there is a good chance that he was a descendant of the Carvajals of our story. If so, he represents an appropriate outcome. It was Baltasar and Miguel who had recognized that there was no longer any Jewish future left as such within the Iberian orbit, whether in the Old World or the New, and they had gone out of it. But Jacob had now perhaps recognized something else which had been part of the original vision of his forebears: that there was some kind of special Jewish future to be realized in the New World after all. This newest realization, however, could only have occurred after the newest developments; for by then, the Western Hemisphere was no longer exclusively under Iberian control. Other European nations were moving into it, and new Americas were coming into being.

18

France Discovers the
Noble Savage

Aᴌᴛʜᴏᴜɢʜ sɪxᴛᴇᴇɴᴛʜ-ᴄᴇɴᴛᴜʀʏ France, the scene of religious massacres
and civil wars, can hardly be considered a model of enlightened tolerance, a distinct urbanity seems nevertheless to arise as we move northward across the Pyrenees, particularly with regard to the relationship
with the New World. A breeze of wit blows up and parts the murky
clouds of Spanish apocalypticism. In the Fourth Book of *Gargantua and
Pantagruel,* the bibulous adventurers unfurl their sails and head for
"Upper India, close to Cathay," along the western route, undaunted by
the great obstacles of land consistently encountered that way, including
by their own countryman Jacques Cartier only a few years before. They
pass through a mythical ocean that is, among other things, replete with
Hebraisms,° and even meet some rabbis and a Jewish oracle; but there
are no Lost Tribes of Israel at the end of the quest, nor any other objects
of glorious conquest for Christianity. There is only the divine *Bacbuc*
(Hebrew for "bottle"), and though there is much drinking, there is no
inebriation of the soul. Far from the spiritual and physical fires of the

---

° Its islands bear names like *Tohu* and *Bohu* ("without form" and "void," in Genesis
1:2), *Ruach* ("wind" or "spirit"), and *Ganavim* ("thieves").

Spanish New World, we are now in a cool Gallic one, where sober spirits crave no flame so much as one that will warm their bodies.

In general, there is something resolutely earthy and practical, a quality gratifyingly prosaic, about the early history of French North America. The country may very well have been first discovered by fishermen: for a long time it was known as "Baccallaos," the Portuguese word for "cod," which only subsequently made its way down, in English translation, to the cape that now commemorates this early northern counterpart to Aztec treasure. But French fishermen may have got there even earlier than the Portuguese, and it seems an appropriate symbol of the history of the area that, when Cartier entered the Gulf of St. Lawrence on his first voyage there in 1534, he found himself being greeted by a fishing ship from La Rochelle. It is not unreasonable to conjecture that such vessels may have been making trips there since the days of the Vikings at least, long before indiscreet "discoverers" began to come along and then advertise to the whole world where a good catch could be found.

Pre-Columbian North America shies away from history, but this was not necessarily because historically minded men did not know about it. The eleventh-century Viking experience of "Vinland," preserved in saga, is now known to have actually occurred. Why, then, did it not have a more palpable impact upon Europe? Knowledge of the New World may even have spread as a result of it, but only reluctantly. Furthermore, some scholars now believe that English ships from Bristol may have begun reaching North American shores as early as 1481; but if this is so, why was there nothing of the clamor over the discovery that followed in the wake of the one made by Columbus eleven years later? Even the well-documented discovery of North America for the English by John Cabot in 1497 did not cause much excitement, nor was it followed by any discernible rush to colonize the new found land. Until the Spaniards finally began to endow it with their characteristically fabulous notions concerning cities of gold and fountains of youth, the image of North America remained dim and largely unappealing to Europeans.

The reason for this seems to lie primarily in the northern landscape, so attractive and ultimately rewarding to sober spirits ready for prolonged efforts of primitive accumulation, but offering little to those who expect immediate gratification, either materially or spiritually. Even the most hopeful of the northern spiritual travelers, the sixth-century Irish monk St. Brendan, found not the Promised Land of the Saints that he had been seeking, but a succession of treeless, rock-covered islands, the windswept retreats of dour hermits, and harsher things as well: an iceberg, and once even a whale, on which he and his companions had ensconced themselves thinking it was an island until it began to move. His adventures are filled with the drizzly chiaroscuro of the kind of landscape commemorated in Celtic literature and legend. An ancient northern European folklore seems to be coming back to life in a slightly new setting in such things as this description, on a Spanish world map of 1544, of the region that was becoming French Canada:

> This land was discovered by John Cabot the Venetian, and Sebastian Cabot his son. . . . The people of it are dressed in the skins of animals; they use in their wars bows and arrows, lances and darts, and certain clubs of wood, and slings. It is a very sterile land. There are in it many white bears, and very large stags like horses, and many other animals; and likewise there is infinite fish, sturgeons, salmon, very large soles a yard long, and many other kinds of fish, and the great number of them are called baccallaos; and likewise there are in the same land hawks black like crows, eagles, partridges, linnets, and many other birds of different kinds.

This is bleak for any who seek their particular vision of paradise, whatever the relative earthliness or spirituality of its nature, in the sundrenched, lushly vegetating south.

Yet it is an ideal enough landscape for some, and the tough, vigorous people who inhabit it — so different in character from languid Fortunate Islanders or luxurious Aztecs — can be viewed as representing a certain vision of the good life. The vision is well represented by an ancient Celtic cradle song, which goes (in Nora Chadwick's translation):

> When thy father went a-hunting
> With spear on shoulder, and cudgel in hand,
> He would call his big dogs,
> "Giff, Gaff": "Catch, catch!": "Fetch, fetch!"
> In his coracle he would spear a fish,
> Striking suddenly like a lion.
> When thy father went up the mountain
> He would bring back a roebuck, a wild boar, a stag,
> A spotted grouse from the mountain,
> A fish from the falls of Derwenydd.
> As many as thy father caught with his spear
> None would escape except those with wings.

With a few variations, this could be a picture of the life of the indigenous North American as Europeans began to see it in the sixteenth century, and as those among them who "went native" began living it. The inhabitants of the northern parts of the New World, in others words, represented something of a pure ancestral way of life that had been lost but not forgotten by northern Europeans, many of whom greatly admired it when they saw it still alive among the Americans. This feeling was no Mediterranean classicist's vision of a simplicity conceived in antiquity by Greeks and Romans, and held up always in a literary middle distance. There were elements of such a classicism in it for those who were so inclined, but it was above all a blood-longing, a kind of primordial self-image. Implicit in its embrace of the northern landscape and of the ideal life led in harmony with it was a rejection of the Mediterranean world, and of the south.°

It is tempting to call such a feeling "Nordic," but the racial feeling underlying the solidarity manifested by some northern Europeans toward the northern New World native seems really to have been more Celtic than Teutonic. One might say that when the French and the English attacked and conquered the American Savage, they were behaving like the Teutonic elements in their own respective histories, violent, restless, uprooted wanderers from the East. But when they admired his rustic tranquillity and unerring grasp of a life in harmony with nature, when they felt compassion for the simplicity of the man of the northwest whom they were now beleaguering, they were harking back to their Celtic ancestry, and being reminded of its surviving enclaves in their own metropolitan north and west — Brittany in France, Ireland, Wales, and Scotland in the British Isles. It is significant that when the British began seeking the earliest possible sources for their claims upon North America, their favorite myths were Celtic: not only St. Brendan, but more emphatically Prince Madoc, a twelfth-century Welshman who was said to have founded an American colony and whose lineage was persistently perceived among some Indians by a tradition of enthusiasts down to very recent times. But we shall have more to say about the English vision of the New World in subsequent chapters.

As for France, most of whose New World explorers and settlers came from the heavily Celtic northwest of the country, the possibility of an inner Celtic feeling of solidarity with the North American *sauvage* may

---

° Such a rejection is implied on the linguistic level in the fact that Frenchmen and Englishmen tended to call the northern New World natives not "Indians" but "Savages" (*sauvages* in French). "Indian" was a Spanish idea, filled with implications of a southern reality and a longed-for East, neither of which was very attractive to northwestern Europeans. "Savage," on the other hand — which was usually "Salvage" in the English of the sixteenth and seventeenth centuries — came ultimately from the Latin *silvaticus* (a standard dialect variation was *salvaticus*), meaning "a man of the woods [*silvae*]," and carried far less of the connotation of cruel ferocity that it has today. Until the latter part of the sixteenth century, the English used "Salvage" almost exclusively for the natives of the American north, and continued preferring it to "Indian" through much of the first half of the seventeenth century. A cultural distance is of course implied in "Salvage," but not a racial one to any significant degree; the latter begins to be implied strongly only with the use of "Indian."

help to explain what is the most outstanding element in the entire history
of the French experience in America: the relative harmony and intimacy
of the relationship with the Indian. This is a subject that has been much
romanticized about, and at the outset it would be salutary to remember
that the French killed Indians too, and that, above all, they would surely
have killed many more had they come to America in numbers as great as
those in which Spaniards and Englishmen came. Until well into the seventeenth century, Frenchmen came to the New World primarily to fish and
to trade with the Indian, and only rarely to establish full-fledged, socially
and economically self-sufficient colonies. The typical French-American of
that epoch was not the householder with his permanent plot of land and
growing family, but the solitary wilderness adventurer seeking to make
his fortune in pelts and then return home to France. The nature of his
commerce required that he live with the Indian on terms as friendly as
possible, and his way of life required that he emulate and learn from the
Indian as much as he could. The French have always been hardy
travelers, and those among them who went to America were often the
hardiest of Frenchmen. For many of them, the journey into the American
forest among the Indians was a return to the ideal world of their Gallic
ancestors, preserved in their racial memory and assimilated into their
newer, merely fifteen-hundred-year-old Romance culture like the elements of a pot-au-feu.

Yet, as with good cookery, the French relationship to the American
landscape had to be developed slowly. There is no Arcadian enthusiasm
in Jacques Cartier's account of his first experience of the Canadian shore
in 1534:

> If the soil were as good as the harbors are, it were a great
> commodity: but it is not to be called the New Land, but rather
> stones and wild crags, and a place fit for wild beasts, for . . .
> I did not see a cartload of good earth: yet went I on shore
> in many places, and in the island of white sand, there is noth-
> ing else but moss and small thorns scattered here and there,
> withered and dry. To be short, I believe that this was the land
> that God allotted to Cain.

He had no intention of sojourning amidst this: in this first voyage, and
again in 1535, he was looking primarily for a way *through* it, a northwest
passage to Cathay. By 1535, he was already looking for something else
as well that would be the main preoccupation of his third and last American voyage in 1541, something in keeping with the Spanish New World
tradition: a fabled kingdom of Saguenay, described to him by Indians,
which would have been a northern Peru had it existed. It was not until

1542 that there arrived, in Cartier's wake, the first serious French attempt to settle in Canada, an expedition commanded by Jean-François de La Roque, the Sieur de Roberval, a nobleman of Protestant inclinations. Roberval's company included a number of high-born ladies and gentlemen, whom he evidently intended to establish as his vassals in a kind of feudal domain; possibly one of the purposes of the colony, which was chartered by François I and which was established on the St. Lawrence a short distance to the southwest of modern Quebec City, was to provide a safety valve for Protestants such as New England later became. But after one harsh Canadian winter had taken its toll in lives and in resolution, Roberval and his colonists returned to France. After that, French-Canadian history was not to be resumed for another sixty years.

The records of this first chapter of French history in the New World do not provide any overwhelming evidence of the special quality of understanding that was later to emerge in the relationship between Frenchmen and Indians. There is no particular fondness to be discerned in Cartier's initial description of the natives, possibly Beothuks, whom he encountered in the Gulf of St. Lawrence:

> There are men of an indifferent good stature and bigness, but wild and unruly: they wear their hair tied on the top like a wreath of hay, and put a wooden pin within it, or any other such thing instead of a nail, and with them they bind certain birds' feathers. They are clothed with beasts' skins as well the men as women, but that the women go somewhat straiter and closer in their garments than the men do, with their waists girded; they paint themselves with certain roan colors: their boats are made of the bark of birch trees, with the which they fish and take great store of seals, and as far as we could understand since our coming thither, that is not their habitation, but they come from the mainland out of hotter countries, to catch the said seals and other necessaries for their living.

The first confrontations between Cartier's men and the Savages show a combination of wariness and would-be friendliness on the part of the Frenchmen that is not palpably different from the comportment of Columbus and his men in 1492 and 1493. But by the time of his second expedition in 1535, Cartier seems to have learned a good deal about relations with the Indian, and his encounters that year up the St. Lawrence, among the relatively sophisticated peoples — possibly Hurons, but there is no certainty about this — living in the villages of Stadaconé and Hochelaga, which correspond to modern Quebec City and Montreal, show the emergence of a considerable warmth. "In which place of Hochelaga," he writes of the latter town,

and all the way we went, we met with many of those countrymen, who brought us fish and such other victuals as they had,
still dancing and greatly rejoicing at our coming. Our captain
to lure them in, and to keep them our friends, to recom-
pense them, gave them knives, beads, and such small trifles,
wherewith they were greatly satisfied. So soon as we were
come near Hochelaga, there came to meet us above a thousand
persons, men, women and children, who afterward did as
friendly and merrily entertain and receive us as any father
would do his child, which he had not of long time seen, the
men dancing on one side, the women on another, and likewise
the children on another: after that they brought us great store
of fish, and of their bread made of millet, casting them into our
boats so thick, that you would have thought it to fall from
heaven. Which when our captain saw, he with many of his
company went on shore: so soon as ever we were aland they
came clustering about us, making very much of us, bringing
their young children in their arms, only to have our captain
and his company to touch them, making signs and shows of
great mirth and gladness, that lasted more than half an hour.

This euphoria prevailed throughout the entire Cartier sojourn that year,
to such an extent that the Frenchmen were allowed to take home with
them several Indian leaders, who volunteered for the honor. The idea was
that they were to become interpreters and eventually return to Canada;
but Cartier could not obtain the king's support for another voyage until
1541, by which time all the Indians he had brought to France had died.
His last sojourn in Canada was marked by tense and increasingly hostile
relations with the Indians; Roberval fared better with them, but it was
a relationship that had no time to develop.

This quality of mere tentativeness continued to dog French efforts to
settle in the New World through the remainder of the sixteenth century.
In 1555 a daring group of French colonists, once again led by a nobleman
of Protestant tendencies, Nicolas Durand de Villegagnon, established
themselves on an island in the mouth of the Rio de Janeiro, and in the
teeth, as it were, of Portuguese Brazil. The Portuguese would not stand
for it, and by 1558 they were able to disperse and destroy the colony,
though their ability to do this was unquestionably aided by the internal
disintegration of *La France Antarctique,* as the colony was called, over
the preceding three years: for the Protestant and the Catholic settlers
were at one another's throats. A more solidly Protestant group of French
colonists then planted themselves in Florida starting in 1562, north of the
Spaniards at the mouth of the St. John's River. There seems to have been
little internal strife among this group of settlers, who represent the nearest

equivalent ever attempted by Huguenots to the kind of Puritan common-wealth established in Massachusetts in the following century, but Spanish power in the area was still too great to permit their enterprise to succeed. In 1565 the colony was wiped out by a Spanish army that came up from St. Augustine, which was founded for this very purpose. A French raid three years later wreaked vengeance upon the new Spanish colony, but nevertheless the history of French Florida was over.

The French colonists showed signs of a special concern for the Indian during both of these short-lived efforts. The Brazilian expedition pro-duced two significant books in later years, one written by a Catholic veteran of it, the other by a Protestant one, and though their main pur-pose was to polemicize with one another over what happened, they nevertheless devoted considerable space to essays into Indian ethnology — essays that, incidentally, seem largely to derive from a common written source. Both of the authors, the Catholic André Thevet, whose *Singular-itéz de la France antarctique* appeared in Paris in 1558, and the Huguenot Jean de Léry, whose *Histoire d'un voyage faict en la terre du Brésil* was published in Geneva in 1577, show a high degree of sympathetic interest in the Indian, although the latter's Protestantism adds an extra dimension to his attitude. Writing about the cannibalism of the Brazilian natives, Léry cannot resist observing that the ritual eating of men who have been honorably killed in battle is not nearly so deplorable as what the Catholics had done five years before at the Massacre of St. Bartholomew. In gen-eral, he seems more sensitive than Thevet to the claims of an outsider people to the validity of their own customs and beliefs.

An even more distinctly Protestant sympathy comes out of one of the most important narratives of the Florida expedition, written in London in 1586 by Jacques le Moyne de Morgues, who had been the colony's map-maker and artist. A heightened solicitousness toward the Indian emerges in one of his very first paragraphs:

> Upon our arrival in New France [in this case, Florida], we found the seashore crowded with native men and women, who kept up large fires. At first we thought it necessary to be on guard against them, but very soon we realized that the last thing in their minds was to harm us. On the contrary, they gave numerous proofs of their friendly intentions. They were filled with admiration when they found that our flesh was so much softer and more tender than their own, and they praised our garments, which were so different from their. The gifts we received from them were the things they valued most, being useful either for the preservation of their lives or for the protection of their bodies. They brought us grains of roasted maize, ground into flour, or whole ears of it, smoked lizards or

other wild animals which they considered great delicacies, and various kinds of roots, some for food, others for medicine. And when they discovered that we were more interested in metals and minerals, they gave us some of these as well. [Our captain], finding that our men were cheating the Indians, forbade on pain of death any trading for gold, silver, or minerals unless it was put in the common stock for the benefit of all.

Eventually, the French colonists in Florida had some trouble with the Indians despite the favorable atmosphere of this opening scene, but mainly because the French were only just learning that to befriend one tribe meant becoming the enemy of another.

Le Moyne, who painted a group of watercolors that provided the most striking set of visual portraits of the North American Indian yet made, was representative of a northern European counterpart to what we have called the pro-Indian intelligentsia of Spain that was emerging in the late sixteenth century. Appearing at various moments in Switzerland, France, the Netherlands, and England, this tendency can be as firmly identified with a strain of Protestant humanism as the Spanish one was with a certain current of New Christian religiosity. But it must be understood that this strain does not correspond to the broad sectarian divisions of the day that have become standardized by posterity.° The true core of this outlook was not in some one of the various religious doctrines that were making their way through Europe like wildfire, but in a distillation of religious and other cultural attitudes that were, for a certain moment at least, primarily French and at least quasi-Protestant, and that were colored by the strongly anti-Spanish attitudes engendered on one ground or another in France, the Netherlands, and England during the late sixteenth century. Perhaps the principal literary source of inspiration for this outlook was Las Casas's *Brief Relation of the Destruction of the Indies,* by now available in the languages of these northern countries, which served to place Spain before the eyes of the world in something like the role that the United States played during the era of the Vietnam War: it was above all resentment or hatred toward the great power involved that

---

° If it seems to have particular strength among French Huguenots of the late sixteenth century, this does not mean that there is anything particularly Calvinist about it: on the contrary, when the Calvinist element is quite strong in any group's religiosity, as among the Puritans of Massachusetts, this particular brand of humanism tends to subside. It is noteworthy that where this tendency had special force in the Netherlands, it was primarily among Remonstrants, those who opposed the strict Calvinism of the religious establishment that took over the country during the course of the long and ultimately successful revolt against Spanish rule. Likewise, in England, the current of pro-Indian humanism generally flowed more freely among Anglicans than among Puritans, despite some notable exceptions among the latter, which we shall consider in their place.

fanned the flames of passionate admiration for the beleaguered non-European people across the sea.

If Las Casas is the principal source, it therefore seems especially appropriate that the outstanding spokesman north of the Pyrenees of this pro-Indian humanism of the late sixteenth century should also have been a descendant of New Christians: Michel de Montaigne. Although his father was of old French aristocratic stock, Montaigne's mother, Antoinette de Loupes, was the daughter of a family of Sephardic refugees whose name had been López. The Bordeaux region, in which Montaigne was born in 1533 and which remained his home throughout his life, had in fact long been a principal refuge for Spanish New Christians, and though the open practice of Judaism was no more legal on French than on Spanish soil, the secret practice of it was considerably easier there. Not that there is a whiff of secret Judaism in Montaigne's family that we know of, but there were on the other hand distinct Protestant tendencies among them, and though the great essayist did not openly throw in his lot with the Huguenots, as two of his brothers did, he nevertheless was sympathetic to their cause. In general, the religious and cultural variety of Bordeaux in that day must have been very influential in the formation of Montaigne's skeptical and cosmopolitan spirit, for which established creeds were merely overly constricting containers imposed upon inner human freedom; and so also were the established cultures that so righteously and unthinkingly sought to inflict themselves upon the ways of life of other men.

Montaigne's view of the Indian, nurtured by his reading of Léry and others, is best summed up by this passage from his essay, *Of Cannibals* (here presented in the translation of the Elizabethan John Florio), which describes also the profound effect upon him of a brief but significant personal experience:

> Three of that nation, ignorant how dear the knowledge of our corruptions will one day cost their repose, security, and happiness, and how their ruin shall proceed from this commerce, which I imagine is already well advanced (miserable as they are to have suffered themselves to be so cozened by a desire of new-fangled novelties, and to have quit the calmness of their climate, to come and see ours) were at Rouen in the time of our late King Charles the Ninth, who talked with them a great while. They were showed our fashions, our pomp, and the form of a fair City; afterward some demanded their advice, and would needs know of them what things of note and admirable they had observed amongst us.
>
> They answered three things, the last of which I have forgotten, and am very sorry for it; the other two I yet remember.

They said: "First, they found it very strange, that so many tall men with long beards, strong and well-armed, as it were about the King's person (it is very likely they meant the Switzers of his guard) would submit themselves to obey a beardless child, and that we did not rather choose one amongst them to command the rest. Secondly (they have a manner of phrase whereby they call men but a moiety one of another), they had perceived, there were men amongst us full gorged with all sorts of commodities, and others which hunger-starved, and bare with need and poverty, begged at their gates: and found it strange, these moieties so needy could endure such an injustice, and that they took not the others by the throat, or set fire on their houses."

I talked a good while with one of them, but I had so bad an interpreter, and who did so ill aprehend my meaning, and who through his foolishness was so troubled to conceive my imaginations, that I could draw no great matter from him. Touching that point, wherein I demanded of him, what good he received by the superiority he had among his countrymen (for he was a Captain and our mariners called him King) he told me, it was to march foremost in any charge of war. Further, I asked him, how many men did follow him. He showed me a distance of place, to signify they were as many as might be contained in so much ground, which I guessed to be about four or five thousand men. Moreover I demanded, if when wars were ended, all his authority expired; he answered, that he had only this left him, which was, that when he went on progress, and visited the villages depending of him, the inhabitants prepared paths and highways athwart the hedges of their woods, for him to pass through at ease.

All that is not very ill; but what of that? They wear no kind of breeches nor hosen.

The calm skepticism of these observations is succeeded by an angrier mood some ten years later, in his essay *Of Coaches*, written by Montaigne after a thorough reading of Las Casas and other writers on the Spanish New World conquests, and during the time of the looming threat of the Spanish Armada:

When I consider that stern-untamed obstinacy [he writes now of the Indians], and undaunted vehemence, wherewith so many thousands of men, of women and children, do so infinite times present themselves unto inevitable dangers, for the defense of their Gods and liberty: this generous obstinacy to endure all extremities, all difficulties and death, more easily and willingly, than basely to yield unto their domination, of whom they have so abominably been abused: some of them choosing rather to starve with hunger and fasting, being taken, than to accept food at their enemy's hands, so basely victorious: I perceive, that whosoever had undertaken them man to man, without odds of arms, of experience or of number, should have had as dangerous a war, or perhaps more, as any we see amongst us.

In the earlier passage, the spirit of the New Christian, with its characteristic anthropological insight and innate sense of the right of any people — whether they wear breeches and hose or not — to be culturally autonomous, is clearly present; so also is that of the classicist, admiring men who seem to have gone on living in the untrammeled purity of an Ovidian golden age. These are attitudes with which we have already become familiar south of the Pyrenees. But the second passage suggests something more distinctly French, not only in its specifically anti-Spanish undertone, but also in its idealization of the vigorous manhood of the Indians: not even Las Casas made such claims about their fighting abilities, and most of their Spanish defenders were inclined to stress their relative physical weakness, at least so far as war was concerned. The element of Celtic romance is present in this latter passage, of eagerness to tout the virility of men who lived, like one's own ancestors, in close harmony with nature. In his set of attitudes toward the Indian, as in his own personal background, Montaigne thus forms a link between the world of the Spanish pro-Indian intelligentsia and that of its Protestant-humanist equivalent to the north. He more than anyone else brought the pro-Indian doctrine into the part of the world that was now seizing the initiative in American discovery and colonization.

19

England Takes on the
Ocean Sea

D URING HIS VOYAGE on the western ocean in the middle of the sixth century, there was a moment when St. Brendan perceived that Satan had taken command of one of the monks in his company. They had all eaten dinner on an island, and then:

> After they had fallen asleep, St. Brendan witnessed the machinations of the Evil One. He saw a little Ethiopian boy holding out a silver necklace and juggling with it in front of the monk.

The Irish holy man, or at any rate the ninth-century hagiographer who wrote down his adventures, was evidently familiar enough with the apocryphal literature from the southeast about St. Thomas and others to know what that little Ethiopian represented. Brendan spent the rest of the night in prayer, but it was to no avail, and as the company was about to depart he was forced to announce to the others that a

> ". . . brother of ours is hiding a silver necklace in his bosom; a devil handed it to him last night."
> At this the monk flung the necklace from him, fell at Brendan's feet, and cried: "Father, I have sinned. Pardon me and pray for me lest I perish."

The rest of the monks cast themselves to the ground and begged the Lord to save their brother's soul. Brendan lifted the culprit to his feet and the rest of the monks stood up — to see a little Ethiopian boy pop out of the culprit's breast and cry out: "Man of God, why are you expelling me from the home I have lived in these past seven years? You are casting me off from my inheritance."

After a final imprecation from Brendan, the guilty monk and the devil both died, the former ascending to heaven in reward for his last-minute repentance, the latter going down to "rest only in Hell."

Thus the black Devil is purged from northwestern waters at the very mythological beginnings of British venture into them. He — or rather, his carnal feminine counterpart — does not reappear in that region until nearly a thousand years later, and then only as a slave. "Of Ane Blak-Moir" ("Of a Blackamoor"), by the Scottish poet William Dunbar, celebrates a jousting contest held in 1506 or 1507 at the court of King James IV of Scotland, at which the ironic guest of honor is one of the undoubtedly very rare pieces of human cargo from the African slaving ships of the day to have made her way this far north. The poem, whose spirit, like the occasion, is a bit of Renaissance horseplay, provides possibly the earliest attempt to describe a Negro in detail that we have in what might roughly be called the English language. It begins in mock courtly tones:

> Lang heff I maed of ladyes quhytt,
> Nou of ane blak I will indytt,
>   That landet furth of the last schippis;
> Quhou fain wald I descryve perfytt,
>   My ladye with the mekle lippis.

("Long have I made [poems] of ladies white" — the "quh" stands for our "wh" throughout — "Now of a black I will indite,/ That landed forth of the last ships;/ Who I fain would describe perfectly,/ My lady with the big lips.")

The last line only hints at what is now to come, for the next two of the poem's five stanzas contain as gross a caricature of Negro traits as any lowbrow, minstrel-mongering American humorist has ever created in more recent times:

> Quhou schou is tute mowitt lyk ane aep,
> And lyk a gangarall onto gaep;
>   And quhou hir schort catt nois up skippis;
> And quhou scho schynes lyk ony saep;
>   My ladye with the mekle lippis.

> *Quhen schou is claid in reche apparrall,*
> *Schou blinkis als brycht as ane tar barrell;*
>   *Quhen schou was born, the son tholit clippis,*
> *The nycht be fain faucht in hir querrell:*
>   *My ladye with the mekle lippis.*

("She who has a protruding mouth like an ape,/ And is like a toad in her gape;/ And whose short cat's-nose turns up;/ And she who shines like any soap;/ My lady," etc. "When she is clad in rich apparel,/ She looks as bright as a tar barrel;/ When she was born, the sun was eclipsed;/ The night wanted to fight in her defense:/ My lady," etc.) With the task of burlesque description out of the way, the poet now proceeds to his ultimately bawdy purpose:

> *Quhai for hir saek, with speir and scheld,*
> *Preiffis maest mychttelye in the feld,*
>   *Sall kis and withe hir go in grippis;*
> *And fra thyne furth hir luff sall weld:*
>   *My ladye with the mekle lippis.*

("Whoever, for her sake, with spear and shield,/ Proves himself most mightily in the field,/ Shall kiss and with her go to grips;/ And shall thenceforth possess her love:/ My lady," etc.) So much for the lucky winner; but as for the loser:

> *And quhai in felde receaves schaem,*
> *And tynis thair his knychtlie naem,*
>   *Sall cum behind and kis hir hippis,*
> *And nevir to uther confort claem:*
>   *My ladye with the mekle lippis.*

("And whoever receives shame in the field,/ And loses there his knightly name,/ Shall come behind and kiss her hips,/ And never to other comfort claim:/ My lady with the big lips.") The atmosphere now takes on a hint of the witches' sabbath, in which the kissing of the hind parts was a regular feature of the ritual. In general, the poem is filled with a kind of forbidden sniggering which was to become widespread in some parts of American society by the nineteenth century, manifesting a mood whereby libidinous and even perverse expressions of a sort that were not permitted in "polite" — that is, white — circles, were given free rein in relation to Blacks.

The long hiatus of British inexperience with Blacks, and with darker southern peoples in general, had produced an atmosphere of unreality in the perception of them. Lacking any of the sophistication about the various racial colorations of mankind that was so natural a part of the Iberian legacy, the British until well into the sixteenth century formed their myths about the Negro without knowing much or anything about him in fact. Dunbar's experience was an unusually concrete one, and he shows it: his vivid caricature of Negro features is the response of a shocked naïf at a sight unlike anything he had seen in his life before. It is nasty, and it does not bode well for the future, but there also hovers over it a certain innocence that would be lost to its Anglo-American counterparts of later centuries. Its most sinister component is the mood of dark licentiousness provoked by its subject that could not have come from Dunbar's own national experience, but was clearly an import from the south, like the Black woman he describes. For all its negative aspects, the poem still by and large represents a moment of unformed relationships and attitudes between Britishers and Negroes: the myths of the south and the East had long before taken their toll in Britain, but experience still had to make its own impression on the issue.

The British lack of sophistication concerning Blacks was still very much present in 1555 when Richard Eden, one of the most learned geographers of his day, whom we have already met as the first English translator of Pigafetta's account of the Magellan voyage around the world, wrote these lines:

> It is to be understood that the people which now inhabit the regions of the coast of Guinea and the middle parts of Africa, as Libya the Inner, and Nubia, with divers other great and large regions about the same, were in old time called Aethiopes and Nigritae, which we now call Moors, Moorens, or Negroes, a people of beastly living, without a God, law, religion, or commonwealth, and so scorched and vexed with the heat of the sun that in many places they curse it, when it riseth.

The fiction of men cursing the sun each morning was to appeal to the Elizabethan imagination; but the identification of a Negro simply as a "Moor," which Shakespeare among others was to accept, bespeaks some vagueness about who these scorched people really were. One suspects that many Englishmen of the time thought blackness of complexion began somewhere just south of Madrid. Undoubtedly Eden himself shared the impression conveyed by Pigafetta's narrative that dark men of the south were pretty much the same in the New World as the Old. In midcentury Britain men were not yet prone to make the distinction between the darker-skinned peoples of the southeast and of the southwest that Iberians had begun making a generation or two before.

The early British sense of the south Atlantic peoples is conveyed in a contemporary account of the voyages of the Plymouth merchant, William Hawkins, father of the more celebrated Sir John Hawkins, who between 1530 and 1532 made three profitable sallies into the Ocean Sea, stopping first at Guinea, "where he trafficked with the Negroes, and took of them elephants' teeth, and other commodities which that place yieldeth," and then at Brazil, where he traded with the Indians. In Brazil, the narrator is happy to tell us, the elder Hawkins

> used there such discretion, and behaved himself so wisely with those savage people, that he grew into great familiarity and friendship with them. Insomuch that in his second voyage, one of the savage kings of the country of Brazil was contented to take ship with him, and to be transported hither into England: whereunto Mr. Hawkins agreed, leaving behind in the country as a pledge for his safety and return again one Martin Cockeram of Plymouth. This Brazilian king, being arrived, was brought up to London and presented to King Henry VIII, lying as then at Whitehall; at the sight of whom the king and all the nobility did not a little marvel, and not without cause; for in his cheeks were holes made according to their savage manner, and therein small bones were planted, standing an inch out from the said holes, which in his own country was reputed for a great bravery. He had also another hole in his nether lip, wherein was set a precious stone about the bigness of a pea. All his apparel, behavior and gesture were very strange to the beholders.

The Brazilian king remained among the English for almost a year, according to the narrative, after which Hawkins brought him along on his third voyage, intending to return him home; "but it fell out in the way that by a change of air and alteration of diet the said savage king died at sea." The life of the pledge, Martin Cockeram, was feared for as a result; but "the savages, being fully persuaded of the honest dealing of our men with their prince," returned him unharmed. It would seem that good old Englishmen could do no wrong in their fair dealings in those days, even with naked savages. Whether this euphoria was as great in fact as in the accounting of it or not, there is at any rate no reason to assume that it was any different on the African than on the Brazilian coast. There was no slave-trading yet, so that the particular hue of the dark cheeks could hardly have mattered. Brazilian and Negro were equally strange, but both evidently were honest merchants as far as William Hawkins was concerned.

Guinea seems to have become a prominent target of English seagoing traders from the very beginning of their more ambitious venturing out on the Ocean Sea. English trading voyages were going there at least as far back as 1482, perhaps because the ancient national intimacy with Portugal attracted Englishmen to its routes, alternately as friends or as rivals. Clearly by William Hawkins's time there was a concerted effort afoot to cash in on the Portuguese Oceanic system, for this was a period of superficial Anglo-Spanish friendship, and it was therefore acceptable behavior for patriotic Englishmen to needle Castile's old competitor. In the 1550s, there were several important English trading voyages to Guinea, by Thomas Windham, John Lok, William Towerson, and others, who produced significant narratives of their experiences and contributed to a suddenly growing English geographical sophistication about this area. Rivalry with Spain was now looming on the scene, but this was accompanied by another element that was far more sinister: the transatlantic slave trade, which was suddenly reaching new lucrative heights in this period after the passage and gradual enforcement of the New Laws of the Indies.

It was during several early voyages to the Canaries that John Hawkins had learned, according to the anonymous narrator of his first voyage from Guinea to the New World, "that Negroes were very good merchandise in Hispaniola, and that store of Negroes might easily be had upon the coast of Guinea." Hawkins resolved — quite illegally, from the official Spanish and Portuguese points of view — to enter into this trade. With his good family connections and obvious talents, Hawkins easily won commercial backing, and sailed from England with a fleet of three ships in October, 1562. Stopping first at Tenerife in the Canaries, "where he received friendly entertainment," he moved on to Sierra Leone on the Guinea coast, "where he stayed some good time, and got into his possession, partly by the sword, and partly by other means, to the number of 300 Negroes at the least, besides other merchandises which that country yieldeth." The "friendly entertainment" at Tenerife and the "other means" of obtaining Negroes and other commodities at Sierra Leone both hint through the otherwise guarded tones of the narrative that at least some Spanish and Portuguese colonial officials, always ready to break the rules for a little personal profit-making, were helping this man officially designated as a pirate by their governments. This would also be true on the other side of the Atlantic, when

> with this prey, he sailed over the Ocean Sea unto the Island of Hispaniola, and arrived first at the port of Isabella: and there he had reasonable utterance of his English commodities, as also of some part of his Negroes, trusting the Spaniards no further, than that by his own strength he was able still to master them. From the port of Isabella he went to Puerto de Plata, where he made like sales, standing always upon his guard: from thence

also he sailed to Monte Christi, another port on the north side of Hispaniola, and the last place of his touching, where he had peaceable traffic, and made vent of the whole number of his Negroes: for which he received in those three places by way of exchange such quantity of merchandise that he did not only lade his own three ships with hides, ginger, sugars, and some quantity of pearls, but he freighted also two other hulks with hides and other like commodities, which he sent into Spain.

He returned home in September, 1563, "with prosperous success and much gain to himself" as well as to his financial backers. Much of the old English innocence was now being lost.

Yet there remains something peculiarly dispassionate and, in the English manner, businesslike in the racial attitudes that seem to permeate this and Hawkins's two subsequent voyages between Guinea and the New World, in 1564–1565 and 1567–1568. The various narratives show no particular animus against the Negroes, and the descriptions of African and of New World natives still tend to treat both equally as exotics. "These people are all black," says one Hawkins narrative about the natives of the Cape Verde region, "and are called Negroes, without any apparel, saving before their privities: of stature goodly men, and well liking by reason of their food, which passeth all other Guineans for kine, goats, pullen, rice, fruits and fish. . . . These men also are more civil than any other, because of their daily traffic with the Frenchmen, and are of nature very gentle and loving." The men thus described seem far more congenial than the Chichimecs of Pánuco in northern Mexico as described by Miles Philips, one of Hawkins's sailors stranded in that region in 1568; he saw them as "a warlike kind of people, which are in a manner as Cannibals, although they do not feed upon man's flesh as Cannibals do. . . . And they use to wear their hair long, even down to their knees; they do also color their faces green, yellow, red and blue, which maketh them to seem very ugly and terrible to behold." Hawkins would no doubt have traded in Chichimecs or any other Indians just as well as in Negroes if they had been what the market demanded. As for the free Negroes he did business with on the Guinea coast, he and his men clearly felt no particular difference between them and any of the other exotics of the southern ocean, in the Old World and in the New. The slaves belonged to a different frame of reference: somewhere along the line they had become commodities, so little thought of in human terms that even their blackness was not held against other men who were not slaves, by Hawkins's generation at any rate. In this moment, there was no moral fury or complexity surrounding the matter-of-fact acceptance of the Portuguese legacy of Black slavery by worldly men like Hawkins; it would take a very different kind of spirit, now waiting in the wings, to come onstage with the idea that the fact of slavery represented a divine decision against Blacks in general.

Nevertheless, Hawkins's deadly brand of matter-of-factness had obviously taken its toll in the history of Atlantic race relations, and the link between him and the future slave system of Anglo-America is obvious as we contemplate his career in the 1560s. Yet in a brief period that immediately followed his ascendancy, a possibility did present itself for an entirely different history of race relations in the English New World.

In the fall of 1568, at the end of his third sojourn in the Indies, Hawkins arrived one day at the Mexican port of San Juan de Ulúa, near Vera Cruz, because some of his ships were badly in need of repair. Presumably he thought that his tried and true technique of bribing Spanish officials would serve him in as good stead here as it had elsewhere, and it almost did; but this was a port of call of the Spanish treasure fleet, which sailed into the harbor only two days after Hawkins's arrival. Hawkins thereupon tried also to buy off the fleet commander, who seemed at first to acquiesce, but who then staged a surprise attack. All but two of the English ships were captured, and one of those that got away, the *Minion,* under Hawkins's command, was left in such bad shape and with supplies so depleted that half its crew had to be unloaded on the coast of Pánuco before it could safely make its way back home. Miles Philips, whose observations on the Chichimecs were quoted just above, was one of the number of survivors of that group who first had to undergo capture by the Spanish and trial before the Inquisition as Protestant heretics before they eventually got free; others did not survive the experience. San Juan de Ulúa became the "Alamo" of Anglo-Spanish relations, marking the unofficial beginning point of a state of war between the two countries that was to last thirty-six years. From now on, Englishmen were to deal with the Spanish overseas empire not by the Hawkins method of feeding upon it, but by assaulting it, and trying to destroy as much of it as possible and replace it with something of their own.

The preeminent figure in this new epoch was Sir Francis Drake, who as a young man in his late twenties had participated in Hawkins's third voyage to the Indies, and had in fact been captain of the *Judith,* the second of the two ships that survived San Juan de Ulúa. In the ensuing years he carried on what seems to have been a personal vendetta for San Juan de Ulúa, waging against the Spaniards a private war from which he emerges as one of the most celebrated seagoing fighters in history. The climax of this phase of his career was a series of raids on the port of Nombre de Dios in Panama, where the treasure from Peru was regularly loaded onto ships heading back to Spain, culminating in his capture of a substantial portion of the treasure in 1573. This escapade is important in the history of England's early overseas race relations as well as in that of her rise to world power: for Drake and his men received crucial assistance in it from the *cimarrones*, or Maroons, of Darien.

Drake's alliance with these communities of escaped Blacks and Indians and their cross-bred children living in the forests of the isthmus, inherited by him from French captains still influential in the area, was a stroke of great cleverness on his part, since no other people at once knew the countryside so well and hated the Spaniards so thoroughly. Yet there also was an element of idealism in it. The son of a preacher, Drake displayed some of the traits of the best kind of Protestant humanism of his generation despite his Puritan tendencies. He left little written testimony to his thinking behind him, but his activities bespeak a conception on his part of an English America that would include free Blacks and Indians living in equality with white men. Not that he imagined an English America with anything like the massive concentrations of population, white and non-white alike, that would already be coming into being there only a century later; he probably envisioned only a network of relatively small English outposts in the New World, holding back the Spanish influence and occasionally reclaiming territory from it. Such territory would include small Black and Indian populations who, as Drake saw it, were to be free under English law. It was a vision of moderate decency, but one that was quite advanced for its day. The streak of English innocence about racial matters was still persisting at this time, and had now reached a generation of moral men whose compassion extended, for the moment at least, not only to the Indian but to the usually forgotten Negro as well. There were literary manifestations of this feeling, in the travel narratives, and also in the publication, in 1569, of Underdowne's translation of Heliodorus' *Ethiopica;* a generation later there would be *Othello*.

It is obvious that certain patterns of profit-making that had become well established in the New World were going to demolish this worthy but feeble structure of racial morality when the time came for Anglo-American colonization; but were there perhaps also conditions in the very culture that produced it militating against it from the outset? There does happen to be a peculiar cultural irony in the Anglo-Spanish relationship at this time. For Englishmen, the sixteenth century was an era of alternating attraction and aversion with regard to Spain, the first half marked primarily by an aristocratic attraction that culminated in the marriage of Queen Mary to the young prince who was soon to be Philip II, the second half mainly by popular aversion and by war. Yet even in the second half, some cultivated Englishmen — and not only Catholics — continued to feel the attraction, discernible in literature, in manners, and in the personality of a man like Drake, who spoke Spanish fluently and devoted his life to a kind of passionate, albeit bellicose, relationship with the Spaniards. Figuratively as well as literally, Drake's customary route to America was the southern one, and his vision of an Anglo-American society that would include free Blacks and Indians was not so much a repudiation of the Spanish-American way as a correction of it. The institution of slavery that it sanctioned was not acceptable to him, but its racial conditions were.

Drake's idea of a multiracial society was far more Spanish than English, however. For a while longer, the English enterprise in North America was to be dominated by men who thought as he did, but eventually it would be taken over by men who felt no such attraction to the Spanish world of the south, and to its particular racial composition. They disliked Spaniards and Blacks just as much as they thought they disliked slavery, and their war against Spanish America was not founded, the way Drake's was, in a desire to take over as much of it as possible and Anglicize its existing qualities, but was fought primarily to prevent its spread into the northern regions that they found more congenial. The irony was that, when Black slavery finally infiltrated their world in spite of themselves, they — or their spiritual offspring — discovered that it was above all Blacks they despised and not slavery, and that in order to shore up their white society against the former they endorsed the latter even more vigorously than the Spaniards had. Drake's vision of a society, multiracial in the Spanish manner but made just by English laws, was in the long run perverted by English racism into a slave system even more unjust than the Spanish one.

Significantly, this antisouthern outlook was finding its own route to America at the very time when Drake was at his height. After finally setting out into the Ocean Sea in earnest, England had soon floated to her natural seagoing level in the north. Indeed, attracted like her old friend Portugal to the Orient, she first concentrated her fleets on the northeast before turning with special emphasis toward the northwest. In 1555 the Muscovy Company was chartered to trade with the tsar by the Arctic Sea route, and for the next twenty years English ships brought back pelts and tales, not only of the tsar's chill Byzantine court, but of wild Samoeds (or Samoyeds) in the Siberian northeast.

By the middle of the seventies, however, the attractions of this trade had brought another idea into being: a revived hope for discovering a northwest passage to Muscovy and Cathay. Consequently, Martin Frobisher made three voyages, in 1576, 1577, and 1578, into the subarctic ice of Baffin Island, mainly exploring the inlet that has since been named Frobisher Bay in his honor, hoping in vain that it would open out into a route to Cathay. In the course of these, he discovered what was thought to be gold on the peninsula south of Frobisher Bay, which he named *Meta Incognita* ("the Unknown Promontory"), and this became an additional incentive for exploring the area. He was followed on this route by John Davis, who made three voyages to the same area between 1585 and 1587. Meanwhile, these advances to the northwest had opened a route of possible colonization in more temperate places just to the south of it: in 1578 and 1583, Sir Humphrey Gilbert made two unsuccessful attempts to colonize the region then known as Norumbega, corresponding roughly to northern Maine and the Maritime Provinces.

The most vivid descriptions of Frobisher's three voyages are from the hand of one of his captains, George Best, in an account first published in 1578. Best had also been to Muscovy, and was an enthusiast about the north, which he clearly envisioned as a whole English hemisphere of influence counterpoised against the Iberian one in the south: he did a sketch map of the world which bespeaks such a notion of symmetry, including a hopeful "Frobisher's Straits" in the far north to parallel Magellan's in the far south. The Spaniards could have their world, as far as Best was concerned; he shared none of Drake's obsession with it. The implied invidiousness of this outlook extends even to his descriptions of the newly encountered pagan peoples. He writes at length about those whom he and Frobisher came across in Meta Incognita, who presumably were Eskimos, and who bore a strong resemblance to the "Skraelings" of the Norse sagas about westward travel to Vinland and adjacent countries. Frobisher, like the Vikings, had some tough skirmishes with the natives of the northwest, and Best's passages on them therefore have a sometimes grudging quality; but his admiration for them shines through all the same, as when he writes:

> Their sullen and desperate nature doth herein manifestly appear, that a company of them being environed by our men on the top of a high cliff, so that they could by no means escape our hands, finding themselves in this case distressed, chose rather to cast themselves headlong down the rocks into the sea, and so be bruised and drowned, rather than to yield themselves to our men's mercies.

A "sullen" nature that chooses death rather than enslavement was, in the long run, bound to win more respect than disapproval from a man like Best, who clearly had in mind the example of heathen peoples who seemed to have behaved in exactly an opposite sen..e.

Best's admiration for the people of Meta Incognita becomes more unqualified when he talks about their abilities as hunters and fishermen — and, above all, about their personal morality. "They are very shamefast in bewraying the secrets of nature," he writes with wholehearted approval,

"and very chaste in the manner of their living." He provides a vivid illustration of this. In their second voyage, Frobisher's men had taken one
man captive, and then later also took a woman "cumbered with a suck-
ing child at her back," and brought the two together in the same quarters.
In the ensuing weeks, watchful English eyes noted how the man and the
woman, shyly at first, began striking up a close and highly dependent
relationship with one another. And yet,

> for so much as we could perceive, albeit they lived continually
> together, yet they did never use as man and wife, though the
> woman spared not to do all necessary things that appertained
> to a good housewife indifferently for them both, as in making
> clean their cabin, and every other thing that appertained to his
> ease: for when he was seasick, she would make him clean, she
> would kill and flea the dogs for their eating, and dress his meat.
> Only I think it worth the noting, the continency of them both:
> for the man would never shift himself, except he had first
> caused the woman to depart out of his cabin, and they both
> were most shamefast, lest any of their privy parts should be
> discovered, either of themselves, or any other body.

A solid, quasi-English morality, this, quite in harmony with the incipient
Puritan and middle-class outlooks of the day, which Best seems to share —
and one is tempted also to call it northern. Spiritual considerations aside,
of course, climate alone would have militated in Meta Incognita against
the nakedness that prevailed in the West Indies. But, whatever the reasons, we can behold these two natives of the far northwest — in the drawings of them made by the artist John White, who went along on the
voyage — wrapped as thoroughly as any good English lady or gentleman
might have been if venturing into the far north. Best stresses their universal northernness when he says:

> These people I judge to be a kind of Tartar, or rather a kind
> of Samoed, of the same sort and condition of life that the
> Samoeds be to the Northeastwards beyond Muscovy, who are
> called Samoeds, which is as much to say in the Muscovy tongue
> as eaters of themselves, and so the Russians their borderers do
> name them. And by late conference with a friend of mine
> (with whom I did sometime travel in the parts of Muscovy)
> who hath great experience of those Samoeds and people of the
> Northeast, I find that in all their manner of living, those people
> of the Northeast, and these of the Northwest are alike.

The wholesale rejection of the south that is implicit in all this emerges
in Best's remarks about complexion. Of the people he has just been
describing, he says:

> They are of the color of a ripe olive, which how it may come to pass, being born in so cold a climate, I refer to the judgment of others, for they are naturally born children of the same color and complexion that all the Americans are, which dwell under the Equinoctial line.

At first sight, these words seem to represent a healthy egalitarianism, stressing the view elaborated by Best at great length elsewhere that climate has no effect whatsoever upon the color of the skin. But his anti-climate theory of race is in fact the opposite of egalitarian, for its ultimate purpose is a condemnation of the Negro more devastating than any we have encountered so far among Europeans.

"I myself," he writes in his extended digression on climate and race, "have seen an Ethiopian as black as a coal brought into England, who taking a fair English woman to wife, begat a son in all respects as black as the father was, although England were his native country, and an English woman his mother: whereby it seemeth this blackness proceedeth rather of some natural infection of that man, which was so strong, that neither the nature of the clime, neither the good complexion of the mother concurring, could anything alter, and therefore, we cannot impute it to the nature of the clime." In its rejection of climate as a cause of skin color, this view of course represents a considerable advance in sophistication over Richard Eden's picture, drawn only twenty-three years earlier, of men cursing the sun that had scorched them black — an advance aided, evidently, by the presence of at least one Negro and possibly more now living in England and marrying there, to the chagrin of Best and no doubt many others. But the talk of "some natural infection" is ominous, and makes one long for the merely skin-deep contempt of Negro traits implied by the relatively innocent climate theory.

What we have here is a new form of the racial antisouthern outlook of Duarte Pacheco Pereira, Gomes Eannes de Zurara, and some of the medieval Arab racial theorists in their notion of a divinely accursed race, now even more vehement in a man for whom the Iberian and Arab worlds also are part of a south that he scorns. For the "natural infection" of the Blacks is, according to Best, ultimately the result of the Devil's work in relation to — and here again, we are on ancient and familiar ground — Noah and his three sons. The "Wicked Spirit," Best tells us, was eager to maintain evil in the world even after the Flood, and so when he found

> none but a father and three sons living, he so caused one of them to transgress and disobey his father's commandment, that after him all his posterity should be accursed. The fact of disobedience was this: When Noah at the commandment of God had made the Ark and entered therein, and the flood-gates of

heaven were opened, so that the whole face of the earth, every tree and mountain was covered with abundance of water, he straitly commanded his sons and their wives, that they should with reverence and fear behold the justice and mighty power of God, and that during the time of the Flood while they remained in the Ark, they should use continency, and abstain from carnal copulation with their wives: and many other precepts he gave unto them, and admonitions touching the justice of God, in revenging sin, and his mercy in delivering them, who nothing deserved it. Which good instructions and exhortations notwithstanding his wicked son Ham disobeyed, and being persuaded that the first child born after the Flood (by right and law of nature) should inherit and possess all the dominions of the earth, he contrary to his father's commandment while they were yet in the Ark, used company with his wife, and craftily went about thereby to disinherit the offspring of his other two brethren: for the which wicked and detestable fact, as an example for contempt of Almighty God, and disobedience of parents, God would a son should be born whose name was Cush, who not only itself, but all his posterity after him should be so black and loathsome, that it might remain a spectacle of disobedience to all the world.

We have come across the curse of Ham before, and even the view that blackness was one of the punishments implied in it, but Best has provided a new wrinkle: Ham's disobedience on the Ark, well before the scene involving Noah's drunkenness and curse that the Bible describes. The provenance of this new version is not clear, but its import is; there is no longer any room for the ambiguity left by the fact that Noah's Biblical curse is specifically against Canaan, and that the burden to be borne is mere servitude — Best's curse is against Cush, blackness is the issue, and God's permanent condemnation is the source of what the author now refers to more amply than before as a "natural infection of blood."

The biological tone here represents a purer racism than any we have seen with reference to the Negro so far, as pure as that which had been attained in Spain with reference to New Christians in the previous century. In rejecting climate as a source of significant differences among men, Best has come up with something deeper and more disturbing, an inborn and ineradicable set of differences that just happen to apply to men born in different parts of the world. There are, on the one hand, "our people of Meta Incognita (of whom and for whom this discourse is taken in hand)," as Best puts it — sober, hardworking and chaste. And on the other hand, there are men living in a place like Africa, which largely consists of "a cursed, dry, sandy, and unfruitful ground, fit for such a generation [meaning 'race'] to inhabit in," apparently because of the greed, insolence, and carnality of an ancestor who has also brought the curse of blackness upon them. How different these sons and daughters of the concupiscent Ham are from the people of Meta Incognita, to William Dunbar's delight and George Best's chagrin! But these are now different manifestations of God's good and bad graces. It is the divine light rather than the sun which has colored Best's conception of the races of man, and the results are far more devastating. In its most high-minded form this outlook preferred not to see either Negroes or slaves anyplace where Englishmen lived and governed. Their ideal world was St. Brendan's, a North Atlantic without any black devils lurking in it. But Black slaves were to arrive in Anglo-America all the same, and thanks to men like George Best, to find a racism already there to accommodate them.

20

Roanoke

BY THE EARLY 1580s a group favoring a program of English colonization in North America had come into being at Queen Elizabeth's court. Led by the ardently anti-Spanish Sir Francis Walsingham, who had been ambassador to Paris at the time of the St. Bartholomew massacre in 1572, it was in some ways a direct northern reaction to the recent experiences of France and Spain. Two cousins who both were named Richard Hakluyt, the elder one a lawyer, the younger a clergyman, both members of the group and geographers by true vocation, had established warm relations with some of the Huguenot leaders of the abortive French Florida colonies of the 1560s, and had seen to the translation of their writings. Closely associated with the Hakluyts was John Florio, the son of an Italian Protestant descended from Spanish New Christians, and a teacher of languages at Cambridge, who translated Montaigne's essays and Cartier's voyage narratives into English. Filled with a sense of Spanish cruelties and French failures at home and abroad, these men regarded themselves as heirs to the Protestant humanist mission in the New World.

But another historical experience, far more concrete and closer to home, and implying somewhat less exalted aims, also formed a significant part of this group's background. Several of its members — in particular the two half-brothers Sir Humphrey Gilbert and Sir Walter Raleigh —

had done military service in Ireland, to help, as Edmund Spenser put it, in the "reducing of that savage nation to better government and civility." The centuries-old aspiration to Anglicize Ireland, however, had proved to be as unmanageable a task as marching in military order through a bog, frustrated not only by the warlike prowess of its people, but also by the perennial tendency of the Anglo-Irish frontier lords to "go native." Efforts to establish an English system of law and land tenure had consistently failed outside the small enclave surrounding Dublin that was known as the Pale. In the more remote parts of the country, the "wild Irish" often seemed as primitive and exotic in English eyes as any heathen people overseas. The Elizabethan chronicler William Camden wrote about the arrival at court of an Irish leader in 1562:

> Now was Shan O'Neal come out of Ireland . . . with a guard of ax-bearing galloglasses [foot soldiers], bare-headed, with curled hair hanging down, yellow surplices dyed with saffron, or man's stale [urine], long sleeves, short coats, and hairy mantles: whom the English people gazed at with no less admiration than nowadays they do them of China and America.

Indeed, there were to be moments in the ensuing history of Ireland and of America when they both would seem to have fallen under the same English gaze. Colonization experiments had been begun by the English in Ireland only shortly before the idea of colonizing in America came to the fore, and during the 1580s, when Raleigh became involved in the Roanoke project we are about to examine, he spent much of the time in Ireland supervising the establishment of a colony there. For years and even for generations to come, Ireland was to be for many English adventurers a kind of way station westward, at which they either stopped for some time before going to America or settled down upon their return.

In some respects, then, Ireland played a role for England similar to that which the Canaries played for Spain. But it was the English Granada as well, for since the death of Queen Mary the Catholicism of Ireland had become a major element in the conflict with Protestant England, somewhat in the way that Islam was the main factor in Granada's conflict with Catholic Spain. And just as Granada had at least the potentiality of powerful religious alliances from the south and east, so also did Ireland obtain, after the days of San Juan de Ulúa, a Catholic ally in Spain. This alliance consistently brought the threat of a large Spanish military presence in Ireland, but never the reality, and therefore in the long run proved more a burden than an advantage for the Irish; for it made the English fight them all the more vehemently. It was in Ireland that the English evolved a pattern of aggression which they were later to apply to the Indians: that of murdering a weaker people — weaker because less developed socially and technologically, however great their courage and strength as individuals — under the self-justifying delusion that they were dealing with one at least as strong as themselves. The English counterpart to the conquests of the Canaries and Granada, dress rehearsals for American conquest, was the devastation of Munster, inflicted in the wake of the rebellion there in the winter of 1580 and 1581, in which more than thirty thousand Irish either were killed or died of starvation and disease. Edmund Spenser, a long-time resident of Ireland, described the scene:

> Out of every corner of the woods and glens they came creeping forth upon their hands, for their legs could not bear them; they looked like anatomies of death; they spake like ghosts crying out of their graves; they did eat of the dead carrions, happy were they if they could find them, yea, and one another soon after, insomuch as the very carcasses they spared not to scrape out of their graves; and if they found a plot of watercresses or shamrocks, there they flocked as to a feast for the time.

It was to Munster, in places a wasteland of rubble and scorched fields, that Raleigh was to come in 1586, his task that of repopulating it with Englishmen — an ominous precedent for American colonization. This was the underside of the Protestant humanism of Walsingham's group.

The cries of the suffering were in Gaelic, but this does not seem, for the moment, to have awakened many guilty memories of Celtic ancestry among Englishmen where Ireland was concerned. It was, rather, to the still-pleasant sounds of America that ears were now attuned for Celtic strains. John Dee, geographer, astrologer, and all-round Renaissance magus, another member of Walsingham's group, revived the story of Prince Madoc as a justification for English claims in the New World; Dee was sure that the descendants of that twelfth-century Welshman and his companions were still living there. Vivid support for this vision came from a simple sailor named David Ingram, probably a Welshman himself, who had been among the members of Hawkins's crew dropped off in Pánuco after the disaster of San Juan de Ulúa. Ingram and two others had, unlike Miles Philips and his companions, made their way northward out of the Spanish sphere and through the wilderness that would eventually be the eastern United States; indeed, he claimed they had marched as far north as the Canadian coast, there to be rescued by a French ship. It was in his encounters with Indians on the way, Ingram said, that he heard Welsh words spoken. This news must have been dear to the hearts of John Dee and the Hakluyts, all three of Welsh descent; but it was not all. His account also depicted glimmers of another Mexico: men wearing rubies four inches long, great quantities of pearls and gold all about, houses "builded with pillars of massy silver and crystal," and the like. Walsingham had the story taken down in 1582 – Ingram himself evidently could not write – and it thereupon became one of the chief sources of inspiration for Sir Humphrey Gilbert's ill-fated expedition of the following year.

Many would soon begin doubting Ingram's story, but other influences now were also at work making North America attractive to Englishmen. The growing resentment against Spain had given rise to an English sense of manifest destiny in opposition to the Spanish one, an ideal of expanding Protestantism pitted against the Spanish Catholic onslaught in the newly discovered parts of the world. This was a gentle ideal for some – even as it had been for some Spaniards – but for others it resounded with a militancy worthy of Cortés. No better expression of the more militant version of this mood can be found than in the opening remarks of an account of Sir Humphrey Gilbert's 1583 voyage written by one Edward Hayes, a Liverpool merchant who had sailed along on it. It is "the preordinance of God," Hayes writes, "that in this last age of the world" the natives of America are to be brought to Christianity, and the English vocation in this is manifest, "it seeming probable by event of precedent attempts made by the Spaniards and French sundry times, that the countries lying north of Florida, God hath reserved the same to be reduced unto Christian civility by the English nation" – very close to Spenser's words about the Irish. A touch of the apocalyptic was now making its way into England, this being perhaps another legacy from the south and the East. Hayes certainly has a clear view, at any rate, of the direction in which the true religion has moved through history; here is how he reflects upon the English mission in the New World:

> Which also is very probable by the revolution and course of God's word and religion, which from the beginning hath moved from the East, towards, and at last unto the West, where it is like to end, unless the same begin again where it did in the East, which were to expect a like world again. But we are assured of the contrary by the prophecy of Christ, whereby we gather, that after his word preached throughout the world shall be the end. And as the Gospel when it descended Westward began in the South, and afterward spread into the North of Europe: even so, as the same hath begun in the South countries of America, no less hope may be gathered that it will also spread into the North.

Destiny and geography have thus come together for the northwestern-most of the European nations, and the implications for the farther North-west — the northern New World — are clear. Hayes anticipates the millenarianism of the Puritans of Massachusetts by two generations — although they, for the most part, will not share his enthusiasm for con-verting the Indians.

A gentler vision of English manifest destiny in America was represented by Richard Hakluyt the younger, who had published a collection of ac-counts of English and French voyages to America in 1582 and then gone on a diplomatic mission to France to be closer to some of his sources of geographical information. In 1584, Raleigh — who now had seized the main initiative in American colonization after the death of his elder half-brother, Sir Humphrey Gilbert — summoned Hakluyt back to London to collect all his knowledge into a memorandum for the queen summarizing all the arguments for their program. The resulting *Discourse of Western Planting*, although it was not published until the twentieth century, can nevertheless be considered the first manifesto of the coming age of English imperialism. American colonies will not only be footholds for a future northwest passage to Cathay, Hakluyt writes in it hopefully, but be part of a growing and flourishing commercial system. New raw mate-rials, such as fish, skins, naval stores, wood, and dyes, would be sent into the home industry by the colonies, which would at the same time develop into new markets for English manufactured goods, not only on their own account but by means of the Indians as well, who would be civilized by them and thereby made into consumers. Furthermore, colonies would be a social safety valve, in America as in Ireland — for Hakluyt, like many of his contemporaries, was convinced that overpopulation was a major source of England's woes.

All of this is a sober, mercantile English vision, highly practical, but unmarked by any particular lust for gold. There is also no apocalypticism in it, although Hakluyt did not neglect to place the conversion of the Indians in his program: he was, after all, a clergyman, although this status seems to have been more for the sake of a living, as in the case of Peter Martyr, than out of a strong sense of vocation. In the matter of religion, Hakluyt's chief concern is with preventing the spread of Ca-tholicism — and of Spanish influence — among the Indians; the saving of souls seems to be a secondary matter for him. Religion is a means of creating a possible alliance with the Indians against the Spaniards that would permeate the entire New World, and it is such an alliance — an idea doubtless inspired by Drake, and by the opposing example of the Spaniards in Ireland — that interests Hakluyt above all. "Now if we," he writes, ". . . would either join with these Savages, or send or give them armor as the Spaniards arm our Irish rebels, we should trouble the King of Spain more in those parts, than he hath or can trouble us in Ireland, and hold him at such a bay, as he was never yet held at." The belief implied here that the Indians would flock to the call from the English for such an alliance comes out of the naïve certainty of some Englishmen at this time that their history in the New World would right the wrongs committed against its peoples by the Spaniards. To buttress this view, Hakluyt quotes at great length from the recent English translation of Las Casas's *Brief Relation of the Destruction of the Indies*, as if to prove English virtue merely by intoning in full the litany of Spanish wickedness.

There is a certain want of Hakluyt's otherwise firm sense of reality in this uncomplicated vision of happy Anglo-Indian relations, a fault dramatized at one point when he suggests in passing that the English might even try allying themselves with the Moors against Spain. We suddenly are confronted with the notion of something like a vast, English-led conspiracy among all of the darker-skinned peoples of the world whom the Spaniards have made their enemies. In its sweep, it deftly averts any steady contemplation of the real relationship about to develop with one of those peoples, the Indians, and of the problems it might entail. The English are, for the time being, still the dilettantes of empire, sneaky competitors from the western fringe of Europe like the Portuguese in the preceding century, free of any continental appetite, resistant to the realities of territorial responsibility into which they are about to plunge, and content to envision a system of world power made up of enclaves more firmly rooted in the open sea than in the lands out of which they are to be carved. The French were not yet really committed to continental power, either; but they were to remain relatively clear of it for a long time. The English, on the other hand, were to find themselves taking it on with a suddenness that would upset their own equilibrium as well as that of the Indians, with a dire effect upon Anglo-Indian relations unforeseen by Hakluyt in 1584.

Earlier in the year in which he summoned Hakluyt from France to prepare this memorandum, Raleigh had sent out two ships, commanded by Philip Amadas and Arthur Barlowe, to scout the coastline between Spanish Florida and French Norumbega for a possible site for a colony. Landing somewhere just north of Cape Hatteras in mid-July of 1584, the Englishmen soon encountered members of the Roanoke tribe, the Algonquian people centered on and near the island that now bears their name.

Barlowe later wrote about this experience in the euphoric terms typical of English New World narratives at that time. The next day after the first chance meeting with a boatload of the local Indians, "there came unto us divers boats," he writes, "and in one of them the King's brother, accompanied with forty or fifty men, very handsome, and goodly people, and in their behavior as mannerly and civil as any of Europe." Granganimeo, the "king's" brother, got off his boat upon landing at the beach, and walked with his men — all clad in simple skins about their loins — over to where the English were anchored:

> When he came to the place, his servants spread a long mat upon the ground, on which he sat down, and at the other end of the mat, four others of his company did the like: the rest of his men stood round about him, somewhat afar off: when we came to the shore to him with our weapons, he never moved from his place, nor any of the other four, nor never mistrusted any harm to be offered from us, but sitting still, he beckoned us to come and sit by him, which we performed: and being set, he makes all signs of joy and welcome, striking on his head, and his breast, and afterwards on ours, to show we were all one, smiling, and making show the best he could, of all love, and familiarity. After he had made a long speech unto us, we presented him with divers things, which he received very joyfully, and thankfully.

The atmosphere seems as ideally English as that surrounding Montezuma's welcome of Cortés into Mexico was Spanish; we are more in Hakluyt's world than David Ingram's. Eight of the Englishmen were taken by their hosts to Roanoke Island, where they entered "a village of nine houses, built of cedar, and fortified round about with sharp trees, to keep out their enemies." There they received an even warmer welcome than before from Granganimeo's wife, who assigned women to wash their clothes and feet before supper. Barlowe could only conclude with a virtual paraphrase of Ovid:

> We found the people most gentle, loving and faithful, void of all guile and treason, and such as lived after the manner of the golden age. The earth bringeth forth all things in abundance, as in the first creation, without toil or labor.

How could honest English yeomen resist a land like this?

Returning home with Manteo and Wanchese, two young Indians from Roanoke who had volunteered to go back to England with them and become interpreters, Amadas and Barlowe created enough excitement to induce Raleigh to try a full-scale colonizing experiment within a year. Raleigh received a patent by act of Parliament to establish colonies in the land that was now named "Virginia" in honor of the queen — a term broader than what was later meant by it, covering the whole part of North America to which the English were now laying claim. The expedition sent out under Sir Richard Grenville consisted of five full-sized sailing ships and two small pinnaces, with over five hundred men aboard, 108 of whom were destined to be colonists — there were no women going just yet to Virginia, which was still thought of primarily in terms of a military colony against Spain. It was not until early July, after some straggling and a stint of privateering to earn its keep, that the fleet reached the Carolina Banks, and that its small boats began a reconnaissance of Pamlico Sound in search of a good place to plant the colony. By the end of the month, Granganimeo had invited the English, in the name of his brother Wingina, the werowance, or chieftain, whom some of the settlers still referred to as "king," to establish themselves at the southern end of Roanoke Island. A fort was built, and Grenville with the large ships then sailed for England, and for a little more piracy on the way.

What happened during the ensuing year is somewhat obscure, but clearly discernible are the outlines of a division between two types of colonists: those, on the one hand, who were inclined to resort to force as soon as possible in the resolution of all problems with the Indians, and those, on the other, who clung to the ideals of gentleness and carefully cultivated friendship that had been advocated by humanists back in England, the heirs of the old Spanish pro-Indian intelligentsia. Unfortunately for our understanding of the situation, the only surviving narrative of events in that first Roanoke colony of 1585–1586 was written by a representative of the get-tough group, Ralph Lane, Raleigh's appointed governor of the colony, who had obtained his training for situations of this sort by doing military service in Ireland.

A first sign of approaching disintegration of Anglo-Indian relations was the defection of Wanchese. We cannot discern exactly when or why he turned against the English after what was, by all accounts, supposed to have been a pleasant year in their midst at home and in England; it has been suggested that he was jealous of Manteo, who apparently "went native" among the English far more zealously and successfully than he. Perhaps Wanchese's defection was simply a sign of problems already emerging between the English and the Roanokes; in those circumstances, he evidently was the one who would feel his first loyalty to be to his people, whereas Manteo, who apparently was of Croatoan* rather than Roanoke origin, was satisfied even then to remain on the English side. Whatever the exact pattern of events, we can see Wanchese as the first of a succession of Roanoke go-betweens to be lost by the English during the course of that disastrous year. The next loss was that of Granganimeo, and after him, that of a friendly elder of the tribe named Ensenore, both of whom died, apparently of natural causes. It may well be that Granganimeo's enthusiasm for the English — which perhaps

* One of the islands then forming the Outer Banks.

cooled a little the second time around, when the latter came to stay — had never been shared by Wingina, who remained notably absent during all the early encounters. In any case, now that these final restraints were gone, Wingina became openly hostile and forbade his people to trade with the English: this was serious, because the English had not yet learned to fend for themselves and relied heavily upon the Indians for food supplies. Harking to an Indian custom of adopting a special name for war, Wingina now began to call himself "Pemisapan."

The situation was tense but unresolved by the end of May, when, according to Lane, he received word through Indian spies that Pemisapan was seeking to make alliances with neighboring tribes for a major attack upon the English, planned for June 10. Seizing the initiative, Lane was able on June 1 to gain entry with several of his men into Pemisapan's village of Dasemunkepeuc, on the mainland shore west of Roanoke Island, with the claim that he wanted to confer on a matter of contention between the English and the Indians. As he stood talking with Pemisapan and seven or eight other Indian leaders, Lane suddenly gave his men a signal, "and immediately," as he later wrote, "those his chief men, and himself, had by the mercy of God for our deliverance, that which they had purposed for us." Pemisapan was shot and lay as if dead for a few moments during the melee, but "suddenly he started up, and ran away as though he had not been touched." He got away into the woods, but not without being wounded by one of Lane's Irish servants. Another, named Edward Nugent, at length caught Pemisapan and delivered a summary sentence of his own. "We met him," Lane writes, "returning out of the woods with Pemisapan's head in his hand." Was this a vicarious form of revenge by one of the "wild Irish" for the treatment his own people had received at the hands of the English? We have already seen examples of this strange but recurring pattern in race relations, a displacement of vindictiveness exercised by one oppressed people against another — New Christian slave traders in São Thomé, Black servants mistreating Indian laborers in Mexico. It is a strikingly ironic ending to the first English effort to live with the Indians in America.

Yet there also had been an entirely different strain running through this history. Some of the colonists were men of considerable learning and technical skill, whose main purpose was the advancement of knowledge; indeed, in one of its aspects, this first Roanoke adventure had the air of a kind of gentlemanly English scientific expedition more common in a later era — one thinks of Darwin on the *Beagle*. There was, for example, Joachim Ganz, a metallurgist born in Prague, who had come along because Amadas and Barlowe, though they had not discovered gold, had found plenty of copper ore. During the entire year of the colony, Ganz smelted copper, which was not only of direct use to the English but a lively article of trade with the Indians. When Pemisapan sought alliances with other tribes against the English, he used his ample store of copper as an inducement. Ganz is remarkable to us in another, wholly different way as well: for he was a Jew, the son of a Jewish scholar of some distinction named David Ganz, who was still living in Prague at this time. It is not known when Joachim arrived in England, but he is known to have been working in the copper industry there by 1581. Later, in 1589, he was to be investigated on charges of blasphemy for denying the divinity of Christ. Apparently he never renounced his Judaism, even though professing Jews were not allowed by law to be in England at this time. Elizabethan England was, in general, rather casual about privately held religious beliefs: Catholics and Protestant dissenters were by and large connived at, so why not a few Jews as well? The upshot is that Joachim Ganz must be considered the first professing Jew to reside in English America, and in the future United States.

But the most prominent members of the learned contingent at Roanoke were two men whose science represented Renaissance humanism in its fullest New World application. Thomas Hariot and John White worked as a team much of the time, for Hariot, an Oxford graduate in his mid-twenties, was a researcher and writer, and White, a surveyor by profession, was an artist by avocation who had gone along on Martin Frobisher's voyage of 1577 to Meta Incognita and done some pictures of Eskimos. Together they compiled a portfolio, which has since largely been lost, of drawings and paintings accompanied by explanatory text, an ambitious collaborative essay in natural history and anthropology.

Among White's Roanoke works that survive are maps and pictures of flora and fauna done with considerable skill; but most striking of all is roughly a score of watercolors depicting Indians and their way of life. We see the men, women, and children of Roanoke and the vicinity, either posing individually for the artist, or engaged severally in the round of their everyday life. White occasionally displays a faulty understanding of the human anatomy, but his sense of Indian physiognomy and character is the best of its time — better even than that of Le Moyne. The depth of White's insight gives these paintings a truthfulness that remains fresh for all time. It is interesting, by the way, that among his other surviving drawings are some fanciful ones of ancient Picts and Britons, who bear resemblances to his Indians. White was born in Ireland of English stock, and the analogy of living among Celts may well have struck him during his stay among the natives of North America.

Thomas Hariot, though no rival to White in artistry, was his equal in humanistic depth. There was, to be sure, an element of detached interest in flora and fauna in Hariot's work as in White's. This had practical as well as purely scientific grounds, for Hariot was compiling a catalogue both of what nature could provide to sustain any future English colonies and of what raw materials could be used in overseas trade. But the study of the Indians clearly was his main interest. Indeed, it is likely that when Manteo and Wanchese had sojourned in England they had spent most of their time with Hariot, exchanging with him their knowledge of Algonquian language and customs for lessons in English. Certainly Hariot came to know Algonquian well, for he eventually compiled a vocabulary of the language; this, unfortunately, has not survived. In fact, a good part of his notes and more finished writings about Roanoke has disappeared; among other things, we are missing a narrative history of the events of that year, promised by him though possibly never even written.

The one work about Roanoke that we do have from his hand, *A brief and true report of the new found land of Virginia,* which was a quick summary of the colony's virtues done for propaganda purposes, gives clear indication that the picture his narrative would have given of Anglo-Indian relations there would have been very different from the one sketched out by Lane. Hariot's few remarks in this brochure about Wingina-Pemisapan are entirely sympathetic. For example, in a context in which he has talked at length about the religious propensities of the Indians, perceiving in them an incipient monotheism and a definite readiness for Christianity, he writes:

> The werowance with whom we dwelt called Wingina, and many of his people, would be glad many times to be with us at our prayers, and many times call upon us both in his own town, as also in others whither he sometimes accompanied us, to pray and sing psalms; hoping thereby to be partaker of the same effects which we by that means also expected.
>
> Twice this werowance was so grievously sick that he was like to die, and as he lay languishing, doubting of any help by his own priests, and thinking he was in such danger for offending us and thereby our God, sent for some of us to pray and be a means to our God that it would please him either that he might live, or after death dwell with him in bliss, so likewise were the requests of many others in the like case.

Hariot is fully aware that he is dealing here with a naïve religiosity that still wants educating; indeed, he refers several times to the disturbing fact that the Indians were often inclined to think of the English as gods themselves, as in this passage in which he also displays his own thoroughly Christian, if not necessarily godlike, readiness to bring the light of science to Virginia:

Most things they saw with us, as mathematical instruments, sea compasses, the virtue of the lodestone in drawing iron, a perspective glass whereby was showed many strange sights, burning glasses, wildfire works, guns, books, writing and reading, spring clocks that seem to go of themselves, and many other things that we had, were so strange unto them, and so far exceeded their capacities to comprehend the reason and means how they should be made and done, that they thought they were rather the works of gods than of men, or at the leastwise they had been given and taught us of the gods.

There are no signs of interracial hostility in this, and though we must allow for the inclination to put Virginia's best foot forward in this public pamphlet meant in part to attract future colonists, Hariot is persuasive when he says that "some of our company towards the end of the year, showed themselves too fierce, in slaying some of the people, in some towns, upon causes that on our part, might easily enough have been borne withal." This is rather frank for a work of propaganda, as is a passage in which he roundly criticizes an unnamed segment of the colonists for their poor behavior in Virginia as well as their slanderous talk of it once they got home:

The cause of their ignorance was, in that they were of that many that were never out of the island where we were seated, or not far, or at the leastwise in few places else, during the time of our abode in the country: or of that many that after gold and silver was not so soon found, as it was by them looked for, had little or no care of any other thing but to pamper their bellies; or of that many which had little understanding, less discretion, and more tongue than was needful or requisite.

Obviously the word had got out that there had been trouble in the colony, so Hariot felt no compunction about discussing the issues directly. Conceding in the end that there was an "alteration of . . . opinions" among the Indians toward the English, he can say only that "it was on their part justly deserved." The implications here even are startling: it is only from Lane that we know of a conspiracy of Pemisapan which he so sneakily nipped in the bud. Was there really one after all?

The death of Wingina-Pemisapan had left the Indians of Roanoke in sufficient disarray that Lane could now feel he had command of the situation; but the colony's days proved to be coming to an end all the same. That spring Raleigh had sent out two relief expeditions to Virginia, one of them a single ship, the other a fleet commanded by Grenville; but the first English ships to reach there were led by Sir Francis Drake, on their way back from a voyage of harassment and plunder through the Spanish colonies during which they had all but completely destroyed St. Augustine. Drake had by this time made his celebrated voyage around the world (from the fall of 1577 to the fall of 1580), and was more determined than ever to snatch empire from the jaws of Spain wherever he could; Raleigh enthusiastically concurred in this aim, and there are signs that Roanoke was meant among other things to be a base for Drake's activities, so that his appearance there in June of 1586 was probably no accident.

From his exploits in the Spanish Indies, Drake had brought along with him a shipload of freed Negro slaves and Indians, evidently planning to establish them as part of the Virginia colony. This is as close as we ever get, however, to the realization of Drake's particular vision of a multiracial English America, for it is not known what happened to these freedmen in the ensuing shuffle of events. Drake intended to leave one of his ships, the *Francis*, at Roanoke for permanent use there — the colony had gone almost a year without any oceangoing vessel at its disposal — and several of the English colonists boarded it to take it over; but then a storm struck, and the next thing anyone knew, the *Francis* had broken away from its moorings and was heading back to England with the colonists aboard. This was a signal for the latent demoralization at Roanoke to become rampant, and the upshot was that Lane and Drake decided to take everybody home. But by the time the ships landed at Portsmouth on July 27, the Black and Indian freedmen were not on them. Where had they debarked? The voyage narratives of this period have many gaps in them owing to the war with Spain and considerations of military sensitivity, and they provide us with no answer to this particular question. The best bet is that these freedmen were left at Roanoke after all. If so, then they must eventually have become absorbed into the surrounding peoples; this would make them really the first "Lost Colony" of Roanoke.

The "Lost Colony" celebrated in history and folklore, however, was the one sent out in the spring of 1587 in three ships: one hundred and fifty English settlers, this time including women and children, who were determined to make another try. As usual, Raleigh, still proprietor of the venture, did not himself make the trip; the governor this time was our old friend John White, who brought along his son-in-law and pregnant daughter. Another member of the group was Manteo, who had returned with Lane and Drake to England the previous year and was now utterly Anglicized. The plan was to leave him in charge at Roanoke as Raleigh's vassal, then move on to Chesapeake Bay and, in accordance with what Lane had recommended on the basis of his explorations, establish a colony there. However, an obscure chain of circumstances ended in the installation of the colony at Roanoke after all. There were some high points in the ensuing weeks: the establishment of warm relations with the Indians of Croatoan, the installation of Manteo as "Lord of Roanoke and Dasemunkepeuc," and the birth of Anglo-America's first offspring, White's granddaughter Virginia Dare; but there were problems as well, and some of the other leaders persuaded White to return to England and plead for more supplies. He sailed on August 27, never again to see his daughter, grandchild, or any of the colonists.

After reaching England in November at the end of a difficult passage, White tried a return trip to Virginia the following April; but his ship was pillaged by a French privateer and had to sail back home. Then history intervened. That summer the Spanish Armada sailed into the English Channel, but Drake and the other great English captains of the day collaborated with the weather to the effect that "the magnificent, huge, and mighty fleet of the Spaniards (which themselves termed in all places invincible) such as sailed not upon the Ocean Sea many hundred years before, in the year 1588 vanished into smoke; to the great confusion and discouragement of the authors thereof." Thus was the event described by Emanuel van Meteren, a Dutch historian, in a passage that Richard Hakluyt quickly had translated for inclusion in his monumental compilation, *The Principal Navigations, Voyages and Discoveries of the English Nation*, published at the beginning of 1590. Together, the defeat of the Armada and Hakluyt's great work signaled the turning that had occurred: the gage of overseas initiative had been passed from Spain to England. But in spite of the rejoicing to be heard from Hakluyt, his party was not to be the one to exploit the triumph. As with the Spaniards a few generations before, the relatively humanistic aspirations of an earlier group of American colonizers were to be largely superseded by the ambitions of harsher men. In the very moment of victory, the failure of Walsingham's group was being demonstrated by the collapse of Raleigh's Virginia enterprise.

For what had happened to the Roanoke colony by the time the smoke had cleared? John White was not able to return there until August, 1590, when he and his companions found the fort in ruins, and entirely empty of humanity. Some goods had been buried in the ground, however, and this and other signs suggested to White that the colonists had left of their own volition and not been taken or killed there. On one tree were carved the letters CRO, and on another CROATOAN, but without the cross that had been agreed upon as a symbol of distress. "I greatly joyed," White later wrote about these clues, "that I had safely found a certain token of their safe being at Croatoan, which is the place where Manteo was born, and the Savages of the island our friends." But a storm was blowing up, and the captains of the fleet in which White had come decided that they could not search at Croatoan right away. One of the ships returned to England immediately, and White's ship, determined at first to winter in the West Indies and then return to Croatoan in the spring, was eventually blown so far out to sea that it, too, returned to England instead.

White apparently made at least one more voyage to find his Lost Colony — and his lost family — but we do not know the outcome. Indeed, the subsequent behavior of Raleigh and other interested Englishmen with respect to the colony remains as mysterious as its own fate. Little effort seems to have been made to find out what happened to it. Perhaps its survivors, too, eventually assimilated with the surrounding peoples; this remains a possibility. As for John White, the only known survivor of this more hopeful day in Virginia, he went at last to his native Ireland and apparently spent the rest of his days there.

21

Dramatic Interlude

B<small>Y THE TIME</small> the second Roanoke colony was established in 1587, young Christopher Marlowe had written

> *Of Tamburlaine, that sturdy Scythian thief,*
> *That robs your merchants of Persepolis*
> *Trading by land unto the Western Isles. . . .*

The character is taken from the late fourteenth century, and the geography is intentionally medieval, but with a sly anachronism. Another passage refers to "East India and the late discover'd isles," and it becomes clear that these isles belong to Marlowe's day. Indeed, it is not hard to see in Tamburlaine, the Scythian upstart and brigand become ruler of the world, the spirit of a rambunctious Elizabethan England asserting itself over all the more ancient and decadent powers to the south and the east. He has a passion to embrace the south and its warmth, but one feels the chill mountain air of his origins breathing proudly on the neck of Zenocrate, his captive Egyptian princess, when he promises her that

> *With milk-white harts upon an ivory sled,*
> *Thou shalt be drawn amidst the frozen pools,*

> *And scale the icy mountains' lofty tops,*
> *Which with thy beauty will be soon resolved.*

Zenocrate marries this former shepherd, yielding to the athletic democracy of the north.

This triumph over Africa enables Marlowe to be in places the poet of the Guinea voyagers, viewing an ancient southern landscape, both mythically and realistically, with the naïve and exuberant eye of an upstart imperialism. In Part Two of *Tamburlaine the Great*, Techelles describes his conquest of that continent to his Scythian lord:

> *And I have marched along the river Nile*
> *To Machda, where the mighty Christian priest,*
> *Call'd John the Great, sits in a milk-white robe,*
> *Whose triple mitre I did take by force,*
> *And made him swear obedience to my crown.*
> *From thence unto Cazates did I march,*
> *Where Amazonians met me in the field,*
> *With whom, being women, I vouchsaf'd a league,*
> *And with my power did march to Zanzibar,*
> *The western [sic] part of Afric, where I view'd*
> *The Ethiopian sea, rivers and lakes,*
> *But neither man nor child in all the land:*
> *Therefore I took my course to Manico,*
> *Where, unresisted, I remov'd my camp;*
> *And, by the coast of Byather, at last*
> *I came to Cubar, where the negroes dwell,*
> *And, conquering that, made haste to Nubia.*

The fascination with the landscape of the southeast extends also to the peoples living in that direction, as in the catalogue given by the Turkish king Orcanes of the troops he has mustered against Tamburlaine:

> *We have revolted Grecians, Albanese,*
> *Sicilians, Jews, Arabians, Turks, and Moors,*
> *Natolians, Sorians, black Egyptians,*
> *Illyrians, Thracians, and Bithynians. . . .*

But Marlowe is particularly interested in the element of the demonic that can be found in all this. Among his prizes from Africa, Techelles presents Tamburlaine with the crown of Fez

> And with an host of Moors trained to the war,
> Whose coal-black faces make their foes retire,
> And quake for fear, as if infernal Jove,
> Meaning to aid thee in these Turkish arms,
> Should pierce the black circumference of hell,
> With ugly Furies bearing fiery flags,
> And millions of his strong tormenting spirits. . . .

Marlowe knows precisely what images from overseas can strike terror in the hearts of his listeners.

Perhaps if he had lived longer he would have done a play with a terrifying Moor in it, as Shakespeare was to do in writing *Titus Andronicus;* but he did at least undertake a thorough exploration of another race of putatively demonic southerners in *The Jew of Malta.* This play deals as unabashedly in the medieval mythology of the villainous Jew as Techelles's speech does in the fright that some Englishmen evidently felt at black complexions; in both cases, the reality is even beside the point, the poet preferring to play upon the popular notions. Barabas is presenting the myth of an entire race rather than any credible personal history when he tells Ithamore:

> As for myself, I walk abroad o'nights,
> And kill sick people groaning under walls:
> Sometimes I go about and poison wells;
> And now and then, to cherish Christian thieves,
> I am content to lose some of my crowns,
> That I may, walking in my gallery,
> See 'em go pinion'd along by my door.
> Being young, I studied physic, and began
> To practise first upon the Italian;
> There I enrich'd the priests with burials,
> And always kept the sexton's arms in ure
> With digging graves and ringing dead men's knells:
> And, after that, was I an engineer,
> And in the wars 'twixt France and Germany,
> Under pretense of helping Charles the Fifth,
> Slew friend and enemy with my stratagems:
> Then, after that, was I an usurer,
> And with extorting, cozening, forfeiting,
> And tricks belonging unto brokery,
> I fill'd the gaols with bankrupts in a year,
> And with young orphans planted hospitals;
> And every moon made some or other mad.

This is a long way from Shakespeare's more human caricature of a Jewish villain, whose sentimental touches would make him a full-blown tragic figure in the eyes of a later age; until his very last works, Marlowe was as unsentimental as the spirit of early Elizabethan drama was in general. Villains were on the stage to make trouble, not to express the depths of their anguish, and a scheming Jew was there to provide a certain convention of villainy, not a case against anti-Judaism.

Nevertheless, Marlowe is not entirely opposed to Barabas, especially during the first two acts (indeed, the last three acts, in which Barabas turns into a hideous monster beyond belief, murdering his daughter and many others besides, are thought by some scholars to have been completed by another hand). The playwright has shown his sneaking admiration of "Machiavel" in other works as well, relishing the power of intellect and will that enables a man to come out on top against all odds, playing at the conventions of an essentially nasty game. Practicing an early version of *épater le bourgeois*, Marlowe likes nothing better than to portray a scoundrel coming from the margins of respectable society and showing it up. There is a feeling of delicious and well-deserved conspiracy among outcasts in the slave-market scene, when Barabas asks the Muslim captive Ithamore:

> *Where wast thou born?*
> ITHAMORE: *In Thrace; brought up in Arabia.*
> BARABAS: *So much the better; thou art for my turn.*

Barabas recognizes this anomalous offspring of both Europe and Asia as a genuine counterpart to the wandering Jew, and buys him to serve as an accomplice in wrongdoing. After they have exchanged life histories with one another, Barabas exclaims:

> *Why, this is something: make account of me*
> *As of thy fellow; we are villains both;*
> *Both circumcised; we hate Christians both. . . .*

The irony of this mutual recognition is aptly conveyed (whether written by Marlowe or not) in a scene near the end of the play, when Barabas, after having by his machinations enabled the Turks to conquer Malta, now welcomes the Turkish governor Calymath with the secret intention of returning the island to Christian rule. "Welcome, great Calymath!" he says, and Ferneze, the Christian governor with whom he has planned this new betrayal, turns to the audience and exclaims: "How the slave jeers at him!" By this time Ferneze, taken first through utter abjection and now to the brink of new triumph entirely by the whim of Barabas, has been to him as a fly to the gods; yet he still calls him "slave." The playwright is having fun here with the shortsightedness and hypocrisy of Christians in relation to peoples they think of as inferior; one thinks of Fray Marcos, being led about by Estévanico, but still imagining him to be a slave.

It is contempt for Christian hypocrisy in particular that enables Marlowe in places to come rather close to a sentimental view of Barabas. In the first act, he shows Barabas being treated with gross injustice by the Christians, who take away all his possessions by an arbitrary government fiat, thus motivating in him a legitimate desire for revenge. When one of the Knights of Malta performing this judicial theft chides him for "thy inherent sin" — a remark that is only a shade removed from George Best's "natural infection of the blood" — the Jew replies:

> What, bring you Scripture to confirm your wrongs?
> Preach me not out of my possessions.
> Some Jews are wicked, as all Christians are;
> But say the tribe that I descended of
> Were all in general cast away for sin,
> Shall I be tried for their transgressions?

Barabas shows glimmers of Shylock here, and would have had a strong case against the racist implications of anti-Judaism had he only said that *some* Christians were wicked and not *all*. Similarly, when he says,

> It's no sin to deceive a Christian;
> For they themselves hold it a principle,
> Faith is not to be held with heretics:
> But all are heretics that are not Jews;

the irony cannot have been without appeal to the more sophisticated members of the audience, but the round assertion that all Christians are heretics would only have alienated them in the end. Marlowe guards his every formulation against the threat of going soft. But the fact remains that, at the end of two acts, he has achieved an interesting moral balance that promises something of greater depth than what the play then becomes. An opportunity to explore the ironies of racial and religious outsiderness more fully has been missed: the tragedy of *The Jew of Malta* is the work itself.

Shakespeare was to do far better with these ironies, but not right away. His first inquiry into them, made in about 1594, some four years after *The Jew of Malta* and a year after Marlowe's death, took up the latter's theme of the demonic racial outsider from the south, but with the Negro rather than the Jew for its subject. Aaron the Moor in *Titus Andronicus* is a more direct offspring of Barabas than Shylock is. Like Marlowe, Shakespeare was still deeply interested in "Machiavel" at around this time — when he also wrote *Richard III* — and he preferred a fascinating villain to some more tragic victim of society's conventions. *Titus Andronicus* is Shakespeare's cruelest and most unsentimental play, and Aaron, if not its cruelest character, is certainly its most relentlessly wicked one, a black devil pure and simple. Indeed, he seems at times to be nothing more than the clever metaphorical construct of a brilliant but still callow poet — blackness as a walking, plotting, fornicating symbol of evil. Often he is just an excuse for a riot of verbal chiaroscuro, as when Bassianus comes upon the Gothic Queen Tamora in the woods just after her tryst with her Black slave and says:

> *Believe me, Queen, your swarth Cimmerian*
> *Doth make your honor of his body's hue,*
> *Spotted, detested, and abominable.*
> *Why are you sequestered from all your train,*
> *Dismounted from your snow-white goodly steed,*
> *And wandered hither to an obscure plot,*
> *Accompanied but with a barbarous Moor,*
> *If foul desire had not conducted you?*

At the end of this first century of English experience with the Negro, Shakespeare seems eager to explore every possibility of language that the situation contains. In this context the word *foul,* used frequently with reference to Aaron throughout the play, is especially significant. It had originally meant only "putrid," "rotting," and, by extension, "dirty." This latter sense was now taking on a visual connotation, and in some contexts actually meant "brown" — especially when contrasted with *fair,* which had once meant only "beautiful," but now also suggested lightness of complexion. The contrast between "fair" and "foul" at this time often was intended as a simple comparison between shades of skin; but the other implications could never have been far behind. The peculiar ambiguities that these two words were taking on clearly were a phenomenon of evolving racial attitudes.

Yet even the raw young Shakespeare could make his games of language plunge to sudden depths of insight. When Aaron proclaims to the audience,

> *Let fools do good, and fair men call for grace;*
> *Aaron will have his soul black like his face,*

he is, in one sense, simply offering the metaphorical rule of thumb by which he can be understood throughout the play; but he also is delivering a wholly warranted fillip to a world that expects him to be its devil. In this he foreshadows Edmund pronouncing the credo of his bastardy, and secret admirers of Machiavel in the audience, however they may have felt about Negroes, must surely have sensed the attractiveness of this wily outsider determined to wreak some havoc upon a society in which everyone is so smugly alike. The word-play of Aaron's exhortation to himself

> *To mount aloft with thy imperial mistress*

achieves a deeper penetration of the ironies of the master-slave — or rather, the "mistress"-slave — relationship than did any of Barabas's words or deeds. And Shakespeare's game of black-and-white imagery becomes for a moment something far more human when Tamora's nurse comes to Aaron with the black child to which their mistress has just given birth:

AARON: *Well, God give her good rest! What hath he sent her?*
NURSE: *A devil.*
AARON: *Why, then she is the devil's dam —*
        A joyful issue.
NURSE: *A joyless, dismal, black and sorrowful issue.*
        Here is the babe, as loathsome as a toad
        Amongst the fairest breeders of our clime.
        The Empress sends it thee, thy stamp, thy seal,
        And bids thee christen it with thy dagger's point.
AARON: *'Zounds, ye whore! Is black so base a hue?*

Suddenly Aaron's usual stance of mocking villainy, so true to the tradition of Machiavel, gives way to something like "Black anger" at this insult, and the threat to the life of his child. For a few moments he is magnificent, a Noble Ethiopian.

But it was not yet precisely Shakespeare's moment to be the Columbus and the Frobisher of the human spirit, to discover reaches of it that had been hitherto undisclosed, and the language soon reverts to mere cleverness when Aaron says:

> *Coal-black is better than another hue*
> *In that it scorns to bear another hue;*
> *For all the water in the ocean*
> *Can never turn the swan's black legs to white,*
> *Although she lave them hourly in the flood.*

Shakespeare evidently was familiar with the story of the Englishwoman and her Black husband and child that George Best had told, or with one just like it, but his interest in the ironies of color that it seemed to imply was still more that of a young man absorbed in metaphorical acrobatics than that of the author of *Othello*. Yet there are glimmers of what is to come.

By the time of *The Merchant of Venice* some two years later, Shakespeare has arrived at a more openly humanistic concept of race. As if expressly to repudiate his own earlier creation of a Black devil, as well as George Best's idea of a "natural infection of the blood," he offers the Prince of Morocco's ruminations for Portia's benefit on the more humane "burnt-skin" theory:

> *Mislike me not for my complexion,*
> *The shadowed livery of the burnished sun,*
> *To whom I am a neighbor and near bred.*
> *Bring me the fairest creature northward born,*
> *Where Phoebus' fire scarce thaws the icicles,*
> *And let us make incision for your love,*
> *To prove whose blood is reddest, his or mine.*
> *I tell thee, lady, this aspect of mine*
> *Hath feared the valiant. By my love, I swear*
> *The best-regarded virgins of our clime*
> *Have loved it too. I would not change this hue,*
> *Except to steal your thoughts, my gentle Queen.*

Apart from the questionable but well-meaning science of the "burnt-skin" theory, the conception presented here of the Negro is entirely free of illusions, either against him or in his favor. His color is merely a matter of outward form, reflecting no condition of blood or of the soul, frightening to some but attractive to those who share it. The Prince also knows perfectly well that Portia may not like it, and, she being nothing more nor less in this respect than the average lady of her time and class, he is right. "If he have the condition of a saint and the complexion of a devil," she tells Nerissa with full understanding both of herself and of the problem, "I had rather he should shrive me than wive me." She, at least, could consider the possibility of confessing to a Black priest, but love is another matter. "Let all of his complexion choose me so," she says with relief after he has selected the wrong casket, thereby losing the chance to claim her in marriage.

Portia is thus by no means color-blind where the Negro is concerned, but she is no racist. And much the same can be said of the attitude of all the aristocratic young people in this play toward the Jew: disliking the conventional Jewish religious and social traits that Shylock seems to evince, they nevertheless harbor no real racial resentment toward him and his breed. They have nothing against Jewish blood, as they demonstrate in their wholehearted acceptance of Shylock's daughter Jessica when she joins the Christians. Indeed, when her deserted father insists that "my daughter is my flesh and blood," Salarino contemptuously replies that "there is more difference between thy flesh and hers than between jet and ivory, more between your bloods than there is between red wine and Rhenish." There could be no more vehement repudiation of any idea of a "natural infection of the blood." That this is by no means a set of attitudes to be taken for granted is shown by the servant Launcelot Gobbo, who, according to Jessica, "tells me flatly there is no mercy for me in Heaven, because I am a Jew's daughter." Shakespeare seems to be suggesting here that the lower classes do not share the apparent view of their social superiors that Jews are not born with a racial taint; Sancho Panza felt just as Launcelot did, and the point is no doubt sociologically sound for its day. It is therefore interesting to learn, as we do a few lines later, that Launcelot has not minded sleeping with a Black woman and getting her pregnant. This was a whole other matter; perhaps Launcelot would as willingly have slept with a Jewish woman as with a Black one, but he probably would not have married either of them.

Shakespeare seems, then, to be presenting a world in which no enlightened person ought to deny the essential anthropological truth of Shylock's celebrated plea:

Hath not a Jew eyes? Hath not a Jew hands, organs, dimensions, senses, affections, passions? Fed with the same food, hurt with the same weapons, subject to the same diseases, healed by the same means, warmed and cooled by the same winter and summer as a Christian is? If you prick us, do we not bleed? If you tickle us, do we not laugh? If you poison us, do we not die? And if you wrong us, shall we not revenge?

One could read "Negro" for "Jew" in this speech, and it would still be presenting the underlying racial outlook of the play. It is the mature Shakespeare's answer to all racial devil theories, Jewish or Black, and is the point at which he leaves Barabas behind as decisively as he has left Aaron the Moor. Shylock may still be the villain of the comedy, but the audience is allowed no easy conscience about him; Shakespeare has shown his side of the question in a more than merely intellectual way. The Marlovian *épater le bourgeois*, the sly insistence that there are other viewpoints than those of smug convention, has developed into a more richly human understanding of the outsider himself, and boyish cleverness has given way to tragic insight of the highest order.

Indeed, it is possible to say that Shylock is the first genuine tragic figure in Shakespeare, and that all the rest, outsiders in one way or another, are descended from him. This makes it most appropriate that, during his period of transcendent creativity, Shakespeare returned to the theme of the racial outsider and made a Black man one of his immortal tragic heroes. Othello seems in a way to be a conscious atonement for Aaron the Moor; he is the very opposite of a devil, and even the passion that leads him to murder his wife is the expression of a heart purer than that of anyone else in the play. He is a true Noble Ethiopian — although his innocence, and the period of American experience in his background, suggest some qualities of the Noble Savage as well. He is in any case the best of the Venetians, no different from them in his eagerness to fight off the Turkish threat from the southeast — Shakespeare has given his Moor the most northern and Christian of souls — but stronger in his resolve and in his ability to do so. We are vividly reminded of this in his great final speech when he points out in his despair, "I have done the state some service, and they know't," and takes his own life upon saying,

> *that in Aleppo once,*
> *Where a malignant and a turbaned Turk*
> *Beat a Venetian and traduced the state,*
> *I took by the throat the circumcised dog*
> *And smote him, thus.*

In that moment of exorcism, of decisive self-separation from the turbaned and the circumcised, Othello had been like Moses, the Egyptian prince, slaying one of his countrymen for persecuting a Hebrew. Who could doubt the fullness of his identification with the Christian cause?

Not that the play is without its devil, for Iago, Shakespeare's most richly developed personification of evil, is the direct descendant of Aaron the Moor, though without any of his sexuality or charm. There is even a quasiracial tinge to the way in which Iago sees himself: he proclaims an alliance between "my wits and all the tribe of Hell," and later invokes "the souls of all my tribe"; but this is only the Devil's race, undefinable by any other trait than its blackness of heart. The terms "devil" and "slave" are used frequently in connection with Iago, and quite appropriately; but the great irony is that the man toward whom he is both these things is of the complexion to which they were usually attributed. Shakespeare makes no brief for slaves or servants in this play, but is on the side of the dignity of status that is earned by true nobility of character. He is turning all popular notions about slaves, devils, and Black men over on their heads.

There seems, in fact, to be a new level of sophistication concerning the Negro at work in this play, which was written in about 1602. The racial attitudes of the Middle Ages have now been left behind, as evidenced not only in Shakespeare's quasimodern liberalism on the subject of color, but in the new kinds of anti-Negro prejudice manifested by some of the characters. Only Brabantio, whose daughter Desdemona has eloped with the Moor, thinks of the latter as a devil in the old-fashioned way, maintaining,

> She is abus'd, stol'n from me and corrupted
> By spells and medicines bought of mountebanks.
> For nature so preposterously to err,
> Being not deficient, blind, or lame of sense,
> Sans witchcraft could not.

But Brabantio is of a dying generation, whereas Roderigo, denouncing "the thick-lips" and "the gross clasps of a lascivious Moor," and Iago, who is the first to inform the deceived father,

> Even now, now, very now, an old black ram
> Is tupping your white ewe,

have a more up-to-date notion of what black deviltry is supposedly all about. New representatives of the sophisticated bigotry of the Arabian Nights, they have, as it were, rejected all the mythic elements in Aaron the Moor save that of his remarkably potent sexuality. They are the link between medieval and modern race prejudice.

Iago, who occasionally toys with the idea that Othello had been sporting with his wife, is so patently obsessed with sexual jealousy of the Moor that it is even possible to think of this as the chief motive for his deadly campaign of deceit. He has a nagging dirtiness of mind where Othello is concerned, betrayed above all when he ruminates in front of the latter about Desdemona's choice of him as a husband:

> Not to affect many proposed matches
> Of her own clime, complexion, and degree,
> Whereto we see in all things nature tends —
> Foh! One may smell in such a will most rank,
> Foul disproportion, thoughts unnatural.

Iago sounds a little bit like Brabantio here, but more vile, since he is trying to tell the Moor to his face that his white wife was perverse for having chosen him, and more ominous, since he is hinting at the one piece of Black witchcraft that will remain convincing to future generations. For Iago and others, Black sexual potency was the true demonism, symbolized by the Negro child of a white mother that figured in George Best's story from real life and in Shakespeare's earlier dramatic fiction. The fear of what that child represented was now spreading among Englishmen in general. It was a legacy being prepared above all for English America, even before the latter had come fully into being.

The New World was again becoming a prominent part of English schemes during the period in which Shakespeare flourished, and he, like other Elizabethan and Jacobean playwrights, responded vividly to its presence. Not that he ever made the American enterprise an explicit part of the action of a play the way George Chapman, Ben Jonson, and John Marston did in their 1605 comedy *Eastward Ho,* with two "adventurers bound for Virginia" among its many characters, and a sea captain who says,

> A whole country of English is there, man, bred of those that were left there in '79 [*sic,* for 1587]; they have married with the Indians, and make 'em bring forth as beautiful faces as any we have in England; and therefore the Indians are so in love with 'em that all the treasure they have they lay at their feet.

But the references abound in Shakespeare all the same. In *The Merchant of Venice,* Antonio's ships go to Mexico among other far-flung places; in *Twelfth Night,* Maria says of the deceived Malvolio that "he does smile his face into more lines than is in the new map with the augmentation of the Indies" — an apparent reference to the map in the second edition of Hakluyt's *Voyages.* In 1595, Raleigh had made his first unsuccessful expedition to Guiana, hoping to establish an English foothold between Spanish and Portuguese settlement in that region and find the fabled gold of El Dorado, and in *The Merry Wives of Windsor* Falstaff says of Mistress Page, "She is a region in Guiana, all gold and bounty." Shakespeare's patron, the Earl of Southampton, was Raleigh's rival at court, and it may well be that Falstaff's remark is not the only place in the plays to make fun of the Guiana adventure: Portia's three caskets, the two worthless ones being of gold and silver, the valuable one being of lead, could very well be a parable about Raleigh's southern pretensions to treasure — it is interesting that the two princes who yield to the false glitter are a Moroccan and a Spaniard — in contrast to the good old sober

English way to New World fortune. Raleigh's *Discovery of Guiana* was undoubtedly Shakespeare's source for Othello's description

> *of the cannibals that each other eat,*
> *The anthropophagi, and men whose heads*
> *Do grow beneath their shoulders,*

even though the latter monstrosity is a standard element in travel litera-ture going all the way back to classical antiquity.

By about 1611, however, four years after the establishment of the first permanent English colony in Virginia, Shakespeare went beyond mere passing references to the New World and wrote, without explicitly stating it as his subject, the most brilliant parable of it that has ever been seen. The specific source of the central idea in *The Tempest* was the shipwreck at Bermuda — which subsequently led to English colonization of that island group — of part of the relief expedition that Sir Thomas Gates had been leading to Virginia in 1609. After the survivors had returned to England the following year, two of them had published accounts of the disaster, and one of these, written by William Strachey, seems to have been studied carefully by Shakespeare; there are several apparent refer-ences to it, including Ariel's remark about "the still-vexed Bermoothes." But the greatest poetic imagination of all time readily rose above mere topical references, and achieved a fictitious construct encompassing all of the hopes and realities of overseas colonization. It is the philosophical Gonzalo, "an honest old councillor," who gives us the Ovidian — and Montaignian — vision of the good life to be led in Arcadia:

> *I' the commonwealth I would by contraries*
> *Execute all things, for no kind of traffic*
> *Would I admit, no name of magistrate.*
> *Letters should not be known; riches, poverty,*
> *And use of service, none; contract, succession,*
> *Bourn, bound of land, tilth, vineyard, none;*
> *No use of metal, corn, or wine, or oil;*
> *No occupation — all men idle, all;*
> *And women too, but innocent and pure;*
> *No sovereignty —*

But Shakespeare knows full well that any such desire "to excel the Golden Age" is just a dream; he also knows that foremost among the realities of Arcadia that contradict it is the violation of its stricture against the "use of service." As the no less philosophical Prospero says about his own native servant,

> *We cannot miss him. He does make our fire,*
> *Fetch in our wood, and serves in offices*
> *That profit us. What ho! Slave! Caliban!*

The underside of the colonial experience is above all represented in *The Tempest* by Caliban (the name is an anagram of "cannibal"), who is Shakespeare's summary vision of the colonized savage, and the last of the eminent racial outsiders in his plays. But one should not look for any of the sentiment that had attached to Shylock or Othello in this long-tailed monster, whom Prospero calls in all sincerity

> *Thou poisonous slave, got by the Devil himself*
> *Upon thy wicked dam,*

and who seems to combine the childlike unruliness of Pigafetta's Patagonians with strange physical traits of the sort that Raleigh and Othello described. Shakespeare's sentiments went out to men and women of the Old World, and not to the exotic beings — whether fancifully or realistically conceived — who inhabited faraway places. Indeed, his view on the colonization of such places seems to be that one should, in the end, do precisely what Prospero does and get out of them, leaving behind for good all the problematical even if profitable relationships that they entail. (Perhaps this, too, was his reading of the career of Raleigh, who now was a prisoner in the Tower of London.) The poet shows no fondness for Caliban, and no faith whatever in the spiritual capacities of this savage who latches on to a pair of drunkards in his clumsy strivings for freedom, and is ready to make gods of them. But he sees Caliban's side of the story all the same: in a sense, we are back to the early, more Marlovian Shakespeare, who can present the case for the outsider dispassionately, without any particular identification with him, on the strength of intellect alone — although now it is a vastly richer intellect, capable of taking on its own kind of emotive force. Caliban is genuinely moving when he recalls some of Prospero's better moments at the very beginning of colonization, evoking memories of Thomas Hariot at Roanoke:

> *Thou strokedst me, and madest much of me, wouldst*
>   *give me*
> *Water with berries in't. And teach me how*
> *To name the bigger light, and how the less,*
> *That burn by day and night. And then I loved thee,*
> *And showed thee all the qualities o' th'isle,*
> *The fresh springs, brine pits, barren place and fertile.*

But he reminds his master that such knowledge from another world is in the end a curse:

> *You taught me language, and my profit on't*
> *Is I know how to curse. The red plague rid you*
> *For learning me your language!*

However ignorant and repulsive the savage may be — Shakespeare is showing us — and whatever benefits civilization may offer him, we cannot deny the ultimate import of his case against it:

> *For I am all the subjects that you have,*
> *Which first was mine own king.*

Colonizer and colonized are equally repulsive to one another, in Shakespeare's vision, which shows the relationship to be hopeless for as long as it exists. Michael Drayton, at around this very time, can urge Englishmen

> *To get the pearl and gold,*
> *And ours to hold,*
> *Virginia,*
> *Earth's only paradise,*

but the weary author of *The Tempest,* having traveled through some of the farthest reaches of the human spirit, would now rather

> *retire me to my Milan, where*
> *Every third thought shall be my grave.*

It was time for yet another generation to take on the joys and agonies of empire, and to encounter the new-found races of mankind.

22

L'Acadie

WITH THE COMING of the seventeenth century there arose a new interest in American colonization among the nations of northern Europe; but it was France, not England, that seized the initiative. In 1598, the year in which he signaled an end to the long civil war by promulgating the Edict of Nantes, King Henry IV granted a patent to a Breton nobleman, the Marquis de la Roche, to colonize Canada in seigneurial fashion. La Roche obtained some forty convicts, brought them to remote Sable Island, about a hundred miles east of Nova Scotia, and returned to France to raise funds for the colony. He did not get back to the island until 1603; finding eleven bedraggled survivors there, he took them home. Meanwhile, a more expressly commercial New World enterprise had begun. In 1600, the king had granted a part of La Roche's rights to Pierre Chauvin, a wealthy merchant of Honfleur on the coast of Normandy. Chauvin sailed right up the St. Lawrence and established a garrison at Tadoussac, at the mouth of the Saguenay River, where he proceeded to carry on a brisk trade in furs with the Indians. He then left a contingent of sixteen men there and returned to France, but when he got back in 1602, he found them nearly extinguished by scurvy, starvation, and the ravages of winter. He was trying to start a new colony when he died at the very beginning of 1603.

Upon hearing of Chauvin's death, Aymar de Chaste, governor of Dieppe and an old friend of Henry IV, asked for and obtained his patent. By March of 1603 he had sent out an expedition to Tadoussac commanded by François Gravé, the Sieur du Pont — generally known as Pontgravé — who had previously sailed with Chauvin, as one of his partners. What is especially notable about this voyage is that it included a young soldier named Samuel de Champlain among its members.

It is a pity we do not know more about the origins of this man who was to dominate the history of New France for the next thirty years, leave an indelible mark upon the map of southeastern Canada and the northeastern United States, and serve for all time as a model of sane European-Indian relations. Born of humble parentage in about 1570 at the seaport village of Brouage, not far from La Rochelle, Champlain may have been baptized a Protestant, but we have no evidence on this point one way or the other. He professed Catholicism later in life, but the Old Testament "Samuel" is a name more likely to have been given by Protestant than by Catholic parents, and La Rochelle was a major Huguenot center. Furthermore, he made his entrance into history as part of an enterprise dominated by Protestants — Chauvin was one, and possibly Pontgravé as well. De Chaste was a Catholic, however, and evidently a true *politique,* as his long-time association with Henry IV would suggest. Perhaps it was the *politique* spirit that in the end represented Champlain's underlying religious orientation. This was, after all, a new era: Philip II had died in the year of the Edict of Nantes, and the shadow of militant, Spanish-style Catholicism had receded with him. In the age of Henry IV, the Protestant humanist tradition could, like the king himself, as easily wear a Catholic mantle as a Huguenot one. As among the New Christians of an earlier time, a fresh synthesis of religious ideals was again possible within Catholicism; and Champlain seems to have been one of its quiet prophets. In any case, Canada was worth a mass.

A new synthesis certainly is suggested by the nature of his first entry into the New World, which occurred in 1599. In that year, after several years in the army, he had shipped out in an expedition commanded by an uncle of his, who was serving Spain. They had gone to the West Indies, and during the entire journey Champlain had kept a record of what he saw, in the form of sketches as well as notes, for he had a certain skill in drawing. The manuscript book that he had composed out of these after his return to France in 1601 — which was not to see print until the nineteenth century — had somehow won the attention of the king, who had thereupon brought Champlain into contact with De Chaste. Champlain was to continue being a prolific writer and sketcher of his New World impressions.

His account of the expedition led by Pontgravé in 1603, which evidently was intended for reconnaissance rather than settlement, shows a high degree of solicitousness toward the Indians of Tadoussac — who, incidentally, were Algonquian, and not the people Cartier had encountered more than sixty years before, now mysteriously vanished. Champlain seems to have shared from the outset the inclination, so strong among Frenchmen, to regard the Indians as equals, and to recognize that one's own ability to cope with the wilderness depended upon respectfully learning from and even identifying with its indigenous inhabitants. This attitude is reflected even in Champlain's account of a conversation about religion, the most vexing of subjects in that era, that he had with a sagamore, or chieftain, named Anadabijou (presumably through an unmentioned interpreter):

> They are for the most part a people that has no law, as far as I could see and learn from the said grand Sagamore, who told me that in truth they believe there is a God, who has made all things. Then I said to him, since they believe in one God only, how had He brought them into the world, and whence had they come? He answered me, that after God had made all things, He took a number of arrows, and stuck them in the ground, whence He drew men and women, which have multiplied in the world up to the present, and had their origin in this fashion. I replied to him that what he said was false; but that in truth there was but one God, who had created all things on earth and in the heavens. Seeing all these things so perfect, without anybody to govern this world beneath, He took the slime of the Earth, and of it created Adam, our first father. While Adam slept, God took a rib of the said Adam, and out of it formed Eve, whom He gave him for his companion; and that it was the truth that they and we had our origin after this manner, and not from arrows as was their belief.

The atmosphere suggests a rustic *lycée*, a scene out of Rousseau; it is a far cry, indeed, from the scenes of idols being smashed and mass baptisms imposed that we associate with the Spaniards in the New World.

Upon their return to France that fall, Champlain and Pontgravé learned that De Chaste was dead, and that the patent was now held by Pierre de Gua, the Sieur de Monts, a Protestant gentleman who had been a partner of Chauvin along with Pontgravé. De Monts had been to Tadoussac with his partners three years before, and was evidently convinced that it was not viable for settlement, so that when he sent out an expedition in the spring of 1604, with Champlain and Pontgravé aboard, it sailed into the Bay of Fundy instead of the St. Lawrence. The new colony was established at an inlet on the southwestern shore of Nova Scotia, and was called Port Royal. Champlain proceeded to explore the waters to the west and south of it, giving to his discoveries such enduring names as Isle au Haut and Isle des Monts Déserts. The entire region was called by the French "l'Acadie," probably at first after the Micmac word *aquoddy* — enshrined in such place-names as Passamaquoddy — meaning "place" or "region," but also no doubt with the echo of "Arcadia," which had been applied to the North American coast before, ringing in their ears.

The Arcadian atmosphere of that bit of French America is best conveyed in the writings of Marc Lescarbot, a lawyer who arrived in Port Royal in 1605, as the colony entered its second year. In a kind of seventeenth century preenactment of the classic flight into the French Foreign Legion, Lescarbot apparently sailed to America to escape creditors, but once there, he became its eager and passionate student, a French Thomas Hariot. A man of taste and classical learning, he was eventually to write a *History of New France,* a delightful work which surveys the events of Cartier's voyages, of Brazil, and of Florida, but which deals primarily with the author's own experiences and observations at Port Royal. Anticipating Rousseau even more vividly than Cartier had, he writes with reference to his American experiences that "those men are indeed to be pitied who, having it in their power to live a quiet life in the country, cultivating the soil which yields such a good return, pass their lives in cities." This is as genteel a vision of life in America as can be encountered in that epoch, and indeed, Lescarbot's view of the savages, of whom he constantly reiterates that they must be treated with the utmost gentleness by Europeans, makes them seem almost more decorative than real. For him, they come out looking a bit like those elegant ladies and gentlemen back at the French court who in these very days would occasionally dress up as Indians for pageants.

Lescarbot even once created a New World pageant of his own, right on the scene. One evening in November of 1606, he presented before an audience of French colonists and local Indian leaders a masque consisting of Neptune, six Tritons, and four Savages — all, including the latter, played by Frenchmen. As part of the amphibious proceedings, the four "Savages" arrived in canoes bearing a quarter of venison, and intoning to the French commander:

> *Nos moyens sont un peu de chasse*
> *Que d'un coeur entier nous t'offrons;*
> *Et vivre toujours en ta grâce*
> *C'est tout ce que nous désirons.*

("What we have is a little something from the hunt/ Which we offer wholeheartedly to thee;/ And to live forever in thy good graces/ Is all that we desire.") This may have been too pretty for Champlain, who was of a less privileged background than Lescarbot's and more grizzled than he by real experience with the Indians: in later years, when they became bitter rivals and authors of competing versions of the history of Acadia, Champlain was to accuse him of never having set foot outside of Port Royal itself. There is undoubtedly a touch of dilettantism in Lescarbot, but this also is something present in the entire French approach to the New World at this time, even in its more rugged manifestations. The French came to trade, not to cultivate as the English were soon to do; the typical successful French colonist of the early seventeenth century was the man who made his fortune in furs and then went back to France to enjoy it. Even those most dashing symbols of New France who were to arise in the next generation, the *coureurs de bois* — "runners of the woods" — bold adventurers who penetrated the wilderness alone on foot and by canoe, dealing with the Indians on terms of the greatest intimacy and proudly living like them, the true ancestors of Natty Bumppo, hardly were expressions of the impulse to settle down and make homes that subsequently created American society.

But not even the French would be able to hold to this romance in all its purity, and Champlain himself soon had to face grim realities in Indian relations. Early on, the pioneers of New France made a fateful decision to be the loyal allies of the Algonquian tribes who straddled the banks of the St. Lawrence, and above all, of the Hurons farther west, the largest of all the nations along the emerging French trade route. The Hurons seem to emerge into history as a veritable French alter ego: they had most likely been the people encountered by Cartier at the villages of Stadaconé and Hochelaga, and the very name they were now coming to be generally known by was French — it meant "men with heads like wild boars," but the French view of them became more benign soon after that christening. In the later course of the seventeenth century, the most heroic stories of all those attaching to the French in North America were to be told about the Jesuit missionaries among the Hurons, many of whom eagerly gave their lives for the sake of this people they had made their own. But disaster also was written into this most noble of European-Indian alliances, for the most implacable of the Huron's native enemies was also the greatest power in eastern North America at the time of the white man's arrival: the five-nation League of the Iroquois. This confederacy, consisting of the Mohawk, Oneida, Onondaga, Cayuga, and Seneca nations, was linguistically related to the Hurons, but since its territory was somewhat to the south of the St. Lawrence and inland from

Acadia, along the westward extension of present-day New York State, the French had hardly come into contact with its members at first. This lack was soon corrected.

After a sojourn back in France, Champlain and Pontgravé had returned to Canada with a new expedition in the spring of 1608 and had this time gone up the St. Lawrence, establishing their colony near the site of ancient Stadaconé and naming it Québec. That fall, after Pontgravé had sailed back home with a large cargo of furs, leaving Champlain and twenty-eight others to man the fort, a chief of the Ottawas, one of New France's Algonquian allies, showed up for a visit. Among other things, the Ottawa was given a display of those new toys that would shake the foundations of Indian life — firearms — and he was so impressed that he made a suggestion. Would the Frenchmen care to go south with a party of Algonquians and Hurons and fire upon their enemies, thereby to frighten them into permanent submission? Champlain agreed — free access to Ottawa as well as to Huron country were prizes he greatly desired — and in June of 1609, after Pontgravé's return, he duly set out at the head of such an expedition, consisting of eleven Frenchmen and perhaps as many as four hundred Indians at first. Before long, a quarrel broke out among the Indians, and about three-quarters of them went home. The remainder of the war party made its way down the western shore of the lake that now bears Champlain's name — although for many years the English colonists were to call it Lake Iroquois — and encountered a group of about two hundred Mohawks in the vicinity of Ticonderoga. Through the night the Mohawks built a barricade for themselves on shore, while the French and their Indian allies remained in their boats, the two sides exchanging loud taunts.

In the morning, Champlain later wrote, "after arming ourselves with light armor, we [that is, the eleven Frenchmen] each took an arquebus, and went on shore. I saw the enemy go out of their barricade, nearly two hundred in number, stout and robust in appearance. They came at a slow pace towards us, with a dignity and assurance which pleased me greatly, having three chiefs at their head." Even in this last moment of an ancient dignity which he was about to violate forever, Champlain, a true Frenchman, could pause to admire it. His allies, outnumbered and outclassed by the enemy, were unflaggingly aware of their secret weapon, however, and after making doubly sure that the gun-wielding Frenchmen would not be far behind, charged with false boldness into the fray. "They began to run for some two hundred paces towards their enemies," Champlain goes on, "who stood firmly, not having as yet noticed my companions, who went into the woods with some savages. Our [Indian] men began to call me with loud cries; and, in order to give me a passageway, they opened in two parts, and put me at their head, where I marched some twenty paces in advance of the rest, until I was within about thirty paces of the enemy, who at once noticed me, and, halting, gazed at me, as I did also at them. When I saw them making a move to fire at us, I rested my musket against my cheek, and aimed directly at one of the three chiefs. With the same shot, two fell to the ground; and one of their men was so wounded that he died some time after." Champlain has further immortalized this fateful moment with a splendid drawing, showing two armies of naked Indians facing each other at the water's edge, their boats on one side, the woods on the other, and himself standing between them in the full battle regalia of a French soldier of the day — including an iron helmet with a white plume — firing his arquebus at the enemy leaders, who fall to the ground.

It was a shot heard round the American Northeast. "The Iroquois were greatly astonished that two men had been so quickly killed, although they were equipped with shields of wood and woven cotton thread which was proof against their arrows. This caused great alarm among them. As I was loading again, one of my companions fired a shot from the woods, which astonished them anew to such a degree that, seeing their chiefs dead, they lost courage, and took to flight, abandoning their camp and barricade, and fleeing into the woods; whither I pursued them, killing still more of them. Our savages also killed several of them, and took ten or twelve prisoners. The remainder escaped with the wounded."

The French had won the day, but ultimately — and probably because of this day above all — they were to lose the war; for the Iroquois were henceforth to be dedicated to destroying them and their allies wherever possible, with whatever allies they could themselves obtain for the task. And providence even had begun sending the cure, deadly in its own right, before the plague. At this very moment, the English captain Henry Hudson was sailing a Dutch ship down the American coast toward the mouth of the river that would eventually bear his name, and that was to become the artery along which firm friendship was to flow between the Dutch and the Iroquois in years to come. As for the nation that was to be heir to this Dutch-Iroquois alliance and thereby the definitive destroyer of French ambitions in North America, it too had established a permanent foothold on these shores at last. The Jamestown colony, such as it was, had thus far survived two years of starvation and disease, and it was not to be lost. The days of North American Arcadia were already at an end, and the scramble for empire was about to begin in earnest.

23

The Adventures of Captain
John Smith

> At his [Smith's] entrance before the King
> [Powhatan], all the people gave a great shout.
> The Queen of Appomattock was appointed to
> bring him water to wash his hands, and another
> brought him a bunch of feathers, instead of a
> towel to dry them: having feasted him after
> their best barbarous manner they could, a long
> consultation was held, but the conclusion was,
> two great stones were brought before Pow-
> hatan: then as many as could laid hands on him,
> dragged him to them, and thereon laid his head,
> and being ready with their clubs to beat out his
> brains, Pocahontas the King's dearest daughter,
> when no entreaty could prevail, got his head in
> her arms, and laid her own upon his to save him
> from death. . . .

THE LEGEND OF JOHN SMITH and Pocahontas stands on these words
written by Smith's own hand, describing events that followed his capture
by Indians along the Chickahominy River in Virginia at around the very
end of 1607. Her selfless act of rescue, even more than her later marriage
to John Rolfe, has given Pocahontas a vivid place in the American imagination and constitutes her claim to being a kind of Doña Marina of the
north. A wide public that knows little else about Smith's prominent role
at the beginning of American colonization cherishes his memory for this
moment alone. The story seems to sum up the most ideal aspects of the
Virginia colony in its early relationship with the Indian — bold, romantic,
and so gentle as to be ready to assume the role of victim before any other.

But this apparently was not the only romantic rescue by a lady that
Smith had experienced in his life. In the Epistle Dedicatory of *The General History of Virginia, New England and the Summer Isles*, from which
the above-quoted passage was taken, he tells his patroness, the Duchess
of Richmond:

Yet my comfort is, that heretofore honorable and virtuous
Ladies, and comparable but amongst themselves, have offered
me rescue and protection in my greatest dangers: even in
foreign parts, I have felt relief from that sex. The beauteous
Lady Tragabigzanda, when I was a slave to the Turks, did all
she could to secure me. When I overcame the Bashaw of Nalbrits in Tartaria, the charitable Lady Callamata supplied my
necessities. In the utmost of many extremities, that blessed
Pocahontas, the great King's daughter of Virginia, oft saved
my life. When I escaped the cruelty of pirates and most
furious storms, a long time alone in a small boat at sea, and
driven ashore in France, the good Lady Madame Chanoyes,
bountifully assisted me.

This certainly is appropriate company for an Indian princess about whom
— when news of her betrothal to John Rolfe was brought back to England — King James wondered if it were proper that she marry a mere
commoner, regardless of their respective races. It also is a dazzling
record of feminine alliances for a man, a mere commoner himself, who
remained a bachelor all his life. What in the world, the reader may have
wondered when this book appeared in 1624, were all these fabulous histories he is referring to? One would not have had to wait too long for the
answer: eagerly cultivating his personal legend by then, Smith went on to
publish his autobiography five years later. *The Travels and Adventures
of Captain John Smith* is the book from which we obtain almost all that
we know about the first twenty-six years of his life, down to the Jamestown expedition.

Born in 1580 in Willoughby, Lincolnshire, of modest but up-and-
coming yeoman stock, John Smith began a life of adventurous wandering when he was about fifteen years of age, according to this narrative.
We see him, first as an apprentice, then as a mercenary soldier, traveling
through the Netherlands, France, and Italy, and finally arriving in Hungary, where he proceeds to fight with the Christian armies against the
Turks. A sturdy, ingenious Anglo-Saxon, Smith quickly displays grace
under pressure to his Austrian and Hungarian comrades, devising a
signal system for them in the heat of battle, creating an elaborate fire-
works scheme with which to harass the enemy, and eventually chal-
lenging three Turks to individual combat, each of whom in turn suffers
defeat and the loss of his head under Smith's fearsome sword. For this
latter exploit Smith, now a captain in the imperial army, is rewarded by
Prince Zsigmond Báthory with an escutcheon showing three Turks'
heads upon it — an appropriate symbol for a man who is soon also to show his
strength before another sometimes troublesome dark-skinned people at
the western end of the world. But difficulties arise: Smith is at last taken

prisoner by the Turks and sold into slavery. Coming into the possession of one "Bashaw Bogall," he has the good fortune to be sent as a gift to that man's "fair mistress," the Lady Charatza Tragabigzanda, in Constantinople. She falls victim to his charms, treats him with kindness, and eventually sends him for an intended brief sojourn with her brother, the "Bashaw of Nalbrits," on the far side of the Black Sea. Smith gets into a fight with the "Bashaw," kills him, and makes his escape across the steppes, his chains still dangling from him. At a remote Muscovite outpost, a governor takes pity on him and removes his chains; Smith also wins the concern of the governor's wife, "the good Lady Callamata," who "largely supplied all his wants." He finally makes his way back to western Europe, has another bout of voyaging, then ships out with a French privateer and gets into a fierce sea battle with two Spanish men-of-war off the west coast of Africa. After this he returns to England; it is 1604, and the voyage to Jamestown lies only two years ahead.

What are we to make of this dazzling world traveler, who seems to have a special way with exotic, highborn women wherever he goes (the French Madame de Chanoyes belongs to a later period of his life) and an incredible ease in strange environments? But this latter trait, so startling in a provincial Englishman of that day, brings to mind a significant point: Smith never tells us how he was able to communicate so readily with men and women of various nations, many of whose names are so thoroughly butchered by him as to suggest a total ignorance of their languages on his part. In fact, many of his spellings of personal and place names have Italian forms when they are literate at all, and this is significant in light of our knowledge that he leaned heavily for some of his background material on an Italian work, *The Wars of Hungary, Wallachia and Moldavia*, by Francisco Ferneza.* This fact becomes particularly striking when, upon close examination not only of Smith's account of the Turkish wars but of the entire book, one perceives that there is remarkably little personal narrative interspersed among a great quantity of historical and geographical information that need not have been based on the author's own experience at all — that, indeed, probably was not, for it is largely routine and impersonal.

We are led, then, to some disturbing questions. What other works of travel and history, not mentioned by Purchas, did Smith perhaps also borrow for use in this purported autobiography? And how are we to take

---

* The original of this — which has disappeared, and may have existed only in manuscript — had been translated into English by Smith's good friend, mentor, and editor, Samuel Purchas, but had not been published by him when he handed it over to Smith for the latter's use. The translation also has since disappeared, but we know of it because Purchas tells us about it in a marginal note to his edition of Smith's autobiography.

the various passages describing his own exploits, which are often so crudely inserted in the text as to form separate short paragraphs between longer ones of impersonal historical narrative? As for the sea battle at the end, it is written in a style so different from the rest that it leads one to wonder whether Smith has not borrowed wholesale somebody else's written account of this adventure. Such are the thoughts aroused by at least one book from the man who also has given us, not only the celebrated story of his rescue at the hands of Pocahontas — the veracity of which has, in fact, been questioned by Henry Adams and other writers — but the largest and most important single account of the early history of Jamestown, our sole source for much that happened there.

But let us leave Smith for a moment and return to the general history of English overseas activity that was to culminate in the Jamestown adventure. In England, as in France, a renewed surge of interest in America had come with the arrival of the seventeenth century, signaled above all by Richard Hakluyt's publication, from 1598 to 1600, of a second and greatly enlarged edition of his monumental compilation of voyages. For a moment, American activity continued to revolve mainly around the figure of Raleigh, who seemed to have recovered from the decline in his fortunes resulting from, among other things, the apparent failure of the Roanoke colony.* His recovery of the leadership in overseas expansion seemed assured by his highly touted though fruitless expedition to Guiana in 1595, and by his participation in the brilliant naval assault on Cadiz the following year. This latter exploit had come hard upon the news that Drake and Hawkins, who had united their forces again at last to make a voyage of harassment to the West Indies, had both fallen sick and died on their ships. It was the end of an era — but Raleigh did not herald the new one, as it turned out, whatever the expectations for him may have been as the new century began.

By 1602, Raleigh had sent several reconnaissance expeditions to Roanoke, but there are signs that he was beginning in that year to lose the initiative in American colonization. That spring, a ship commanded by Bartholomew Gilbert, a son of Sir Humphrey Gilbert, and by Bartholomew Gosnold sailed to "the North part of Virginia" and established a trading colony of several months' duration on Cuttyhunk, one of the Elizabeth Islands southwest of Cape Cod. Gilbert was Raleigh's nephew, but Gosnold's family had been closely associated with Essex, and when

---

* Another setback had been the queen's disapproval upon learning in 1592 that he had secretly married Elizabeth Throckmorton, one of her ladies-in-waiting — an indiscretion that had cost him several months in the Tower of London. But his return to favor at the court was certain by 1601, when his young rival Essex was beheaded for having tried to lead a coup d'état.

this expedition became known to Raleigh after the fact, he at first disapproved of it. At least two other major reconnaissance voyages, also without Raleigh's involvement, were made to that region in the ensuing three years, one in 1603 commanded by Martin Pring, and the other in 1605 under George Waymouth, who paid particular attention to the Maine coast, right in the teeth of the new French establishment at Port Royal. But Raleigh had in the meantime become reconciled with Bartholomew Gilbert, who made yet another voyage to the Roanoke and Chesapeake Bay areas for his uncle early in 1603, and lost his life there. Raleigh was at that moment still in the Anglo-American picture, and perhaps still even dominated it; but now it was to change precipitously.

Queen Elizabeth died in March of that year and the new king, James I, wasted no time about showing a great dislike for Raleigh, who had opposed his claim to the succession. Raleigh's enemies at court convinced James that he had even planned a conspiracy to prevent the new king from ascending the throne. James also wanted to end the long war with Spain as soon as possible, and therefore was amenable to the idea of disposing of that country's foremost surviving English enemy. By November Raleigh had been arrested, and at the end of a trial that has lived on in infamy was found guilty of treason. His life was spared, however, and he was sent to the Tower of London, where he was to spend the next twelve years.

Raleigh's demise signaled even more decisively than the death of Drake and Hawkins the end of an era where American colonization was concerned. Whatever his faults, Raleigh had represented the aspirations of that Protestant humanist tradition that had been passed on from France to England in the latter half of the sixteenth century, and had been the trademark of the group of advocates of American initiatives gathered around Walsingham in the 1580s. Walsingham had died in 1590, and the condemnation of Raleigh now seems to have delivered a final blow to the energies of that group's survivors. Hakluyt is the member of the group whose profile suggests a dramatic rising and falling of enthusiasms: the new edition of his *Voyages* was followed, after Raleigh's trial and imprisonment, by a sudden and permanent retreat into the shadows.

For Thomas Hariot, the situation became even more extreme. Shortly after returning home from Roanoke in 1586, he had obtained the patronage of one of the most powerful nobles of the realm, Henry Percy, the ninth Earl of Northumberland — a direct descendant of Shakespeare's Hotspur — and had gone to live and do research on his estate. True to the recent traditions of his family, Northumberland was a Catholic, but this had not been a disability when James first came to the throne. James was tolerant of Catholics, and for a moment there had even been hopes for a Catholic initiative in American colonization, as evidenced by George

Waymouth's 1605 voyage, which had Catholic backing. In this brief dawn of religious reconciliations promised by the death of Philip II, the end of the war with Spain, and the reign of Henry IV in France, a new Catholic humanism, close in spirit to the Protestant one, stepped to the fore in England as in France: it was such a spirit that made the atmosphere of the Northumberland estate congenial to a man like Hariot. But it suddenly was forced into retreat with the uncovering, in November of 1605, of the abortive plot, led by some Catholics, to blow up Parliament. English anti-Catholicism thereupon found a new lease on life, and the Earl of Northumberland, accused of complicity in the plot, became Raleigh's neighbor in the Tower of London. Hariot thereby was given two reasons for staying out of the foreground of affairs.

In the spring of 1606, as if to emphasize that a new era had begun, two Virginia Companies were chartered by the crown to take up the task of American colonization: Raleigh's old seigneurial approach was now being replaced by a capitalistic one. On the surface of it, at least, the old gentlemen of colonization and their associates were either in jail or in retreat, and the task was being taken up by representatives of the rising middle classes, by men for whom the strain of relatively easygoing humanism that had flourished at Roanoke in spite of everything was a luxury not to be readily tolerated. But the changing of the guard was not, in fact, to be accomplished so smoothly.

According to the terms of their charters, the Virginia Company of London was to colonize the southern part of Virginia, that of Plymouth the northern part. The Plymouth Company got started first, sending out Martin Pring later that year to explore the Maine coast for a site. Both companies then sent out colonizing expeditions that reached their respective destinations in May of 1607, but the Plymouth Company's colony, established at the mouth of the Kennebec River — then called the Sagadahoc — gave up after a harsh winter and returned to England the following year. The London Company's colony at Jamestown is another story.

More so than its sister at Plymouth, the London Company had quietly maintained some links with the recent colonial past. Sir Thomas Smythe, chairman of the East India Company and one of the eminent merchants of the day, was a central figure among the London Company's shareholders, and he was an old friend of Raleigh's. Richard Hakluyt's name also was on the list of the company's patentees, and though he was never to be clearly visible during the subsequent course of events, his presence is often discernible: surely it was his hand at work, for example, at the point in the company's instructions to the colonists when they are urged,

"In all your passages, you must have great care not to offend the naturals, if you can eschew it."

The recent history of American colonization and exploration also seems to have been summed up in the remarkably varied assemblage of one hundred and forty-four men who sailed aboard three ships out of the Thames on December 20, 1606, heading for Virginia in the name of the London Company. The commander of the expedition was Captain Christopher Newport, a Drake-like figure who had risen from humble origins and achieved fame as a privateer against the Spaniards, primarily in the West Indies, where he had lost an arm in battle. The second-in-command was Bartholomew Gosnold, of the Cuttyhunk expedition of 1602, an important moral leader among the members of the expedition who, unlike Newport, was going to stay with the colony once it had been established. Among the prospective colonists, but holding no evident official position, was George Percy, the twenty-six-year-old younger brother of the Earl of Northumberland, seeking his fortune in the wide world as the younger brothers of nobility were so often forced to do in that era of unrelenting primogeniture. We do not know if Percy was a Catholic like his brother, but there was at least one highborn Catholic aboard that we know of. This was Edward Maria Wingfield, whose grandfather had been a diplomat in the service of Henry VIII, and whose father had remained steadfast in his loyalty both to that queen and to that Virgin whose name in common he had given to his son. Wingfield brought two servants with him on the voyage, and soon made enemies with his airs of social superiority as well as with his religious convictions, which he apparently made little effort to conceal.

Indeed, the fleet had barely left port when he became the center of a shipboard controversy over religious matters. The final upshot is not clear, although we know definitely of one casualty among the several persons who became involved. This was John Smith, who had made his way onto the expedition through a series of personal and family connections leading to Bartholomew Gosnold. Smith, "suspected for a supposed mutiny," evidently for the way he had involved himself in the conflict against Wingfield, was placed in confinement at around this time and held as a prisoner for the remainder of the long voyage.

But then the story takes a remarkable turn. One night late in April, 1607, having reached the desired shores of Chesapeake Bay but not yet having chosen an exact site for the colony, Captain Newport opened the sealed instructions of the London Company and read off the names of those who had been appointed to the governing council in Virginia. The list not surprisingly included the three ships' captains — Newport himself, Bartholomew Gosnold, and a mysterious character who called himself

John Ratcliffe but whose name turned out to be really Sicklemore. It also included Wingfield, who was well connected at the London Company — indeed, whose connections in high places were probably better than those of anyone else on the expedition, with the possible exception of George Percy, who was notably *not* named to the council, even though he was at this time keeping a diary that seems too much the opposite of casual not to have had some kind of official basis. The surprise came with the three other names on the list of seven council members: John Martin, George Kendall — both of them men of obscure origins who were to play significant roles in the campfire politics of Jamestown — and John Smith.

Wingfield must have been astonished at the inclusion of Smith. He later was to say that, back in England, he would never have let it come about that his "name should be a companion" to such a man — though there are indications that he had known Smith before this expedition; for we know that he was to accuse Smith of once having "begged in Ireland like a rogue, without a license." Wingfield, then, had served in Ireland, like so many other English pioneers in America; but what about Smith? This statement makes it sound as if he had done the same apprenticeship, and perhaps had misbehaved; but there is not a word about Ireland in his memoirs, written more than twenty years after the events at Jamestown.

Meanwhile, how had Smith achieved this sudden eminence among the Jamestown settlers? Surely his connection with Gosnold was the secret. Gosnold evidently was the London Company's fair-haired boy, their answer to any suspicions of the Raleigh taint that might still attach to them, a potential English Champlain. He was entitled to have his own men and Smith was one of them, made even in the master's image to some extent, albeit of somewhat poorer quality material. This was the relationship that would eventually, after Gosnold's death from illness only three months later, enable Smith to rise to eminence and, in the end, immortality; but Smith, still a prisoner, had not achieved real power just yet. The majority of the council was still favorably disposed toward Wingfield, and they elected him the first president of the colony.

The site of the colony was established on the James River, and Newport, after leading a preliminary scouting expedition upriver and back, set sail with two of the ships for England on June 22, 1607. He intended to return with new supplies as soon as possible, but meanwhile the colony of one hundred and four men that he had left behind was in a situation already deteriorating rapidly, from hunger, illness, troubles with the Indians, and internal squabbling. In the ensuing six months, all but thirty-eight of the colonists died, mainly from sickness and starvation; but the struggle for survival exacerbated rather than dulled the spirit of contention among this remarkably varied group of strong-willed men. With Newport gone, and after Gosnold's death in August, Wingfield was left without his principal backing, and the hostility toward him that had never been far beneath the surface among the colony's leaders quickly erupted. Smith accused him to his face of taking more than the agreed-upon allotment of food for himself and his servants out of the common store, of which he was in charge, and this was concurred in by two other council members, John Ratcliffe alias Sicklemore, and John Martin, whose son had come along on the expedition and had just died of starvation. The idea also spread among Wingfield's enemies that, since he was a Catholic, he probably was plotting with the Spaniards to overthrow the colony. Finally, in September, a triumvirate made up of Smith, Ratcliffe, and Martin succeeded in removing Wingfield from office, and installed Ratcliffe as president in his place. Wingfield was held prisoner, but nothing worse was done to him because he still had friends and defenders in the colony: George Percy evidently was still on his side, though he remains in the shadows of this affair as with so many others.

Shortly after these events, in December, John Smith — in his capacity as "cape merchant," or chief trader with the Indians — made the trip up the Chickahominy River that has since become immortal for his capture by the Indians and the Pocahontas episode. When he returned in late December or early January, he found himself confronted with a radically different situation at the fort than had prevailed at his departure. For yet another rambunctious personality now appears on the scene, this time one Gabriel Archer, a man who also had old associations with Gosnold — he had gone along on the 1602 voyage to Cuttyhunk commanded by Gosnold and Bartholomew Gilbert, and had written the account of it that survives to this day — and who perhaps had become resentful of the stature that his fellow disciple Smith had attained in the colony. Ratcliffe and Martin had both fallen ill, and during Smith's absence Archer had persuaded them to let him take command. Now, upon Smith's return, Archer demanded that his rival be brought to trial for negligence in the deaths at the hands of Indians of two of the colonists who had accompanied him up the Chickahominy. Smith's life therefore was hanging in the balance when, suddenly, Newport returned with the supply ships from England, bringing much-needed sustenance, and placating everyone enough, Smith later wrote, that "for a while these plots against me were deferred." Ratcliffe recovered, things in the colony took a better turn, and when Newport sailed for England again in April, he brought Wingfield and Archer with him to air their grievances back in London.

This is the point at which Smith begins to emerge as something of a man of letters and, above all, as an overseas hero of the English people, particularly in his relations with Indians. In the immediate wake of New-port's departure, there doubtless was a surge of feeling in the colony that Wingfield and Archer should not be allowed to present their stories back home uncontested: they would certainly be at odds with one an-other, and it was desirable that there be some third position between their attitudes of self-serving strife, representing the colony itself, such as it now was in their absence. Furthermore, the public at large, and not just the directors of the London Company, ought to be able to hear about what Englishmen were accomplishing at Jamestown against great odds. Now Smith, as it turns out, had been keeping a journal that would prove satisfactory to these requirements, and furthermore, an opportunity pre-sented itself for getting that journal back to England at about the same time as Wingfield and Archer arrived there, but without their knowledge. For after Newport's departure in April, the *Phoenix*, another of the sup-ply ships that had come with him from England, finally straggled into Jamestown after long delays at sea. It was the *Phoenix*, then, that re-turned to England in the summer of 1608 bearing the manuscript of John Smith's *A true relation of such occurrences and accidents of note as hath happened in Virginia*, which was published in August.

The possibility remains that Smith had placed his manuscript aboard the *Phoenix* entirely on his own initiative, but somebody sailing on the ship had to be persuaded to carry out this mission, and this probably required more influence than Smith alone would have had. Further-more, there clearly were people back in London who were eager to see his work through the presses, even though the personal aggrandizement of Captain John Smith was not necessarily the first reason in their minds for wanting to do so. Indeed, the pamphlet had to have a third printing before Smith's name even appeared on it.* Evidently, some person or persons took their time deciding whether they wanted to tout the man named John Smith at all.

For the name of the narrator of *A true relation* was one that was bound to enjoy a certain glory. His account portrays a scene of hardship met by Englishmen with an indomitable will to succeed, and of tension and tentativeness with the Indians gradually turning into accommodation and the ability to deal with them. There are internal conflicts among the colonists, but at the center of them all stands a sturdy man of the people, a worthy successor to Gosnold, tough and ingenious, steadfast in his loyalty to the enterprise though often misunderstood, shrewd and un-

---

* On the first printing, its author was simply "a gentleman of the said colony," and on the second a "Thomas Watson," though there was no one by that name in James-town. Even the third version had to be corrected, for it said at first "Captain Smith Coronell [i.e., Colonel] of the said colony"; the "Coronell" was subsequently changed to "one."

afraid in his relations with the Savages, toward whom he seems ever to
know exactly when to be kindly and when to be tough — in short, an
English Champlain. The high point of the narrative is Smith's capture by
the Indians, which at last brings him face-to-face with the great Powhatan, the "emperor" — as the English often called him — of a loose
confederation of most of the tribes of the region, about whom the settlers
had often heard, but whom none of them had met until this moment:

> Arriving at Weramocomoco, their Emperor proudly lying
> upon a bedstead a foot high, upon ten or twelve mats, richly
> hung with many chains of great pearls about his neck, and
> covered with a great covering of rahaughcums [raccoon skins].
> At [his] head sat a woman, at his feet another; on each side
> sitting upon a mat upon the ground, were ranged his chief men
> on each side the fire, ten in a rank, and behind them as many
> young women, each a great chain of white beads over their
> shoulders, their heads painted in red: and with such a grave
> and majestical countenance, as drave me into admiration to see
> such state in a naked Salvage, he kindly welcomed me with
> good words, and great platters of sundry victuals, assuring me
> his friendship, and my liberty within four days.

There then ensues a long, leisurely and rather detailed conversation between the Indian ruler and his English captive.

The scene is as vivid as a John White painting, and as inspiring a one
as could be desired at the very beginning of Anglo-American history: if
only relations between white man and Indian could always have been
like this! But, alas, we cannot accept this account uncritically; disturbing
questions crowd in upon it. We must take note, for example, that this is
the very scene in which the episode of Smith's near execution and his
rescue by Pocahontas was to be inserted in a version published by him
sixteen years later.* Where is that story now? The editor of this pamphlet, who signs himself only "I.H.," tells us in a preface that "somewhat
more was by him written, which being as I thought (fit to be private) I
would not adventure to make it public"; but would this consideration
apply, given the obvious purposes of the pamphlet's publication, to so
good a piece of copy as the Pocahontas story?

The questions do not end here. The long conversation between himself and Powhatan, described by Smith without any indication that an
interpreter may have been present, also is puzzling. How could he have
attained such a knowledge of the Algonquian language in so short a

---

* Roughly, it would appear after "their heads painted in red" plus some additional
embellishments.

time? A few years later, as an appendix to one of his books, he was to publish an Algonquian vocabulary, but even this is hardly extensive enough to have covered the rather sophisticated points he exchanged with Powhatan that day at the very end of 1607 or beginning of 1608. Furthermore, there are passages scattered throughout this pamphlet over which the same question must be reiterated, such as this one describing his encounter, during the captivity that ultimately brought him before Powhatan, with the werowance of Paspahegh:

> I presented him with a compass dial, describing by my best means the use thereof: whereat he so amazedly admired, as he suffered me to proceed in a discourse of the roundness of the earth, the course of the sun, moon, stars and planets.

In an instant, this remarkable man has become a veritable Prospero, teaching Caliban how to "name the bigger light, and how the less" — or, even more to the point, a Thomas Hariot, who had introduced the natives of Roanoke to "mathematical instruments, sea compasses," and the like.

Indeed, the shadow of Thomas Hariot rests so heavily on this and other passages that one must assume a palpable influence, upon the writing of them if not necessarily upon the original acts they describe. No doubt Smith had read Hariot's *Brief and true report,* a work which certainly would have heightened his understanding of the Indian and have fired his eagerness to pull out compass dials before astonished werowances. But would it have given him an ability to describe Indians with a great skill and keenness of observation — as in the above-quoted passage on Powhatan — that often vanishes without a trace elsewhere in his writings? Smith may have read Hariot, but he had not studied with him.

In short, the text of John Smith's pamphlet of 1608 abounds with hints of a presence or presences other than his own amidst the personal and often solitary adventures depicted by the author. One can even go a step further than this; for there are stylistic inconsistencies, sudden jumps from a less to a more cultivated literary hand, as in the passage on Powhatan, which begins with "arriving at Weramocomoco" and then leaves the participle dangling as it moves into a realm of better syntax. Smith seems to have embellished his own recollections with some outside literary materials.

Nor do we have to look very far for a probable source of such materials. We know that, though only the merest fragments of them have survived, George Percy was keeping records of observations made at Jamestown by himself and others; and who was a likelier bearer than he of the intellectual tradition of Thomas Hariot? After all, it really is inconceivable that Hariot's potentially very useful body of observations at Roanoke should have gone by the board, especially with Hakluyt still a presence in the Virginia enterprise. But who besides Percy would have inherited it among the men at Jamestown? He above all of them was the representative of the pro-Indian humanist tradition that White and Hariot had stood for. It was during the years of his childhood and adolescence at the Northumberland estate that Hariot had lived there, and now here he was at Jamestown displaying, among other things, signs of a thorough familiarity with the Algonquian Indian language, as we can readily see in his writings. Surely Hariot had been his teacher.

This probable discipleship is well displayed in the fragments that we have of the journal kept by Percy during at least the early months of the expedition. Evident throughout is an eagerness to cast the glow of Hariot and White over Anglo-Indian relations at Jamestown, as in this passage describing the adventures of a scouting party led by Newport during the first days of the fleet's arrival in Chesapeake Bay:

> The next day, being the fifth of May, the Werowance of Rapahanna [Rappahannock] sent a messenger to have us come to him. We entertained the said messenger, and gave him trifles which pleased him. We manned our shallop with muskets and targeteers sufficiently: this said messenger guided us where our determination was to go. When we landed, the Werowance of Rapahanna came down to the water side with all his train, as goodly men as any I have seen of Savages or Christians: the Werowance coming before them playing on a flute made of a reed, with a crown of deer's hair colored red, in fashion of a rose fastened about his knot of hair, and a great plate of copper on the other side of his head, with two long feathers in fashion of a pair of horns placed in the midst of his crown. His body was painted all with crimson, with a chain of beads about his neck, his face painted blue, besprinkled with silver ore as we thought, his ears all behung with bracelets of pearl, and in either ear a bird's claw through it beset with fine copper or gold. He entertained us in so modest a proud fashion, as though he had been a prince of civil government, holding his countenance without laughter or any such ill behaviour. He caused his mat to be spread on the ground, where he sat down with a great majesty, taking a pipe of tobacco: the rest of the company standing about him. After he had rested awhile he rose, and made signs to us to come to his town. He went foremost, and all the rest of his people and ourselves followed him up a steep hill where his palace [sic, for wigwam] was settled. We passed through the woods in fine paths, having most pleasant springs which issued from the mountains. We also went through the goodliest corn fields that

ever was seen in any country. When we came to Rapahanno's town, he entertained us in good humanity.

Allowing for touches of idealization, this is as keen an anecdotal description of Indian life as can be found in the early English literature on the subject, and it bespeaks a mind that, in addition to being highly cultivated in a general way, has already achieved a particular sensitivity toward this kind of material.

The solicitousness toward the Indian continues in Percy's journal even down through its description of the first major crisis in the relations between the two races at Jamestown, later that month. This occurred during the scouting expedition that Newport led up the James River before his departure for England; Percy and Smith both were on this expedition, whereas Wingfield and Gosnold stayed behind at the chosen site of the colony to supervise the construction of a fort. The fragment of Percy's journal dealing with the journey upriver has survived in manuscript, and was not included in the parts that were published a few years later in Samuel Purchas's celebrated collection of travel narratives; but though it bears no author's name and has been attributed by most scholars to Gabriel Archer, who also was on the expedition, it clearly belongs to Percy's journal. The crisis appears in this narrative fragment as follows:

> Wednesday we went ashore at Point Winauk [Weyanoke], where Nauiraus [the Indian guide for the journey] caused them to go a-fishing for us, and they brought us in a short space good store: These seemed our good friends, but (the cause I know not) here Nauiraus took some conceit, and though he showed no discontent, yet would he by no means go any further with us, saying he would go up to King Arahatek [Arrohattoc], and then within some three days after he would see us at our fort. This grieved our Captain very deeply, for the loving kindness of this fellow was such as he trusted himself with us out of his own country, intended to come to our fort, and as we came he would make friendship for us, before he would let us go ashore at any place, being (as it seemed) very careful of our safety.
>
> So our Captain made all haste home, determining not to stay in any place as fearing some disastrous hap at our fort. Which fell out as we expected, thus.

And Percy goes on to describe the scene as they found it back at the fort, where, indeed, an Indian attack had occurred, doing considerable damage to the unfinished construction, killing a servant boy, wounding many other Englishmen, including "our president Master Wingfield (who showed himself a valiant gentleman) [who] had one shot clean through his beard, yet scaped hurt." The relationship between Nauiraus and the attack remains unclear, but except for one cautious parenthetical "as it seemed," Percy shows a strong inclination to give him the benefit of the doubt.

The attitude is somewhat different in the account of this incident given by John Smith in *A true relation*. He writes:

> That night passing by Weanock [Weyanoke] some twenty miles from our fort, they [the Indians] according to their former churlish condition, seemed little to affect us, but as we departed and lodged at the point of Weanock, the people the next morning seemed kindly to content us, yet we might perceive many signs of a more jealousy in them than before; and also the hind [that is, servant, referring to Nauiraus — the usage is uncomplimentary] that the King of Arseteck [Arrohattoc] had given us, altered his resolution in going to our fort, and with many kind circumstances left us there. This gave us some occasion to doubt some mischief at the fort, yet Capt. Newport intended to have visited Paspahegh and Tappahanock, but the instant change of the wind being fair for our return we repaired to the fort with all speed. . . .

Here there is suspicion from the outset, and a touch of scorn at the end for what the writer clearly regards as Newport's overly trusting attitude, enabling him for a moment to consider going on with the journey despite the signs that something may have gone wrong back at the fort. Surely these words are not by the same man who lectured on compass dials to the werowance of Paspahegh and discoursed so amiably with the fearsome Powhatan. This is a tough-minded son of the people, surly and suspicious toward alien races, not an aristocratic student of exotic cultures.

And in the long run, the Smith of *A true relation* as a whole — the John Smith of legend — was a blend of the two. It is unlikely that he could have written the pamphlet without Percy's close cooperation, and contrary to the look of things at first sight, there are good reasons why Percy might have given it. Things had reached such a pitch at Jamestown by the time the *Phoenix* was getting ready to return to England that Percy may well have been eager to lend his vital services in the making of Smith into another Champlain. He was a friend and distant relative of Wingfield's, to be sure, but he probably hated Archer, and besides, he seems to have been a man for whom no personal loyalty could rival his devotion to the enterprise. He knew better than anyone that it was badly in need of a hero at this moment, and that he, with his retiring personality and tainted associations, could hardly have played the role. A Gosnold was needed but, lacking him, a Smith would do. These are the grounds on which this prodigal offspring of Shakespearean lineage may have begun the building of our first American legend, even before Pocahontas lent a hand.

The Adventures of Captain
John Smith, Continued

THE JAMESTOWN CAREER of Captain John Smith reached its apogee immediately after the departure of the *Phoenix* with his manuscript aboard in June of 1608. That summer he led two voyages of exploration along the shores of Chesapeake Bay and its environs and, upon his return from the second one in September, was elected to succeed Ratcliffe as president of the colony. He seems to have carried out this task creditably in the ensuing months, although it is extremely difficult to judge this point, since all we have are his own accounts written in later years, which inflate his role to that of Jamestown's savior.

Meanwhile, however, the fate of the colony was being determined back in London, the real center of its power if not the spearhead of its survival. Wingfield and Archer were heard out by the company's directors, other problems were considered, and by the beginning of the following year the London Company had been reorganized and merged with that of Plymouth. The presidency of the colony was replaced by a governorship, which was awarded to a distinguished nobleman, the Lord De la Warr (whose name is the origin of "Delaware"). De la Warr was not yet ready to sail to Virginia, however, and so in May an acting governor, Sir Thomas Gates, was sent out in his place, with a fleet commanded by Christopher

Newport. One of its passengers was Gabriel Archer, who evidently had achieved some kind of decision in his own favor; Wingfield stayed home. But the flagship, with Gates, Newport, and the writer William Strachey aboard, was soon foundering off Bermuda, to provide eventual inspiration for the colonizing of that island and, through the medium of Strachey's account of the shipwreck, for *The Tempest*. The other four ships of the fleet reached Jamestown, and Archer, who arrived on one of them, immediately began to agitate for Smith's deposition. Smith resisted; the days of the presidency were numbered, to be sure, but nobody knew yet when a governor would arrive, and Smith wanted to hold onto power as long as he could. But just as the end of his elected term was approaching, a powder bag he was holding accidentally exploded, and he was left disabled. Badly in need of medical attention, he reluctantly sailed back to England in October. George Percy was elected acting president in his stead.

The tenuousness of Jamestown's existence was by no means at an end, however. Percy evidently was far less gifted an administrator than he was a scientist and writer, and there was not much anyone could have done in that moment when inexperience, hardship, and anarchy conspired to bring the colony's fortunes to their lowest ebb. Powhatan remained unpredictable despite the contact that had been established with him, and there were still skirmishes with Indians, to such an extent that even Percy seems to have lost some of his patience with them at this point. Yet, so far as is possible to make out — all we have for this period is the merest fragment of a manuscript, written years later by his own hand — he remained a force for reconciliation with the Indians even in the worst moments, in opposition to the uncontrollable brutalities of a Captain James Davis, who had arrived with the rump of Gates's fleet, evidently the company's choice as a keeper of law and order. Gates finally arrived, and so did De la Warr, but both of them soon returned home, leaving the management of the troubled colony — which, at one point, had been almost completely abandoned out of despair — in Percy's weary hands once again. Relief finally arrived in May of 1611, in the form of yet another fleet sent out by the now resolute company, under the command of a military leader, Sir Thomas Dale. Authoritarian to the point of unconscionability, Dale soon brought viability to Jamestown, organizing it like a military garrison, and forcing the settlers to grow their own food instead of relying, as they had in the past, almost completely upon trade with the Indians for their sustenance. The Virginia adventure was on a solid footing at last by the spring of 1612, when George Percy sailed home. Like Smith, he was never again to see the colony he had done so much to help create.

Percy's work on behalf of Jamestown was not quite at an end, however. We may safely assume that he returned to England with a large accumulation of papers, the product of six years of observation and inquiry, though not necessarily all of it; some papers had probably gone back to England already, and some had perhaps even been entrusted to John Smith in palmier days, in the form of duplicates at least. He also returned just after the man who clearly was the choice of himself and his circle — still far from eager to publicize themselves — to succeed Smith as the chief propagandist of the Jamestown enterprise: the writer William Strachey. A Cambridge man, an aspiring litterateur, a friend of Ben Jonson and of Thomas Campion, a devout humanist, Strachey had sailed with Gates to be secretary of the Jamestown colony after a spotty career as a lawyer and a diplomat; he was obviously suited to do the job that now devolved upon him. A little over a year after his arrival home, he had turned out a tentative draft of a work based not only upon his own experiences, but also clearly upon material he could only have obtained from Percy and from Hakluyt, as well as upon some already published sources. Making three copies of his *History of Travel into Virginia Britannia,* he sent one of them, with a dedication, to Percy's brother, the Earl of Northumberland, who was still a prisoner in the Tower. But the manuscript was unfinished, and had obviously been wound up in haste. Why had this crucial work, which undoubtedly was as much Percy's as it was Strachey's, been suddenly released in such a half-baked condition? The reason seems to lie in the sudden reappearance, at this very moment, of Captain John Smith.

We do not know what Smith had been doing for most of the three years since his return to England, but he assuredly had spent at least part of the time seeking to advance his own fame. Energetic and ambitious, he had even gained a group of supporters all his own, and it was with their help that he was able to publish his second book in the fall of 1612. Smith's volume, *A Map of Virginia,* included a full-length literary work as well as a map per se. The text was divided into two parts, and must therefore have been doubly startling to Percy, Strachey, and their associates when they first got wind of it. The second or narrative part, which deals not only with the year covered by A *true relation,* but with the entire period that Smith was at Jamestown, and which purports to be the work not of Smith himself but of several of the colonists — all of whom are otherwise little known to history — presents a new and greatly inflated hero for the world to admire. Incidents described in the 1608 narrative reappear, greatly expanded, their particulars taking on more impressive dimensions as in a big fish story. Suddenly Smith is no longer merely the shrewd and plucky Cape merchant of old, unaccountably competent in the Algonquian dialects, but a kind of philosopher-king, who lectures to Powhatan and other Indians in long set speeches, and ponders their similarly lengthy replies. Evidently inspired by the experience of 1608, Smith was now exploring new heights of exaggeration and personal myth-making. Percy must surely have recognized, when he saw this, that it was his own fault; his propagandistic chickens had come home to roost.

But this was only the half of it. The first of the two textual parts of *A Map of Virginia* was a descriptive tract, purportedly by Smith himself, on the geography, flora, fauna, and Indians of Virginia, in the manner of Thomas Hariot — indeed, it was worthy of that author, but for a reason: passage after passage of it was either very close to or identical with passages in Strachey's *History of Travel into Virginia Britannia!* Nowadays, it is widely assumed among scholars who are willing to put faith in Smith in spite of everything that Strachey copied from him, and not the other way around. Yet even on the basis of internal evidence alone this view is not entirely tenable, since in virtually every parallel set of passages Smith's is the shorter one and Strachey's is far more detailed.[*] Rather, what the circumstantial evidence suggests above all is that this coincidence of texts was due to their authors' use of a common source — the provenance of which, once again, could only have been that most astute compiler of the natural and moral history of Jamestown, George Percy. Surely it is no accident that Smith manages never to use Percy's name even once in this descriptive part of his book, not even in a passage that Strachey tells us was based on an eyewitness account of his. This oversight is hardly worthy of the generosity Strachey shows to Smith, of whom he writes at one point: "Sure I am, there will not return from thence [Virginia] in haste, any one who hath been more industrious, or who hath had (Captain George Percy excepted) greater experience amongst them [the Indians], however misconstruction may traduce him here at home, where is not easily seen the mixed sufferances both of body and mind, which is there daily, and with no few hazards, and hearty griefs undergone." The exception in the name of George Percy was evidently too great a one to be borne by the mounting ego of Captain John Smith, who seems to have been preparing his betrayal at the very moment these words were written.

But how did Smith get hold of Percy's material so that he could pirate it in this way? It is quite clear that Smith and Strachey were in touch

---

[*] Indeed, even one eyewitness observation of Indian customs that Strachey readily attributes to Smith — but not to *A Map of Virginia* — is more detailed in Strachey than in Smith, suggesting that the source may have been a deposition made by Smith long before, which he preferred to use instead of his own recollection, and which was at least as available to Strachey as it was to him.

during the period when Strachey was back in England writing his book, for Strachey makes in it a number of appreciative references to Smith's map of Virginia — that is, to his *map* properly so called, and not to the book of that name that Smith was to publish along with it. Percy and Strachey must have been delighted when they saw this first detailed depiction of the Chesapeake Bay area, and evidently they showed their appreciation by letting Smith see their own material. Perhaps Smith even asked them if he could draw upon some of it as an accompanying text for the forthcoming published version of his map; they would certainly have agreed to such a request, not knowing what they were in for as a result.

All of this indicates that Smith, in the four years since his launching as a public figure with Percy's probable help, and especially in the three since his return from Virginia, had become quite well ensconced within the network of geographical popularizers and proponents of American colonization that ultimately had its origin in Raleigh's initiatives and that was still — in spite of everything — dominated by the venerable figure of Richard Hakluyt. It remains possible, even through the obscurity covering most of Smith's career in this period, to see some of the connections. Undoubtedly there were some direct relations with Hakluyt himself, since Smith had returned to England as Percy's fair-haired boy. But Hakluyt was still staying in the shadows, and Smith made his most solid connections in this network with a group that would probably not have participated so enthusiastically in it had Raleigh still been active. For what we see gathering around Smith is a group of Puritan divines — to use the word "Puritan" for a period before it had yet come to designate a separate party, but when it already represented a distinct tendency — whose view of the Virginia enterprise was closer to the spirit of militant Christianity that had been expressed by Edward Hayes in his account of Sir Humphrey Gilbert's last voyage back in 1583 than it was to the more relaxed humanism of Raleigh's old circle. The editor of Smith's *A Map of Virginia*, for example, was the Reverend William Symonds, a London preacher who had attracted a good deal of attention three years earlier with a sermon exhorting Englishmen to plant themselves in Virginia like the Israelites in Canaan.

The most important of all these associations for Smith, however, was with a man who was now on his way to becoming the foremost keeper of the record of the "American Genesis" in this epoch, the Reverend Samuel Purchas. Born in around 1575 in the village of Thaxted, in Essex, Purchas was a man of humble origins, like Smith. A good scholar, he had gone to Cambridge and studied for the clergy, but had started out in his career on the lowest rung of the ladder despite this background: his marriage license, drawn up in Purleigh, Essex, in 1601, describes him and his bride as "household servants" in the home of the parson. From 1604 to 1613 he was in a better position, holding a vicarage in a nearby town, but evidently he burned for the kind of distinction that only literary work could bring; and in 1613 he published a book that made his reputation. Called *Purchas his Pilgrimage,* this folio volume of more than six hundred pages was a peculiar distillation of its author's two intellectual passions, religion and geography. Purchas evidently had set for himself the task of writing the religious history of the entire world, but his approach to it turned into a kind of continent-by-continent historical geography. In his acknowledgment of sources, Purchas even makes note of his special debt to the works of Hakluyt; perhaps he was already beginning to envision himself as an author in the tradition of this other, most eminent, clergy-man-turned-geographer.

Hakluyt himself evidently saw it that way, at any rate: for, among the substantial rewards suddenly heaped upon Purchas for this maiden literary effort — which included a chaplaincy under the Archbishop of Canterbury, to whom the book had been respectfully dedicated, and a rectorship in the London suburb of Ludgate — were the attentions of the great editor himself. We do not know precisely what went on between the two clergymen in the months following the publication of Purchas's book, but one may justly assume that Hakluyt, perhaps already feeling the oncoming exhaustion of his days — he was to die in less than three years — was most eager to find a successor to his life's work, and had decided that Purchas was the man. It does not seem to have been anything against the new Rector of Ludgate in Hakluyt's eyes that he had become a warm admirer — though not necessarily a personal friend just yet — of Captain John Smith, from whose *A Map of Virginia* he had quoted liberally in his own book. Obviously, none of the taint of Smith's literary piracy attached to Purchas, and Hakluyt may have been willing to regard the whole matter as beside the point anyway. The Smith image remained worth having for the enterprise, just as the Purchas one was now worth getting. These two men of the people, patriots and Protestants to the core, could provide just the breath of fresh air that was needed to clear away the bad odor surrounding the old Raleigh and Northumberland crowds.

The upshot was that Purchas came away from his distinguished admirer with so much new material, a lot of it pertaining to Virginia, that he immediately set to work on a new edition of his book. It appeared the very next year, 1614, with the additional acknowledgment, "Now in this edition I have been much beholden to Mr. Hakluyt for many written treatises in this kind." This debt particularly shows itself in the chapter on Virginia, now considerably longer than before and filled with additional data not only about early voyages to North America but also about the life and customs of the Indians. This was the high point in relations between Purchas and the Hakluyt circle; but they broke down very quickly thereafter, for reasons about which we can only conjecture.

The main reason may lie in a new and surprising development that had occurred in John Smith's career. In the very year of Purchas's second edition, Smith had shipped out as an officer on a whaling voyage to the coast of "North Virginia," and had not wasted this opportunity to achieve further fame as an explorer and adventurer. During the voyage he had made some side trips of his own in small boats up and down the coast, presumably recording his impressions, and, to top it all off, had been captured by French pirates on the way home. This all was material for another book, *A Description of New England*, which Smith published in June, 1616, some six months after his return. What may have been grievous to Hakluyt is the fact that, sandwiched between the brief accounts of Smith's personal adventures that appear at the beginning and at the end of the book, is a geographical treatise on New England that culminates in an exhortation to Englishmen to plant there. The whole thing is a kind of updated, would-be *Discourse of Western Planting*, and it is just too good, too full of detailed knowledge beyond what anyone could have obtained within a single voyage devoted primarily to whaling, to have come from anything but a sophisticated archive like that compiled by Richard Hakluyt. And if this is Hakluyt's material, then it is a good guess that Smith obtained it through his now devoted friend, the Reverend Samuel Purchas.

If Smith had indeed obtained the use of some of the Hakluyt papers in Purchas's possession, this suggests that a significant historic development was quietly taking place: for Purchas and the other Puritan divines who were now busy making Smith the outstanding hero of the American adventure were men with a distinct philosophy of the English manifest destiny. The fact that they were taking New England as their target instead of Virginia — one can now use these terms in something closer to their modern senses — indicates that Puritan aspirations to make that region specifically their own had distinctly arisen even four years before the landing of the Pilgrims at Plymouth. Something entirely new was shaping up within the bosom of the American colonization movement, and Hakluyt must have fully perceived, by the time he succumbed to his final illness in the fall of 1616, that it was a monster he had himself created. But evidently he sought to make amends, and he died refusing to cooperate any longer with Purchas, who was forced to write of him in the acknowledgments to yet another edition of *Purchas his Pilgrimage* the following year: "Although in this third edition, I could not obtain like kindness from him, I know not how affected or infected with emulation or jealousy: yet shall his name live while my writings endure."

Purchas was not to let the matter go at that; but meanwhile, a new element in the John Smith legend, ultimately to be the most celebrated of all, was beginning to take shape. Although Smith had not mentioned Pocahontas in his 1608 account of his first meeting, as a prisoner, with Powhatan, he had spoken of her elsewhere in that pamphlet, and with avid interest. In one place he describes her as "a child of ten years old: which, not only for feature, countenance, and proportion, much exceedeth any of the rest of [Powhatan's] people: but for wit and spirit, the only Nonpareil of his Country." And he was not the only Englishman at Jamestown to have been struck by the charm of this Virginia princess even before she had reached womanhood. William Strachey, in his *History*, remembered her as

> a well-featured but wanton young girl, Powhatan's daughter, sometimes resorting to our fort, of the age then of 11 or 12 years, [who would] get the boys forth with her into the marketplace and make them wheel, falling on their hands, turning their heels upwards, whom she would follow, and wheel so herself, naked as she was, all the fort over. . . .

We do not hear of this girl again until 1613. By this time the Virginia colony was clearly showing its viability, but relations with Powhatan were still unresolved and the Indian situation was as chaotic as ever. That spring — according to an account published in London in 1615 by Ralph Hamor, one of the Jamestown colonists — Captain Samuel Argall, a newly arrived trader, was making a voyage up the Potomac when he found Pocahontas visiting that area. Sensing a unique opportunity, he lured her aboard his ship by a ruse and took her back to Jamestown as a hostage. She was treated well there, both by the governor, Sir Thomas Gates, and by Sir Thomas Dale, the military commander of the colony, who placed her in the custody of a minister after she had, as we are told, expressed a desire to learn about Christianity. It was during this apparently gracious captivity that she met another recently arrived colonist, John Rolfe, a widower in his late twenties, who, perhaps as much for the sake of policy as for love, soon expressed a desire to marry her.

The prospect of the first legal marriage between the races in Anglo-American history was not one to be taken lightly. After all, no less eminent a supporter of the Virginia adventure than the Reverend William Symonds, John Smith's friend and editor, had spoken out against such alliances in his celebrated sermon of 1609, when he said:

Out of the arguments by which God enticed Abram to go out of his country, such as go to a Christian plantation may gather many blessed lessons. God will make him a great Nation. Then must Abram's posterity keep to themselves. They may not marry nor give in marriage to the heathen, that are uncircumcised. And this is so plain, that out of this foundation arose the law of marriage among themselves. The breaking of this rule may break the neck of all good success of this voyage, whereas by keeping the fear of God, the planters in a short time, by the blessing of God, may grow into a nation formidable to all the enemies of Christ and be the praise of all that part of the world, for so strong a hand to be joined with the people here and fear God.

It is not likely that even baptism would have qualified an Indian woman to become exempted from this rule of Ezra in Symonds's eyes, but Pocahontas's apparent desire to become a Christian was the burden of a letter written by Rolfe early in 1614 to Sir Thomas Dale — but evidently also to the English public at large, to whom it was soon released in print — carefully defending his proposal to marry her. Rolfe clearly has men like Symonds in mind when he writes that he is not "ignorant of the heavy displeasure which Almighty God conceived against the sons of Levi and Israel for marrying strange wives," but that he is ready to accept eternal damnation

if my chiefest intent and purpose be not to strive, with all my power of body and mind, in the undertaking of so mighty a matter, no way led (so far forth as man's weakness may permit) with the unbridled desire of carnal affection: but for the good of this plantation, for the honor of our country, for the glory of God, for my own salvation, and for the converting to the true knowledge of God and Jesus Christ an unbelieving creature, namely Pocahontas.

Yet the religious issue alone patently was not the end of the matter as far as many Englishmen were concerned. The matter of "carnal affection" mentioned by Rolfe seems to have been a prominent part of the range of criticisms with which he had to deal. Further on in his letter he writes:

Now if the vulgar sort, who square all men's actions by the base rule of their own filthiness, shall tax or taunt me in this my godly labor: let them know, it is not any hungry appetite to gorge myself with incontinency; sure (if I would, and were so sensually inclined) I might satisfy such desire, though not without a seared conscience, yet with Christians more pleasing to the eye, and less fearful in the offense unlawfully committed.

Rolfe evidently was not the only colonist to have sought an Indian mistress, but he seems to have been the first ever to have wanted to marry her. This was to result in a certain open-mindedness among Virginians where Indians were concerned: William Byrd of Westover, among others, was to regard intermarriage between whites and Indians as a good idea, and the number of aristocratic Virginians who have, in effect, blessed the union of John Rolfe and Pocahontas by claiming descent from their son is legendary. Rolfe seems to have been one of the persons chiefly responsible for bringing about this attitude. But in his effort to do so, we can glimpse a moment at the very beginning of American history — and before the arrival of the Negro — when the Indian evidently did not look very different from the Negro in the eyes of some white men. Rolfe even grants in his letter that Pocahontas is from a "generation [that is, race] accursed" — a notion not far removed from George Best's idea of a "natural infection" in Blacks, or from late-medieval Spanish notions about Jews and New Christians. The original religious climate within which all such ideas were engendered is still present, but it is beginning to fade and leave a modern, secular racism in its wake.

Baptized with the Christian name of Rebecca, Pocahontas was married to John Rolfe in April of 1614. The union was blessed by Powhatan, who granted the couple a tract of land and became an avowed friend of the colonists at last. The Chickahominies, the most formidable of Powhatan's enemies, thereupon feared a possible alliance against themselves, and they, too, made overtures to the English: in general, a new era of Anglo-Indian relations seemed to have begun. In 1616, Sir Thomas Dale invited the Rolfes and their infant son Thomas to accompany him on a visit to England, and they sailed that spring with an entourage of some ten or twelve Indians. The "Indian Princess," who by now affected a completely English manner and style of dress, became something of a sensation in London, although a few evidently were critical of her "tricking up and high style and titles," as the letter writer John Chamberlain put it. Eventually the Rolfes were presented to the king and queen, whose guests they subsequently were at a gala production of Ben Jonson's masque, *The Vision of Delight,* on January 6, 1617.

Not all was well, however. The dank air of Old World cities had often proved a problem for visiting native Americans, and during the course of their stay in London the Rolfes had been forced to retire to a suburb because of it. Pocahontas was quite ill by the time they set out on their return to Virginia in March, and she died aboard ship even before it had left the Thames. She lies buried in England to this day, at the parish church of St. George in Gravesend.

John Rolfe, a widower once again, returned to Virginia without his small son,* remarried — this time, as the first, to an Englishwoman — and settled down to the life of an assiduous farmer. He soon became celebrated for pioneering the cultivation of tobacco as a cash crop, the first source of real wealth for Virginia — and, in time, grounds for the mass importation of cheap labor that would ultimately lead to the slave trade. Rolfe could not have foreseen this; but, coincidentally, his name also is attached to the sentence that announces the beginning of Black slavery, and of Black history, in Anglo-America: "About the last of August," he apparently wrote in his journal for 1619 (although this reaches us only by John Smith's hand, the original having since disappeared), "came in a Dutch man-of-war that sold us twenty Negars [*sic*]." By a strange irony, then, the figure of one of the first men to bring light to Anglo-Indian relations in America casts an ominous shadow over the Black destiny that was to ensue.

But this is not the only irony of John Rolfe's later years. For a while, relations between the English and the Indians reached new heights at Jamestown and the smaller settlements it now was spawning nearby; prosperity and peace seemed so abundant that the number of colonists exceeded four thousand by the beginning of 1622. Plans were laid for the establishment of an Indian college at Henrico, about fifty miles up the James from the parent colony; at the center of these plans stood a man named George Thorpe, the most recently arrived representative of a humanist approach to the Indians, who apparently was ready to devote his life to the cause of friendship between the races. But Powhatan had died in 1618, ominously to be succeeded by his younger brother Opechancanough, who had never ceased to look upon the English with hostility. Alarmed by the growing population of intruders, he planned an attack, and finally struck in March of 1622. In a series of ambushes, about 350 of the colonists were killed; among the dead were George Thorpe and John Rolfe.

In the wake of the disaster, more than two thousand of the would-be colonists returned to England, and by 1624 the mortally wounded Virginia Company had been dissolved; Jamestown and its offspring were then placed directly under control of the crown. The euphoria about the Indian that had attended the visit of Pocahontas was now at an end, and John Smith could candidly show the true nature of his racial outlook by writing, at the end of his account of the 1622 attack:

> Thus have you heard the particulars of this massacre, which in those respects some say will be good for the plantation, be-

---

* Thomas Rolfe received an English education and did not return to his native Virginia until he was twenty years old.

cause now we have just cause to destroy them [i.e., the Indians] by all means possible: but I think it had been much better it had never happened, for they have given us an hundred times as just occasions long ago to subject them. . . . Moreover, where before we were troubled in clearing the ground of great timber, which was to them of small use: now we may take their own plain fields and habitations, which are the pleasantest places in the country. Besides, the deer, turkeys, and other beasts and fowls will exceedingly increase if we beat the Salvages out of the country: for at all times of the year they never spare male nor female, old nor young, eggs nor birds, fat nor lean, in season or out of season; with them all is one. The like they did in our swine and goats, for they have used to kill eight in ten more than we, or else the wood would most plentifully abound with victual; besides it is more easy to civilize them by conquest than fair means; for the one may be made at once, but their civilizing will require a long time and much industry. The manner how to suppress them is so often related and approved, I omit it here: And you have twenty examples of the Spaniards how they got the West Indies, and forced the treacherous and rebellious infidels to do all manner of drudgery work and slavery for them, themselves living like soldiers upon the fruits of their labors. This will make us more circumspect, and be an example to posterity: (But I say, this might as well have been put in practise sixteen years ago as now).

One should, in all fairness, attribute some of the energy of these monstrous remarks to the high feelings of the moment; but there also are signs here — and not in the last sentence alone — of notions that have been harbored a long time.

Indeed, Smith had really always been a get-tough man with reference to the Indians: this would have been prominent among the reasons why Percy apparently had lighted upon a Smith-image — albeit a doctored and, in this respect, somewhat softened one — as preferable to his own back in 1608, and this was now the main reason why Purchas was doing his best to bring that image to the heights that gave it immortality. For the sudden appearance of the Captain John Smith of 1624, after several more years of shadows pierced by only occasional rays of light, can only make one gasp. His book of that year, *The General History of Virginia, New England and the Summer Isles,* is not only the most ambitious single work on Anglo-American history that had yet been published, and to this day the most definitive on Virginia for the period 1608–1624; it is also an uncannily rich compendium of original sources — such as the above-mentioned journal of John Rolfe — that have since disappeared, and that could only have reached Smith's hands through the intervention of someone with a good deal more influence than his own. Now this, once again, cannot have been anybody but Samuel Purchas, who also was preparing his own greatest literary triumph at this very moment: for Purchas had finally obtained the entire Hakluyt collection of manuscripts, "not without hard conditions" from the estate, he tells us, but under circumstances that will otherwise forever remain obscure. It was therefore in an entirely proprietary frame of mind toward the hero and the book that were now primarily his own creations that Purchas wrote a prefatory poem to Smith's *General History*, which ends significantly with the couplet:

> *Smith's forge mends all, makes chains for Savage Nation,*
> *Frees, feeds the rest; the rest read in his book's relation.*

The title of Purchas's own monumental work speaks for itself: *Hakluytus Posthumus, or Purchas his Pilgrims*. With only a few exceptions, the contents of this immense anthology of the world's travel literature from antiquity down to the author's own day is of little interest to us, but its spirit is most relevant to our concerns. For it depicts the history of geographical expansion as the unfolding of a divine purpose, culminating in the mission of Protestant England in the wilderness of the New World. This idea is conveyed not only in the arrangement of the materials, but in the editor's abundant commentaries, to be found in the preface and the conclusion of the work, and above all in the marginal notes that he has placed throughout. "Divine things," he tells us in his preface, "are . . . not the peculiar argument of this work, which notwithstanding being the labor of a professed divine, doth not abhor from the same; but occasionally everywhere by annotations, and in some parts professedly by special discourses, insinuateth both the history and mystery of Godliness, the right use of history, and all other learning." This is a large promise, but Purchas's ensuing efforts to deliver on it lack nothing in vigor, and if their shallowness is no surprise, their vindictiveness toward the Savages standing in the way of the new English Joshua may shock the reader who comes to them unprepared.

"These Savages are naturally great thieves," writes Purchas in the margin alongside George Percy's straightforward, nonmoralizing description of a theft, and when Smith drives a hard bargain the editor puts down a rousing cheer: "How to deal with the Savages." But he does not confine himself to brief remarks, and when Smith writes disapprovingly of some generous gifts presented by Newport to Powhatan, saying "We had his favor much better only for a plain piece of copper," Purchas observes:

Civility is not the way to win Savages, nor magnificence and bounty to reclaim barbarians. Children are pleased with toys and awed with rods; and this course of toys and fears hath always best prospered with wild Indians either to do them, or to make them good to us or themselves.

This sermonizing reaches a height at a point when Smith, back in 1608, momentarily detains Opechancanough, one day to be author of the great massacre; Purchas writes:

Opechancanough taken prisoner amidst his men. If this course had been taken by others Virginia by this had been out of her cradle, and able to go alone, yea to trade or fight. But names of peace have bred worse than wars, and our confidence hatched the miserable massacre by this perfidious Savage. And would God a Dale or Smith, or some such spirit were yet there to take this, that is the only right course with those which know not to do right, further for fear of suffering it enforceth.

The mounting fury reaches fulfillment in the editor's conclusion to the work, in which he writes of Virginia at the present moment (1625):

His Majesty is . . . pleased to send a running army of soldiers to scour the country of the unneighborly malicious naturals. . . . I fear not but so bright a sunshine will quickly produce blessed effects.

Purchas thus vents his godly wrath on Canaanites, but these are not the only villains of the piece; for throughout the work there also is an ongoing criticism, explicit and implied, of the kind of men once represented by Raleigh, now dead, whom the pious editor sees as mere dilettantes of the holy task of colonization. In his preface, he writes scornfully — and quite pointedly, though no names are mentioned:

As for gentlemen, travel is accounted an excellent ornament to them; and therefore many of them coming to their lands sooner than to their wits, adventure themselves to see the fashions of other countries, where their souls and bodies find temptations to a twofold whoredom, whence they see the world as Adam had knowledge of good and evil, with the loss or lessening of their estate in this English (and perhaps also in the heavenly) Paradise and bring home a few smattering terms, flattering garbs, apish cringes, foppish fantasies, foolish guises and disguises, the vanities of neighbor nations . . . without furthering their knowledge of God, the world, or themselves.

Purchas also wastes no opportunity to echo these sentiments in his marginal notes, with comments like "Vanity of effeminate planters," "Vanity of self-seeking gloriosos," "Misery of base idleness," and the like, and alongside a passage in Percy's journal about a somewhat mysterious figure at Jamestown named William White, a possible survivor of the Lost Colony, who had "lived with the natives," Purchas writes simply: "He was a madman."*

This feeling extends to Percy himself, whose journal appears in Purchas's book as a mangled fragment that is finally cut off in the middle of a sentence with the remark, scornful and unconsciously significant at the same time: "The rest is omitted, being more fully set down in Capt. Smith's Relations." Percy, who went off to fight against the Spaniards in the Netherlands at around this very time, must have known full well what was now being done to him and everything he stood for; this probably was when he sent his brother an account of his own — which also only survives in fragments — about events in Jamestown during his whole time there and a letter bemoaning the fact "that many untruths have been formerly published wherein the author hath not spared to appropriate many falseties and malicious detractions not only of this part and time which I have selected to treat of but of former occurrences also. . . ." Thus blaming everything on his creature Smith at last, Percy went forth to pursue noble causes once again, and lost a finger in battle.

In a sense, the passing of the John Smith legend from the creative hands of George Percy to those of Samuel Purchas represents the transition taking place in the thrust of American history at that very moment, from early Virginia to early New England, from the Protestant humanism of a Hakluyt and a Hariot to the harsh Puritanism of many of the men who made Massachusetts, from a more or less aristocratic approach to one closer to the hearts of the rising middle classes. There can be no doubt that Purchas and Smith both now looked to New England as the place where the mistakes of Virginia would be corrected, and where men and attitudes of the stamp they now held up to the world would prevail. "I rejoice . . . to hear," Purchas writes in his conclusion, "that the affairs of New England are thriving and hopeful, which two colonies of Virginia and New England (with all their neighbors) God make as Rachel and Leah, which two did build the house of Israel, that they may multiply into thousands." A few years later, Smith placed in his *Advertisements for the Unexperienced Planters of New England, or Anywhere* the following advice, hopefully directed to John Winthrop:

---

* The note literally reads: "He was a made man"; but this surely was a printer's error. In the spelling of the day, "mad" was "madde"; the inadvertent dropping of a "d" is a far more reasonable explanation than any of the ones that must be undergone if we take "made" at face value.

Who is it that knows not what a small handful of Spaniards in the West Indies, subdued millions of the inhabitants, so depopulating those countries they conquered, that they are glad to buy Negroes in Africa at a great rate, in countries far remote from them; which although they [that is, the Negroes] be as idle and as devilish people as any in the world, yet they [that is, the Spaniards] cause them quickly to be their best servants. Notwithstanding, there is for every four or five natural Spaniards, two or three hundred Indians and Negroes; and in Virginia and New England more English than Savages that can assemble themselves to assault or hurt them, and it is much better to help to plant a country than unplant it and then replant it: but there Indians were in such multitudes, the Spaniards had no other remedy; and ours such a few, and so dispersed, it were nothing in a short time to bring them to labor and obedience.

How completely at odds with both morality and history is this, one of Smith's very last literary statements on his lifelong preoccupations! Now he has decided that enslavement of the Indians is more desirable than killing or transporting them, even though it was the latter that Anglo-Americans were for the most part going to do; and as for the Negro slavery to which he found the Indian kind preferable, that was exactly what was to come into being and thrive in his old stamping grounds. In the last analysis, Smith the man was not merely cruel-minded, but pathetically irrelevant. The manufacturers of his legend had, in the end, taken only what they wanted of him, and left him behind — as subsequent American tradition has done.

But what of the Pocahontas whose glory, if not her love, caused Smith to loom large in history after all? The lie now seems almost too obvious: the rescue story did not appear anywhere in his published writings until 1622, the year that Rolfe died; by dint of hearsay, at least, he had been the last possible witness. There is supposed to have been a letter from Smith to Queen Anne, James's wife, about Pocahontas and the rescue, written at the time of her visit to England; but we have this information, and an abstract of the purported letter, only in Smith's *General History,* published after Queen Anne — yet another witness of sorts — also had died. The final, inflated version of 1624 clearly forms a part of the entire mesh of exaggeration and falsehood that Smith, with the aid and encouragement of Samuel Purchas, has woven into the earlier accounts that were published under his name. We have seen the various reasons why Purchas and other influential friends of Smith may have been eager to have him as their own kind of hero; as for Smith, an obvious passion for self-aggrandizement suffices to explain his behavior. But can we discern something else at work in him besides, something ineffable and, dare one say, romantic? The Pocahontas of the *General History*, whose age is not now given, appears frequently as an attractive and apparently ripe young woman. In particular, there is this most memorable passage of all of Smith's writings, describing an idyllic moment at the fort, which does not appear in the earlier versions:

> Pocahontas and her women entertained Captain Smith in this manner.
>
> In a fair plain field they made a fire, before which, he sitting upon a mat, suddenly amongst the woods was heard such a hideous noise and shrieking, that the English betook themselves to their arms, and seized on two or three old men by them, supposing Powhatan with all his power was come to surprise them. But presently Pocahontas came, willing him to kill her if any hurt were intended; and the beholders, which were men, women, and children, satisfied the Captain there was no such matter.
>
> Then presently they were presented with this antic; thirty young women came naked out of the woods, only covered behind and before with a few green leaves, their bodies all painted, some of one color, some of another, but all differing; their leader [presumably Pocahontas] had a fair pair of buck's horns on her head, and an otter's skin at her girdle, and another at her arm, a quiver of arrows at her back, a bow and arrows in her hand; the next had in her hand a sword, another a club, another a pot-stick; all horned alike; the rest every one with their several devices.
>
> These fiends with most hellish shouts and cries, rushing from among the trees, cast themselves in a ring about the fire, singing and dancing with most excellent ill variety, oft falling into their infernal passions, and solemnly again to sing and dance; having spent near an hour in this masquerade, as they entered, in like manner they departed.
>
> Having reaccommodated themselves, they solemnly invited him [i.e., Smith] to their lodgings, where he was no sooner within the house, but all these nymphs more tormented him than ever, with crowding, pressing, and hanging about him, most tediously crying, Love you not me? Love you not me?
>
> This salutation ended, the feast was set, consisting of all the savage dainties they could devise: some attending, others singing and dancing about them; which mirth being ended, with firebrands instead of torches they conducted him to his lodging.

These are pretty recollections for a forty-four-year-old bachelor! The stern — and solidly married — Purchas wrote in the margin alongside this account as it appeared in his own work of 1625, "A wild Diana Actaeon in one person" (another chapter would be needed to ponder *that* remark); but Smith in his 1624 *History* had simply noted at the same place: "A Virginia Maske." A pleasant thought: was this fabricated hero of a group of stern Puritans using them, in the end, to help him indulge in erotic fantasies? Or maybe there even was something, long ago, on some wild moonlit night in Virginia, that either he or George Percy — or both of them, who knows? — had genuine cause to remember, even to embroider a little. But that other lifelong bachelor, Smith's alter ego in some ways after all, was as silent, in his own name at least, on this subject as on most others. Whatever the secret may have been, the two brought it to their graves not long after this literary outburst, and within a year of one another: Smith died in 1631, Percy in 1632. In some ways, tidily repressed and sublimated onto literary battlefields, it was a thoroughly Yankee story, as different from the preceding history of Europe in America as Smith, Percy, and Pocahontas were from Cortés, Las Casas, and Doña Marina.

25

Squanto: The Story of a
Pilgrim Father

In some ways the Indian Squanto, a solitary wanderer without a home, is austere New England's counterpart to the romantic lady Pocahontas of Virginia. Like her, he was a quiet sacrificial victim to the earliest successful colonization efforts by Englishmen in America, and an unwitting bone of contention among opposing camps of intruders who saw in him the means to their various goals of self-justification.

Squanto's story begins a few years before the founding of Plymouth, with an ominous incident occurring in the early morning of New England history. Thomas Hunt, master of one of the whaling ships with which Captain John Smith had sailed to New England in 1614, lingered behind the others when their work was done and performed an act of treachery against some natives that outraged even the thick-skinned veteran of Jamestown's racial skirmishes. In Smith's words, Hunt "betrayed four and twenty of those poor Salvages aboard his ship: and most dishonestly, and inhumanely, for their kind usage of me and all our men, carried them with him to Maligo [sic, for Málaga], and there for a little private gain sold those silly Salvages for Rials of eight." He had thus behaved in violation of English custom in the New World — not by kidnapping Indians, which was common enough, but by selling them on foreign markets — and "this vile act kept him ever after from any more employment in those parts." The culprit then all but disappears from history, but "Hunt's wickedness," as even Samuel Purchas was moved to call it, was not to be quickly forgotten in either of the Englands, Old or New.

As for the victims, there were as many as twenty-seven of them, according to some reports — seven Nausets from Cape Cod, and twenty Wampanoags from Patuxet, which stood at the site of what was soon to be the Plymouth colony. We know that the intervention of some friars in Spain — true spiritual descendants of Bartolomé de las Casas — caused most or all of them to be released from captivity; but from then on we lose sight of all but one, a Wampanoag who, perhaps having stayed aboard Hunt's ship at Málaga, is seen to turn up in London. The name of this lone exile was Tisquantum, but this usually became Squanto on the lips of Englishmen, the Latin declensions of schooldays evidently never ceasing to echo in their ears. Squanto went into the service of a London merchant named John Slany, treasurer of the Newfoundland Company.

In this way, the kidnapped Wampanoag became yet another in a small but notable succession of Indians who, since the beginning of the century, had sojourned in England under the wings of various New World activists, as in the days of Roanoke and Thomas Hariot. Indeed, this bespoke a surviving connection between those days and the present ones. Among Squanto's predecessors, for example, were five natives of the Maine coastal region who had been brought back to England by George Waymouth on his voyage of 1605, three of whom had lived for a time in the custody of Sir Ferdinando Gorges, governor of the fort at Plymouth, England. A member of a distinguished family that was related by marriage to the Raleighs and the Gilberts, Sir Ferdinando was a founder and guiding spirit of the Virginia Company of Plymouth, and decidedly belonged to the old aristocratic school of American colonization. He counted Thomas Hariot among his friends, and it was in tones worthy of that great humanist that he wrote of the three Maine Indians who became his charges in 1605: "I observed in them an inclination to follow the example of the better sort, and in all their carriages manifest shows of great civility far from the rudeness of our common people." It is hard to imagine Samuel Purchas, somewhat closer to the rudeness of the common people than Sir Ferdinando was, coming across words like these without bristling. No doubt the three Indians thus described figured prominently in the Plymouth Company's Sagadahoc expedition of the following year. If that colonization attempt had succeeded, the history of New England might have been something far different from what it became; it would have been more French than Puritan, more Gorges than Purchas — but that was not to be.

Years later, Gorges's memory was to persuade him that one of his three

Noble Savages of 1605 had been Squanto, but this cannot have been so. Nevertheless, it would seem that Squanto, during his sojourn among the English in the years immediately following 1614, did become part of a circle surrounding Gorges, and therefore an instrument of the latter's continuing aspirations to achieve hegemony in New England. Squanto was still in John Slany's employ when he made a trip to Newfoundland in 1615, but Gorges was involved in the Newfoundland Company and it was one of his men, Captain Thomas Dermer, who brought the Wampanoag back to England the following year.

In 1619 Dermer, still working for Gorges, sailed once more to New England to fish and trade along the coast, and brought Squanto with him as a guide. It was during this voyage that Squanto was able to revisit his home village at last; but a great shock awaited him. A plague had raged through New England in 1616 and 1617, and had taken its greatest toll among the Wampanoags, few of whom were left alive anywhere; as for Squanto's native Patuxet, its entire population had been wiped out. Thus by an irony of circumstance, this already somewhat anglicized Indian had become a wandering exile even in his homeland, and was forced to be even a little more like his captors as a result.

As chance would have it, another turn to his already peculiar destiny was now being shaped for him unwittingly in the hands of other exiles, back across the ocean. The congregation of Brownists — Separatists from the Anglican Church — that had been founded at Scrooby in Nottinghamshire in 1606 and had by now lived for some years in Holland, first briefly at Amsterdam, then at Leyden, had recently decided to try making a life for themselves somewhere in the New World. After having considered various possibilities — including Guiana, and an offer from the Dutch to settle in an as yet undefined New Netherland — they had reached an arrangement with the Virginia Company of London, whereby they would establish a second major colony somewhat to the north of Jamestown. Accordingly, a group of the Leyden congregants sailed from Holland in July of 1620 on a rickety vessel called the *Speedwell*, and put in at Southampton to meet the *Mayflower*, which was coming down from London with a second shipload of settlers. This latter group was not Brownist at all, but consisted of ordinary English Protestants from various walks of life, and therefore was no different from any of the shiploads of persons that were regularly leaving for Jamestown by this time. It formed the majority of the passengers who finally crowded onto the *Mayflower* after the *Speedwell*, returning to port twice for repairs, was at last declared unfit for the transatlantic passage. Of the one hundred and two men, women, and children who were to found the historic settlement at

Plymouth that December, then, only about one-third were "Pilgrims" in the sense intended by this label that a later generation was to attach to them.

Indeed, there were conflicts aboard ship between the Pilgrims and the "strangers," as they were called, not all of whom shared the Brownists' loyalty to the Virginia Company of London. Some of them apparently still honored the claims of Sir Ferdinando Gorges's old Plymouth Company, now reorganized as the Council for New England, over the region to which they were headed.° The dissidents are not named for us in the sources, but a possible leader among them was Stephen Hopkins, a wealthier man than most of the others — he had two indentured servants with him, as well as his wife and four children — who had apparently been to the New World before. The profile we can obtain of him suggests a personality somewhat in the Gorges image: he was, for example, to show signs at the colony of a thorough sympathy with the Indians. The quarrel among the colonists was settled by the drafting of the celebrated "Mayflower Compact," which united them in a "civil body politic" of their own, but this ended what was really only the first round of a struggle that was to last two more decades, pitting Gorges and his followers against the steadily growing Puritan leadership of New England. Sir Ferdinando apparently did not even mind Puritans very much, but they minded him; they despised him for his seigneurial ambitions and High Church outlook, nor could they forget the fact that he had betrayed Essex, whom many of them had admired, at the time of the latter's rebellion in 1599. They also did not care for his cavalier approach, at an ocean's remove, to relations with the Indians.

No doubt the Plymouth colonists had prepared themselves for hard confrontations with the natives, but, as it turned out, fortune spared them these to a large extent, and enabled them to become a little bit cavalier themselves. In November, before the landing at Plymouth, there was a skirmish with the Nausets along Cape Cod — perhaps one or two of the *Mayflower* passengers even knew why Nausets harbored a particular anger toward Englishmen — but by the time they had begun building their homes alongside the still-intact cornfields of Patuxet the following month, they were given ample reason to believe that Providence had, for their sake, all but cleared the entire countryside of its native population. Now and then, small groups of Indians could be seen to appear and then vanish hurriedly in the distance, and tools occasionally

---

° It is perhaps owing to their demands that the name Plymouth stuck for the place colonized by the *Mayflower* people. It had already borne this name on the map of New England published by John Smith in 1616, but it could have been given a new one had the settlers so chosen.

disappeared during the night, but these forlorn instances gave small indication of any significant presence lurking behind them.

The eerie silence was at last broken one Friday in March, a balmy day of oncoming spring, when a group of the men had repaired to an open area alongside the settlement to practice formations under the direction of their military commander, Captain Miles Standish. About a month earlier, while holding just such a drill, they had spotted two Indians in the distance, who had disappeared when Standish and Hopkins had approached them. And now, this time as well, "we were interrupted again," according to an anonymous narrator of these early days in the colony, "for there presented himself a Savage, which caused an alarm." But from this point on the story was to be different. The new visitor, who carried a bow and two arrows but was otherwise stark naked, did not run away, but "very boldly came all alone and along the houses straight to the rendezvous, where we intercepted him, not suffering him to go in, as undoubtedly he would, out of his boldness." Such brash behavior was only to be a lesser source of the Englishmen's astonishment, however, for suddenly, as William Bradford later wrote, he "spoke to them in broken English, which they could well understand, but marvelled at it."

The surprise visitor turned out to be a sort of immigrant himself, a native of Monhegan Island — where the Waymouth expedition of 1605, among others, had sojourned for a time — who had become well acquainted with the English fishermen who frequented there. Indeed, the very name with which he now introduced himself, Samoset, may not have been an Indian one but an English nickname (e.g., Somerset?) that they had given him. Samoset proceeded to endear himself somewhat among his curious listeners by displaying a knowledge of the names of "most of the captains, commanders and masters that usually come," and, since he "was a man free of speech, so far as he could express his mind, and of a seemly carriage," the conversation soon became affable. The Englishmen would still not go so far as to invite him into the village, but when, no doubt vividly recalling old experiences of Anglo-Saxon conviviality, he asked for some beer, they brought him not only "strong water" — the beer supply was short — but also "biscuit, and butter, and cheese, and pudding, and a piece of mallard, all which he liked well." When the wind rose a little, they took one more opportunity to assimilate him a jot with their favors by casting a horseman's coat about his shoulders.

Samoset described the situation in this part of the country, mentioning the plague of some four years before and claiming that, as a result, there were now only some sixty Wampanoags living in nearby villages and a little more than a hundred Nausets on Cape Cod. He told of how the Nausets were, in the anonymous narrator's paraphrase, "ill affected towards the English, by reason of one Hunt, a master of a ship, who deceived the people, and got them under color of trucking with them, twenty out of this very place where we inhabit, and seven men from the Nausets, and carried them away, and sold them for slaves like a wretched man (for twenty pound a man) that cares not what mischief he doth for his profit." But as for Patuxet, where the English now were settled, Samoset assured them that none of its population had survived except "another Indian whose name was Squanto, a native of this place, who had been in England and could speak better English than himself."

The whole afternoon thus passed in largely reassuring conversation, but the Englishmen, in spite of all this pleasantry, wanted Samoset to take his leave when night approached. He, however, was determined to stay until morning. Still reluctant to let him into the village, they thought of rowing him to the *Mayflower* for lodging, but the waves proved too rough for the landing boat. Finally, they "lodged him that night at Stephen Hopkins' house, and watched him." Perhaps they watched Hopkins, too.

Samoset took his leave the next morning, heading for the Wampanoag village of Sowams (now Warren, Rhode Island) to the southwest, and promising to return with some Indians to trade in beaver skins. The English sent him on his way with gifts of a knife, a bracelet, and a ring, and with instructions that any Indians he brought back with him would have to leave their bows and arrows in the woods, about a quarter of a mile from the settlement. He returned the very next day with "five other tall proper men; they had every man a deer's skin on him, and the principal of them had a wildcat's skin, or such like, on one arm. They had most of them long hosen [i.e., leggings] up to their groins, close made; and above their groins to their waist another leather: they were altogether like the Irish trousers. They are of complexion like our English gypsies, no hair or very little on their faces, on their heads long hair to their shoulders, only cut before, some trussed up before with a feather, broadwise, like a fan, another a fox-tail hanging out. . . . Some of them had their faces painted black, from the forehead to the chin, four or five fingers broad; others after our fashions, as they liked."

The English on the whole remained wary before this sudden onrush of native Americans, but the latter gave them no grounds for such an attitude. They had left their bows and arrows in the woods as instructed, and, furthermore, had brought with them all the tools that their tribesmen had stolen during the winter. In general, they "made semblance unto us of friendship and amity; they sang and danced after their manner, like antics." They also "did eat liberally of our English victuals," even though they had brought along some ground corn of their own. But the occasion did not quite come off; they had arrived with only three or four skins, and besides it was Sunday. The English eagerly sent them off, with gifts, and with urgings to bring more ample goods for trading the next time.

Samoset stayed on again, claiming he was ill, and presumably was lodged again at Hopkins's house. He finally left on Wednesday, and that afternoon, as if to bring home to the English that they should take firm hold upon the friendships they had now acquired, they had a tense encounter with a few unknown Indians. It occurred once again during a military drill — obviously, these exercises always were unintentional provocations. This time, two or three Indians appeared at the top of a nearby hill and "made semblance of daring us, as we thought." For a few moments they "whetted and rubbed their arrows and strings, and made show of defiance," but when Miles Standish and another man advanced toward them with muskets, they ran off.

The next day the entire picture changed. "About noon," the anonymous narrator writes, "we met again about our public business, but we had scarce been an hour together, but Samoset came again, and Squanto, the only native of Patuxet, where we now inhabit, who was one of the twenty captives that by Hunt were carried away, and had been in England, and dwelt in Cornhill with Master John Slany, a merchant, and could speak a little English with three others, and they brought with them some few skins to truck, and some red herrings newly taken and dried, but not salted." Thus Squanto is reunited with Englishmen pilgrim meeting Pilgrim; but where had he been in the meantime? We know that by this time his English companion, Captain Dermer, had already been to Jamestown and back to New England, had been mortally wounded by unfriendly Indians on Martha's Vineyard, and had returned to Jamestown to die. But though Squanto evidently had been with him during one adventure on Cape Cod, interceding for his life among the Nausets, he does not seem to have accompanied the Englishman in all his travels since 1619. Presumably he had lived awhile among the Wampanoags at Sowams, for he was now arriving as their emissary, bringing the news that "their great sagamore Massasoit was hard by, with Quadequina his brother, and all their men." It was a great moment for him. An hour later Massasoit "came to the top of a hill over against us, and had in his train sixty men, that we could well behold them and they us."

What Squanto had brought with him was nothing less than the turning point in relations between Englishmen and Indians at Plymouth, the first establishment of real contact between them and, as it turned out, the beginning of a time of peace. The ensuing scene can therefore be looked upon as a worthy fulfillment in his troubled career. Unfortunately, it can also be seen to contain foreshadowings of his eventual downfall. At this first startling moment of confrontation, the anonymous narrator goes on, "we were not willing to send our governor [John Carver] to them, and they unwilling to come to us, so Squanto went again unto him, who brought word that we should send one to parley with him, which we did, which was Edward Winslow, to know his mind, and to signify the mind and will of our governor, which was to have trading and peace with him."

Now, the twenty-five-year-old Edward Winslow — the probable author of the anonymous narrative from which we have been quoting, which was sent to England along with several others for publication a year later — seems to have been a most significant choice for this mission. On the basis of age and experience, Stephen Hopkins would have been the more likely choice, but it is clear that the Brownist leaders of Plymouth were by now eager to replace him in precisely this role with someone more congenial to their own way of thinking. And Winslow had much to recommend him. Born in Droitwich, Worcestershire, probably of well-to-do parentage, he had not joined the Separatist congregation until 1617, in Leyden, after having traveled for a time on the European continent. He was thus more cosmopolitan than most of his fellow settlers, but was, since his conversion at least, no mere dilettante where spiritual matters were concerned; in future years, he was to be a bulwark of Puritanism. Soon to show considerable skill at acquiring a knowledge of the Indian language and customs, he nonetheless remained a man who could not easily be swayed from the stolid English middle-class way of looking at things by any sentimental notions concerning the Noble Savage. He would truly prove to be an unexpected weapon in the moral arsenal of Samuel Purchas and company, far more gifted for the purpose than Captain John Smith ever was.

Winslow went up the hill to Massasoit bearing a pair of knives, and a copper chain with a jewel in it, as gifts. He also brought gifts to Quadequina, "a knife and a jewel to hang in his ear, and withal a pot of strong water, a good quantity of biscuit, and some butter, which were all willingly accepted." Speaking in English with Squanto and Samoset as his interpreters, Winslow told Massasoit "that King James saluted him with words of love and peace, and did accept of him as his friend and ally, and that our governor desired to see him and to truck with him, and to confirm a peace with him, as his next neighbor." Massasoit, "a very lusty man, in his best years, an able body, grave of countenance, and spare of speech," whose face was oiled and painted red, and who wore around his neck a chain of white bone beads with a tobacco pouch hanging from it, "liked well of the speech and heard it attentively, though the interpreters did not well express it." The last remark is a startling intrusion. Undoubtedly Samoset's broken English is part of its target, but the observation clearly is meant above all in criticism of Squanto, an arrival from the world of Sir Ferdinando Gorges, who was no doubt already being looked upon by some of the Brownists with suspicion. This is the first hint of an antagonism between Winslow and Squanto that was to become deadly before long.

But for the moment it is only a fleeting shadow across a glowing tableau of peacemaking. After hearing Winslow's speech, Massasoit decided to go over to the English in person. Leaving Winslow with Quadequina as security, he crossed the brook with a train of twenty Indians — probably including Squanto and Samoset — who left their bows and arrows behind them. They were met on the other side by Captain Miles Standish, who took six or seven of them into custody as hostages for Winslow. Massasoit, the narrative goes on in detail — if Winslow indeed wrote it, the information is here being conveyed to him by another party — was conducted to "a house then in building, where we placed a green rug and three or four cushions. Then instantly came our governor with drum and trumpet after him, and some few musketeers. After salutations, our governor kissing his hand, the king kissed him, and so they sat down. The governor called for some strong water, and drunk to him, and he drunk a great draught that made him sweat all the while after; he called for a little fresh meat, which the king did eat willingly, and did give his followers. Then they treated of peace."

In the written treaty, the two peoples agreed that they would do no injury to one another, and that each would hand over from its midst any individual who had offended against the other; they also vowed to aid one another in any case of an unjust attack by a third party. The Indian leaders promised to return all stolen tools, and to leave their bows and arrows behind whenever they came to visit the colony, "as we should do our pieces when we came to them." The peace thus drawn up between Plymouth and the Wampanoags was to remain in force one way or another for more than fifty years; but perhaps it was as much a sign of the abject condition to which circumstances had reduced the Indians of the area as it was of any particularly good intentions and diplomatic skill on the part of the settlers. As for sheer power, Plymouth had little military muscle, but the Wampanoags had even less. Our anonymous narrative says that Massasoit, all the while that he sat by Governor Carver negotiating with him, "trembled for fear." The agreement they arrived at was assuredly a concurrence of the tremulous.

After the ceremonies, the Indians took to the woods, with two exceptions. "Samoset and Squanto, they stayed all night with us," and the following morning still showed no sign of being about to leave. But whoever felt uneasy at this did not yet fully recognize what a boon had come to the people of Plymouth. At noon, Squanto went "to fish for eels; at night he came home with as many as he could well lift in one hand, which our people were glad of. They were fat and sweet; he trod them out with his feet, and so caught them with his hands without any other instrument." These were services to which even the usually grudging anonymous narrator had to give credit.

Nor were they the end of the matter, for whereas Samoset did leave after a few days and eventually return to Maine, Squanto stayed on, as if to serve as destiny's emissary from the old Patuxet to the new Plymouth, guiding the creators of the latter to viability upon the ghostly paradigm that the former had left behind. His role as such became particularly evident a month after his arrival, when the settlers, in William Bradford's words, "began to plant their corn, in which service Squanto stood them in great stead, showing them both the manner how to set it, and after how to dress and tend it. Also he told them except they got fish and set with it (in these old grounds) it would come to nothing; and he showed them that in the middle of April they should have store enough come up the brook, by which they began to build, and taught them how to take it, and where to get other provisions necessary for them; all which they found true by trial and experience." In general, Bradford wrote elsewhere, Squanto "continued with them, and was their interpreter, and was a special instrument sent of God for their good beyond their expectation . . . and never left them till he died." The author of this encomium — a man too sincere to be swayed by mere political considerations when judging a fellow human being — was to be elected governor of the colony only a few days after the start of that first planting, upon Carver's death from a fever, and was to remain Squanto's stoutest supporter through all that would follow.

The second of the anonymous narratives published in the so-called *Mourt's Relation* of 1622, from which we have been quoting, describes an episode that seems to represent not only the first challenge to the eminence that Squanto had now achieved at Plymouth, but also a final dismissal of any claims on the part of Stephen Hopkins to a special relationship with the Indians. It is an account, unquestionably written by Edward Winslow — for it sounds the highly intelligent and slightly ironic tone that would always characterize his writing, especially when dealing with the Indians — of a journey to Massasoit's village of Sowams undertaken in July of 1621 by Winslow and Hopkins, with Squanto as their guide. Carrying a "horseman's coat of red cotton, and laced with a slight lace," as a gift for Massasoit, and a copper chain as a pledge of the friendship that had been signed at Plymouth that spring, the three emissaries made their way on foot and, thanks to Squanto's urging, reached their destination at the end of two days.

Massasoit was not at home when they arrived, but he was sent for immediately. "When news was brought of his coming," Winslow writes, "our guide Squanto requested that at our meeting we should discharge our pieces." Evidently, the treaty requirement that the English leave their muskets behind upon entering a Wampanoag village had already been forgotten. This problem does not seem to have bothered Winslow; rather, what obviously concerns him here is Squanto's relish for a display of English might. "But one of us going about to charge his piece," he continues, "the women and children, through fear to see him take up his piece, ran away, and could not be pacified till he laid it down again, who afterward were better informed by our interpreter." The Narragansett Bay area, in which this village was located, had long been frequented by French ships as well as English ones, and its peoples were quite familiar with the effects of the Christians' godlike weapons.

But the villagers evidently became reconciled to the prospect of some ceremonial thunder when their sagamore arrived. "Massasoit being come," Winslow writes, "we discharged our pieces, and saluted him, who after their manner kindly welcomed us, and took us into his house, and set us down by him, where, having delivered our foresaid message and presents, and having put the coat on his back and the chain about his neck, he was not a little proud to behold himself, and his men also to see their king so bravely attired." Massasoit and the Englishmen then exchanged, with Squanto as interpreter, renewed pledges of friendship and peaceful commerce.

Winslow then goes on to describe wryly the subsequent course of Wampanoag hospitality. Massasoit smoked tobacco with his guests and talked deferentially of King James throughout the evening, but he did not offer them supper, "for indeed he had not any, being he came so newly home." When the time came for sleeping, the sagamore "laid us on the bed with himself and his wife, they at the one end and we at the other, it being only planks laid a foot from the ground, and a thin mat upon them. Two more of his chief men, for want of room, pressed by and upon us, so that we were worse weary of our lodging than of our journey." The next morning, upon the urging of some of Massasoit's sachems, the Englishmen gave a display of their firearms by shooting at a target, presumably to Squanto's delight; but breakfast was no more forthcoming than supper had been. Finally, however, at "about one o'clock, Massasoit brought two fishes that he had shot; they were like bream but three times so big, and better meat. These being boiled, there were at least forty looked for share in them, the most ate of them. This meal only we had in two nights and a day, and had not one of us brought a partridge we had taken our journey fasting."

Massasoit wanted them to stay a few more days, but since it was Thursday, Winslow and Hopkins were able to excuse themselves by saying they wanted to get home by Saturday night so as to awaken to the

Sabbath in their own homes. Privately, they "feared we should either be light-headed for want of sleep, for what with bad lodging, the savages' barbarous singing (for they use to sing themselves asleep), lice and fleas within doors, and mosquitoes without, we could hardly sleep all the time of our being there; we much fearing that if we should stay any longer, we should not be able to recover home for want of strength." Accordingly, after managing one more night with Massasoit, the two Englishmen took their leave before dawn on Friday.

But they left without Squanto. Winslow writes that Massasoit retained the survivor of Patuxet so as to send him "from place to place to procure truck for us," and that he appointed an Indian of Sowams, "called Tokamahamon, in his place, whom we had found faithful before and after upon all occasions." Are we seeing here a concerted effort to down-grade Squanto? For we know from subsequent events, not only that Winslow disliked him, but that Massasoit had never really become recon-ciled to the presence of this stranger — albeit a Wampanoag — in his midst. Perhaps Squanto was a bit too English for the sagamore's liking, just as he was too much identified with a certain group of Englishmen for Win-slow's; and both of them undoubtedly perceived that he was becoming too ambitious. This would explain their evident eagerness here to promote Massasoit's man Tokamahamon in his place. But meanwhile, what about Hopkins? He may well have been on Squanto's side, but he becomes a strangely anonymous figure in this narrative, as though Winslow, writing it the following year for an English public that included people who knew something of Squanto and of Hopkins as well, was giving clear notice of what were the forces now being superseded in New England. By the time Winslow and Hopkins reached home Saturday night with their new guide, a quiet victory had been won by the Brownists over the "strangers" in the all-important realm of Indian affairs. From now on, Massasoit's friend Winslow was to be the dominant figure in it, while Hopkins, though he even was to be assistant governor for a time, fades steadily out of the picture.

But Squanto, on the other hand, was not to be defeated so easily. He soon found an opportunity to recover his old eminence by playing a vital role in a crisis that arose toward the end of that same month of July. A young boy of the colony named John Billington had got lost in the woods, and after five days of wandering and living mainly on berries, had been taken in by Indians, who then conveyed him to the Nausets on Cape Cod. Why he was given over to the Nausets and why they wanted him remain a mystery; but it is a good guess that they still, some six years after Hunt's perfidy, felt they had some scores to settle with the English, and that they and their friends saw an opportunity for doing so in the lost boy.

If this was the case, then their method of carrying it out ought to have served as a model for Englishmen.

Plymouth learned through Massasoit where young Billington was, and ten Englishmen were dispatched to Cape Cod in a boat, accompanied by two Indian guides: "the one," according to the anonymous narrator of this episode, also published in *Mourt's Relation*, "was Squanto, our interpreter, the other Tokamahamon, a special friend" — this sounds like Winslow once again. After running into a storm the first day, the party put in for the night at Cummaquid, the site of present-day Barnstable, and there the next morning they encountered representatives of a local sachem named Iyanough, who invited them to come eat with him. Six of the Englishmen went, probably accompanied by the two Indian guides, and they were warmly entertained; but they also were provided with an unexpected reminder as to why they had little reason to expect leniency toward their own from the Nausets. For while they were with Iyanough, they were suddenly confronted by "an old woman, whom we judged to be no less than a hundred years old, which came to see us because she never saw English, yet could not behold us without breaking forth into great passion, weeping and crying excessively. We demanding the reason of it, they told us she had three sons who, when Master Hunt was in these parts, went aboard his ship to trade with him, and he carried them captives into Spain (for Squanto at that time was carried away also), by which means she was deprived of the comfort of her children in her old age." One wonders what was going through Squanto's own mind while he interpreted these words. The English replied that they "were sorry that any Englishmen should give them that offense, that Hunt was a bad man, and that all the English that heard of it condemned him for the same; but, for us, we would not offer them any such injury though it would gain us all the skins in the country. So we gave her some small trifles, which somewhat appeased her." Small consolation, indeed, coming from men who were about to get their own child back.

Having learned that the Billington boy was at Nauset, the site of present-day Eastham, the Englishmen proceeded there in their boat, now accompanied by the hospitable Iyanough and two of his men. It was these three Nausets, in fact, accompanied by Squanto, who went off when they arrived at Nauset to treat with Aspinet, the sachem of the village, while Tokamahamon and all the Englishmen waited back at the boat. It proved to be a long, tense vigil, but finally, "after sunset, Aspinet came with a great train, and brought the boy with him, one bearing him through the water. He had not less than a hundred with him, the half whereof came to the shallop side unarmed with him, the other stood aloof with their bows and arrows. There he delivered us the boy, behung with beads, and made peace with us, we bestowing a knife on him, and like-wise on another that first entertained the boy and brought him thither. So they departed from us." It was a stirring example of how the Nausets could behave toward a people that had wronged them. It also was a moment of triumph for Squanto, who alone had stood for the English in arranging the settlement.

But now the history both of Squanto and of Plymouth's relations with its Indian neighbors becomes more vexed. The settlers had not yet had any dealings with the Narragansetts, a larger and more warlike people than any they had yet encountered, who lived in the lands westward of the bay that now bears their name. Suddenly, however, on the voyage to redeem young John Billington, the English expeditioners heard rumors of a Narragansett attack on Sowams. Returning to Plymouth, they found not only that this was true, but that "Corbitant, a petty sachem or governor under Massasoit (whom they ever feared to be too conversant with the Narragansetts), was at Nemasket [a Wampanoag village some fifteen miles west of Plymouth], who sought to draw the hearts of Massasoit's subjects from him, speaking also disdainfully of us, storming at the peace between Nauset, Cummaquid, and us, and at Squanto, the worker of it." Corbitant also made known his anger at two other Indian go-betweens — Tokama-hamon, whom we have met, and Hobomock, another of Massasoit's men who had recently come to live among the English, "a proper lusty man," according to Governor Bradford, "and a man of account for his valour and parts amongst the Indians, . . . [who] continued very faithful and constant to the English till he died."

Tokamahamon, evidently the least of the offenders in Corbitant's eyes, went to the rebel leader to plead with him in person, while Squanto and Hobomock made their way secretly into Nemasket to see what they could learn. Not secretly enough, however, for they "were discovered to Corbitant, who set a guard to beset the house [in which they had been hiding], and took Squanto (for he had said, if he were dead the English had lost their tongue)." In the scuffle, Corbitant also "offered to stab Hobomock; but being a lusty man, he cleared himself of him, and came running away all sweating and told the governor what had befallen him, and he feared they had killed Squanto, for they had threatened them both, and for no other cause but because they were friends to the English, and serviceable unto them."

The colonists acted with dispatch. Taking a nearby petty sachem as hostage for Massasoit — whose condition was not yet known — they sent fourteen armed men to Nemasket, with Miles Standish as their captain and Hobomock as their guide, and with instructions to cut off Corbitant's head if it turned out that he had killed Squanto. Upon reaching the village, the soldiers marched straight to the house in which they knew Corbitant to have been staying, and surrounded it; but he was no longer there. A few of the villagers made a show of protest at this incursion, but the discharge of two muskets into the air was sufficient to quiet them down. Standish learned from the Indians that Corbitant and his most loyal followers had fled, and that Squanto was still alive. With that, "Hobomock got on the top of the house and called Squanto and Tokamahamon, which came unto us accompanied with others, some armed and others naked." In the sequel, Massasoit turned out to be safe, and Corbitant was never to be any trouble again.

But the Narragansetts continued to be a problem, creating an atmosphere of tension at Plymouth that ultimately cast a cloud of suspicion over Squanto in particular. In December, shortly after the first supply ship, the *Fortune,* had come and gone, bringing wherewithal and new settlers to Plymouth, a messenger arrived at the colony from Canonicus, chief sachem of the Narragansetts. He asked for Squanto, but seemed relieved when he was informed that the latter was not in the village at the moment. He had brought a strange missive, consisting of a bundle of arrows wrapped in a rattlesnake skin, but when he wanted to leave it for Squanto and be off, the English detained him. Standish and Winslow took him aside and, with Tokamahamon as their interpreter, plied him with questions into the night. From him they obtained details about another messenger who had gone back and forth between Canonicus and Governor Bradford several times the previous summer, and who had so delayed and misrepresented various communications as to turn a potential atmosphere of understanding between them into one of growing suspicion and hostility. It is clear, though nothing is explicitly said in the sources to this effect, that Standish and Winslow suspected Squanto of having been behind this misbehavior.

The next morning the Narragansett messenger was sent home. When Squanto returned to Plymouth later that day, he was shown the missive, and "signified to the governor," in Winslow's words, "that to send the rattlesnake's skin in that manner imported enmity; and that it was no better than a challenge." Bradford responded firmly, sending back the snakeskin, but this time stuffed with powder and shot. Canonicus apparently was so terrified by this "message" that he refused to touch it, and eventually it made its way back to Plymouth unopened.

Meanwhile Winslow, with Standish now sharing his viewpoint in this respect, continued to look with wary eyes upon Squanto. By this time, the lone survivor of Patuxet was becoming decidedly indiscreet in the ways that he flaunted his special position among the English before other Indians. He claimed to have knowledge, for example, that the English had the plague buried underneath the floor of their storehouse, "which, at our pleasure, we could send forth to what place or people we would; and destroy them therewith though we stirred not from home." It may well be, of course, that Squanto was simply giving a not unreasonable account of the gunpowder that was indeed to be found in the storeroom, but Winslow did not give him the benefit of the doubt. Rather, he describes in his own account of this episode, how he enlightened Hobomock one day when the latter came asking if it was true, as Squanto said, that the English had the plague in their possession. He told Hobomock that it was not true, but rather that "the God of the English had it in store: and could send it at his pleasure; to the destruction of his and our enemies." Was this really any better than Squanto's version?

By this time Hobomock evidently had — for reasons that are not clear — replaced Tokamahamon as the favorite of both Winslow and Massasoit, and one sign of the fact is a growing rivalry between him and Squanto. This reached a point of crisis in March of 1622, when a group of the colonists were preparing to go north on a trading expedition among the Massachusetts, a people with whom relations were still uncertain. Hobomock began to spread a rumor that the Massachusetts were in league with the Narragansetts against the English, and that Squanto was an in-strument in their machinations. Warning that an ambush was being planned against the English traders, Hobomock implored them not to go on the expedition; but though some were ready to listen to him, the ever-plucky Standish argued in favor of going through with the plan, and won the day. Accordingly, early in April, a small boat set sail for Boston Bay, with Standish, Winslow, and eight other Englishmen aboard, as well as the two Indian rivals, Squanto and Hobomock, presumably to prove themselves against one another.

"But we had no sooner turned the point of the harbor, Gurnet's Nose," Winslow writes, "but there came an Indian of Squanto's family, running to certain of our people that were from home, with all eagerness, having his face wounded, and the blood still fresh on the same, calling to them to repair home; oft looking behind him, as if some others had him in chase: saying, that at Nemasket . . . there were many of the Narragansetts, Massasoit our supposed friend, and Corbitant our feared enemy, with many others; with a resolution to take advantage, on the present opportunity, to assault the town in the Captain's absence. Affirming that he received the wound in his face for speaking in our behalf, and by slight escaped; looking oft backward, as if he suspected them to be at hand." Three guns were fired immediately to summon the boat home, and in a short while Standish and his companions were back in the village. Confronted by the accusations of Squanto's relative — which Winslow has already, by some stylistic devices, made suspect for his readers — Hobomock flatly said he was lying. After some discussion it was decided that

Hobomock's wife would be sent to Sowams to determine the facts of the matter. Hardly an impartial witness herself, she went and came back with the information that Massasoit was there at home and engaged in no wrongdoing — indeed, that he had been deeply offended upon hearing of the accusation that had been made against him.

"Thus, by degrees," Winslow concludes, "we began to discover Squanto; whose ends were only to make himself great in the eyes of his countrymen, by means of his nearness and favor with us: not caring who fell, so he stood." It is not absolutely certain that Hobomock was right and Squanto wrong in this situation, but even Bradford had to admit that by now, in general, Squanto clearly "sought his own ends, and played his own game, by putting the Indians in fear, and drawing gifts from them to enrich himself; making them believe he could stir up war against whom he would, and make peace for whom he would." Some Indians even were beginning to seek protection from Squanto instead of their nominal overlord Massasoit. For a moment, Squanto emerges as a kind of would-be Estévanico; but this forlorn survivor of Patuxet, this seventeenth-century Last of the Mohicans, who apparently strived to use his tenuous bit of Englishness in rivalry against the legitimate authority of Massasoit over the pathetic remains of the Wampanoags, hardly had the diabolical strength to play such a role.

Among the men who held real power at Plymouth, Squanto seems by now to have no longer had any other friend but Bradford: this one member of the colony's leadership who had been with the Scrooby congregation from its very beginning, on the whole somewhat less sophisticated in his understanding of the Indians than Winslow was, and perhaps less realistic about them than Standish, was simply that most decent-minded sort of Englishman who could hold firm to a debt of personal gratitude in spite of everything. And he soon had occasion to prove this quality where Squanto was concerned. Standish and his trading party — including even Squanto despite the incident — went ahead on their expedition among the Massachusetts, and it proved to be a success; but by the time they returned home, Massasoit was at Plymouth, justifying himself before Bradford and pouring out his wrath concerning Squanto. Bradford pacified him for the moment and he left, but a message soon arrived from him demanding that Squanto be put to death. The governor replied to him diplomatically, saying for his benefit that Squanto indeed deserved to die, but urging mercy and pointing out that he was still most urgently needed for proper verbal communication between the English and the Indians. Massasoit promptly sent back several messengers, demanding that Squanto be turned over to them in accordance with the treaty, and serving notice that they carried his own knife, with which they were to "cut off [Squanto's] head and hands, and bring them to him." They also had brought "many beavers' skins for his consent thereto," but Bradford refused this bribe, telling them that "it was not the manner of the English to sell men's lives at a price; but when they had deserved justly to die, to give them their reward." Squanto was summoned, and he, confronted with his would-be executioners, "accused Hobomock as the author and worker of his overthrow; yielding himself to the governor, to be sent or not, according as he thought meet."

Bradford seemed about to give in at last, according to Winslow's narrative of the incident, since the alternative was a probable breakdown of relations with Plymouth's only Indian ally. But then, we are told, an almost incredible *deus ex machina* suddenly came to Squanto's rescue. For "at the instant when our governor was ready to deliver him into the hands of his executioners, a boat was seen at sea to cross before our town, and fall behind a headland not far off. Whereupon, having heard many rumours of the French, and not knowing whether there were any combination between the savages and them, the governor told the Indians he would first know what boat that was, ere he would deliver him into their custody. But, being mad with rage, and impatient at delay, they departed in great heat." The ship turned out to be English, but the excuse it provided had worked even better than Bradford may have anticipated; for, from now on, we hear nothing more of Massasoit's demands against Squanto. There was, in fact, nothing more to be feared from him.

Having been thoroughly discredited, Squanto was now in effect free from the taint of his old associations with the Gorges circle, and nothing now remained for him but to try to prove himself as a man — which, undoubtedly, was all he had ever wanted to do in the first place. As it happened, he even found a chance to do so in the little time now remaining to his unhappy life. The English ship that had arrived on that fateful day had brought a new group of settlers, who subsequently founded a second colony in Boston Bay, and the suddenly increased demand for supplies caused the two colonies to fit out a trading expedition to Cape Cod later that year. "All things being provided," Bradford writes, "Captain Standish was appointed to go with them, and Squanto for a guide and interpreter, about the latter end of September; but the winds put them in again, and putting out the second time [Standish] fell sick of a fever, so the governor went himself."

Guided by Squanto, a veteran of Cape Cod expeditions, the boat made its way down the eastern shore of the Cape. Its ultimate destination was the southern shore, but the difficult shoals forced the party to put in for a night at Manamoyack, the site of present-day Chatham. There Bradford and his men received a strange welcome, for though the natives of the place welcomed them with food, "yet their joy was mixed with much jealousy," as Winslow observed. "For, at first, they were loath their dwellings should be known; but when they saw our governor's resolution to stay on shore all night, they brought him to their houses: having first conveyed all their stuff to a remote place, not far from the same; which one of our men, walking forth, occasionally espied; whereupon, on the sudden, neither it nor them could be found. And so, many times, upon conceived occasions, they would all be gone, bag and baggage." But Squanto came to the rescue, explaining the situation to the people of Manamoyack, and allaying their fears; and "being afterwards, by Squanto's means, better persuaded, they left their jealousy, and traded with them."

Pleased with his triumph, Squanto now was determined to move on and guide the boat along the southern shore as originally intended. But this further display of his abilities was not to be; for God, as Winslow writes, "had otherwise disposed, who struck Squanto with sickness; insomuch as he there died." This terse conclusion to a life history is improved upon in Bradford's account:

> In this place Squanto fell sick of an Indian fever, bleeding much at the nose (which the Indians take for a symptom of death), and within a few days died there; desiring the governor to pray for him, that he might go to the Englishmen's God in heaven, and bequeathed sundry of his things to sundry of his English friends, as remembrances of his love; of whom they had a great loss.

Squanto was no hero of his people, nor protagonist in any cause but that of his own survival, when all was said and done; he was simply a man, which was a very hard thing for an Indian to be once he had fallen into English hands. Surely it is a sign of how hard it was that no one else but Bradford seems to have wept over his grave.

26

Light and Vain Persons

On a return trip to England in 1624 to raise money and moral support for the Plymouth colony, Edward Winslow published a sequel to his earlier anonymous narratives. *Good News from New England* contains the whole story of Squanto's demise; but this is not its only subject matter, and other aspects of it were even more interesting to Samuel Purchas, who included a portion of it in the last volume of his *Pilgrims*. Winslow, sounding more Puritan in it than ever before, states in his preface that he has written the book to encourage potential settlers of "upright life and conversation: which doctrine of manners ought first to be preached, by giving a good example to the poor savage heathens, amongst whom they live." On the other hand, it is a warning to "light and vain persons" to stay away from New England, for "what great offense hath been given by many profane men; who, being but seeming Christians, have made Christ and Christianity stink in the nostrils of the poor infidels; and so laid a stumbling block before them."

These angry words refer primarily to one Thomas Weston and the short-lived colony he had established in Boston Bay, to which the largest part of Winslow's book is devoted. Weston was a London merchant, and though he did not have any apparent connection with Sir Ferdinando Gorges, he nevertheless represented the kind of dilettantes of American colonization that were being more and more reviled by men of Puritan stripe. The Brownists of Plymouth had actually known Weston even before their voyage to the New World, for he had been involved in some of the early negotiating between Leyden and London that ended in their decision to colonize for the Virginia Company. He had even put up some money for them, but then had withdrawn it upon seeing no immediate return in the offing — an act that hardly helped endear him to them. Weston was not interested in building godly new societies in the wilderness; he wanted to make money trading in skins with the Indians, as the French did; and he finally sought to implement this aim by obtaining a patent and sending out colonists of his own in 1622. It was the first of Weston's arriving ships that had appeared in Plymouth harbor at the very moment when Squanto was about to be sentenced, and had thereby caused him to be spared. Perhaps Winslow, when he described the incident in this way, had seen it as an example of how rogues can be of service to one another even when they do not intend to be. After their landing at Plymouth, Weston's men had moved on northward to establish themselves at a place the Indians called Wessagusset.

Weston, who planned to join the colony in person the following year, admitted in a letter to Bradford at the time that there were some "rude fellows" among the sixty or seventy men he had sent out; but their subsequent behavior, which scandalized the straitlaced leaders of Plymouth, and furthermore threatened to use up all the available food supplies in New England, was more dissolute than he had foreseen. "It may be thought strange," Bradford wrote of them, "that these people should fall to these extremities in so short a time, being left competently provided when the ship left them, and had an addition by that moiety of corn that was got by trade, besides much they got of the Indians where they lived, by one means and another. It must needs be their great disorder, for they spent excessively whilst they had, or could get it; and, it may be, wasted part away among the Indians (for he that was their chief was taxed by some amongst them for keeping Indian women, how truly I know not). And after they began to come into wants, many sold away their clothes and bed coverings; others (so base were they) became servants to the Indians, and would cut them wood and fetch them water, for a cap full of corn; others fell to plain stealing, both night and day, from the Indians, of which they grievously complained."

This was going native with a vengeance; indeed, the scene at Wessagusset, as viewed through Plymouth's eyes, begins to turn into a kind of Conradian heart of darkness. Winslow tells of "one of Master Weston's company" who, having escaped to Plymouth with all his goods in a bundle on his back, "made a pitiful narration of their lamentable and weak estate, and of the Indians' carriages. Whose boldness increased abundantly, insomuch as the victuals [the Englishmen] got, [the Indians] would take it out of their pots and eat before their faces; yea, if in anything they gainsaid them, they were ready to hold a knife at their breasts." "In the end," Bradford concludes, "they came to that misery, that some starved and died with cold and hunger. One in gathering shellfish was so weak as he stuck fast in the mud, and was found dead in the place. At last most of them left their dwellings and scattered up and down in the woods, and by the watersides, where they could find ground nuts and clams, here six and there ten. By which their carriages they became contemned and scorned of the Indians."

Stories of this sort were reaching the ears of the Plymouth settlers in the wake of the news from Virginia of Opechancanough's destructive campaign against the English the year before. The Massachusetts were hardly comparable in size or strength to Opechancanough's confederacy, but the Plymouth people were in no mood to wait for this point to be proved. They needed only a small excuse for action; and it came — from their old friend Massasoit.

In March, 1623, word reached Plymouth that Massasoit was mortally ill; and since there also was news that a Dutch ship had run aground at the mouth of the Taunton River near Sowams, it was decided that Winslow should go down there, simultaneously to pay his last respects and find out what the Dutch were up to. Traveling with Hobomock, Winslow learned en route that the Dutch ship had left, but that Massasoit, whom they at first feared dead, was still alive. Winslow's description of the ensuing scene is an opportunity for him to show his readers the kind of intimacy and understanding he had by now obtained with Plymouth's Indian friends. When he arrived with Hobomock at the sagamore's house, he found it crowded with men praying for their leader, "making such a hellish noise," he writes with characteristic bite, "as it distempered us that were well; and therefore unlike to ease him that was sick." Massasoit was lying in bed, his arms and legs being rubbed by several women. Told of the arrival of "Winsnow" — "for they cannot pronounce the letter l; but ordinarily n in the place thereof" — he asked to see his English friend.

"Then he said twice, though very inwardly, Keen Winsnow?, which is to say, 'Art thou Winslow?'

"I answered, Ahhe; that is, 'Yes.'

"Then he doubled these words, Matta neen wonckanet namen Winsnow?, that is to say, 'O Winslow, I shall never see thee again.'"

But thanks to Winslow's medical skills, Massasoit did not die, and the sagamore rewarded him for the cure by informing him that a plot was being organized against Weston's colony by the Massachusetts, with the collaboration of some of the less friendly Nauset sachems. Furthermore,

Massasoit went on to say, after wiping out the colony at Wessagusset, they were then going to do the same against Plymouth; indeed, they had tried to enlist his cooperation in this scheme, he told Winslow. Armed with this news, Winslow and Hobomock rushed back to Plymouth, and before long the redoubtable Miles Standish was leading a military party to Boston Bay.

Standish found the Englishmen at Wessagusset living in the abject condition that had been described in reports; and some of them, he learned, had even begun to fear the worst at the hands of the Indians, who went freely in and out of the settlement. The Plymouth captain tried to pretend that he had come to trade while he sounded out the situation, but eventually an Indian spy discovered the truth and reported it back to his leaders. One of them sought out Hobomock, who had come along, and revealed to him that the Indians knew Standish had come to kill them. "Tell him we know it," he said, "but fear him not, neither will we shun him. But let him begin, when he dare; he shall not take us at unawares."

The tension mounted rapidly. Groups of Indians, or even solitary individuals, would often walk boldly into the village and up to Standish, "where they would whet and sharpen the points of their knives before his face; and use many other insulting gestures and speeches." Wituamat, thought to be the leader of the conspiracy, came before the captain and "bragged of the excellency of his knife," which had a woman's face carved at the end of the handle. "But," he said, "I have another at home, wherewith I have killed both French and English: and that hath a man's face on it; and by and by, these two must marry." He also said of the knife, Winslow's narrative goes on, "*Hinnaim namen, hinnaim michen, matta cuts,* that is to say, 'By and by it should see; and by and by it should eat, but not speak.'" Another Indian leader, Pecksuot, came to Standish and taunted him for his shortness of stature, saying "Though he were a great Captain, yet he was but a little man. And said he, 'Though I be no sachem, yet I am a man of great strength and courage.'

"These things the Captain observed; yet bore with patience for the present."

But the seething threat of violence finally erupted the next day, when Wituamat and Pecksuot, accompanied by another man and a boy of about eighteen, entered Standish's room and began taunting him again. Suddenly the captain, who had Hobomock and two or three other Englishmen — probably including Winslow — in the room with him, ordered the door to be shut. "And the door being fast shut, began himself with Pecksuot; and, snatching his own knife from his neck, though with much struggling, killed him therewith: the point whereof, he had made as sharp as a needle, and ground the back also to an edge. Wituamat and the other man, the rest killed; and took the youth, whom the Captain caused to be hanged." Winslow describes the scene with evident satisfaction, although he cannot help but marvel at how many wounds Wituamat and Pecksuot were able to take before they died, "not making any fearful noise, but catching at their weapons and striving to the last."

As for Hobomock, he "stood by, all this time, as a spectator and meddled not: observing how our men demeaned themselves in this action." It would seem that, though willing enough to collaborate in the murder of Massachusetts, he was not inclined actually to take up arms against fellow Indians. But he was quite ready to gloat over the outcome, saying to Standish: "Yesterday, Pecksuot, bragging of his own strength and stature, said, 'Though you were a great Captain, yet you were but a little man.' But today, I see you are big enough to lay him on the ground." The reader of all this must pause for a moment to wonder: is it possible that Massasoit had, with Hobomock's connivance, invented this whole story of a conspiracy at Wessagusset? We saw much taunting of Englishmen there, provoked in the first place by the assiduous incompetence of Weston's men, but little real indication of an impending attack.

But the main thing was that Plymouth and Sowams had both been given a much-desired opportunity to render the already weakened Massachusetts completely ineffectual; and this above all is what was achieved in the general fight that broke out after the struggle in Standish's room. Englishmen were killed as well as Indians, but in the end, muskets prevailed over bows and arrows as always, and the rump of the Massachusetts were put to flight. As for the Wessagusset colonists, they dispersed, some of them going to the trading outpost on Monhegan Island, others returning with Standish to Plymouth. The little captain led the way home triumphantly bearing the head of Wituamat, which was set up on a spike in a public place by the colony.

The men of Wessagusset had been a sorry example, indeed, of the sort of dilettantes of colonization that Winslow's preface denounced, but their demise did not put an end to the arrival of such "profane men" in New England, in spite of his book. That very autumn, a group of colonists was brought to the Wessagusset site by Robert Gorges, a son of Sir Ferdinando, who sponsored the expedition through his Council for New England. To make matters worse, Robert claimed for himself, with his father's sanction, the title of governor general of New England. This was a sign of troubles to come, but as it happened, in this particular instance at least, the Gorges challenge proved to be no problem. In both Old and New England, Robert Gorges had trouble getting his claims taken seriously, and he returned home in a year. As for the colonists he left behind, they were family people, solid middle-class English Protestants like the residents of Plymouth, and not at all offensive in the latter's eyes once young Gorges had departed. Soon Plymouth and the colony at Wessagusset — now renamed Weymouth — were the best of friends.

But the threat against which men like Winslow and Purchas had fulminated was not yet gone; rather, the most vivid example of it was only now about to occur. Sometime in 1625, according to Bradford, "there came over one Captain Wollaston (a man of pretty parts), and with him three or four more of some eminency, who brought with them a great many servants, with provisions and other implements for to begin a plantation; and pitched themselves in a place within the Massachusetts, which they called, after their Captain's name, Mount Wollaston." The place they had come to, called Passonagessit by the Indians, was just a few miles north of Weymouth, within the bounds of present-day Quincy. Not much good was likely to come of this outpost of male adventurers as far as the leaders of Plymouth were concerned, and it is with no surprise that Bradford writes that, after a while, "not finding things to answer their expectations, nor profit to arise as they looked for, Captain Wollaston takes a great part of the servants, and transports them to Virginia, where he puts them off at good rates, selling their time to other men." Staying on in Virginia, Wollaston then wrote to one of his partners back at the colony, a man named Rasdall, telling him to come down with more of the servants to sell, and to leave another member of their group, a man named Fitcher, in charge of the few who would remain. This is the point at which yet another of the Wollaston colonists, one Thomas Morton, suddenly appears at the center of the stage.

Bradford tells us that "this Morton abovesaid, having more craft than honesty (who had been a kind of pettifogger, of Furnefell's Inn), in [Fitcher's] absence, watches an opportunity (commons being but hard amongst them), and got some strong drink and other junkets, and made [the remaining servants] a feast; and after they were merry, he began to tell them he would give them good counsel. You see (saith he) that many of your fellows are carried to Virginia; and if you stay till this Rasdall return, you will also be carried away and sold for slaves with the rest. Therefore I would advise you to thrust out this lieutenant Fitcher; and I, having a part in the plantation, will receive you as my partners and consociates; so may you be free from service, and we will converse, trade, plant, and live together as equals, and support and protect one another, or to like effect. This counsel was easily received; so they took opportunity, and thrust lieutenant Fitcher out of doors, and would suffer him to come no more amongst them, but forced him to seek bread to eat, and other relief from his neighbors [at Weymouth], till he could get passage for England."

Who was this backwoods pre-Jacobin, Thomas Morton? Unfortunately, little is known about his life prior to these events. Clearly he was a lawyer, as Bradford tells us rather scathingly, but by his own testimony he was of the more distinguished Clifford's Inn rather than Furnefell's. There seems to have been some crime, or suspicion of one, in his past, and Morton's detractors then and more recently have suggested that it may have been murder. He also has left testimony that he had already once been in New England before 1625, and his words suggest that he must have been with Weston's colony — which certainly would have been no surprise to the leaders of Plymouth. It also would have been no surprise to them if he were already associated with Sir Ferdinando Gorges, which is entirely possible, since he was to be associated with him in the future. Morton also was something of a would-be litterateur and, eventually at least, could count Ben Jonson among his friends. Undoubtedly, he was a bit of a scoundrel, although Bradford probably exaggerates the disrepute in which he had been held from the outset by Wollaston's men in writing that he "had little respect amongst them, and was slighted by the meanest servants." But he seems also to have been a man of considerable charm, as humane in his attitudes toward servants and Indians as any Englishman of his day, and one gets the impression that there is even an occasional glint of admiration in Bradford's eye while contemplating him.

Yet for all the evident touch of Elizabethan liveliness in Bradford, Morton went too far even for him. After the ejection of Fitcher, Bradford writes, Morton and the rebellious servants "fell to a great licentiousness, and led a dissolute life, pouring out themselves into all profaneness. And Morton became lord of misrule, and maintained (as it were) a school of Atheism. And after they had got some good into their hands, and got much by trading with the Indians, they spent it as vainly, in quaffing and drinking both wine and strong waters in great excess, and, as some reported, £10 worth in a morning. They also set up a Maypole, drinking and dancing about it many days together, inviting the Indian women for their consorts, dancing and frisking together (like so many fairies, or furies rather), and worse practises. As if they had anew revived and celebrated the feasts of the Roman goddess Flora, or the beastly practises of the mad Bacchanalians. Morton likewise (to show his poetry) composed sundry rimes and verses, some tending to lasciviousness, and others to the detraction and scandal of some persons, which he affixed to this idle or idol Maypole. They changed also the name of their place, and instead of calling it Mount Wollaston, they call it Merrymount, as if this jollity would have lasted ever."

But even these bacchanalia alone, described by Bradford with startling gusto, might not have been sufficient to induce Plymouth to put an end to Merrymount. The problem was that Morton, a would-be French-style trader, was committing a sin of Frenchmen even worse in Plymouth's eyes than the ones just described. For, as Bradford goes on to say, "to maintain this riotous prodigality and profuse excess, Morton, thinking himself lawless, and hearing what gain the French and fishermen made by trading of pieces, powder, and shot to the Indians, he, as the head of this consortship, began the practise of the same in these parts; and first he taught them how to use them, to charge and discharge, and what proportion of powder to give the piece, according to the size or bigness of the same; and what shot to use for fowl, and what for deer. And having thus instructed them, he employed some of them to hunt and fowl for him, so as they became far more active in that employment than any of the English, by reason of their swiftness of foot, and nimbleness of body, being also quicksighted, and by continual exercise well knowing the haunts of all sorts of game. So as when they saw the execution that a piece would do, and the benefit that might come by the same, they became mad, as it were, after them, and would not stick to give any price they could attain to for them; accounting their bows and arrows but baubles in comparison of them."

It requires little imagination to see why the trading of firearms to Indians was a sin worse than Satanism for settlers of the Plymouth type, and by this time there were several minuscule colonies in the area, in addition to Weymouth, that saw matters the same way. By late 1627, they had banded together on this issue and were sending letters of protest to Morton. But the lord of Merrymount, standing on his professional training, stumped them in the exchange, for they had invoked a proclamation of King James forbidding "disorderly trade" with the Indians of New England, and his reply was, correctly, that this had no status as law. When they thereupon invoked the possibility of the king's displeasure, he replied, ominously, that "the king was dead and his displeasure with him." For indeed, James, no friend to men of Puritan bent by any means, had died in 1625 and been succeeded by his son Charles, whose wife was Catholic and French, and whose fondness for both of those elements in her makeup threatened to know no bounds. One can hear the New England woods echoing, in this moment, with its own first rumblings of oncoming warfare between Cavalier and Puritan.

In the face of Morton's obstinacy, Bradford goes on, the colonists opposed to him "resolved to proceed, and obtained of the Governor of Plymouth to send Captain Standish, and some other aide with him, to take Morton by force. The which accordingly was done; but they found him to stand stiffly in his defense, having made fast his doors, armed his consorts, set diverse dishes of powder and bullets ready on the table; and if they had not been overarmed with drink, more hurt might have been done. They summoned him to yield, but he kept his house, and they could get nothing but scoffs and scorns from him; but at length, fearing they would do some violence to the house, he and some of his crew came out, but not to yield, but to shoot; but they were so steeled with drink as their pieces were too heavy for them; himself with a carbine (overcharged and almost half filled with powder and shot, as was after found) had thought to have shot Captain Standish; but he stepped to him, and put by his piece, and took him. Neither was there any hurt done to any of either side, save that one was so drunk that he ran his own nose upon the point of a sword that one held before him as he entered the house; but he lost but a little of his hot blood." Morton was sent back to England on the next ship. A short time later, when John Endicott, a true representative of a greater Puritan militancy now forthcoming in New England, arrived to establish the Salem colony, he went down to Merrymount and "caused that Maypole to be cut down." Some of the more severe-minded of the colonists, Endicott's spiritual kin, renamed the place "Mount Dagon," as if that infamy would have lasted ever.

This was the crux of Morton's history, although New England had not heard the last of him. In 1629 he reappeared, this time in the employ of Sir Ferdinando Gorges, staying first with a friend in Plymouth and then moving on to his old haunts. But his enemies contrived once again to have him sent back home, where he at length obtained his revenge by writing a book that scathingly summarized his American adventures. *The New English Canaan,* as he slyly called it, represents his moment of greatest triumph in general, for shortly before he wrote it Gorges had succeeded in having New England proclaimed a crown colony with himself as its governor general. This was never to be effectuated, and the Puritan victory over the king in years to come would put an end to the Gorges claims there for once and for all, but for the moment at least, New England was in a state of consternation and Morton could revel in the overflowings of his patron's glory.

Following a literary convention well established by this time, Morton's book was divided into three parts, the first of which was devoted to a description of the Indians of New England, the second to its flora, fauna, and geographical features, and the third to a history of the author's experiences there. Written with Elizabethan gusto, and filled with puns and bawdy asides, it is a thoroughly amusing piece of work, which even has its serious side in its constant pleas on behalf of the Indians; but its status as either an anthropological or a historical document is questionable. Its descriptions of Indians come largely from another book, *New England's Prospect,* by William Wood, and are otherwise often unreliable; as for the narrative part, it is better regarded as a kind of freewheeling *roman à clef* than as a true account. With these reservations in mind, one can certainly enjoy such things as the references to Standish as "Captain Shrimp," to Bradford as "Master Bubble," and to Endicott as "Captain Littleworth," or passages like this one about a certain beaver skin with a tail that

> is of such masculine virtue that if some of our Ladies knew the benefit thereof they would desire to have ships sent of purpose to trade for the tail alone: it is such a rarity, as is not more esteemed of than reason doth require.

Fun, yes; but how one could have wished for a little more high seriousness! For Morton does not miss his opportunities to sermonize on the one issue to which he carries real moral weight, saying, for example, that "I have found the Massachusetts Indian more full of humanity than the Christians," or that, from what he has written, "you may easily perceive the uncivilized people are more just than the civilized." These could have been the observations of a New World Marlowe or Shakespeare, but in the context of the book and the personality it presents, they emerge as hardly more than a flippant game of *épater le bourgeois* being indulged in by a seventeenth-century playboy. What has happened by now to the Hariots and the Percys, or even to the promise once held out by a Gorges? Circumstances seem to have given them decadent offspring, even though, heaven knows, the Indians of New England could have used a defender with real moral authority in this moment above all. For the year in which the book appeared, 1637, was also the one in which the Pequot Massacre took place.

27

The Massacre of the Pequots

W HEN THE FIRST GROUP of about nine hundred founders of the Massachusetts Bay colony reached its destination in the summer of 1630, the area of the future state bearing that name had an English population of about three hundred, most of them living at Plymouth. This was the total for ten years of settlement; but in another ten years, the figure would be some fourteen thousand, and Plymouth would be dwarfed by the colony that was eventually to absorb it.

A similar growth was to take place elsewhere in the English colonies as well during that decade from 1630 to 1640,° for the "Great Migration" of the period, often thought of only with reference to New England, in fact reached out to all westward horizons and even covered Ireland. Land-hunger and the desire for material self-improvement were as much motives for this exodus as religious aspirations were, and New England was far from the only place where they could be satisfied. Furthermore,

---

° The number of settlers in Virginia, for example, increased from three to nearly eight thousand in this decade. The most dramatic growth of all was in the West Indies: the English population of Barbados, zero at the beginning of 1625, was more than eighteen thousand by 1640. In that moment it was the largest of the English colonies, and St. Kitts was third in size, not far behind Massachusetts Bay, at more than twelve thousand.

even in New England, the great majority of the settlers were drawn no less by the generous terms for land allotment there than by religious ideals. Yet the fact remains that Massachusetts Bay, which, along with its offspring in Connecticut, Rhode Island, New Hampshire, and Maine, was far and away the giant of continental Anglo-America in this epoch, contained the lion's share of the colonial traits that would ultimately develop into the American character. Predominantly Puritan as well as land-hungry, restless and consumed with both worldly and spiritual ambitions, the New England settlements were the principal seedbed not only of a nation's democratic ideals, but of its peculiar brand of empire as well. Some aspects of the latter are well summed up by a man who was no hero to Puritans but very much an Englishman of the incipient age of expansion, Sir Thomas More, who wrote of the continent his Utopians colonized whenever their own island became overcrowded:

> The natives there have more land than they can use, so some of it lies fallow. The Utopians permit the natives to live in the colony if they wish, since their acceptance of Utopian laws and customs means they are easily assimilated, which benefits both peoples. The Utopian way of life makes the land fruitful enough for both groups, though previously it was too poor and barren for either. All natives who refuse to live under Utopian law are driven out of the colony and war is waged on the natives who resist. Utopians regard a war as just if it is waged to oust a people who refuse to allow vacant land to be used according to the very law of nature.

This Anglo-Saxon self-assurance about nature's laws reverberates down through the ages, passing through the Puritan leaders of early New England into recent American history.

Indeed, if there were any differences between More and the Puritans on this point, it was only in ways that were yet more ominous for the future of Anglo-Indian relations in America. More spoke of assimilation, but New England would always be far less prone to make the Indians its own than Virginia or, to be sure, Spanish America had been. Furthermore, whereas More looked upon colonization as a tentative thing, the men of Massachusetts Bay, who had spirited away their colonial charter with them, had an entirely different outlook. No seekers of mere enclaves, as the Portuguese had been in their own first era of expansion, and as the English had been until now, they quickly turned out to be in possession of a full-fledged continental appetite; in this respect they were like the Spaniards, with whom they also shared a common religious zeal and innate sense of manifest destiny. But, far from reaching out to the Indian as the Spaniards did — albeit with an embrace that often was deadly — the hermetic Protestants of Massachusetts and Connecticut never ceased to encounter him as though his presence were some unfortunate accident. Having no particular taste either for *encomienda* or for miscegenation, they really longed for endless horizons as emptied by Divine Providence of their aboriginal populations as the Massachusetts coast had been. In their quieter moments, they wanted only to behave toward the Indian in a spirit of live and let live, as Plymouth had tended to do before them. But their spirits were unquiet, and when circumstances brought them into conflict with the natives, they proved at least as ready to lend Divine Providence a helping hand as Miles Standish had been at Wessagusset in 1623. They may have doled out their cruelties with greater hesitancy and misgiving than the Spaniards did, but in the end they doled them out all the same. For all the differences between the slaughterers of Cholula and those we are about to see at Mystic Fort, there remains a final point of reckoning at which, however strangely and ironically, they come together; the dead of both places would hardly quibble over the distinctions between English and Spanish national character.

The Puritans do not give the impression, as Spaniards did, of having charged with swords drawn the moment they set foot on the American continent. It took them a few years to discover their great hunger for it, and until about 1634, Anglo-Indian relations at Massachusetts Bay were rather sedate; indeed, they seem almost idyllic, even allowing for the extent to which this situation was due to the near extinction of the local native population. That early mood comes through in such a writer as the Reverend Francis Higginson, who could say in 1630 of the Massachusetts Indians:

> They do generally profess to like well of our coming and planting here; partly because there is abundance of ground that they cannot possess nor make use of, and partly because our being here will be a means both of relief to them when they want, and also a defense from their enemies, wherewith (I say) before this plantation began, they were often endangered.

This hopefulness becomes euphoric in William Wood's *New England's Prospect*, published in 1634, which sings the praises of the Massachusetts, and sums up their attitudes toward various Europeans like this:

> The Spaniard they say is all one *aramouse* (*viz.*, all one as a dog), the Frenchman hath a good tongue, but a false heart: the Englishman all one speak, all one heart; wherefore they more approve of them than of any nation.

Wood, who seems in many ways to have been a kind of Hariot or Percy of New England, also wrote of the Pequots that they "be a stately warlike people, of whom I never heard any misdemeanor."

It did this idyll no harm that, in the fall and winter of 1633–1634, a smallpox plague raged among the Indians of New England — for the bacteria brought to America by the Europeans were often even deadlier than their guns — and cleared the land of several thousand more of its original population. But the atmosphere of race relations soon was darkening all the same. By 1634, Francis Higginson was dead and William Wood, evidently just another dilettante of colonization after all, had gone back to England for good. New settlers were coming by the thousands, and the relentlessness of expansion was made more ferocious by a newly heightening political and religious anxiety. Sir Ferdinando Gorges was reaching the pinnacle of his ambitions concerning New England, and the Puritan leaders there became convinced that he was about to send over an invading force; this was when John Endicott made his celebrated gesture of defiance, tearing the red cross out of an English flag before the eyes of an assemblage of settlers. To make matters worse, religious authoritarianism was tightening back home under Charles's newly appointed Archbishop of Canterbury, William Laud, and the leaders of Massachusetts Bay, which was becoming a yet more eagerly sought refuge of Puritans as a result, responded by bringing their own streak of doctrinal authoritarianism to the surface in the next few years, first against Roger Williams, then against Anne Hutchinson and the Antinomians. This was the climate within which Indian troubles first arose among the tiny outposts of New England settlement that had begun to gather along the Connecticut River.

A concerted English effort to settle that borderland region between Dutch and English colonization was not made until 1636, when a total of about eight hundred English men, women, and children established themselves in the settlements of Windsor, Wethersfield, Saybrook, and Hartford during the first half of the year. The Indians living right along the river had proved to be no problem for them; but this was not to be the case with the Pequots, whose country was somewhat to the east. The Pequots had been a source of tension for the English colonists ever since an incident that had occurred at the beginning of 1634, when a confrontation at the mouth of the Connecticut between a few of them and Captain John Stone, a trader from Virginia, had ended in the death of Stone and some of his men. The leaders of Massachusetts Bay, regarding the Connecticut River as their jurisdiction, had spent the next two years trying to obtain full satisfaction for this, and in the summer of 1636, now that there were colonies in the area, they sent the governor's son, John Winthrop,

Jr., on a mission for this purpose. The younger Winthrop put in at Saybrook, at the mouth of the Connecticut, but the roughly forty men and women living there apparently did not welcome him with open arms; already anxious about the Indian situation, they regarded his mission as a provocation. It was in July, during his sojourn there, that an incident occurred that brought about a heightening of the tension.

John Gallop, a trader from Massachusetts Bay, was sailing from Connecticut to Long Island, when a storm took him off his course to Block Island instead. There he spied a small pinnace, which he recognized as that of another Massachusetts trader, named John Oldham; but, upon drawing near, he found the deck to be crowded with Indians. As soon as they saw that they were spotted, the Indians set sail, aiming Oldham's ship for Narragansett Bay, but Gallop pursued them, ramming the ship and boarding it with his men. After a furious battle, during which most of the Indians leaped into the sea — and two others were thrown into the water after being bound by Gallop's men — the body of John Oldham was found under a fishing net, "stark naked, his head cleft to the brains, and his hand and legs cut as if they had been cutting them off, and yet warm." When the news of this reached Massachusetts Bay there was great consternation, for Oldham was no Stone, who had been a Virginian and something of a scoundrel; he was, rather, a highly respected fellow citizen, a man prominent in the community's affairs — it was he, for example, who had sailed Thomas Morton back to England in 1628.

This was obviously a Narragansett affair, and indeed, the English heard through their intelligence of a plot against Oldham that had been organized by all the Narragansett sachems except two — Canonicus, now become a friend of the English, and a younger man named Miantanomo. The Narragansetts had not been particularly troublesome to the colonists since the early days at Plymouth, but recently the latter had begun hearing rumors of a possible alliance between this people and the Pequots. This was greatly feared by the English, who also, however, now had a very effective instrument for peace with the Narragansetts in the person of Roger Williams. Among the unacceptable ideas that Williams had aired at Massachusetts Bay and for which he had been forced to leave the colony at the end of 1635 were not only his well-known strictures about the civil limitations of religious authority, but also his conviction that the land of the New World belonged to the Indians and could be obtained from them only by treaty and purchase. He was the Indians' first good friend among the leaders of New England, and he had no sooner established his Providence colony — on land purchased from the Indians — in early 1636 than he began devoting himself to the cause of harmony between the races. Steadily acquiring proficiency in the Narragansett dialect of the Algonquian language, Williams had developed close relations with Canonicus and Miantanomo, and it was he and they who now interceded after the Oldham incident to seek a satisfactory solution to the crisis. Miantanomo secured the release of two boys who had been taken from Oldham's boat and held prisoner on Block Island, a Narragansett preserve, and Canonicus obtained assurance that the other sachems of his people would not ally themselves with the Pequots against the English. The Puritan leaders were further placated, at least for the moment, with the reminder that virtually all of those responsible for Oldham's death had been killed in the fight with Gallop. Unfortunately, a few of those who survived it had, it was learned, taken refuge among the Pequots; and this knowledge rankled.

Precisely what happened next is not clear, but in only a matter of days, rash counsel prevailed at Massachusetts in spite of everything. In Governor John Winthrop's journal, the very next entry after the one describing the peaceable assurances from Canonicus, dated only twelve days later, opens thus:

> The governor and council, having lately assembled the rest of the magistrates and ministers, to advise with them about doing justice upon the Indians for the death of Mr. Oldham, and all agreeing that it should be attempted with expedition, did this day send forth ninety men, distributed to four commanders — Capt. John Underhill, Capt. Nathaniel Turner, Ensign [William] Jennison, and Ensign [Richard] Davenport; and over them all, as general, John Endicott, Esq., one of the assistants, was sent. . . . They had commission to put to death the men of Block Island, but to spare the women and children, and to bring them away, and to take possession of the island; and from thence to go to the Pequots to demand the murderers of Capt. Stone and other English, and one thousand fathom of wampum for damages, etc., and some of their children as hostages, which if they should refuse, they were to obtain it by force.

One suspects that Endicott had a good deal to do with the making of this foolish decision.

Block Island itself gave little satisfaction to the thirst for Indian blood in Endicott and his group of volunteers. After an initial skirmish upon landing, in which nobody was killed, the English discovered all the inhabitants to have fled into the underbrush. "When they had spent two days in searching the island," Winthrop writes, "and could not find the Indians, they burnt their wigwams, and all their mats, and some corn, and staved seven canoes, and departed." Next they went to Saybrook, which was to serve as a base for their mission against the Pequots, but Lyon Gardiner, who was in command there, was anything but overjoyed to find out why they had come. As far as he was concerned, the men of Massachusetts Bay were more troublemakers than helpers in this region so far from where their own homes had to feel the consequences of their acts: "You come hither," he told Endicott, "to raise these wasps about my ears, and then you will take wing and flee away." This would not be the first time they had acted that way; John Winthrop, Jr., after coming here to provoke the Pequots, had already gone with his wife back to Massachusetts Bay, where she was to be delivered of her first child, "and though you say he shall return," Gardiner had written angrily to the leaders there, "yet I know if you make war with these Pequots, he will not come hither again, for I know you will keep yourselves safe as you think, in the Bay, but myself with these few, you will leave at the stake to be roasted, or for hunger to be starved."

These telling remarks seem only to have served as a provocation to Endicott, who in another four days was leading his men, along with a few reluctant volunteers from Saybrook, to Pequot Harbor at the mouth of the Pequot River (now the Thames). As they approached their destination, according to John Underhill's account, "the Indians spying us came running in multitudes along the waterside, crying, What cheer, Englishmen, what cheer, what do you come for?" In that era, "what cheer" was a standard English salutation, but in this situation it could only have sounded mocking to the ruffled emissaries of Massachusetts Bay. "We thinking it the best way, did forbear to answer them," Underhill goes on, "but they, seeing we would make no answer, kept on the course and cried, What, Englishmen, what cheer, are you hoggery, will you cram us? That is, are you angry, will you kill us, and do you come to fight?" The English put up for the night in their boats, but the Indians, uncertain as to what was happening, "made fire on both sides of the river, fearing we would land in the night."

The next morning, the English were greeted at the water's edge by "an ambassador, a grave senior, a man of good understanding, portly carriage, grave and majestical in his expressions." The English inquired about the death of Stone, but "they being a witty and ingenious nation," Underhill writes, "their ambassador labored to excuse the matter, and answered, We know not that any of ours have slain any English." Finally, after much prodding, he did concede that, yes, there had been some such incident, but that it was in revenge for acts that the Dutch had committed against the Indians. "We distinguish not between the Dutch and the English," he said, "but took them to be one nation." This drew protests from his interlocutors, but he reiterated firmly: "We know no difference between the Dutch and the English; they are both strangers to us." This striking and irreproachable reply won some grudging respect from Underhill, who was impelled to remark of the Pequots in general

THE MASSACRE OF THE PEQUOTS

in this context that "from the first beginning to the end of the action, they carried themselves very subtilely."

At length, the English demanded to see the sachem of the Pequots, Sassacus, and not just his ambassador, but the result was only a series of ceremonious delays that kept the English waiting by their boats for several hours. When their patience was exhausted, they decided upon a show of pomp. "Marching into a champaign field, we displayed our colors," Underhill says, "but none would come near us, but standing remotely off did laugh at us for our patience." Perhaps the expressions on the Indians' faces had been misinterpreted, but in any case, the English took this apparent mockery as the final provocation, and went on a rampage. "We suddenly set upon our march, and gave fire to as many as we could come near, firing their wigwams, spoiling their corn, and many other necessaries that they had buried in the ground we raked up, which the soldiers had for booty. Thus we spent the day burning and spoiling the country. And the next day too." Yet even in their fury, the expeditioners proved not to be as effective as they may have hoped. They succeeded in killing only two Indians, which is the figure Winthrop gives; Gardiner later claimed it was only one, and that this had been the work not of an Englishman, but of one of the two Massachusetts Indians that had been taken along as interpreters: "and thus," he wrote in utter disgust, "began the war between the Indians and us in these parts."

Gardiner, at any rate, was entitled to his bitterness: no sooner had Endicott and his band returned to Massachusetts Bay than the incidents at Saybrook began to mount. Once, pursuing some Indian attackers in the forest, Gardiner and his men were astonished to hear one of them calling out in English: "We are Pequots, and have killed Englishmen, and can kill them as mosquitoes, and we will go to the Connecticut and kill men, women, and children, and we will take away the horses, cows, and dogs." As if starting out to deliver on this promise, the Pequots staged a number of ambushes, in the course of which they took one man and roasted him alive; another, one John Tilley, was taken and "they cut off his hands, and sent them before, and after cut off his feet. He lived three days after his hands were cut off; and themselves confessed, that he was a stout man, because he cried not in his torture."

The fear of atrocities was aggravated by the suspicion that the Pequots were again trying to ally themselves with the Narragansetts, in the wake of Endicott's performances at Block Island and Pequot Harbor, which had provided these two peoples with ample common justification for hostility toward the English. In this matter, Roger Williams came once again to the rescue. The leaders of Massachusetts Bay appealed by letter to this man whom they had ejected from amongst them, asking him to use his good offices and persuade the Narragansetts to remain on the English side; Williams immediately set out for Miantanomo's village. There he found a Pequot embassy already arrived for the purpose that the English feared. "Three days and nights my business forced me to lodge and mix with the bloody Pequot ambassadors, whose hands and arms, methought, reeked with the blood of my countrymen, murdered and massacred by them on Connecticut river, and from whom I could not but nightly look for their bloody knives at my own throat also." Williams's counsel prevailed, and within a week or two Miantanomo was in Boston at the head of a Narragansett delegation, declaring to the youthful new governor, Henry Vane, and the other assembled magistrates and ministers: "That they had always loved the English. . . . That they would now make a firm peace, and two months hence they would send us a present." And they proceeded to do just that, paying special attention in their treaty to provisions for common English and Narragansett action in the event of a war with the Pequots. The promised gift arrived at last in March, some five months later: it consisted of "forty fathom of wampum and a Pequot's hand."

In the meantime, Massachusetts Bay turned to its more godly preoccupations. This was the period in which the so-called Antinomian controversy came to the fore, led by Mrs. Anne Hutchinson. The doctrinal issues involved in the controversy are too complex and remote to concern us here, but we may note that included in Mrs. Hutchinson's personal outlook, which in its gentle, inspirational religiosity anticipated Quakerism to a large extent, was a feeling of warm friendship toward the Indians, matched among the prominent figures of this period only by that of Roger Williams, another religious dissenter. We should not go so far as to suppose from this that all of those who abided by Mrs. Hutchinson's "Covenant of Grace" were apostles of sweet reasonableness toward the Indians: John Underhill, as we shall see, was living proof that this could not have been so. Yet there probably were fears among the orthodox Massachusetts leaders that the Antinomians were a subversive element in their struggles with Pequots as in their struggles with the Devil: Mrs. Hutchinson was clearly an ally of the latter in their eyes, and as for the Pequots, a people so determined to extirpate the white man from the soil of New England — for this was what the more alarmist settlers now believed — could not have been anything else. The mood, compounded by the disasters true religion was enduring back in England, under King Charles and Archbishop Laud, and in Europe, where Catholics and Protestants were at the height of the mutual slaughter we now call the Thirty Years' War, was reflected one day in February, 1637, when "a general fast was kept in all the churches" of Massachusetts Bay, according to Winthrop. "The occasion was, the miserable estate of the churches in Germany; the calamities upon our native country, the bishops making havoc in the churches, putting down the faithful ministers, and advancing popish ceremonies and doctrines, the plague raging exceedingly, and famine and sword threatening them; the dangers of those at Connecticut, and of ourselves also, by the Indians; and the dissensions in our churches." This was no time for gentleness when danger reared its head.

And danger seemed truly in the offing at the end of April, when a Pequot attack on the Connecticut River colony of Wethersfield took the lives of six men and three women, as well as of twenty cows and a mare; furthermore, two young girls were carried away. The attack had not been unprovoked: Pequot aid had been enlisted by the sachem of a small local tribe, the Wongunks, who had been forced off certain of their lands by the Wethersfield settlers in violation of an earlier treaty made between them. At a later time, Massachusetts Bay was even to recognize the Wongunk claim as valid, but for the moment the mood was only one of vengefulness. The leaders of the Bay colony called for the mobilization of troops against the Pequots. Plymouth was also enlisted in the cause, even though Edward Winslow, who came to Boston to represent his colony in the matter, registered some objections at first to the treatment his community had suffered at the hands of the expansive giant to the north, and pointed out that the Pequots were not really even Plymouth's enemy.

While all this preparation was going on, the Englishmen in Connecticut, gripped by a sudden hysteria, took matters into their own hands. Convening at Hartford on May 1, the Connecticut General Court, representing all the colonies along that river, declared war on the Pequots and called for the levying of troops. A force of ninety men was mustered under the leadership of Captain John Mason, a former Massachusetts colonist who had been one of the founders of Windsor, and a true representative of the now burgeoning imperial mentality of Puritan New England. Captain John Underhill was also present in the area with a force of twenty men from Massachusetts, having been sent to Saybrook the previous month to stand by for possible troubles both with the Indians and with the Dutch. These combined forces were added to by some Indian auxiliaries, contributed not only by the Narragansetts, but also by the Mohegans, a small people who had just entered upon the scene. Along with the Pequots, the Mohegans had once been part of the Hudson Valley tribe of Mohicans — the difference in name is only a matter of dialect. Late in the preceding century, the combined Pequot-Mohegan group had broken away from the parent community and settled to the east of the Connecticut River, but a very recent factional struggle had led to the secession of the Mohegans under their chief, Uncas, who was now the Pequots' avowed enemy. In the skirmishing along the Connecticut River that took place in the two weeks following the declaration of war against the Pequots, Uncas quickly proved himself an able warrior and the most ardent Indian friend the English had known since the days of Squanto and Hobomock.

By the middle of May the English in Connecticut were able, through the intercession of some friendly Dutch traders who were momentarily on good terms with the Pequots, to obtain the release of the two Wethersfield girls who had been kidnapped in the previous month's raid: according to one story, their Indian captors had hoped they would know how to make gunpowder, and had eagerly released them when it turned out that they did not. They "had been well used by the Pequots," according to Winthrop, "and no violence offered them," but the English thirst for revenge had not been assuaged, particularly since, as Captain Mason saw it, "those Pequots were a great people, being strongly fortified, cruel, warlike, munitioned [sic!], etc., and the English but an handful in comparison." The Pequots were, in fact, fewer than a thousand men, women, and children, but of course, the Connecticut English were fewer still at this point; and in this moment, they were naturally inclined to think of themselves as alone rather than as an outpost of the rapidly growing giant of Massachusetts Bay. It is important for the understanding of Anglo-Indian relations in this period to realize that, in many of the hostile confrontations, the settlers thought of themselves as merely the equal of the natives in strength; this was the same self-justifying delusion that had been harbored in Ireland on the eve of Munster. As to the question of whether the English settlers were even so much as equal to the Indians in courage, this had not yet been proven to anyone's satisfaction, for there had never, anywhere on American soil, been an all-out, face-to-face confrontation between English and Indian fighting men. Doubts remained on both sides whether the English could, in fact, stand up to the Pequots, with their fearsome reputation, and these doubts were often rubbed in: in one of the attacks on Saybrook earlier in the year, some of the Pequots had obtained English clothes and put them on, "and came to the fort jeering of them, and calling, come and fetch your Englishmen's clothes again; come out and fight, if you dare; you dare not fight; you are all one like women." Such taunts were bound to backfire dangerously.

By the last week in May, the English at Saybrook had decided upon a major attack, but not against Pequot Harbor, where they were expected. Rather, after sailing to Miantanomo's village on Narragansett Bay, where they added several hundred warriors to their invading force, they marched overland to the Pequot fort at the mouth of the Mystic River, a few miles east of Pequot Harbor. There were about four hundred Indians at Mystic Fort at this moment, including women and children, and a group of about one hundred and fifty warriors who had just arrived to prepare for a large-scale attack upon the English: their triumphant songs reached the nervous ears of the arriving invaders, who made camp for the night in the woods nearby. At one o'clock the next morning, May 26, 1637, the march toward the fort began; but suddenly, the several hundred Narragansetts, who had continued taunting the English along the way, according to Mason, with remarks that "we durst not look upon a Pequot, but themselves would perform great things," all took to flight. Whether this was out of fear, or a last-minute display of lingering solidarity with their erstwhile Pequot friends, is impossible to say. Apparently some of the Mohegans in the force also fled — though not Uncas himself, who knew exactly where his future lay. The English tried to persuade some of the deserting Indians at least to stand by and watch, "at what distance they pleased, and see whether Englishmen would now fight or not."

In the final approach, the two commanders divided whatever forces remained to them, and Mason moved in from the west, Underhill from the north. Penetrating the palisades that surrounded the fort, the two contingents — or some of them, at any rate — rushed from their respective sides to the wigwams in which the unsuspecting Pequots still slept. They broke inside, and suddenly the Pequot warriors were awake and in action. Mason was hit by "many arrows against his headpiece," Underhill later wrote. "God preserved him from many wounds. Myself received a shot in the left hip, through a sufficient buff coat, that if I had not been supplied with such a garment, the arrow would have pierced through me. Another I received between neck and shoulders hanging in the linen on my headpiece." Underhill could not but be impressed at the prowess of an Indian enemy unlike any encountered in New England before: "Most courageously these Pequots behaved themselves," he wrote.

But there was to be no final decision between the two sides on grounds of chivalry. Suddenly the fort had been set afire, possibly by Mason himself, who was much more determined than Underhill to carry out "the just judgment of God" against the Pequots without any interference from considerations of fair play. Indeed, it is very likely that the fire was a prearranged plan, for the flames spread very quickly — so quickly that, according to William Bradford's account made from eyewitness reports, more of the Pequots "were burnt to death than was otherwise slain" — and yet the English were able to assemble themselves outside of the fort unscathed, ready to deal with all those who rushed to escape. Not many escaped, however. The great majority of the Pequots in the village must have perished in their sleep, but there also were many warriors who preferred the agony of the flames to the instantaneous sentences being meted out by the waiting muskets. "Many courageous fellows were unwilling to come out," wrote the astonished Underhill, "and fought most desperately through the palisades, so as they were scorched and burnt with the very flame and were deprived of their arms — in regard the fire burnt their very bowstrings — and so perished valiantly." The Englishmen gaped in horror at their work. "It was a fearful sight," in Bradford's words, "to see them thus frying in the fire, and the streams of blood quenching the same, and horrible was the stink and scent thereof." When the smoke had died down at last, and the English reentered the fort, some of them recoiled "to see so many souls lie gasping on the ground, so thick in some places, that you could hardly pass along." Most of the long-dreaded Pequot nation now lay smoldering at their feet.

"Mercy did they deserve for their valor, could we have had opportunity to have bestowed it," was Underhill's judgment; but this was not shared by Mason, who said that the Pequots had brought "the mischief they plotted, and the violence they offered and exercised, upon their own heads in a moment: burning them up in the fire of His wrath, and dunging the ground with their flesh: It was the Lord's doings, and it is marvelous in our eyes!" Memories of Amalek clearly are in Mason's head as he concludes his account with the words: "Thus we may see how the face of God is set against them that do evil, to cut off the remembrance of them from the earth." Even Underhill finally sees fit to quiet his conscience with the kind of Old Testament consolations to which Puritans notoriously were prone. "It may be demanded," he begins, in a troubled philosophical digression, "why should you be so furious? (as some have said). Should not Christians have more mercy and compassion?" But militant Puritanism comes up with the same answer as militant Catholicism had. "I would refer you," he goes on, "to David's war. When a people is grown to such a height of blood and sin against God and man, and all confederates in the action, there He hath no respect to persons, but harrows them, and saws them, and puts them to the sword, and the most terriblest death that may be. Sometimes the Scripture declareth women and children must perish with their parents. Sometimes the case alters; but we will not dispute it now. We had sufficient light from the word of God for our proceedings." One hears a final cough in the recollected smoke of the burning fort; but the irritation is quickly assuaged with a dose of the kind of godly arrogance without which New England, as we know it, probably could not have been built.

The confidence in God's judgment increases as we move farther from the original scene, to those who did not have to choke upon its horrible reality. At Plymouth, the normally gentle-spirited Bradford cleared away the stink of his own characteristically vivid description of the holocaust at Mystic Fort by saying that "the victory seemed a sweet sacrifice, and they gave the praise thereof to God, who had wrought so wonderfully for them, thus to enclose their enemies in their hands, and give them so speedy a victory over so proud and insulting an enemy." Edward Winslow also thought it was "God's just judgment." At Massachusetts Bay, Philip Vincent, a somewhat more worldly man than most residents of the colony, invoked not God but all the human provocations that had led up to this violent outcome. Awakening the terrifying memory of Virginia in 1622, which was never far beneath the surface of the settler's attitudes, he wrote: "The long forbearance and too much lenity of the English towards the Virginian salvages, had like to have been the destruction of the whole plantation. These barbarians, ever treacherous, abuse the goodness of those that condescend to their rudeness and imperfections." And, as a final philosophical underlining of his message, he adds: "Mercy mars all sometimes; severe justice must now and then take place." But surely more typical of the outlook at Massachusetts Bay than these careful reasonings is the remark of Edward Johnson, author of the *Wonder-working Providence of Sion's Saviour in New England*, to the effect that "the Lord in mercy toward his poor churches . . . thus destroyed these bloody barbarous Indians." Even more to the point is the statement he makes with respect to the following year, after Anne Hutchinson, at the end of a despicably unfair trial, had been banished from the colony: "The peace of this little Commonwealth being now in great measure settled," he writes, "by the Lord's mercy, in overthrowing the Indians, and banishing of certain turbulent spirits." We do not know how Anne Hutchinson felt about the way the Pequots had been dealt with only a short time before judgment was then delivered upon her, but we do know that Roger Williams registered a virtually lone objection. He had not liked the Pequots, but what had happened was another matter. "I . . . fear that some innocent blood cries at Connecticut," he wrote.

The delivering of God's judgment had not quite ended at Mystic Fort. A few hundred more Pequots were still alive, but the tribe was now not going to be allowed to survive as such. Scattered groups and individuals were pursued through the forests, some of them to be taken prisoner, most of them killed, in the ensuing weeks. Some of them had fled to neighboring Indian tribes once considered friendly; but English law now prevailed through the land in the wake of victory, and many of these Pequot refugees were killed or returned. Sassacus, the Pequot sachem, had fled to the Mohawks with some of his men; but he and they were killed by these erstwhile allies, who sent their scalps to the English. There was a final engagement near the Dutch line in July, at which some two hundred and eighty Pequots surrendered, the last significant rump of this devastated people.

Prisoners were distributed mainly among the various tribes of New England, among whom they were to live ostensibly in servitude, but at any rate without the privilege of calling themselves Pequots again. The very word "Pequot" was eliminated from the map, the river of that name becoming the Thames, the village of the same name becoming New London. Some Pequots apparently were kept as bondsmen by the English, but it was found preferable to have the remnants of Amalek out of sight altogether. Seventeen of the captives — fifteen boys and two women — were sent to be traded off as slaves in the West Indies. John Winthrop tells us this, and also writes, in an entry for the following February, that the captain, William Pierce, who had taken out this cargo of Pequots, "returned from the West Indies after seven months. He had been at Providence [Island], and brought some cotton, and tobacco, and Negroes, etc., from thence, and salt from Tertugos." In other words, the remnant of New England's dreaded enemy had been bartered for, among other things, some Negro slaves. This is another of our history's fateful configurations.

28

Islands of the Sable Venus

It is to the west indies that we must look for the true beginnings of Black slavery in English America. The notorious "twenty Negars" that arrived in Jamestown in August of 1619 came from there, as did the Black slaves brought back to Massachusetts Bay in February, 1638, by Captain William Pierce. Furthermore, whereas there were only a little over three hundred Negroes in Virginia by around 1650, forming some two percent of the colony's total population, there were over 20,000 in Barbados at the same time, fully half of the total population. This English colonial picture was a valid reflection of the international one: even through the subsequent two hundred years of the transatlantic slave trade, the great bulk of the Negroes brought to the New World would land in the region between the tropics, whereas the number of those brought to the territory of the United States did not add up to more than five percent of the final total, according to the most careful modern estimate. The North American continent was only an outpost of the hemispheric slave system.

The true heart of that system in the middle of the seventeenth century was Brazil and those island colonies in the Caribbean that had, after the general decline of the traditional Spanish gold supply, discovered a new source of wealth in the cultivation of sugar. There could be no more vivid

symbol than this sweet cane of the way in which the old Mediterranean
had projected itself into the Atlantic during the previous two hundred
years. It was during that first great wave of colonial expansion, the
Crusades, that Europeans discovered sugar, which had been brought to
the Holy Land from the farther East by the Arabs. After the fall of the
Christian principalities there, sugar cultivation began to move westward
over the Mediterranean, flourishing mainly on the islands of Cyprus,
Crete, and Sicily, often under the hands of Venetian and Genoese colonial
entrepreneurs. The Portuguese became the heirs to this movement as they
did to the whole Mediterranean westward expansion, and sugar cultivation was brought by them — often with Genoese help — out into the
Atlantic, to Madeira, to the Cape Verde Islands, to São Thomé, and
finally to Brazil. The Spanish followed the same course, planting sugar
first in the Canaries, then bringing it over to the West Indian islands, to
Mexico, and to Peru. Sugar had always required fairly large-scale agricultural labor, but it was in the sixteenth century that improved methods of
production and increasing European demand combined to bring about
vast plantation systems in this industry. The Portuguese, first in São
Thomé and the Cape Verde Islands, and then in not very distant Brazil,
did not hesitate to draw upon their own well-established slave trade to
supply Black Africans to the growing plantations. The Spaniards gradually renounced the use of Indian labor, after patterns that we have
glimpsed, and also turned to the Negro supply. When the northern colonial powers — primarily the Netherlands, France, and England — finally
began establishing themselves in the Caribbean in the first part of the
seventeenth century, they soon resorted to the prevalent source from
which the burgeoning need for agricultural labor was being filled in that
region. This represented a fundamental geographical and cultural migration at last, a movement from a North Atlantic to a Mediterranean frame
of reference, as transferred to the shores of the New World, and it was
not achieved without significant problems of adjustment.

The transition into a slaveholding mentality was a rather sudden one
for the English, and the conditions of it must remain somewhat mystifying
for all time. We have seen the very different outlook of a Sir Francis
Drake, and we can in fact note the presence of an attitude similar to his
among Englishmen engaged in significant imperial activity as late as
1620. In that year, a "Company for the Countries of Guinea and Benin"
sent a ship, the *Syon* (i.e., "Zion") to the Gambia River in an attempt to
get at the sources of the West African trade hitherto dominated by Portugal and Spain, but it was interested in gold and other inanimate commodities, not slaves. According to Richard Jobson, commander and narrator of the expedition, some traders offered him Negroes and he refused,
saying, "We were a people who did not deal in any such commodities,

neither did we buy or sell one another, or any that had our own shapes." Jobson writes with great disapproval of the half-Portuguese mulattoes encountered by him in the region, whom he condemns for a life of indolence and dishonesty, and for their willingness to trade in Black slaves; obviously, this is not a phenomenon he could conceive of as occurring in a world dominated by Englishmen.

In general, Jobson's book, *The Golden Trade*, written with the encouragement of our old friend Samuel Purchas and published in 1623, stands as a significant representation of attitudes toward the Black African at the very moment when, at the other side of the Atlantic, English America was at last beginning to take shape. Jobson's extensive descriptions of the character and customs of the peoples he meets along the Gambia are no different in tone from the most favorable descriptions of Indians that we find being written by Englishmen at this time. He writes respectfully of their religion, which is a somewhat modified and primitive form of Islam, and which he most likely would not have appreciated so much in its more sophisticated manifestations. With few exceptions, he admires their looks, and in the case of the Fulbies, "a tawny people," he finds the cleanliness of their women to be far superior to that of the women of Ireland. He says of the Gambians in general that "there is, without doubt, no people on the earth more naturally affected to the sound of music than these people; which the principal persons do hold as an ornament of their state, so as when we come to see them, their music will seldom be wanting, wherein they have a perfect resemblance to the Irish rimer, sitting in the same manner as they do upon the ground, somewhat remote from the company."

The only mildly discordant element in Jobson's hymn of friendliness toward the Negro comes in a digression on the latter's sexual prowess; suddenly we hear echoes of George Best and Iago. Trying to justify the fact that the married men of Gambia have concubines, Jobson writes:

> For undoubtedly these people originally sprung from the race of Canaan, the son of Ham, who discovered his father Noah's secrets, for which Noah awakening cursed Canaan as our holy Scripture testifieth; the curse (as by Schoolmen hath been disputed), extended to his ensuing race, in laying hold upon the same place where the original cause began, whereof these people are witness, who are furnished with such members as are after a sort burdensome unto them, whereby their women being once conceived with child, so soon as it is perfectly discerned, accompanies the man no longer, because he shall not destroy what is conceived to the loss of that, and danger of the bearer, neither until she hath brought up the child, to a full and fitting time to be weaned.

Under such circumstances, the services of concubines are no less than acts of mercy. But here we see the now hoary myth of the curse of Canaan taking a startlingly specific turn in the direction of one of the most significant modern manifestations of anti-Negro racism, a direction we have already seen being tried out in various specimens of Elizabethan writing. George Best made it clear enough that, as far back as 1578, some Englishmen considered Ham's offense to have come out of his overweening sexual appetite, and by the time of *Titus Andronicus* and *Othello* the Negro has emerged as a sexual prodigy who can be both fascinating and terrifying. Jobson now carries this idea a step further by frankly taking note of the Black man's "burdensome" organ, the very manifestation of Noah's curse (or blessing, as inclination may have it), which had been directed at "the same place where the original cause began." In the context, this seems to be an explicit admission that Ham, in viewing his father's nakedness, had shown a perhaps unseemly interest in the part that sired him; but it could also be a reference to the story of his transgression aboard the Ark, told by Best, but not by Jobson, possibly because he assumes his audience already knows it.

In any case, Jobson's version of the curse and its consequences is a far less unflattering one than Best's, or Zurara's, for that matter. Neither complexion nor condition of servitude is at issue for Jobson, and there is no talk of a "natural infection" to be heard from him. Nature's sole manifestation of the curse in his eyes is a "burden" that is only dubiously so, and one suspects that the robust captain felt more admiration for it than pity. The myth of Black superiority in this respect became widespread in that era and persists in some quarters to this day, but no final decision has been made as to any possible basis for it in fact. It has been suggested that the constant sight of the Black man in his nakedness — something that European males did not so often vouchsafe one another — was what inspired this notion, but it is noteworthy that few Europeans had such an idea about the Indian, who was seen just as often in his natural state as the Negro was, but who was widely considered to be only of modest or even feeble sexual prowess. If we can isolate a purely subjective factor in the evolution of this particular mythology, it surely has to do with innate northern- and southern-oriented prejudices: northerners, whatever their complexion, are considered chaste, and southerners are thought of as lewd. Jobson provides hints not only of this set of attitudes, but also of the possibility that an Englishman could harbor them and still find the south perfectly congenial.

Of course, Jobson is the representative of a dying era, a final exponent of the enclave mentality. At the very moment he wrote his book, Jamestown and Plymouth were still only enclaves, and Newfoundland and Bermuda remote Atlantic outposts; but the English overseas world was about to undergo a dramatic change. Jobson undoubtedly dreamed of English factories along the African coast, like those of the Portuguese only more virtuous, and like the North American colonies being touted and cautioned by his friend Purchas, but this was a far more tentative vision of English empire than the reality was now rapidly to become. In the ensuing decades, English ambition could be satisfied only in ways that had to enclose large, relatively defenseless populations in its embrace: on the American continent, Englishmen would begin wanting more land than nature had cleared of its native populations, and in the West Indies, they would begin requiring more cheap labor than either the natives or their own homeland could provide. In a sense, Jobson represents a moment of equipoise when Africa and America could mean virtually the same thing to Englishmen with overseas ambitions: they were faraway places at which to sojourn rather than settle down for good, full of natural resources to be brought home, and of natives with whom to trade, and who were otherwise to be left alone. But circumstances were rapidly rendering this moment obsolete.

Spain and Portugal had been united under the Spanish crown since 1580, but by the early years of the seventeenth century the import of this combination was merely that their power had been declining together. In particular the Dutch, pitted against the power that had once ruled them, were leading the assault against the outposts of the Iberian world empire. They had already made significant inroads into the transatlantic slave trade, and had been established as planters in the Caribbean region, at Surinam, since 1616. The swath that they cut from Africa to the Caribbean was an opening for other Protestant powers, especially England, which was on terms of warm friendship with the Netherlands during most of the early years of the century.

Raleigh's old vision of an English move into the soft underbelly of the Spanish New World empire was not dead, even though Raleigh himself now was; it was appropriate that a new move into a region further weakened by the Dutch was tried by a former member of his 1618 Guiana expedition, Roger North, who organized an Amazon Company in 1620. North hoped to colonize in Guiana, as the Dutch had done, and plant tobacco, which was by now proving successful in Virginia, but though he actually got to set sail and reconnoiter for a prospective site, his charter was quickly revoked by a king who was still susceptible to Spanish pressures. The expedition was not wasted, however, for one member of it, an enterprising young man of affairs named Thomas Warner, was so struck by the Caribbean as a place for English colonization that he sailed there with some companions only two years later to find a site. Certain islands of the Lesser Antilles had remained unoccupied by the Spaniards, and some of them were even devoid of any native population, but they usually offered striking natural conditions for prospective planters of cash crops. Warner chose the island of St. Christopher — also known today by the more Dutch form of its name, St. Kitts — and stayed there for a season, to plant and raise an experimental tobacco crop. He was able to return to England the following year with reports of success, and was back at the island in January of 1624 with a group of planters for a permanent colony. This proved to be the first permanent settlement of non-Spaniards in the islands of the West Indies.

Later that same year, the Dutch captured Bahia, and though this occupation was to last only a year, it worked as a signal for further Protestant movement into the region. This halcyon era of English friendship with the Netherlands was marked by the existence of a number of large Anglo-Dutch business firms, and one of these was the Courteen Brothers of London and Middelburg, which had intimate connections with the illicit Atlantic traders of its two parent nations, as well as with individual Spaniards in both the Old World and the New who were more profiteer than patriot. It was sometime in 1624 that the commander of one of the ships trading for the Courteen Brothers in Brazil, Captain John Powell, saw the possibilities of the uninhabited island of Barbados, for the planting of crops and for the exploitation of its already abundant natural resource of dye-wood. Powell took formal possession of the island in January, 1625, returned to England to proclaim his idea, and the Courteens soon were sponsoring an expedition to Barbados of eighty colonists, under the supervision of Powell's brother, Henry. This first group landed in February, 1627, and was followed by another group of ninety settlers in May; their efforts to adjust to toil in a hot climate were supplemented by the arrival of a group of Arawak volunteers from Guiana, encouraged by Dutch settlers there to go and help found a new way of life in the Americas. For the moment, Barbados hoped that it would be different from the Spanish and the Portuguese colonies, and that, like New England's, its efforts could be founded primarily on a system of free labor. This hope melted away in the tropical sun.

New England, which traded with the British West Indies from the outset, found its most intimate link there with an island far from the others, in the teeth of Spanish continental power. By the time of the great Puritan migration that founded Massachusetts Bay in 1630, the West Indies was as inviting a place for some religious refugees as New England was, and in that same year a group of Puritan planters founded a colony at Providence, off the coast of Nicaragua. The subsequent eleven years of its history seem to provide an image contradictory to the conventional one concerning Puritanism. Providence developed a standard West Indies planter class, which freely owned Negro slaves, and which, most surprisingly, formed close links with the growing buccaneer colony at Tortuga, a tiny island just north of Hispaniola — that most astonishing outcome of the Protestant, anti-Spanish privateering tradition of Sir Francis Drake, now manifested as an anarchical international colony of freebooting roughnecks. Puritanism cut across lines of class as well as of personality, and it is likely that Providence Island attracted, in the long run, more of those among its adherents who were of an aristocratic stamp, socially or temperamentally, than New England did. Old-fashioned aristocracy walked out of Massachusetts Bay when young Henry Vane, after a stint as governor and as a futile supporter of Mrs. Anne Hutchinson, sailed home to England for good in the wake of the Pequot Massacre. Men who flinched at the killing of Indians did not necessarily scruple to hold Negro slaves, and these were the sort, Puritan and Anglican alike, who found Barbados, St. Christopher, or Providence Island more attractive places to reside than Massachusetts or Connecticut. But the Puritan experiment in the Caribbean did not have time to prove what it was to become, for Spanish soldiers put an end to it in 1641, sending its roughly four hundred English men, women, and children back to their home country, and rounding up its six hundred Negroes for their own slave markets.

By the time the Providence Island colony was dispersed, the English enterprise in the West Indies had spread to several more islands of the Lesser Antilles and, after a brief fling at the system of large-scale indentured servitude to which the North American planters continued primarily to adhere, had turned to the untrammeled exploitation of Black slave labor that had long prevailed in the Spanish and Portuguese colonies of the region. This was the line of least resistance, and it seems to have been all but inevitable. The English did not invent Black slavery or initiate its arrival into the Western world, but having betaken themselves to a region in which it had long ago become one of the foundations upon which wealth was built, they hesitated only a moment before staking out their corner of it and ultimately becoming one of its foremost builders. The isolated voice of Richard Jobson could barely be heard before the clamor of colonizing in hot climates had begun.

In spite of the protestations of a Jobson against the buying and selling of human beings, the enslavement of the Negro was as morally neutral an issue for most Englishmen in this epoch as it was for most Spaniards. This was just another of the several ways in which the English, thinking of themselves as morally superior to the Spaniards, proved to be no better in their doings in the harsh world "beyond the line." Indeed, they had even shown themselves capable of enslaving Indians, and would continue to do so from time to time well into the eighteenth century; and if they proved rather resistant to doing this on the whole, they never, on the other hand, produced an equivalent to Las Casas. Slavery remained repugnant to a good many Englishmen on both sides of the Atlantic, but this was more for cultural than for moral reasons: for they regarded the presence of Blacks and slaves as something appropriate only to a world of Spaniards and Saracens, not to their own clean northern climes. For them, the offense committed by the West Indian planters was that they had become southerners, their Englishness dissolving in the sweat of indolence and a steam of racial ambiguity, like the Portuguese traders along the African coast with their mulatto children, whom Jobson had found so despicable.

Indeed, the most dramatic of the cultural revolutions that the New World represented for Englishmen in this period can be seen in the relationship between the white planter of the West Indies and his female slaves, as well as his mulatto children. The British West Indies attracted from the outset, far more than the North American colonies did, a planter class that tended to look upon the New World more as a place within which to sojourn and make one's fortune than as an adoptive homeland. These were the dilettantes of colonization who had been, by and large, rejected by New England. A characteristic type of English colonist arrived in the West Indies young and without family, intending to remain that way until he returned to England a rich man. Under these conditions, the slave mistress came to mean a great deal to the white planter, far more than to his southern American equivalent, for in the West Indies this relationship was often likely to become a sentimental one. It is significant that, whereas the southern colonies quickly decided that the mulatto children of Black women were the same as other Blacks, the West Indies eschewed such a decision and in places gradually moved toward an improved status for mulattoes, both slave and free. A mood that prevailed in the West Indies from the beginning is conveyed as late as 1793 by the Jamaican white planter Bryan Edwards, when in writing his plea for greater equality for mulattoes he says:

> The accusation most generally brought against the free people of Color, is the incontinency of their women; of whom, such as are young, and have tolerable persons, are universally maintained by white men of all ranks and conditions, as kept mistresses. The fact is too notorious to be concealed or controverted; and I trust I have too great an esteem for my fair readers, and too high a respect for myself, to stand forth the advocate of licentiousness and debauchery. Undoubtedly, the conduct of many of the whites in this respect, is a violation of decency and decorum; and an insult and injury to society. Let it not offend any modest ear, however, if I add my opinion, that

the unhappy females here spoken of, are much less deserving reproach and reprehension than their keepers.

Edwards doth protest too much in his condemnation of "licentiousness and debauchery"; and indeed, he proves far more candid about his true feelings a few pages later in his *History of the West Indies* when he reproduces an "ode" — written, he tells us, by a "deceased friend," whom he does not name — "in which the character of the sable and saffron beauties of the West Indies, and the folly of their paramours, are portrayed with the delicacy and dexterity of wit, and the fancy and elegance of genuine poetry." Called "The Sable Venus," the poem is a hymn to that lady, who is first sought out in her native Angola:

> *O sable queen! thy mild domain*
> *I seek, and court thy gentle reign,*
> *   So soothing, soft and sweet;*
> *Where meeting love, sincere delight,*
> *Fond pleasure, ready joys invite,*
> *   And unbought raptures meet.*

She is then followed across the Atlantic in a chariot far more elaborate than the seashell in which her pale namesake rode, but more revealing of its lovely cargo than Cleopatra's barge:

> *Her skin excelled the raven plume,*
> *Her breath the fragrant orange bloom,*
> *   Her eye the tropic beam:*
> *Soft was her lip as silken down,*
> *And mild her look as ev'ning sun*
> *   That gilds the Cobre stream.*
>
> *The loveliest limbs her form compose,*
> *Such as her sister Venus chose,*
> *   In Florence, where she's seen;*
> *Both just alike, except the white,*
> *No difference, no — none at night,*
> *   The beauteous dames between.*

Here is the racial vision of the West Indian white gentlemen at its most idyllic and revealing: in it, the carnal women of the Renaissance travelers have been tamed and have come to the Fortunate Islands at last. The earthly paradise may be a scene of chastity for those who want it so, but there are other ways of construing it. This is the feminine side of the sexual prowess that Jobson and others had imputed to Black men. The vision makes the West Indian planter seem somehow more humanly appealing than those northern colonists who remained more resistant to slavery than he did, but who, like Samuel Sewall of Massachusetts writing against slavery in 1700, regarded the Negro as "a kind of extravasate blood" in the body politic. A New England that spilled Indian blood sooner than take it into the social organism was even more vehemently opposed to a significant Black presence, slave or otherwise. Men like Bryan Edwards, the spiritual nephews of George Percy and even of that buffoon Thomas Morton, though they remained indifferent to whether the classes that served and toiled for them were technically slave or free, were far readier to take on the great New World adventure of racial multiplicity. But they were outside the mainstream of American history.

But granting this element of adaptation on the part of some Englishmen to a southern New World social climate that had largely been tempered by Spaniards and Portuguese, the question still remains: how did slavery become accommodated into a legal tradition in which it had not existed? This point has mystified some modern observers; but there does not seem to have been anything in English law specifically opposed to slavery as such — certainly Thomas More, for example, had nothing against it in principle — whereas the tradition was always amenable to the demands of custom. And custom was strong on this point in the New World by the beginning of the seventeenth century. Some significant comments were made to this effect in a letter written by Luis Brandão, rector of a Jesuit college in Angola, to Alonso de Sandoval, a Spanish Jesuit who had begun to worry about the legality of the methods whereby slaves were acquired from Africa. "We and the fathers of Brazil," Brandão declared,

> buy these slaves for our service without any scruple. Furthermore, I declare that if anyone could be excused from having scruples it is the inhabitants of those regions, for since the traders who bring those Negroes bring them in good faith, those inhabitants can very well buy from such traders without any scruple, and the latter, on their part, can sell them, for it is a generally accepted opinion that the owner who owns anything in good faith can sell it and that it can be bought.

The buying and selling of Negroes as a commodity in good faith had been practiced by Englishmen since John Hawkins's slave-trading days in the 1560s, so why should the permanent ownership claimed by the planter be any less valid than the transient ownership enjoyed by the dealer? At the very moment when custom was deciding this question in the English planter's favor, the eminent Dutch jurist Hugo Grotius — certainly no authority to be repudiated by Protestant nations — was accepting slavery as legal within international law; and it must be said that the Dutch, whose sensibilities had perhaps been conditioned in favor of slavery by several generations of Spanish rule, were the most active instruments in spreading New World slavery beyond the bounds of Iberian hegemony. Indeed, the main reason why the English, entering tentatively into the slave trade at first, became its most zealous practitioners by the end of the century was their eagerness to seize Atlantic commercial predominance from the Dutch in this as in every other respect. The law on which slavery came to be built in English America was that of the marketplace.

Not that there were not some characteristically English scruples. Slave-raiding, which had all but disappeared since its heyday even among the Spanish and Portuguese, was not allowed by English colonists, who tried to prevent by law the purchase of slaves known to be obtained that way. The process had to be "laundered," to use a highly contemporary term. Theoretically, there were legally acceptable methods by which the wretched human commodities of the slave markets had been obtained in the first place — capture in warfare, for example, or voluntary personal commitment to slave status, or birth in slave status, any of these would do — and this applied to the preferably remote frontiers from which the few Indian slaves were obtained as well as to the African and West Indian sources of Negroes; but above all, the English slaveowner did not want to have to see or ponder how the dirty work had been done. In this respect, he was somewhat like the pious resident of Massachusetts Bay rejoicing in God's judgment against the Pequots at a comfortable distance from the scene of the slaughter. Anglo-Saxons are much less capable than Spaniards of contemplating the bloodier parts of the foundations upon which their social edifices are built. But there were also, as the slave system suddenly came rushing in through the door, the scruples of honest realists, who wondered whether, in purchasing members of the darker-skinned races, they were not just extending to them the established English principle of indentured servitude. This question, the product of a certain hesitancy to enslave men in spite of everything, rankled for some time in the southern colonies; but in Barbados, at any rate, it was quickly resolved. There the governor and the council passed a resolution in 1636 specifically stating that "Negroes and Indians, that came here to be sold, should serve for life, unless a contract was made before to the contrary." There was to be no benefit of the doubt for those who had been brought in and sold as slaves; in effect, color was becoming fixed as a *conditio sine qua non* of lifetime servitude.

The process of English immersion into the West Indian cauldron was rapidly completed after the passing of the midcentury, when the Protectorate was established under Oliver Cromwell after the execution of

Charles I, and Dutch power suddenly went into a rapid decline. None of the old fond feelings for the Dutch had rubbed off among the Puritan leadership of England, who soon turned against them in the scuffle over Atlantic hegemony, and reestablished the ancient national alliance with the Portuguese, of all people, again independent of Spanish rule since 1640. A rapid succession of outposts, both in Brazil and in Africa, that the Dutch had taken from the Portuguese earlier in the century were now recaptured by their original rulers. The English joined the onslaught by passing the celebrated Navigation Act of 1651, which forbade the importation into their country of goods from America, Africa, and Asia in any but English ships. This was ultimately to offend the colonists, but for the moment the offense was aimed primarily against the Dutch, who felt it severely, and the result was the Anglo-Dutch war of 1652 to 1654.

The outcome of the war in England's favor led to a burgeoning of imperial ambitions there, and Cromwell had soon conceived a great "Western Design," which involved trying to snatch away a good portion of the Spanish New World empire. To implement this, an expedition was sent out at the end of 1654 under Admiral William Penn — whose son and namesake was to be the founder of Pennsylvania — and General Robert Venables. Their attempt to take Hispaniola proved to be a fiasco, but when they went on to Jamaica, they found a Spanish population that had dwindled to some fifteen hundred, and a population of Indians and Blacks who were only too willing to collaborate in the overthrow of the slavemasters. Jamaica was invaded by the English force in May of 1655 and soon conquered. Edward Winslow, who had returned to England to stay in 1646, and who was ever a link between different aspects of the English New World enterprise, took part in this expedition and died in it.

This newest and largest component of the English West Indian empire soon went the way of the rest. Indeed, it so increased the demand for slaves that Englishmen were impelled to organize themselves for the trade as they never had before. The Spanish crown, imagining itself still to be ruler of the Indies, tried to revive the old *asiento de negros* in 1662, duly granting this monopolistic privilege to trade in slaves across the Atlantic to a Genoese firm. The English were ready for this challenge with a Company of Royal Adventurers Trading to Africa founded in 1660, which was then reorganized and expanded into the Royal African Company in 1672. Slaves were not the only commodity dealt in by the company, which nevertheless achieved predominance in this trade as in others. There continued to be an international struggle over the official prize of the *asiento*, but when the English at last won it by treaty in 1713, it was only a fiction; for by then they had been the chief slave suppliers to the New World for four decades.

29

Slavery Comes to
North America

The notorious sentence, relayed to us by Captain John Smith from the journals of John Rolfe, "About the last of August [1619] came in a Dutch man-of-war that sold us twenty Negars," has received more attention than it can answer to, and one of the questions most often raised about it has been: what precisely was the status of those twenty Blacks? Were they sold in Virginia as slaves pure and simple, or — what was much more common there at the time — as indentured servants? Historians who have argued for their status as indentured servants have mainly been motivated by the desire to absolve the South of having plunged into a slave system, single-handedly and without hesitation, before any other English continental colonies even existed to collaborate in the guilty work. They can find strong circumstantial support for their argument. The twenty Blacks arrived more than two decades before we have any distinct signs that slavery was obtaining a foothold in Virginia. On the other hand, Jamestown, almost as soon as it became entrenched and developed tobacco as a cash crop, had begun a large-scale importation of indentured labor — of men and women bound by contract (the "indented" shape of the perforations at which it was torn in two halves is what gave it its popular name) to serve for a limited period of years, usually around five — that was to remain, throughout the colonial period, almost as significant a means of obtaining workers in the South as the slave market was. Furthermore, in 1619 almost all of the buying and selling of labor in the colony was still being done by the Virginia Company rather than by private individuals: if this was the case with the twenty Blacks, then, isn't it more likely that they were the company's indentured servants rather than its slaves?

But these questions, though important, do not really deal with the problem of the genesis of slavery in North America. For there is one thing about which we can be fairly certain: those twenty Blacks had been a cargo of slaves while they were aboard the Dutch ship, and Virginia had nothing to do with this. No matter what they became when they stepped off the gangplank, the Negroes had arrived — from the West Indies, according to all indications — as offerings of the international slave market. But the fact that the Virginia colony was now dealing with this market does not have to be viewed as a sin of the future South manifesting itself early. It was, rather, an established sin of New World commerce, accepted by Englishmen as far back as Sir John Hawkins — when there was no Virginia yet — and inevitably reaching the shores of another colony where labor was in demand. Virginia was the first Anglo-American colony to receive Black slaves, not because it was the future South, but because it was the first Anglo-American colony.

After all, Massachusetts Bay, the next English continental colony of major size, did not hesitate to enslave Pequots and trade some of them for Black slaves when the moment came to do so, as we know. Furthermore, it is fairly clear that there was Black slavery in the colony well before then, perhaps from the very beginning. William Wood, writing his *New England's Prospect* in 1634, tells in it an anecdote about a "Black-moor" in the colony who was brought back to "his master" after a mishap in the woods: this is not likely to have been an indentured servant. Samuel Maverick of Chelsea was known by 1638 to have had Negro slaves for some years, and it is entirely possible that he, having arrived in the area as one of Sir Ferdinando Gorges's men in 1624, owned some of them even before the mass colonization began in 1630. These lone documented examples need not have been the only cases in fact, for it is well known that some of New England's Puritan leaders had no objections to slavery in principle. In 1645, Emanuel Downing of Salem wrote to his brother-in-law, John Winthrop, about new troubles that were then brewing with the Narragansetts:

> If upon a just war the Lord should deliver them into our hands, we might easily have men, women and children enough to exchange for Moors, which will be more gainful pillage for us than we conceive, for I do not see how we can thrive

until we get into a stock of slaves sufficient to do all our business, for our children's children will hardly see this great continent filled with people, so that our servants will still desire
freedom to plant for themselves, and not stay but for very
great wages. And I suppose you know very well how we shall
maintain 20 Moors cheaper than one English servant.

One could find no more vivid presentation of the reasons why white
planters preferred slaves over indentured servants; as for the preference
for "Moors" over Narragansetts, colonists everywhere seemed convinced
by now that Negroes were harder workers than Indians, and besides, it
was inviting trouble to keep Indians captive too close to their native
habitats.

If in the long run, then, New England proved far more resistant than
the South to a mass influx of Negro slaves into the colonies, this was
hardly owing to any superior moral scruples about slavery. James
Truslow Adams has made the celebrated point that the difference was
simply a matter of landscape, and of the respective economies that the
soil would yield in New England and in the South. This certainly is true
to a large extent, but another factor besides physical geography may be
found in the differing cultural geography of north and south. As we have
seen, the south in general — of which the American South was marginally
and ambivalently a part — was less resistant to a racially varied social
environment than the north was. If one wants to judge the seventeenth-
century American South on its racial record, its relationship with the
Indian should be considered alongside that with the Negro. The Negro
was badly treated everywhere — and was being enslaved everywhere —
but relations with the Indian in English America were nowhere so good,
relatively speaking, as in Virginia, Maryland, and even the Carolinas after
they were founded in the 1660s. As if to prove her hesitancy to become an
aggressor against the Indians, Virginia fell victim to a second large-scale
Indian attack in 1644 before she at last resorted to some of the more conventional frontier behavior of Europeans. True offspring of George Percy
and John Rolfe, Virginians like William Byrd of Westover could go right
on into the eighteenth century advocating intermarriage between whites
and Indians.

New England, on the other hand, was perfectly capable in 1640 of
entertaining thoughts of having "the Indians rooted out, as being of the
cursed race of Ham," according to John Winthrop: this is a rare instance
of that notion of racial taint being applied to the Indian. But more often
such a notion applied to Blacks for New Englanders, too, among whom a
certain kind of middle-class Protestantism, descended from men like
George Best, was as at home in a northern landscape and climate as it

was alien to the kind of "extravasate blood" that Samuel Sewall was to refer to in 1700. It is significant that John Saffin, the Massachusetts slave-owner against whom Sewall directed the antislavery polemic in which he used this term, really agreed with his opponent on what was perhaps the central issue. Saffin said he could accept the abolition of slavery in the colony, provided that the owners be reimbursed, and that the Negroes "be all sent out of the country, or else the remedy would be worse than the disease; and it is to be feared that those Negroes that are free, if there be not some strict course taken with them by authority, they will be a plague to this country."

No Southern plantation owner could have provided a clearer statement to show how any innate distaste for slavery among Anglo-Saxons was overcome by an even greater distaste for racial mingling. Indeed, one of the earliest North American slave laws on record was passed in Massachusetts in 1641, and it makes what is ultimately the same point, saying that "there shall never be any bond-slavery, villenage or captivity amongst us; unless it be lawful captives taken in just wars, and such strangers as willingly sell themselves, or are sold to us." One could not keep one's own in perpetual servitude, neither according to the Old Testament nor to English custom; but on the other hand, the Bible, Aristotle, and current international law all allowed the enslavement of "strangers," which by now meant racial outsiders — that is to say, for Massachusetts in 1641, Negroes and Indians. In other words, from the standpoint of the Massachusetts General Court in 1641, it was permissible to enslave racial outsiders when they fell as captive labor into your hands, and from the standpoint of John Saffin in 1701 it was more than desirable to keep them enslaved. But clearly, as far as decent New Englanders of that era like Samuel Sewall were concerned, the best thing to do was not let them into your midst in the first place.

And this, above all, is what New England was able to do relative to the South; in no way superior to the latter on either the issue of slavery or that of race, New England was able to resist a large-scale influx of Black slaves, partly out of an unreadiness both moral and topographical in basis to enter into the kind of cash-crop economy that was conducive to such an influx, and partly out of a greater unwillingness to admit "strangers" for any reason whatsoever. In the South, on the other hand, once Virginia had made its choice for a tobacco economy, and Maryland had followed suit after its founding in 1634 — a choice deplored by such an outstanding Virginian as the historian Robert Beverley as late as 1705 — they had to go the way of the mass importation of cheap labor, a way that seems, in the whole variety of settings in which it presents itself in that era, to have led all but inexorably into a slave system. For a while, this could still mean enslaving Indians as well as Blacks, but in the long run, even in situations in which there were none of the moral qualms about enslaving native Americans that some settlers felt, Indians simply were not available in the vast quantities that the market desired and that the international trade in Blacks was able to fulfill. By Robert Beverley's time, it was possible for him to predicate without qualifications that "Slaves are the Negroes" (even though there were, in fact, still a few Indian slaves in the colony), distinguishing them from servants, who did not serve in perpetuity and presumably all were white. But for Beverley as for his New England contemporaries Saffin and Sewall, there is an implied distaste for both sides of the equation, Negro and slave, a subtle condemnation of the entire alien complex that the white North American colonist has accepted into his body politic from Iberian hands that he considered unclean; blackness and slavery both are symptoms of the infection.

In the end, the South created a problem all its own by being an ambivalent culture, hanging indecisively between the sharply contrasting ones of the far north and the far south of the English New World, too much like Jamaica in some respects and too much like New England in others. Virginia, the country of John Rolfe, undoubtedly had its own votaries of the Sable Venus even as far back as the seventeenth century, but their influence, sufficient to open wide the doors of the colony to a Black presence, was not to be the dominant one in the public morality. Throughout the seventeenth century in the South, it seems always to be an element more or less West Indian in character — indeed, specifically connected with the West Indies in the case of the Carolinas — that draws the main outlines of the society, but an element closer to the middle-class, Protestant spirit of New England — indeed, Puritans from New England in the case of part of Maryland — that proceeds to fill in the spaces with everyday custom, morality, and law. The end of the process was a biracial society in which the great majority of whites, inclined to dislike Blacks every bit as much as their New England counterparts were, loathed them all the more for fear of being engulfed by them. The Slave Codes were a frantic effort to turn all that "extravasate blood'" into a scab.

Yet there continued for a time to be men, largely anonymous but a perceptible presence all the same, who resisted the inexorable pull of a slave system. We have almost nothing but scattered and often mystifying pieces of legislation, court rulings, and other legal documents by which to trace the emergence of that system in the South during the seventeenth century, but, as many historians have rightly noticed, they are pervaded with a long-lasting indecisiveness as to the category of servitude in which Blacks were to be placed. Clearly, a lot of white masters, who had paid good money for whites just as they had for Negroes, were releasing the latter after specified periods just as they did the former. One can see in them the same reluctance to make slavery an institution among English-men — whether of "strangers" or anyone else — as was manifested in 1652 by the Rhode Island legislature, still under the living influence of one of the most humane men of his time, Roger Williams, when it passed a law forbidding any "black mankind or white" to be held in servitude more than ten years or beyond the age of twenty-four if they had been bought at under fourteen years of age. (Slavery held on in Rhode Island all the same, but insignificantly.) There even are instances to be found in early Virginia of freed Negroes who had themselves become slaveholders, a privilege reluctantly accorded them although they were forbidden to have white indentured servants. Undoubtedly, slave status was the most typical one for Blacks even in the early years in Virginia and Maryland, as in any other colony, but the final decision summed up in Beverley's terse equation was to be made only slowly, and evidently over the resistance of some whites.

A classic instance that appears to illustrate this situation is the case of John Punch, which occurred in Virginia in 1640. In that year, three "servants" — two of them white, one Black — of a planter named Hugh Gwyn ran away and were caught. All three were given a whipping, but whereas the sentence handed out to the two whites, "Victor, a Dutchman, the other a Scotchman called James Gregory," was an additional period of servitude beyond the term of their original contracts, the court ordered that "the third being a Negro named John Punch shall serve his said master or his assigns for the time of his natural life here or elsewhere." It would seem that John Punch had been in for only a limited term of service prior to the offense, and that it was only when this opportunity offered itself that the white society reduced him to the condition of permanent servitude in which the majority of Blacks were undoubtedly to be found by then in Virginia. The case offers us an example of at least one of the ways in which the last obstacles to enslaving virtually the entire Negro serving population were overcome within a system of English law. But the question arises: how had John Punch, either him-self a purchase from the international slave market or the son of one, become an indentured servant rather than a slave in the first place? Obviously, a court ruling was required for Hugh Gwyn to make him un-equivocally into the chattel slave that either he or a forebear surely once had been. This means either that Gwyn had been prepared to manumit him until the court decided to prevent the entry of another frisky free Negro into the general society, or — what is more likely — that Gwyn had bought him from another planter, who insisted that the contract of pur-chase stipulate only a limited term of servitude. In either case, we can see two opposing camps, one of whites who are ready or even eager to treat Negroes like Englishmen (or "Dutchmen," or "Scotchmen") on the fundamental issue of personal liberty, the other of whites doing everything in their power to oppose this aim.

The latter camp won because, in the last analysis, race was the issue, not slavery. From the standpoint of the great majority of whites, those masters who manifested their dislike for this system of servitude by allowing some of the Negro element to flow free into the general society were only making matters worse. Clearly, there were racially adventurous settlers in Virginia and Maryland — more than were likely to have been found in New England — but they were overwhelmed by others who were not prepared to tolerate anything like the racial commingling and sexual promiscuity (the two often went together, as John Rolfe himself had suggested) that Spaniards and Barbadian planters went in for. For, though the white settlers assuredly found the free Blacks in their midst irritating for many reasons, the main issue, as always when racism begins reaching its highest refinement, was sexual union and its consequences. The angriest of the scattered early documents involving Blacks are always focused on this point. In Virginia in 1630, for example, a man named Hugh Davis was sentenced "to be soundly whipped, before an assembly of Negroes and others for abusing himself to the dishonor of God and shame of Christians, by defiling his body in lying with a Negro." It has been suggested that the Black partner here could have been a male, though this is not likely, since outraged Christians in that day were willing to be quite explicit in describing any offense; in any case, the court's emphasis seems to suggest that what was perverse about the act was its interracial aspect. This would also be the import of subsequent instances known to us, in which fornication was punished with what seems to have been a special vehemence if it occurred between white and Negro; the matter was worse if the union produced a child.

Resentment on this issue reached fruition in 1662, when Virginia passed a law that said in part:

> Whereas, some doubts have arisen whether children got by any Englishmen upon a Negro woman, should be slave or free, Be it therefore enacted, that all children born in this country shall be held bond or free only according to the condition of the mother, And that if any Christian shall commit fornication with a Negro man or woman, he or she so offending shall pay double the fines imposed by the former act.

We do not have records, by the way, of the doubtless relatively infrequent cases of fornication between white women and Black men, but there do seem to have been marriages in this category: in 1664, Maryland

banned marriages between white women and Black slaves, on grounds
that these produced too many legal embarrassments, and Virginia finally
prohibited all interracial unions in 1691. The way was left open for almost
nothing but the easy illicitness of the male master–female slave relationship so far as union of the races was concerned, and the threatening issue
of such alliances was cut off from the general society by the kind of law
that Virginia passed in 1662. Laws limiting miscegenation and rein-
forcing slavery were collaborating to prevent Negroes and mulattoes —
who, unlike Indians, did not have an aloof social order of their own —
from becoming part of the settlers' society.

Race had been the problem all along, and it has remained so down to
our own time. Some historians have taken the view that the obvious
superiority of the Latin American countries to the United States in race
relations today is due to a relatively humane slave system in their past,
the offspring of centuries of legal slavery in Spain and Portugal, which
English Americans did not have. Slaves had rights in medieval Iberia,
whereas Englishmen, once they got into the unfamiliar territory of slaveholding, seem to have been unable to conceive of the human beings they
owned in any other legal terms than those applying to property. It certainly is noteworthy that the Virginia law of 1662 already cited above
also provides that

> if any slave resist his master (or other by his master's orders
> correcting him) and by the extremity of the correction should
> chance to die, that his death shall not be accompted felony,
> but the master (or that other person appointed by the master
> to punish him) be acquit from molestation, since it cannot be
> presumed that prepensed malice (which alone makes murder
> felony) should induce any man to destroy his own estate.

One might as well be talking about horses. But what in the last analysis
makes it possible for one group of human beings to reduce another
group to such a condition is not so much a juridical category as a sense
that the latter is made up of absolute "strangers."

Englishmen may have so loathed the system of slavery they inherited
from the Spanards and the Portuguese that, when they finally embraced
it, they could only kick it farther into the dust; but they feared the Negro
that they inherited with it, and this ultimately was the more violent
emotion. Iberia had reacted badly enough to the terrifying southern
legacy that was really part of its own identity, represented by the Moorish past; for Englishmen, at a much farther northerly remove, the south
was Catholic and Moorish alike, and being far more alien, was all the

more repulsive when some of its elements became part of their world. It is no accident that the final, and most severe, wave of the antiwitchcraft craze that arose in the late seventeenth century was particularly strong in the northern countries — Spain and Portugal, like Italy, hardly knew it at all — and strongest of all among Englishmen, at home and in America. Egypt, in its fullest mythological meaning for Englishmen in that day, had sent up its darkest and most loathsome offshoots. Edmund Spenser saw it all in this passage from *The Faerie Queene:*

> As when old father Nilus gins to swell
> With timely pride above the Aegyptian vale
> His fattie waves doe fertile slime outwell,
> And overflow each plaine and lowly dale:
> But, when his later spring gins to avale,
> Huge heaps of mudd he leaves, wherein there breed
> Ten thousand kindes of creatures, partly male
> And partly femall, of his fruitful seed;
> Such ugly monstrous shapes elsewher may no man reed.

> The same so sore annoyed has the knight,
> That, welnigh choked with the deadly stinke,
> His forces faile, ne can no lenger fight:
> Whose corage when the feend perceivd to shrinke,
> She poured forth out of her hellish sinke
> Her fruitfull cursed spawne of serpents small,
> Deformed monsters, fowle, and blacke as inke,
> Which swarming all about his legs did crall,
> And him encombred sore, but could not hurt at all.

Certainly, above all, the English knight could not be hurt by black creatures whom he had burned, hanged, or put in chains.

Nevertheless, resistance to the infection was better than any of the palliatives, and even the southern colonies tried to be like New England for a time and resist the influx of Negro slavery — until the 1660s, when the world began rapidly to change. The England that ensued upon the Restoration of the Stuart monarchy in 1660 was, as it were, more West Indies than New England in spirit, and its overseas enterprises developed accordingly. The English slave trade grew, as we have seen, and so also did the slave colonies, above all in the West Indies, which finally expanded so energetically that they even reached the continental American South. Virginian tobacco had tried somewhat to resist the way of Barbadian sugar, but the outcome of the struggle was arrived at between them, with Carolinian rice. South Carolina was founded in 1663 largely by planters from Barbados, high-born gentlemen who had no compunctions about bringing in the large masses of Negro slaves they wanted for the rice plantations they founded there.

The South was thereby transformed, and Virginia and Maryland legislated all the more ardently to shore up their white societies against the Black influx, above all by strengthening the wall of slavery. But it was Carolina itself, untroubled by the moral problems of the more northerly colonies, that provided them with the most unequivocal formulation to date of the system that was now taking shape in their midst. "The Fundamental Constitutions of Carolina," drawn up in 1669 under the direction of its absentee proprietor, Lord Ashley, the first Earl of Shaftesbury, simply stated that "every freeman of Carolina, shall have absolute power and authority over his Negro slaves." This is no surprising representation of the viewpoint of the kind of haughty men of the world who invested their energies and their fortunes in the colony; it is a surprise, however, when we realize that the principal author of the "Fundamental Constitutions" was John Locke. At this moment, the Black slave was morally invisible even to a man who was soon to emerge as one of the great libertarians of his generation. His views were to change in the ensuing twenty years, as did those of Las Casas after an initial blindness on the subject of Negro slavery; indeed, during that period and especially after the revolution of 1688, a small but articulate number of the finest spirits in England and her colonies were to turn suddenly and vehemently against the institution. But all this only dramatizes the utter darkness into which the English conscience had plunged concerning the slavery question by around 1660.

30

A Lost Tribe Discovered in New York

IN SEPTEMBER, 1644, a Portuguese Marrano named Antonio de Montezinos arrived in Amsterdam after having lived for some years in South America, and proceeded to tell the leaders of the recently established Jewish community there a story that caused them to think of him as a latter-day Eldad the Danite. Two and a half years before, he told them, while traveling in the wild mountains of Quito, he had heard some of his Indian guides remark that the natives of that country deserved all the suffering they had undergone at the hands of the Spaniards. When he asked them to explain why they thought such a thing, they had replied mysteriously that it was because "we so badly treated a holy people, the greatest in the world." Nothing more had been offered by them on this point, but later in the same conversation, Francisco, one of the Indian guides, had declared that his countrymen would be avenged upon the Spaniards in time anyway, "by means of a people now hidden." The two references apparently were to the same people, but Montezinos, not seeing their full meaning in that moment, had put the whole matter out of mind for the time being.

Upon his return to Cartagena, the Judaizing Montezinos had found himself accused by the Inquisition and put in prison. Praying for salvation in his cell one day, he was reciting what was by then a standard formula among New World Marranos, "Blessed be the name of the Lord, Who has not made me an idolater, a barbarian, a Negro, an Indian . . . ," when suddenly be stopped. "Those Indians," he told himself, "they are Hebrews!" Pondering this thought incredulously and yet with growing conviction, he resolved that if he ever was released he would seek out the Indian Francisco and try to learn the truth.

Montezinos's story, unclear as to the circumstances of his incarceration, is equally unclear as to those of his release. But released he was, and he immediately went to Francisco. Revealing himself as a Jew, Montezinos proclaimed his conviction that Francisco's hidden people were of the same race as he. Would Francisco lead him to them?

The two men were soon back in the rugged mountains in which Francisco had made his initial revelation, marching relentlessly for a week before they finally came to a halt. It was a Saturday, Montezinos makes a point of telling us, and they had come to a river "larger than the Duero"; are there echoes of the Sambatyon in all of this? "Here," Francisco announced, "is where your brothers will be seen."

Waving a banner high in the air, the Indian guide soon was greeted by a puff of smoke far beyond the other bank of the river, in response to his signal. The two men waited. Eventually a canoe appeared, bearing three men and a woman, all of them Indians, to the place where Francisco and Montezinos were standing at the water's edge. The woman got off and spoke to Francisco in an Indian tongue that Montezinos could not understand, although he could perceive that he was being identified in the conversation. She then turned to her male companions to explain the situation. Upon hearing her words they rose, went over to Montezinos and, to his utter astonishment, said: "*Shema, Yisroel, Adonai Elohenu Adonai Ehod*" ("Hear, O Israel, the Lord our God, the Lord is One"). They had recited, in Hebrew, the fundamental credo of Judaism.

A brief conversation then ensued in their common ancestral tongue, according to Montezinos, whose fluency in it is almost as perplexing to the reader of his narrative as is that of his three mysterious new companions. They told him that they were themselves of the tribe of Reuben, and that the tribe of Joseph lived on an island nearby. The day when they were at last to issue forth into the world was coming soon, they explained, but in the meantime they could not allow visitors to cross over to them. They were willing to make an exception in the near future, however, on account of their need for education: for, though they spoke Hebrew, they could not read or write it. Would Montezinos send them twelve bearded men to be their teachers? He said he would. The four strangers returned to their canoe, paddled back across the river, and disappeared from view.

Francisco told Montezinos all he knew about these people from his own traditions. His ancestors, to their eternal shame, had indeed made war on them and persecuted them. Only the sorcerers of his tribe had perceived that they were a special people, and had given warning that they should be left alone. "The God of these children of Israel is the true God," they had said, "and everything inscribed on their tablets is true. At the end of days, they will be lords of all the nations of the earth. One nation will come bringing many things to this land, and after we have all been provided for, these children of Israel will go forth from where they now are and reign over the whole earth, as they once did." With this final flourish, Montezinos had turned his tale of the Lost Tribes into a bit of propaganda for the Dutch conquest of Brazil at the same time.

The story was received with enthusiasm by the Jews of Amsterdam, above all by Rabbi Manasseh ben Israel, one of the most prominent and representative men among them. The Netherlands and its Jews had both come out from under the Iberian yoke toward the end of the last century and had embraced one another in the cause of repudiating it. And now that the Dutch were approaching the end of what would be called their "Eighty Years' War" against Spain in a blaze of triumph, the Jewish community of Amsterdam — which had responded to the most tolerant religious climate in Europe by throwing off its Marrano cover in 1596 — was emerging as the most brilliant and influential in world Jewry.

Manasseh ben Israel was the son of Marrano parents who had lived in Portugal, then Spain, and then in the Madeira Islands, where he had been born in 1604 under the Christian name of Manoel Dias Soeiro. From there, the family moved to La Rochelle, a city not far from the Madeiras by dint of commerce as well as geography, but where the predominance of the Huguenots held out the promise of greater religious toleration. By this time, however, it was evident that the Netherlands were the only country in northwestern Europe where one could be an openly professing Jew and still flourish, and it was to Amsterdam that the Soeiros moved while Manoel was still a small child. There the father and his two sons underwent circumcision and changed their name officially to "ben Israel," a Hebrew designation so conventional as to be nearly anonymous, at least until it emerged as a virtual title for the son who became the most famous Jew of his day. Pursuing another convention, this time Biblical, the father named himself Joseph and his two sons Ephraim and Manasseh. They probably had already borne all these names in secret during Marrano days.

The former Marranos who established the Amsterdam community had followed a tradition of recent times and invited learned rabbis from Jewish communities that had never left the fold to be their teachers and religious leaders. Consequently, by the time young Manasseh went to school, Amsterdam Jewry had developed a splendid Jewish educational system, presided over by Sephardic rabbis from North Africa and Ashkenazic rabbis from central and eastern Europe. Under this tutelage Manasseh flourished, becoming an outstanding Hebraist though never precisely the master of Talmud that one can be only by having imbibed it with mother's milk. But what he had was sufficient to advance his star rapidly: the Portuguese part of the community was so delighted at this first appearance of a true Jewish scholar from their own ranks that he was quickly accorded an important place in the learned hierarchy. At the age of seventeen he was appointed as a Hebrew teacher and published his first book, a grammatical work. Success manifested itself in other ways, too: at nineteen he married an Abravanel, a daughter of the family that boasted Queen Isabella's minister Don Isaac Abravanel as one of its ancestors, still one of the most distinguished lineages in Sephardic Jewry and several cuts above Manasseh's own. In 1639, when the various congregations of Amsterdam Jewry finally combined into a single one and began laying the groundwork for the great synagogue known to later generations, Manasseh was appointed to the third position in its rabbinical hierarchy.

One of Manasseh's sideline business activities was a printing press, and with it he published a number of his own works, in Latin and in Spanish — this language still being the standard vernacular of Sephardic Jews everywhere — that were now beginning to reach an audience outside of the Netherlands, of Christians as well as Jews. In particular, his book *The Conciliator,* an effort to reconcile all conflicting passages in the Old Testament, and written in Spanish, had a special appeal for the growing number of learned Protestants in northern Europe and in Britain among whom Hebrew studies were an endeavor of fundamental religious significance. Such men were eager to obtain the rabbinical viewpoint on Old Testament questions, and Manasseh, part Christian himself by upbringing, and not so steeped in Talmud as to have a religious sensibility alien to the kinds of Biblical issues with which non-Jews were concerned, was an almost ideal fulfillment of their wishes. Having a popularizing turn of mind, and being the best-known and most personable Jewish scholar in a city that was now a cynosure for Protestants from all over Europe, Manasseh became an apostle to the Gentiles, a sort of Nathan the Wise of his day, eagerly sought out in letters or in person by Christians searching for religious truths. Englishmen in particular were drawn to him, but he was not without honor in his own country either: Rembrandt illustrated one of his books.

In the months and years following the appearance of Montezinos in 1644 — and his disappearance from history immediately thereafter — Manasseh ben Israel became his story's chief enthusiast. More and more of Manasseh's correspondence and conversation was to be devoted to it, and to its eschatological implications. And in the late 1640s both Jews and Protestants were particularly sensitive to these implications: it was a time of theological anguish and millennial expectations. Some Jewish calculators had appointed 1648 as the messianic year, and since that proved to be the year in which the protracted horrors of the Thirty Years' War came to an end, and in which a second civil war broke out in England, culminating in the execution of Charles I, many Protestants, especially in England, where the Fifth Monarchy sect was at its height, were convinced that they had indeed entered apocalyptic times. Something like apocalypse certainly struck for Jews that year, when the Hetman Bogdan Chmelnitzky led his Cossack followers in a revolt against Polish overlordship that turned its severest attacks upon the Jews of eastern Europe, bringing rape, injury, and violent death to tens of thousands and all but extinguishing the hitherto brilliant light of Polish Jewry. Also in that year, as if in response to this disaster, a young Jew of Smyrna (Izmir) in Turkey announced to a startled congregation that he was the Messiah, and though it was to be some time before many would take Sabbatai Zevi's claim seriously, he was eventually to be the leader of a movement that would send shock waves through all of world Jewry. And the year Sabbatai's followers chose for his messiahship, 1666, was one that Christian calculators had chosen for the Second Coming.

The idea now being popularized by Manasseh ben Israel, that the Lost Tribes were to be found in the New World, among other places, and that they were getting ready for their appearance in the imminent Final Days, was bound to be of particular appeal to an English Puritanism that not only was reaching a hysterical pitch but was keenly aware of its own special relationship with the American continent. It was an English chaplain residing in The Hague, John Dury, who first began spreading Manasseh's new theories among his countrymen, one of whom, Thomas Thorowgood, a clergyman in England, soon was relaying them to friends both at home and in the New World. By this means, they reached the Reverend John Eliot, minister of the town of Roxbury in Massachusetts Bay, who had begun to do missionary work among the Indians in 1646.

A true disciple of Roger Williams in this respect, Eliot, a Cambridge graduate who had come to Massachusetts in 1631 at the age of twenty-seven, was now learning the Algonquian language as part of his effort to bring the Christian message to the natives of the area at last, a calling to which the Puritans had been notoriously slow to respond. Eliot probably had already begun to suspect that there were Hebraic elements in the Indian language and customs, but Thorowgood's correspondence to him on the subject of Manasseh's ideas provided a certainty that led him to see millennial significance in his mission. Writing shortly after Eliot's death in 1690, Cotton Mather, an admirer of the man but not of his intellect, was to say mockingly that the minister of Roxbury "saw some learned men looking for the lost Israelites among the Indians in America, and counting they had thorow-good reasons for doing so. And a few small arguments, or indeed but conjectures, meeting with a favorable disposition in the hearer, will carry some conviction with them, especially, if a report of a Manasseh ben Israel be to back them." But Mather certainly recognized the power of a vision that eventually enabled Eliot to translate the entire Bible into the Algonquian tongue, a great though inevitably obscure effort of early American literature, which surely reflects on every page Eliot's sense of the deep-lying affinities between the Indian language and Hebrew, between the Indian and the Jewish spirits.

This mood at its height is vividly conveyed in a pamphlet describing Eliot's activities that was written in London in 1649 by our old friend Edward Winslow, who had arrived there three years earlier on a mission for the recently organized New England Confederation. "There are two great questions," Winslow writes in his preface, "which have much troubled ancient and modern writers, and men of greatest depth and ability to resolve: the first, what became of the Ten Tribes of Israel . . . ? The second is, what family, tribe, kindred, or people it was that first planted, and afterwards filled that vast and long unknown country of America?" Winslow, who does not seem to have troubled his thoughts with such questions back in Plymouth's early days, now not only ponders them, but believes he has the answer. "A Godly minister of this city," he goes on, probably referring to Thorowgood, has written "to Rabbi ben Israel, a great Doctor of the Jews, now living at Amsterdam, to know whether after all their labor, travels, and most diligent enquiry, they did yet know what was become of the Ten Tribes of Israel?" Manasseh had answered that at least some of them were in America, and Winslow, who had himself often observed customs among the Indians of a purportedly Judaic character, such as the rigid separation of the women during their menstrual periods, was now convinced that this was so, "especially considering the juncture of time wherein God hath opened [the Indians'] hearts to entertain the Gospel, being so nigh the very years in which many eminent and learned divines have from Scripture grounds . . . foretold the Conversion of the Jews."*

---

* Winslow, whose pamphlet was instrumental in causing Parliament to create the Society for the Propagation of the Gospel in New England later that year, may not have been writing these words with complete disingenuousness. He had arrived in England to deal with the challenge being hurled at the Puritan colonies by Samuel Gorton, a troublesome figure who had agitated for a kind of radical Protestantism successively at Massachusetts Bay, Plymouth, Providence, and finally at his own miniature colony of Shawomet, where he declared himself subject to no civil authority

The apocalyptic view expressed here is most dramatically emphasized in a postscript to the pamphlet, in which one "J.D." — probably John Downame, one of the parliamentary supporters of the Society for the Propagation of the Gospel — writes: "It is the expectation of some of the wisest Jews now living, that about the year 1650, either we Christians shall be Mosaic, or else that themselves Jews shall be Christians." Was Manasseh one of the wise Jews who had dropped this idea in the midst of some euphoric conversation? He certainly had felt the English Puritans' excitement by now, as in a letter he received from a minister named Nathaniel Holmes, who promised to write a book declaring that the Millennium was at hand and the Jews were about to have a central role in it. This alone must have made it seem high time to Manasseh that he round up and publish his ideas on the subject in a single book, but literary provocation was added to Millennium by the publication, in 1650, of Thorowgood's book, *Jews in America, or, Probabilities that those Indians Are Judaical.* This was full of Manasseh's name and ideas; and so the world was now ready for the rabbi himself.

Manasseh published his *Hope of Israel* that same year, in simultaneous Latin and Spanish editions. In true rabbinical fashion, the book is, in effect, a text with commentary — the text being Montezinos's deposition before the Jewish leaders of Amsterdam, with which the book begins, and the commentary being Manasseh's learned and philosophical development of its implications. Manasseh begins the latter with a discussion of the various current theories on the origin of the American Indians, and rejects all of them but the one maintaining that they had come from Tartary over an ancient land bridge now covered by the "Strait of Anian" — a vague term in use then, long before the Bering Strait had become clearly known and named, for the narrow body of water conceived to be separating the extreme of Asia from that of North America. In effect, his theory on this fundamental point was the same as the one most widely held today, except that the latter places the migration across the strait much earlier than he did. Manasseh, of course, considered the

---

but that of the crown back home. Gorton had, furthermore, mingled his own cause with that of the Narragansett Indians. Seized on a pretext, he had been sent back to England, where he now was continuing his role as a left-wing-Protestant successor to Thomas Morton, and agitating against the Indian policies of the New England Confederation.

It may well be, then, that the sudden interest in the conversion of the Indians now evinced by the Puritans in 1649 was partly aroused by Gorton's gadfly activities: they had to prove to a suspicious English leadership that they *were* concerned about the Indians' welfare, and they were doing it in the only way they knew how — by means of Christian militancy. In this context, the appearance of Manasseh ben Israel and his ideas was most welcome on a political level as well as meaningful to the Protestant millenarian mentality.

migration to have occurred somewhat after the Assyrian conquest of the northern Kingdom of Israel and the dispersion of its Ten Tribes; but, on the other hand, he does not think that the migrants consisted exclusively of their descendants, and in this respect his theory touches once again upon the modern one. For he maintains that most of the migrants were pure Tartars, and it is his belief that the ancestral tradition described by the Indian guide Francisco refers to an ancient persecution by the Tartars of the Jewish tribes in their midst.

But the Ten Lost Tribes remain Manasseh's principal concern, and his discussion now focuses upon them. Pursuing the eschatological implications of their dispersion, he undertakes an extended examination of the text of II Esdras 13, the "man from the sea" passage. It is revealing of Manasseh's personality, and of the kind of Judaism he represented, that he continued finding this heterodox and mystical text to be of major concern even after his return to rabbinical traditions. The heretical New Christian religiosity was still there beneath the surface; indeed, we may consider Manasseh to be the last outstanding representative of that quasi-religion of geographical messianism extending all the way back, through Columbus and Las Casas, to Abraham Cresques and Master Jacome of Majorca. It is entirely significant that, though learned orthodox Jews throughout the ages, down to Manasseh's time and beyond, continued to locate descendants of the Lost Tribes in various parts of the world, Manasseh was the only member of this tradition, the only ordained rabbi, ever to place them in America. On this issue at least, his was not the voice of normative Judaism speaking at all. He looked westward for redemption, as the heretical New Christians had done.

Perhaps Manasseh sensed this, and it may have been out of a desire to make a concession to more conventional Jewish ideas that he stressed the presence of the Lost Tribes in other remote places as well as America, ready to gather in all the corners of the world at the final Redemption. But America was his main interest, and all the reports he now proceeded to give confirming the existence of the Lost Tribes were from the New World — or, at least, from the southern part of it. For it is striking that this descendant of Iberian Marranos never betrayed, in his writings at least, any of the interest in the Indians of the north that his English friends so passionately showed. How drab and provincial the North American natives, in their bark wigwams, must have seemed to his southern and crypto-*converso* soul! Only in the southern part of the Americas could such a story be heard as the one brought to him of "a white people, with beards and long robes, of great wealth, and abundant in gold, silver and emeralds, who live in populous walled cities, where some Indians of the Orinoco have gone, bringing back with them much treasure." Not that Manasseh settled only for stories of the fabulous, however: sometimes, the ungainly was what betrayed a possible Jewish presence, such as the report brought to him from the mountains of Quito, Montezinos's territory, of "a white people, tall in stature and well formed, with full-grown beards like Spaniards, very brave, but who do not know how to handle canoes, even though all the Indians of that country do not go around any other way." All this evidence is quite persuasive to Manasseh, who nevertheless regrets that it cannot be examined more closely and verified — for a certain Fleming who once was about to undertake an expedition for this purpose, hired by a group of wealthy and interested Jews, "died shortly thereafter, apparently because God would not permit such discoveries until the End of Days." But Manasseh, convinced that the recent Jewish recovery from the long night of suffering under the Spaniards has eschatological significance, assures his readers that they do not have long to wait for this event.

The publication of this work was received enthusiastically by the left wing of English Protestantism, both in the Old World and in the New, where the inspiration it provided was to extend into the sixteen-seventies and -eighties among the Quaker founders of West New Jersey and Pennsylvania, who were to be the best friends the Indians had yet known among the English colonists. The Protector Oliver Cromwell became attracted to Manasseh's views, which included a belief that the time had come for a Jewish return to England. On this point, the mystical and the practical came together in Manasseh's spirit, for he urged it not only on the ground that the Jews had first to be dispersed in all the countries of the world before the final Redemption could come, but also because England's growing commercial empire could benefit greatly from Jewish skills. Indeed, it was an empire that the English were now inheriting from the Spaniards by way of the Dutch, so why not inherit the services of their Jews as well?

To this end, Manasseh was invited by Cromwell in 1655 to come present his views on Jewish emigration to England. His arguments appealed to the Protector but not to Parliament, which was stirred up against them by such anti-Jewish voices as that of the Puritan pamphleteer William Prynne. The bid for Jewish entry was rejected, and a disappointed Manasseh, though consoled by Cromwell with the promise of a yearly stipend of one hundred pounds, died on his return voyage home.

The matter of Jewish entry into England was resolved in the ensuing years, English-fashion, by connivance rather than any sweeping, official act. Jews quietly resettled there, and even as early as December, 1656, a group of them in London were able, without interference, to rent a house and use it explicitly as a synagogue. By 1664, when an accusation was brought against them that their services were in violation of that year's Conventicle Act, which permitted only Anglican religious assemblages,

372 LOST TRIBES AND PROMISED LANDS

the restored King Charles II himself came to their rescue, and took them under his official protection. Jews in England had become an acknowledged fact.

Meanwhile, a Jewish presence also made its way into the English colonies, and by the same route, from Iberian persecution over the bridge formed by the Dutch. We may look for the origins of the Jewish community of the future United States in the colony of Recife in Brazil, which had been taken by the Dutch from the Portuguese in 1630. Recife was, in terms of economic geography, more a part of the West Indies at this time than part of the South American continent, and its Jewish community — which consisted of about a thousand persons at its height, some one-third of the total European population there — had become thoroughly integrated into the West Indian economic life. The Jews of Recife, many of whom were of Portuguese Marrano descent, were in a variety of occupations, but these tended in one way or the other to be related to the colony's main industry, sugar. Historians have even suggested that New Christians were the first to bring sugar to Brazil, from São Thomé, the Canaries, or the Madeiras; in any case, there were Jewish sugar planters in Dutch Recife, although they do not seem to have been among the largest landowners. These planters owned Negro slaves just as their Christian counterparts did. In fact, some Jews of the colony found a particular outlet for their commercial talents as brokers in the slave trade. Technically, the trade was a monopoly of the Dutch West India Company, but in practice, the company's ships found it convenient to deposit large consignments of slaves at the port and leave the retailing of them to middlemen rather than sell them directly to the planters, and it was in the intermediate operation that a number of Jews found their métier. Later, when Jewish communities were established in other parts of the West Indies, some of their members continued to pursue this form of business activity.

This fact has often caused bewilderment among observers from a different era: how, they ask, can a people just emerging — and in other places not yet emerging — from centuries of persecution have so readily become collaborators in the persecution of another people? The answer lies in the appalling truth we have so often had occasion to contemplate in these pages, that Black slavery — in which there even were Black collaborators in the trade on the African shores — was a matter of conscience for very few men in this epoch.

In January, 1654, Recife was retaken by the Portuguese, mainly because the Dutch fleet was too preoccupied with the war against the English to be able to defend it — an interesting irony from the standpoint of those Recife Jews who were to end up living under the British flag as a result. The Portuguese conquerors imposed their usual brand of religious tyranny tempered by second thoughts and a touch of *Schlamperei*, requiring that all Protestants and Jews leave the colony, but giving them three months to do so peacefully. The departing Jews were able to find various satisfactory asylums in the Old World and the New: some sailed to the Netherlands, but many stayed closer to their recent home, settling primarily in the West Indian colonies of the Dutch, the French, and the English. One group of four men, six women, and thirteen children, however, made its way up to the farthermost north of the Dutch New World, and in September, 1654, arrived aboard the French ship *Ste. Catherine* in the harbor of New Amsterdam.

The Province of New Netherland, whose government was centered in the village at which the twenty-three Jewish refugees had arrived, was as anomalous among the English colonies on either side of it as it was different from them in nationality. Established in 1623 on the basis of the claim made by Henry Hudson's voyage fourteen years earlier, it had none of the continental ambitions and hopes to create a new way of life on earth that now characterized the colonies of both New England and the South. Rather, it was primarily just a collection of trading outposts of the Dutch West India Company, in one respect a far northern extension of the Caribbean network, in another, a counterpart to the French enterprise in Canada, manifesting its equivalent to the *coureurs de bois* in some of the adventurous patroons and their comrades in the north. The European population of New Amsterdam in 1654 was no more than about fifteen hundred. The home country of Dutchmen, unlike that of Englishmen, was prosperous, relatively untroubled by internal strife, and not so heavily populated as to seem to leave no breathing space for even the only moderately ambitious; its natives did not surge forth after new horizons. New Netherland was therefore largely a place for the type of colonist who, whether from the Netherlands, France, or England, usually went to the West Indies or Canada, more in search of adventurous profiteering than of a new homeland.

One result of this in New Netherland was the kind of ease in racial matters that characterized the French of Canada with respect to the Indian, and the West Indian planter with respect to the Negro. The Dutch, like everyone else, had their bad moments with the Indian; but on the whole, race relations along the Hudson were so good that the Dutch friendship with the Iroquois, later inherited by the English, was to turn into the longest-lasting and most powerful European-Indian alliance in all of the Americas. In the matter of Black slavery, which flourished more in New Netherland than in any other colony north of Maryland and Virginia, its record also is characterized by a spirit that seems rather relaxed for that time and place. The slaves, who tended to work side by side with whites in a variety of occupations, obtained manumission with relative ease, mainly through a "half-freedom" status worked out with the West India Company, whereby they could live in effect as free individuals in exchange for certain services and a modest annual tribute. All of this took place in an atmosphere that was unusually cosmopolitan for a New World colony; it was said that sixteen different languages could be heard among the settlers in New Amsterdam. In short, one can discern in the Manhattan Island village in particular some of the outlines of the future New York, and, as such, a likely place for Jewish refugees.

Not that the twenty-three refugees from Brazil were welcomed with open arms. New Amsterdam had tolerated the separate arrivals of two Jewish settlers from the Netherlands just a few weeks earlier, but a whole miniature community was another matter. "These people have no other God than the Mammon of unrighteousness," the New Amsterdam Reverend Johannes Megapolensis wrote to his colleagues back home, "and no other aim than to get possession of Christian property, and to overcome all other merchants by drawing all trade towards themselves. Therefore we request your Reverences to obtain from the Messrs. Directors [of the West India Company], that these godless rascals, who are of no benefit to the country, but look at everything for their own profit, may be sent away from here. For as we have here Papists, Mennonites and Lutherans among the Dutch; also many Puritans or Independents, and many atheists and various other servants of Baal among the English under this government, who conceal themselves under the name of Christians; it would create a still greater confusion, if the obstinate and immovable Jews came to settle here." This, at least, was not racial fear; and indeed, after Governor Peter Stuyvesant had sent back to the company in Amsterdam for instructions concerning the refugees, and the latter had settled down to await the reply, Dominie Megapolensis showed that his bark was worse than his bite by helping to tide them over with funds from the Dutch Reformed Church.

A response from the company in favor of the refugees probably was inevitable, not only on the moral grounds that religious toleration was right and had proven its viability in the Netherlands, but on the practical grounds that the commercial skills of Jews with connections all over the West Indies could be most useful. Furthermore, what was probably the most important factor of all, there were Jews among the investors in the company. A group of Amsterdam Jewish leaders petitioned the company, urging that the refugees be admitted and the company at length wrote back that "these people may travel and trade to and in New Netherland and live and remain there, provided the poor among them shall not become a burden to the company or to the community, but be supported by their own nation."

Thus began a Jewish community life in the future New York, replenished by the arrival in the next few years of more Jewish settlers from the West Indies and the Netherlands, and rooted by the purchase of a communal burial plot — traditionally the first manifestation of the establishment of a Jewish community. Disabilities remained, however: for a long time, the Jewish settlers could not buy real estate, bear arms, engage in trade with the Indians or even in retail trade — nor could they publicly hold religious services. Indeed, the size of the New Amsterdam Jewish community had begun to dwindle under these restrictions by the time the four historic English men-of-war arrived in the harbor in August, 1664, and took over the colony without firing a shot.

But from then on, Jewish life in New York began to flourish, like that in London, while Christian gentlemen looked the other way. By 1700, the Jews of the city were entering into the economic pursuits that had been forbidden them by the Dutch, and were freely worshipping according to their faith in various rented houses. In 1730, organized as Congregation Shearith Israel ("The Remnant of Israel"), they built the first synagogue in North America. By then, there were Jewish communities in other parts of the country as well — in Newport, in Philadelphia, in Charleston; soon there would be one in Savannah — and scatterings of individual Jews in all the colonies.

It was an English fulfillment; but the way to it had been opened in the Amsterdams, Old and New, and primarily through the efforts of Manasseh ben Israel and others of his generation who saw themselves as engaged in the final round of a struggle begun by their ancestors in fourteenth-century Spain. They had expected apocalypse, and some equivalent to what Christians were calling the Millennium; but when the moment passed, what came instead was a quiet conclusion to a millennium and a half of Jewish searching for some corner of the world in which to live in relative peace, equality, and religious freedom. From time to time, men would continue to seek evidence among the Indians of the latter's descent from the Lost Tribes of Israel; but whatever that ancient history would prove to have been, a latter-day lost tribe, at least, had assuredly now led the way to an American promised land for themselves and future generations of Jewish refugees from Old World persecution.

Of the various racial questions we have dealt with, then, it was the Jewish one alone that had found something of a solution in the New World by the end of the seventeenth century. Indeed, it was for the Jews alone among the racial outsiders that white America at its inception represented a fulfillment rather than a violation. This was because, within the Dutch and Anglo-Saxon societies that accepted them — above all the latter, which had scarcely known them at all during four centuries of heightening racial consciousness in Christendom — the Jews were little thought of as a race, and had become an almost purely religious minority instead. This was a particular advantage in North America, which proved to be as amenable to a Jewish presence as it was to that of any other group of European religious refugees; but in England as in the New World, religion was an area in which Anglo-Saxon liberalism was prepared to show one of its better sides as the eighteenth century began.

Race was still another matter. We have seen how the English of the sixteenth and seventeenth centuries, for all their vaunted notions of being morally superior to the Spaniards, proved not to be so in the domains of race and slavery. The offenses now were to continue even into an age in which the better spirits on both sides of the Atlantic would sound their protests against them with growing vehemence. The Indians of North America, whether they had ever been the Lost Tribes of Israel or not, were at any rate largely to be reduced to the state of a lost and wandering people in their own country. In the case of the Blacks, a promised land for white Europeans turned out to be an Egypt that held them in bondage for more than two hundred years; and even the nineteenth-century Emancipation hardly turned it overnight into a promised land for them. Today, at least, we can be reasonably satisfied that the worst excesses of domestic racism are behind us; but we still are a long way from having proven that this country can represent — on the level of dignity and mutual respect, if no other — a just end to the wanderings of all the peoples who have come together on its soil.

Acknowledgments

THIS BOOK WAS first conceived in the fall of 1968, during the New York Teachers' Strike. My wife was a member of the teachers' union, and it was impossible for us, as for many others, not to feel strongly the sudden conflict that then had seemed to emerge between old loyalties. In that struggle between the representatives of a Black community and the leaders of a labor union, and in the tension that ensued between Blacks and Jews in New York, we watched with dismay the apparent breakdown of what we had long taken to be a coalition of common interests. Along with many others, I then saw clearly for the first time that the problems and aspirations of various underdogs are not always identical. Coming in the wake of the riots that had recently broken out in one northern Black ghetto after another — reminders that the North had grave racial problems, too — the strike brought home to me at last the realization that American minority-group history was more complex than many of the liberals of my generation had believed. I then embarked on an inquiry which ultimately took me back to times and places far removed from Ocean Hill–Brownsville in 1968; yet nevertheless, I must begin these acknowledgments with a nod to the protagonists in that soul-rending struggle. Whatever else History may finally decide about their achievements or failures, I can at least say this with certainty: without them, this particular history would not have been written.

Struck by the ironies of a confrontation between two anciently oppressed ethnic groups — one of them still the sufferers of grievous racial inequities here in the United States, the other only recently the victims, in Europe, of the most murderous racist policy in history — who had from time to time found significant things in common with one another, I began a philosophical study of American racial history that soon leaped dizzyingly in two directions at once, backward in time and laterally in scope. I realized that what I wanted to discover involved going back to the very beginnings of American history and earlier, and widening my subject matter to include that crucial figure so easily forgotten by a child of eastern urban culture like myself, the American Indian. In the network of concerns that was thus growing for me, a most important role was played by the writings of that great explorer of American consciousness and group identity, Leslie A. Fiedler. In particular, I want to thank him for two works, one an article, "Negro and Jew — Encounter in America," which first appeared in *Midstream* in the late 1950s and was reprinted in *The Midstream Reader*, edited by Shlomo Katz (New York, 1960), and the other a book about the Indian, *The Return of the Vanishing American* (New York, 1968).

My sense of the Indian was heightened greatly during a trip that my wife and I took to the American Southwest in the spring of 1972, and of the many rewarding encounters that then took place, I want to hold up two of them for special expressions of gratitude. One was with Oswald White Bear Fredericks of the Hopi nation, associate author, with Frank Waters, of the *Book of the Hopi* (New York, 1963), who provided us with a morning of illuminating and unforgettable conversation. The other was a venerable Navaho who, during the long lift we gave him, spoke no more than the dozen or so words of English that he knew, but who gave us an image of the nobility of his heritage more vivid than what a shelf of books could have given.

There are few environments in which the particular network of themes in this book could have been evolved other than that of *Midstream* magazine in the late sixties and early seventies, when Shlomo Katz was still its editor. The relationships between different ethnic identities were always of special concern to him, and his conviction was strong that a proud and authentic Jewishness necessarily entailed a moral identification with other minorities who have suffered, especially Black Americans. Under his editorship, I was free to write articles exploring this conviction in myself, and to extend it to include the American Indian as well. I am deeply grateful for that apprenticeship.

Another personal relationship that was crucial for me in the entire evolution of this book was with my friend, Jervis Anderson, whose book *A. Philip Randolph: A Biographical Portrait* (New York, 1972) and whose many articles on Black history and culture in *The New Yorker* and elsewhere have deepened the understanding of so many of us on these subjects. In addition to providing countless valuable insights in conversations over the years, he also had the kindness to read and comment upon parts of the manuscript.

For reading and commenting upon the manuscript, I also want to thank Michael T. Gilmore, of the faculty of Brandeis University; Stanley G. Eskin, who was then on the faculty of the University of Massachusetts, Boston; Roger Donald, of Little, Brown and Company; Elisabeth Gleason Humez, also of Little, Brown; and my wife, Beverly, who was, as ever, so much more than can be expressed by these words or any others.

I conducted my own research, so I have only myself to blame for its faults; but for whatever I have achieved in this respect I owe a special debt of thanks to the staff of the New York Public Library, and in particular to those who work in three of its divisions: American History, Rare Books, and the Jewish Collection. These people are among the unsung heroes of our culture, and their library one of the glories of America.

Bibliographical Notes

Turning now to the bibliography and references, I must begin with a disclaimer or two. It would not be possible to cite every text, many of them forgotten, that has gone into the shaping of this work. Nor is it possible to give more or less definitive bibliographies in the various subject areas covered by the book, both for reasons of space and because I could not, in many of them, claim enough competence to try to offer such lists. This book perforce sails into many different regions, and I entered most of them as no more than a deeply concerned amateur, whose homework will nevertheless, I hope, prove at least minimally adequate to experts in them. The main purposes of the chapter-by-chapter bibliographical notes that follow are to give some indication of the homework I have done and, above all, to give credit where it is due: for I want to thank as many as I can of the authors, living or dead, who have palpably aided me in this effort.

In fact, there are a few authors whose works have been so useful, not only as references for various passages throughout the book, but also as sources of inspiration for some of its underlying conceptions, that I want to mention them here at the top of the list. No study of Black-white relations in the period I have covered could dispense with these two books among its points of departure: Winthrop D. Jordan, *White Over Black:*

American Attitudes toward the Negro, 1550–1812 (Chapel Hill, 1968); and David Brion Davis, *The Problem of Slavery in Western Culture* (Ithaca, 1966). I disagree with some of the viewpoints and conclusions of both these authors, but it is a tribute to their works that one's positions on the subject matter, whether in agreement with theirs or not, must in any case be taken up with them in mind. Another pair of authors provided equally basic reading for me in a field essential to the framework of this book, that of Renaissance exploration and discovery: they were Boies Penrose, whose *Travel and Discovery in the Renaissance, 1420–1620* (Cambridge, Mass., 1955) is a delight to read as well as a rich mine of information, and of course, Samuel Eliot Morison, about whose two volumes of *The European Discovery of America* (New York, 1971, 1974) the same and more must be said. And in this vein, two classic collections — thoroughly ransacked by me, as readers of the ensuing bibliography will observe — should also be mentioned here: the *Original Narratives of Early American History*, New York, edited by J. Franklin Jameson back in the early years of this century; and the volumes of re-printed or translated sources in the history of travel that have been put out virtually every year since 1846 by the Hakluyt Society, London. For the Jewish history running through the whole first half of this book, the indispensable point of departure was Yitzhak Baer, *A History of the Jews in Christian Spain* (2 vols., Philadelphia, 1971).

In the bibliographical notes that follow, I have given two publication dates in cases where the edition I have used is substantially different or of a much later date than the original; in such cases, the latter date — as is also the case in all citations giving a single date — is that of the edition I used, and not necessarily that of the most recent edition of the work. I have rarely given any title more than once, even though it may very well apply to other chapters besides the one under which it appears. The reference notes for each chapter usually give only an author's name or the equivalent if the source being cited is in the bibliography for the same chapter; the references to the same source in subsequent chapters will give its title in an abbreviated but clearly recognizable form. *HS* will always be used to designate Hakluyt Society volumes, *ON* for *Original Narratives of Early American History*, and *BAE* for the *Biblioteca de Autores Españoles*, Madrid. Passages in the text quoted from foreign editions are in my own translations.

Chapter-by-Chapter Bibliographies
and Reference Notes

PROLOGUE: *The Catalan Atlas.* On the Atlas itself, which is in the Bibliothèque Nationale, Paris, and its maker, the basic texts are J. A. C. Buchon and J. Tastu, *Notice d'un Atlas en langue catalane, 1375,* which is a descriptive catalogue of the work, published by the Bibliothèque Nationale in 1839; and G. de Reparaz, *Mestre Jacome de Malhorca, Cartografo do Infante* (Coimbra, 1930), the masterly monograph, written in Portuguese, that definitively identifies Master Jacome as Jafuda Cresques, and also provides rich information on his father, and on Majorcan cartography in general, along the way. I worked with two reproductions of the map itself: one is a full-size, full-color facsimile, produced in a limited edition in Barcelona in 1959 by J. Vernet and David Romano; the other, a small but clear black-and-white, half-tone reproduction in Leo Bagrow, *History of Cartography,* revised and enlarged by R. A. Skelton (Cambridge, Mass., 1966), plates XXXVII–XXXIX. A good descriptive analysis of the Catalan Atlas is provided by G. R. Crone in *Maps and Their Makers* (New York, 1966), pp. 39–47.

On the geographical conceptions and techniques of that era, I made use of John Kirkland Wright, *The Geographical Lore of the Time of the Crusades* (New York, 1925; 1965); C. R. Beazley, *The Dawn of Modern Geography* (3 vols., London, 1897–1906); E. L. Nordenskiöld, *Facsimile-*

Atlas to the Early History of Cartography (Stockholm, 1889; New York, 1973); E. L. Stevenson, *Portolan Charts: Their Origin and Characteristics* (New York, 1911); and the works cited by Penrose, Bagrow, and Crone. On medieval Africa and its geography: E. W. Bovill, *The Golden Trade of the Moors* (Oxford, 1958; 1970), a reworking of his *Caravans of the Old Sahara*, which some still prefer; C. de la Roncière, *La Découverte de l'Afrique au moyen âge* (3 vols., Cairo, 1924–1927); Raymond Mauny, *Tableau géographique de l'ouest africain au moyen âge* (Dakar, 1961); and for a concise general survey of African history, the Penguin *Short History of Africa* by Roland Oliver and J. D. Fage (Baltimore, 1962) is as good as any.

The great work on the Alexander legends is George Cary, *The Medieval Alexander*, edited by D. J. A. Ross (Cambridge, England, 1956; 1967). These also are dealt with in Norman Cohn, *The Pursuit of the Millennium* (New York, 1957, subsequently revised and expanded), the major work on medieval chiliasm; the equivalent Jewish moods are chronicled in Abba Hillel Silver, *A History of Messianic Speculation in Israel* (New York, 1927; Boston, 1959). To my knowledge, the only book-length study of the history of the Lost Tribes idea existing at this moment of writing is Allen H. Godbey, *The Lost Tribes a Myth* (Durham, 1930; New York, 1974), which, as its title indicates, spends a lot of energy refuting the various theories. What is needed is a full-length scholarly study of the history of this idea in its various ramifications, which so far only has been handled in an old series of articles, "Where Are the Ten Tribes?" by Adolph Neubauer, in the *Jewish Quarterly Review*, 1 (London, 1888–1889): 14–28, 95–114, 185–201, 408–423; this is an admirably learned piece of work, but it is really only a catalogue, lacking in a much-needed analysis of the materials.

Some valuable concepts, particularly the "Greater Mediterranean" idea, were provided for this prologue and elsewhere by Fernand Braudel's monumental work, *The Mediterranean and the Mediterranean World in the Age of Philip II* (2 vols., New York, 1972–1973). Some reminders on the background of the period were found in Edouard Perroy, *The Hundred Years War* (New York, 1965).

CHAPTER 1: Master Jacome of Majorca. Spain goes in for monumental studies of its own history, and two at which I paid homage are the unfinished, multivolume *Historia de España*, which was being edited by the great Ramón Menéndez Pidal until his death at more than a hundred years of age — particularly, for this chapter, Volume VI, *España Cristiana, 711–1038*, by Justo Pérez de Urbel and Ricardo del Arco y

Garay (Madrid, 1964); and Rafael Altamira y Crevea, *Historia de España y de la civilización española* (4 vols., Barcelona, 1913), the gist of which has been conveniently reduced to one volume in English, *A History of Spain*, by Charles E. Chapman (New York, 1918; 1965). Another characteristic Spanish literary form is the historical essay, or *ensayo*, summing up the general outlines of the national development, and I used three outstanding specimens of those: Ramón Menéndez Pidal (whose name will appear here yet a few more times, as it must in any bibliography on Spanish history), *The Spaniards in Their History*, translated by Walter Starkie (New York, 1950; 1966); J. Vicens Vives, *Approaches to the History of Spain*, translated by Joan Connelly Ullman (Berkeley, 1972); and Américo Castro, *La Realidad histórica de España* (Mexico City, 1973). Castro, throughout his writings, was ever sensitive to the possibilities of New Christian identity in various Spanish historical figures, and I confess to having let myself be sensitized in this direction primarily by this man, who was widely considered to be the dean of Hispanic studies in the United States during his teaching career.

On medieval Islam and Moorish Spain, I used Bernard Lewis, *The Arabs in History* (New York, 1960); Carl Brockelmann, *History of the Islamic Peoples*, translated by Joel Carmichael and Moshe Perlmann (New York, 1973); R. A. Nicholson, *A Literary History of the Arabs* (Cambridge, England, 1907; 1969); E. Lévi-Provençal, *Histoire de l'Espagne musulmane* (3 vols., Paris, 1950–1967), the definitive work, though unfinished, superseding the classic one by R. Dozy, *Histoire des Musulmanes d'Espagne* (revised ed., Leyden, 1932); and, also by Lévi-Provençal, *La Civilización árabe en España* (Madrid, 1969).

On medieval Jewish and Spanish-Jewish history, one begins, as on most periods of Jewish history, with the classic nineteenth-century work by Heinrich Graetz, *History of the Jews* (6 vols., Philadelphia, 1967), in this case especially with Volumes III and IV. One also tends to fall back upon Max Margolis and Alexander Marx, *History of the Jewish People* (New York and Philadelphia, 1959), surely the most comprehensive one-volume work on the subject, very useful for reference though a little tedious to read. The classic works on Spanish-Jewish history alone are E. H. Lindo, *The History of the Jews of Spain and Portugal* (London, 1848; New York, 1970), dated, but still useful; and José Amador de los Ríos, *Historia social, política, y religiosa de los Judíos de España y Portugal* (Madrid, 1875–1876; 1970), fresh and richly informative to this day. The key modern works are Solomon Katz, *The Jews in the Visigothic and Frankish Kingdoms of Spain and Gaul* (Cambridge, Mass., 1937; New York, 1970), on the pre-Muslim Middle Ages; Eliyahu Ashtor, *The Jews of Moslem Spain* (Philadelphia, Vol. I, 1973; Vol. II forthcoming), on the Muslim period, along with the very fine essay by S. D. Goitein, *Jews and Arabs: Their Contacts Through the Ages* (New York, 1964); and for the Christian period until 1492, the great work by Yitzhak Baer, already cited.

On the Khazars, the standard work still is D. M. Dunlop, *The History of the Jewish Khazars* (Princeton, 1954; New York, 1967), even though a livelier discussion has since been provided by Arthur Koestler, *The Thirteenth Tribe* (New York, 1976). There are many works on the history of anti-Semitism, but the best is Léon Poliakov's four-volume *Histoire de l'antisémitisme* (Paris, 1958–1970), which has yet to appear in English in its entirety; his volume on medieval Europe, consulted for this chapter, has appeared in English as *The History of Anti-Semitism: From the Time of Christ to the Court Jews,* translated by Richard Howard (New York, 1974).

On the aspects of Christian history relevant to this chapter, I made particular use of Steven Runciman, *A History of the Crusades* (3 vols., New York, 1964–1967); Henry Charles Lea, *A History of the Inquisition of the Middle Ages* (3 vols., New York, 1888), the still-indispensable classic on the subject, not to be confused with the same author's work on the Spanish Inquisition to be cited below; and Marcelino Menéndez Pelayo, *Historia de los heterodoxos españoles* (Madrid, 1880–1882; 2 vols., 1965), another monumental work of historical self-examination by one of the greatest of Spanish scholars, full of the ambivalences of the liberal of his generation.

For the literary history of the period covered in this chapter, I consulted George Tyler Northup, *An Introduction to Spanish Literature,* third edition revised and enlarged by Nicholson B. Adams (Chicago, 1925; 1971). Among the literary texts I used were Ramón Menéndez Pidal's edition of the *Poema del Cid,* which has been reprinted in various forms, including an American edition with English translation on the facing pages by W. S. Merwin (New York, 1959); Judah Ha-Levi, *Selected Poems,* in Hebrew, with English translations by Nina Salaman, edited by Heinrich Brody (Philadelphia, 1924; 1974); Ha-Levi's *Kuzari,* translated by Hartwig Hirschfeld, introduction by Henry Slonimsky (New York, 1964); and the Penguin edition, *The Jewish Poets of Spain,* translated by David Goldstein (Baltimore, 1965).

REFERENCES: The H. C. Lea quotation is from his *Moriscos of Spain: Their Conversion and Expulsion* (New York, 1901; 1968), p. 13. The *kharja* is quoted and transliterated on p. 140 of Samuel Miklos Stern, *Hispano-Arabic Strophic Poetry* (Oxford, 1974), a collection of essays by the scholar who achieved the definitive reading of these remarkable specimens of early Spanish verse. The Abd-er-Rahman I poem is in Nicholson, p. 418. The quoted passage from the Hasdai ibn Shaprut letter is on p. 29 of

Elkan N. Adler, *Jewish Travellers* (London, 1930; New York, 1966). A reproduction of the picture of the two troubadours in the manuscript of the *Cantigas* can be found on pp. 84–85 of Bradley Smith, *Spain: A History in Art* (New York, 1966). It was Hasdai Crescas who wrote that "the Lord bent his bow," etc., quoted in Baer, *Jews in Christian Spain,* II, 96. The list of Jews baptized in Majorca in 1391 can be found in Baltasar Porcel, *Los Chuetas mallorquines* (Barcelona, 1971), pp. 59–62. The passage on Master Jacome by Duarte Pacheco Pereira is in the latter's *Esmeraldo de Situ Orbis,* translated and edited by George H. T. Kimble (*HS,* 1937; Liechtenstein, 1967), pp. 100–101.

CHAPTER 2: The Fortunate Islands. On the general history of Portugal, I read A. H. de Oliveira Marques, *History of Portugal* (2 vols., New York, 1972), the most up-to-date large-scale work in English; and H. V. Livermore, *A New History of Portugal* (Cambridge, England, 1969), a concise, revised version of the author's earlier *History of Portugal.* On the Portuguese explorations, some of the most outstanding secondary works are Edgar Prestage, *The Portuguese Pioneers* (London, 1933; New York, 1967); Charles R. Boxer, *The Portuguese Seaborne Empire, 1415–1825* (New York, 1969); and, on the guiding spirit of it all, C. R. Beazley, *Prince Henry the Navigator* (London, 1895; New York, 1968), still one of the most valuable of the many biographies of its subject. The main primary sources on the discoveries in this period are the writings of Prince Henry's official chronicler — a "kept" historian, alas, who was none too objective — Gomes Eannes de Zurara (spelled "Azurara" in many editions), especially his *Chronicle of the Discovery and Conquest of Guinea* (2 vols., *HS,* 1896–1899; recent reprint, New York, n.d.), translated by C. R. Beazley and Edgar Prestage. Zurara's account of "The Conquest of Ceuta," our sole source on the subject, is excerpted and translated in Azurara, *Conquests and Discoveries of Henry the Navigator,* edited by Virginia de Castro e Almeida, translated by Bernard Miall (London, 1936).

Early possible circumnavigations of Africa: a translation of a Greek version of Hanno's account of his voyage is in B. H. Warmington, *Carthage* (New York, 1960), pp. 62–64; the passage in Herodotus about the Phoenician circumnavigation is in Book IV, Chapter 42. The idea of the circumnavigability of Africa appears in various places in Pliny, *Natural History* (Loeb Classics, 10 vols., London and Cambridge, Mass., 1967), as does that of the Fortunate Islands; Plutarch's passage on the latter is in "Sertorius" in *Plutarch's Lives,* translated by John Dryden, revised by Arthur Hugh Clough (Modern Library edition, New York, n.d.).

Boccaccio's account of the 1341 expedition to the Canaries was not discovered until the nineteenth century and does not appear in his Collected Works. It has been reprinted in various places in the original Italian, and a translation of it appears in the introduction to R. H. Majors's edition of the source account of Bethencourt's conquest, *The Canarian*, by Pierre Bontier and Jean le Verrier (*HS*, 1872; New York, 1971).

REFERENCES: The Plutarch quote is in the Modern Library edition, p. 683. The Boccaccio passages are from *The Canarian*, pp. xiii–xv, xvi, xviii–xix. The "killed many natives" quote is in *The Canarian*, p. 75.

CHAPTER 3: Prester John; or, The Noble Ethiopian. A very lively and illuminating study of the entire Prester John legend is Robert Silverberg, *The Realm of Prester John* (New York, 1972), to which I owe a special debt of thanks for its helpfulness in the formulation of the first part of this chapter. The indispensable classic study, filled with many sample texts in the original languages, is Friedrich Zarncke, "Der Priester Johannes," a two-part article in the *Abhandlungen der philologisch-historischen Classe der königlich sächsischen Gesellschaft der Wissenschaften*, Vol. 7 (1879), and Vol. 8 (1883). Some relevant sorces on the legend are *The Travels of Marco Polo* (various editions); *The Travels of Sir John Mandeville* (various editions; I used the 1964 Dover reprint from the London edition of 1900); Francis M. Rogers, *The Travels of the Infante Dom Pedro of Portugal* (Cambridge, Mass., 1961), which contains a translation of the fictitious narrative on this subject published in Spanish in 1515 by Garci Ramírez de Santisteban; and "An Abridgement of the Medieval Legend of Prester John," a 1507 English version of the celebrated letter, reprinted in Edward Arber, editor, *The First Three English Books on America* (London, 1885; New York, 1971).

On the early history of slavery, I used William L. Westermann, *The Slave Systems of Greek and Roman Antiquity* (Philadelphia, 1955); R. H. Barrow, *Slavery in the Roman Empire* (London, 1928); Isaac Mendelsohn, *Slavery in the Ancient Near East* (New York, 1949); and the work by David Brion Davis cited above. And on Blacks in ancient literature: Frank M. Snowden, Jr., *Blacks in Antiquity* (Cambridge, Mass., 1970).

REFERENCES: The reference to Prester John in *The Canarian* is on p. 94, and the one from Zurara is in *Guinea*, I, 55. All the quotes from the reconstructed original Prester John letter are from the English translation of the Zarncke version given in Silverberg, pp. 41–45. The "great king of Israel" is in the 1507 version of the letter quoted in Arber, p. xxxiv. The quotes from Eldad the Danite are from Neubauer, "Ten Tribes," pp. 100–102. On the Sambatyon, besides Eldad: the Josephus passage is in the Loeb Classics edition of his works, III, 534 (Greek), 535 (English translation by H. St.J. Thackeray); the Pliny passage is in *Natural History*, xxxi, 18:24, in Vol. VIII of the Loeb Classics edition, 392 (Latin), 393 (English translation by W. H. S. Jones); and the statement from the Great Midrash is *Midrash Rabboth*, Gen. 73, quoted in Neubauer, p. 20. The quote from Homer on the Ethiopians is from the W. H. D. Rouse translation, p. 11 of the Mentor edition (New York, 1949); and the one from Herodotus is iii, 20, of *The Persian Wars* in the George Rawlinson translation (various editions). The *Satyricon* passage is from the Loeb Classics Petronius, pp. 244 (Latin), 245–247 (English translation by W. H. D. Rouse), and Pliny's gymnosophists are in *Pliny*, vii, 2:22, in Vol. II of the Loeb Classics edition, pp. 520 (Latin), 521 (English translation by H. Rackham). For the *Ethiopica* of Heliodorus, I used the Moses Hadas translation (called *An Ethiopian Romance*), published by the University of Michigan Press, Ann Arbor, 1957; the quotations are from pp. 277, 294, 255, and 274, respectively, of that edition. For *The Romance of Alexander the Great*, I used the translation from the Armenian version done by Albert M. Wolohojian (New York and London, 1969); the quotations are from pp. 135, 136, and 132.

CHAPTER 4: The Guinea Trade. On the general history of the African slave trade: Daniel P. Mannix, with Malcolm Cowley, *Black Cargoes* (New York, 1965); and Basil Davidson, *The African Slave Trade* (original title, *Black Mother*; Boston, 1961). An admirable effort at a satistical history of the subject is Philip D. Curtin, *The Atlantic Slave Trade: A Census* (Madison, 1969). The indispensable source collection is Elizabeth Donnan, *Documents Illustrative of the History of the Slave Trade to America* (4 vols., Washington, 1930). On the early trade, a classic work is Georges Scelle, *La Traite negrière aux Indes de Castille* (2 vols., Paris, 1906). The great work on the medieval European slave trade is Charles Verlinden, *L'Esclavage dans l'Europe médiévale* (Brugge, 1955), although this is only the first volume, dealing with France and the Iberian Peninsula, of a projected two-volume work.

On the Arab background in this chapter, I used J. Spencer Trimingham, *A History of Islam in West Africa* (Oxford, 1962); and Bernard Lewis's brilliant monograph, *Race and Color in Islam* (New York, 1971).

REFERENCES: The Herodotus passage is Rawlinson's translation of iv, 196; and Hanno's voyage is in Warmington, *Carthage*, pp. 62–64. Sa'id al-Andalusi is quoted in Lewis, *Race and Color*, p. 36. The *Arabian Nights* passage is on p. 6 of the Modern Library edition (New York, 1932). Ibn Haukal and Ibn Battuta are both quoted in Bovill, *Golden Trade*, pp. 62

and 95, respectively. The "Moor" at Ceuta is in Zurara, "Ceuta," p. 99. The quotations from Zurara, *Guinea,* are located as follows: Prince Henry "reflected with great pleasure": I, 83; "And certainly his expectation": I, 83; Stevam Affonso: II, 181; "On the next day": I, 81; "sons of Adam": I, 81; "five or six Black Moors" and Noah's curse: I, 54. The quotations from *The Voyages of Cadamosto,* translated and edited by G. R. Crone (*HS,* 1937; Liechtenstein, 1967), are from pp. 41, 28, 49, and 60, respectively.

CHAPTER 5: Jews and New Christians. As always, the main secondary source for the Jews in this period is Yitzhak Baer's great work. Also useful were Cecil Roth's classic, *A History of the Marranos* (New York and Philadelphia, 1959); and Antonio Domínguez Ortiz, *Los Judeoconversos en España y América* (Madrid, 1971). On the Inquisition, the indispensable classic is once again by Henry Charles Lea, *History of the Inquisition of Spain* (4 vols., Philadelphia, 1905; New York, 1966); but this is well supplemented by Henry Kamen's brilliant and more concise modern work, *The Spanish Inquisition* (New York, 1965). Cecil Roth, *The Spanish Inquisition* (London, 1937; New York, 1964), also is useful. A good recent source presentation is: Haim Beinart, editor, *Records of the Trials of the Spanish Inquisition in Ciudad Real: Volume I, 1483–1485* (Jerusalem, 1974), in which the introduction and notes are in English, and the records themselves in the original Spanish. The basic work on the *limpieza* statutes is: Albert Sicroff, *Les Controverses des statuts de 'pureté de sang' en Espagne du XVe au XVIIe siècle* (Paris, 1960). On the general history of Spain in this period, I consulted, in addition to the relevant works cited for Chapter 1, J. H. Elliott, *Imperial Spain, 1469–1716* (New York, 1966); and William H. Prescott's classic, *Ferdinand and Isabella* (2 vols., various editions), which can still be read with profit.

REFERENCES: The Fray Vicente Ferrer story is told by the chronicler Gonçales Davila, quoted in the appendix of "Notas para la historia de astronomía en la España medieval: el Judío salmantino Abraham Zacut," by F. Cantera Burgos, in the *Revista de la Academia de Ciencias Exactas, Físico-Quimicas y Naturales de Madrid,* October, 1931, pp. 63–398. Ibn Verga's passage on Halorki is in his *Shevet Yehuda* (Tel Aviv, 1946, in Hebrew), p. 94. Vol. II of Baer, *Jews in Christian Spain,* is the source for the possibility that the Messiah was fourteen hundred years old, p. 179; for "Jews appeared in Tortosa," pp. 210–211; for Master Juan the Elder, p. 160; for Pedro de la Cavalleria, p. 277. The satire on the Marranos is in H. Pflaum, "Une Ancienne Satire espagnole contre les Marranes," in the

Revue des Études Juives, 86: 144–150. The quotation "If you know or have heard" is in Henry Kamen, pp. 165–166.

CHAPTER 6: *Enter Columbus.* Of the many modern works on Columbus, the ones I specifically made use of were Salvador de Madariaga, *Christopher Columbus* (New York, 1940; 1967); and Samuel Eliot Morison, *Admiral of the Ocean Sea* (Boston, 1942). Morison did a two-volume scholarly edition, hard to obtain today, and a one-volume edition, which is virtually the same text without the notes; I used the latter. Another study crucial for my own approach to Columbus was Meyer Kayserling's *Christopher Columbus and the Participation of the Jews in the Spanish and Portuguese Discoveries* (Budapest, 1893; New York, 1968), translated by Charles Gross; Kayserling, who wrote long before suspicions arose as to Columbus's own possible New Christian identity, was the first to notice the remarkably large presence of Jews and *conversos* in the whole Iberian enterprise of overseas exploration. The main accounts of Columbus by his contemporaries, in the form I used them, are to be found in *The Life of the Admiral Christopher Columbus by his Son Ferdinand,* translated and annotated by Benjamin Keen (New Brunswick, 1959); Bartolomé de las Casas, *Historia de las Indias* (3 vols., Mexico City and Buenos Aires, 1965); Peter Martyr d'Anghera, *De Orbe Novo,* translated from the Latin by F. A. MacNutt (2 vols., New York, 1912; 1970); and Gonzalo Fernández de Oviedo, *Historia general y natural de las Indias* (5 vols., *BAE*, CXVII–CXXI). Columbus's copy, with his annotations, of Pierre d'Ailly, *Imago Mundi,* is in the Biblioteca Columbina, Seville, but there is a limited edition of it in photographic reproduction, made in 1927 by the Massachusetts Historical Society; also, a French translation of the text and the annotations, made by Edmond Buron, was published in Paris in 1930.

REFERENCES: Columbus obtained "the basic rudiments," according to Las Casas, I, 31; and "the wars and factions of Lombardy" are mentioned in Ferdinand Columbus, p. 5. Columbus's note on the "reprobate Jews" is given as quoted in Madariaga, pp. 134–135. Columbus's signature is given in Morison, p. 356, and Madariaga, p. 403, among other places.

CHAPTER 7: *The Other 1492.* On general Spanish history in this period, in addition to the relevant works already cited, I consulted: R. B. Merriman, *The Rise of the Spanish Empire in the Old World and the New* (4 vols., New York, 1918–1934; 1962). On the Conquest of Granada,

I consulted these source works: Hernando del Pulgar, *Crónica de los Señores Reyes Católicos,* and Andrés Bernáldez, *Historia de los Reyes Católicos,* both in *Crónicas de los Reyes de Castilla* (*BAE,* LXX); and Diego Hurtado de Mendoza, *Guerra de Granada* (Madrid, 1970). On the Jewish history of this period, in addition to the relevant works already cited, I read B. Netanyahu, *Don Isaac Abravanel, Statesman and Philosopher* (Philadelphia, 1953). On Abraham Zacuto (often spelled Zacut): F. Cantera Burgos, *Abraham Zacut, Siglo XV* (Madrid, 1935), as well as the same author's article, "Notas para la historia de astronomía," etc., cited under Chapter 5; Abraham A. Neuman, "Abraham Zacuto, Historiographer," in *American Academy for Jewish Research: Harry Austryn Wolfson Jubilee Volume,* Vol. II (Jerusalem, 1965), pp. 597–629; and the sixteenth-century Portuguese chronicler, Gaspar Correa, in *The Three Voyages of Vasco da Gama,* translated and edited by Henry E. J. Stanley (*HS,* 1869; recent reprint, New York, n.d.). Of Zacuto's own writings, the principal ones read were *Almanach Perpetuum,* the Spanish version of which is reproduced in the Cantera Burgos article cited above; and the *Sefer Yuhasin,* edited by Herschel Filipowski (London, 1857; Frankfurt a. M., 1924), selections from which, as they appear in this chapter, either are in my own translations or those of Abraham Neuman, the latter often revised by me.

On Columbus, an interesting theory of a Columbus "mission" to find a refuge for New Christians is in Simon Wiesenthal, *Sails of Hope: The Secret Mission of Christopher Columbus* (New York, 1973). Columbus's journal of his first voyage to America is available in an English edition, *The Journal of Christopher Columbus,* translated by Cecil Jane, with an appendix by R. A. Skelton (London, 1968); but I used the original Spanish text given by Navarrete, the great nineteenth-century archivist and collector of Columbus and other voyage materials, in the *Obras de Don Martín Fernández de Navarrete* (3 vols., *BAE,* LXXV–LXXVII). A convenient English translation and abridgement of the journal, as well as other source writings on Columbus, is in the Penguin edition, *The Four Voyages of Christopher Columbus,* edited and translated by J. M. Cohen (Baltimore, 1969).

REFERENCES: The opening narrative from Pulgar is in the *BAE* edition, pp. 510b–511a; and the Mendoza passage is on p. 402 of the edition cited. The translation of the Expulsion decree from which I have quoted is that of Lindo, on p. 277. The quotes from the *Sefer Yuhasin* of Zacuto are from the Filipowski edition, as follows: "Israel is exemplified by stars": p. 1a; "And so, too": p. 223a; persecutions of 1412: p. 225b; fall of Málaga: p. 227a; conquest of Alhama: p. 226b; Inquisition begun: p. 226b; "In 1492": p. 227a; and, further on, "Some of the Jews": p. 227a. Columbus's preamble is in Navarrete, I, 86. The Bernáldez passage on the Jewish departure is in the *BAE* edition, pp. 652b–653a. Cecil Roth's observation about Columbus and Tisha b'Av is in prefatory note to the revised (1967) edition of Madariaga, *Columbus,* p. xii.

CHAPTER 8: Columbus's Golden World. For this chapter, I consulted all the relevant works cited under the previous two chapters, as well as: R. H. Major, translator and editor, *Select Letters of Christopher Columbus, with Other Original Documents Relating to the Four Voyages to the New World* (*HS*, 1847; New York, 1961).

REFERENCES: The first three Columbus quotes are all from Navarrete: "This high sea": I, 91b; "I, in order that": I, 95b; "Then they came swimming": I, 95b–96a. All the remaining quotations, with the exception of the Peter Martyr passage, are from Major (I have sometimes revised his translations in the light of the texts in the original that he gives at the bottom of each page): "They manifest great love": p. 7; "They practise no kind of idolatry": pp. 8–9; "I did not find . . . most vividly": pp. 13–14; "When I sailed from Spain": p. 127; "When I reached . . . in the temperature": pp. 128–129; "I have always read . . . (. . . terminate)": pp. 129–130; "When I was off . . . long, smooth hair": pp. 132–133; "The Holy Scriptures . . . Canaries": pp. 135–136; "I have already . . . will of God": pp. 136–137; "I have never read": p. 138; "The more I reason": p. 142. The Peter Martyr passage is from *De Orbe Novo,* First Decade, Book 2, but not in the translation by F. A. MacNutt that is used for other passages; this one is from the fuller rendition of the passage made by Richard Eden in 1555 and reprinted in Arber, pp. 70–71.

CHAPTER 9: Black Devils. Travel literature: *The Letters of Amerigo Vespucci,* translated and edited by Clements R. Markham (*HS*, 1894; New York, n.d.); *The Voyage of Pedro Álvares Cabral to Brazil and India,* translated with introduction and notes by William Brooks Greenlee (*HS*, 1938; Liechtenstein, 1967); on the Magellan voyage, I used two versions of the Antonio Pigafetta narrative, one being Richard Eden's 1555 translation from the Italian reprinted in Arber, and the other being the 1525 French version reprinted in *The Voyage of Magellan: The Journal of Antonio Pigafetta,* translated on facing pages by Paula Spurlin Paige (Englewood Cliffs, 1969). Sacred literature: *The Apocryphal New Testament,* translated by Montague Rhodes James (Oxford, 1924; 1972); and Jacobus de Voragine, *The Golden Legend,* translated and adapted from the Latin by Granger Ryan and Helmut Ripperger (London, 1941;

New York, 1969). Among the early sources on witchcraft are Thomas Wright, editor, *A Contemporary Narrative of the Proceedings against Dame Alice Kyteler* (Camden Society, 1843; New York, 1968), the first full account we have of a witchcraft trial, occurring in Ireland in 1324 (the text is in Latin); the 1485 diatribe by Heinrich Kramer and James Sprenger, *The Malleus Maleficarum*, translated and edited by Montague Summers (London, 1928; New York, 1971); and the 1585 attempt by Reginald Scot, in English, to prove that witches did not exist, *The Discoverie of Witchcraft* (London, 1930; New York, 1972). Among more modern works on witchcraft, one should always read, for all its romanticism, Jules Michelet, *La Sorcière* (Paris: Garnier-Flammarion, 1966; and various editions), known in English as *Satanism and Witchcraft* (various editions); and the remarkable work by Margaret A. Murray, *The Witch-Cult in Western Europe* (Oxford, 1921; 1971), along with Norman Cohn's reply to it in his article, "Was There Ever a Society of Witches?" (*Encounter*, December, 1974).

REFERENCES: The d'Ailly quote is on p. 16 of the 1483 edition of *Imago Mundi*. The two passages by Dr. Chanca and the ones by Columbus on the Cannibals and on the women of Matenino are all in R. H. Major, on pp. 25, 30–31, 81–82, and 15 respectively. The two short quotations and the long passage by Vespucci are all in his *Letters*, but I have revised the first of the short quotes and retranslated the long passage in accordance with the Latin and Spanish versions of these given in Navarrete, II, on pp. 152a and 163–164, respectively. The "Grand Feminie" is in Arber, p. xxxiii; and the Caminha description of some women of Brazil is in *The Voyage of Cabral*, pp. 20–21. Michelet's "monstrueux sacrements" is on p. 120 of the French edition cited of *La Sorcière*; and the identification of Zoroaster with Ham is to be found on p. 15a of the *Malleus Maleficarum*, Summers translation. The two passages from the *Acts of Thomas*, from "the Sixth Act" and "the Seventh Act," respectively, are on pp. 390 and 394 of *The Apocryphal New Testament*; the "black, sharp-faced" devil of St. Bartholomew is on p. 468 of the same volume as part of "The Apostolic History of Pseudo-Abdias, Book VII: St. Bartholomew," and the version of it in *The Golden Legend* is on p. 482 of the latter book. The quotation from Alice Kyteler's trial is on p. 3 of the *Proceedings*. The first few references to the Pigafetta narrative are from the 1525 French edition: "grabbed it": p. 9; long breasts: p. 13; "those who sail . . . on account of custom": p. 6. The remaining Pigafetta quotes are from the Eden translation in Arber: "He was of good corporature": p. 251; "giant of somewhat greater stature . . . to his company": p. 251; Magellan's deceit: p. 252; "On a time": p. 252; "They say that": p. 252. Caliban's reference to Setebos is in *The Tempest*, I, ii, 372–373.

CHAPTER 10: The End of Prester John. Two classic works on Jewish and Marrano history in Portugal are Alexandre Herculano, *History of the Origin and Establishment of the Inquisition in Portugal,* translated from the Portuguese by John C. Branner (Stanford, 1926; New York, 1972); and J. Mendes dos Remedios, *Os Judeus em Portugal* (2 vols., Lisbon, 1895–1928). On Vasco da Gama, the source volumes I used were *A Journal of the First Voyage of Vasco da Gama, 1497–1499,* translated and edited by E. G. Ravenstein (*HS,* 1898; New York, n.d.); and Gaspar Correa, *The Three Voyages of Vasco da Gama,* translated and edited by Henry E. J. Stanley (*HS,* 1869; New York, n.d.); one should also read Luis de Camoens's epic poem, *Os Lusíadas* ("The Lusiads" — there are many translations in and out of print), for the making of the da Gama voyage into a Portuguese national myth. On the Portuguese in Africa, I used the following editions of source narratives: *Europeans in West Africa, 1450–1560,* translated and edited by J. W. Blake (*HS,* 1942; Liechtenstein, 1975); Francisco Álvares, *The Prester John of the Indies,* translated by Lord Stanley of Alderley, revised and edited, with additional material, by C. F. Beckingham and G. W. B. Huntingford (2 vols., *HS,* 1961; 2 vols. in 1, Liechtenstein, 1975) — an edition of Lord Stanley's translation that supersedes the one published by the Hakluyt Society in 1881.

REFERENCES: The two quotations from Zacuto — "Time without limit" and "In that year" — are, respectively, from pp. 227a and 227b of the *Yuhasin.* The passage by Ruy de Pina is in Blake, pp. 86–87; and the chronicler's description, "It caused Manuel . . . heart-rending scenes," is in Lindo, pp. 326–327. The passages in Correa on Zacuto are located as follows: "Because it was fitting": p. 17; "good science . . . discovery of India": pp. 18–19; "Sire": pp. 24–25; "received from him much information": p. 59; "died in the error": p. 25. The description of Gaspar da Gama's first appearance is on p. 84 of the *Journal of the First Voyage,* but see also Correa, p. 247. The quotations from Álvares are located as follows: "It is unbelievable": pp. 320–321; "travelled by land": p. 375; "was given a wife": pp. 375–376. Those from Duarte Pacheco Pereira: "For a poor horse": p. 86; "The inhabitants": p. 89; "A great multitude": p. 62; "almost beasts": p. 2; "Many of the ancients": p. 136.

CHAPTER 11: Isles Far Off. On the general history of Spanish colonialism in this period, two standard works are: C. H. Haring, *The Spanish Empire in America* (New York, 1947; 1963); and Salvador de Madariaga, *The Rise of the Spanish American Empire* (New York, 1947; 1965). Specifically for the colonial history of the West Indies, pertaining to other powers as well as Spain, the classic work is A. P. Newton, *The European*

Nations in the West Indies (London, 1933; New York, 1967), which is part of the old Pioneer Histories Series, along with Edgar Prestage. Two other volumes in that series are valuable for the history of discovery and conquest dealt with in this and subsequent chapters: F. A. Kirkpatrick, *The Spanish Conquistadores* (London, 1934; New York, 1969); and John Bartlet Brebner, *The Explorers of North America, 1492–1806* (London, 1933; New York, 1964). On the pro-Indian reform movement, the best modern work is Lewis Hanke, *The Spanish Struggle for Justice in the Conquest of America* (Philadelphia, 1949). The best modern account of the *encomienda* is Lesley Byrd Simpson, *The Encomienda in New Spain* (Berkeley, 1966).

Among the source works used for this chapter, in addition to the Mac-Nutt translation of *De Orbe Novo,* and Las Casas's *Historia de las Indias,* both already cited, were Fray Ramón Pané, *Relación acerca de las antigüedades de los Indios,* edited by José Juan Arrom (Mexico City, 1947); and Bartolomé de las Casas, *Brevísima relación de la destruición de las Indias* (in *BAE,* Vol. CX, which is Volume V of the *Obras escogidas de Fray Bartolomé de las Casas*), of which there are various English translations.

REFERENCES: The quotations from Fray Ramón Pané are in the *Relación* as follows: "a poor hermit": p. 21; "these ignorant people": p. 47; the Taino prophecy: p. 48. The Guanche prophecy is on p. 54 of Fray Alonso de Espinosa, *The Guanches of Tenerife,* translated and edited by Clements Markham (*HS,* 1907; Liechtenstein, 1972); and the Moluccan prophecy is in *De Orbe Novo* (MacNutt translation), II, 161. All the other passages quoted from *De Orbe Novo* are also in the MacNutt translation: "And in this": I, 176; "debauchees . . . as such was honored": I, 142; "It is gold alone": I, 181; "Each industrious Spaniard": I, 181–182; "Yet amidst all these marvels": I, 376; "It is stated": II, 254–255; "Thus perished": II, 270–271. Las Casas's remark, "without compass or chart," is from the *Brevísima relación,* as quoted by Simpson, in *Encomienda,* p. 179.

CHAPTER 12: Interlude: In a Garden. The definitive edition of *La Celestina* is the one edited for the *Colección "Clásicos Hispánicos"* by Manuel Críado de Val and D. G. Trotter (Madrid, 1965); I used the reprint of this published by Editorial Bruguera (Barcelona, 1974), edited by Angeles Cardona de Gibert, and my page references are to this latter volume. There are numerous translations of *La Celestina,* which has been widely known in English since the sixteenth century as *The Spanish Bawd;* a good recent one, under that title, is by J. M. Cohen (Baltimore,

1964). Among the questions pertaining to this mystifying work that have been debated for centuries is: is it a play or a novel? In any case, it is *sui generis*, and I have preferred sidestepping the question by calling the book a "romance in dialogues."

There also are various editions of *Amadís de Gaula*, but it appears conveniently between the same covers as Montalvo's *Las Sergas de Esplandian* in Vol. XL of the *BAE*, *Libros de Caballerías*.

The literature on *La Celestina* is vast, but I confined myself to Stephen Gilman, *The Art of "La Celestina"* (Madison, 1956), and the same author's *Spain of Fernando de Rojas* (Princeton, 1972); María Rosa Lida de Malkiel, *La Originalidad artística de La Celestina* (Buenos Aires, 1962; 1970); and Fernando Garrido Pallardó, *Los Problemas de "Calisto y Melibea"* (Madrid, 1957); as well as a fine chapter on *La Celestina* in Gerald Brenan, *The Literature of the Spanish People* (New York, 1967).

REFERENCES: The quotations from *La Celestina* are in the Bruguera edition as follows: "Entering a garden . . . human heart": pp. 71–73; poem with acrostic: pp. 61–64; "Surely, if the fires . . . and I serve Melibea": p. 76; the girdle: p. 158; "For whom did I": p. 316; "If he wants": p. 276. Gerald Brenan's reference to "the raciest conversation" is on p. 133 of his book, cited above. Montalvo's description of the women of "California" is on p. 539b of *Libros de Caballerías*.

CHAPTER 13: Amadis of Mexico. Among modern works, one must always begin with that great classic of American literature, William H. Prescott's *The Conquest of Mexico* (various editions; I used the Modern Library one, New York, n.d.). I also used Salvador de Madariaga, *Hernán Cortés* (Buenos Aires, 1973); Lesley Byrd Simpson, *Many Mexicos* (Berkeley, 1941; 1974); and Benjamin Keen's remarkable study, *The Aztec Image in Western Thought* (New Brunswick, 1971). The source literature is as dramatic as nonfiction writing has ever been: Bernal Díaz del Castillo, *Historia verdadera de la conquista de Nueva España* (of the many editions, I used the one in the Colección Austral, Madrid, 1968); Francisco López de Gómara, *Historia general de las Indias* (2 vols., Barcelona, 1966), which, in its part dealing with the Conquest of Mexico, has been translated by Lesley Byrd Simpson under the title *Cortés: The Life of the Conqueror by his Secretary* (Berkeley, 1966); Hernán Cortés, *Cartas de relación* (Mexico City, 1971), which has recently been translated by A. R. Pagden under the title *Hernán Cortés: Letters from Mexico* (New York, 1971); "The Anonymous Conqueror," that is, an unknown member and recorder of the Cortés expedition, *Narrative of Some Things of New Spain*, translated and edited by Marshall H. Saville (New York,

1917; 1969); Pascual de Andagoya, *Narrative of the Proceedings of Pedrarias Dávila*, translated and edited by Clements R. Markham (*HS*, 1865; New York, n.d.); *The Discovery of Yucatán by Francisco Hernández de Córdoba*, edited and translated by Henry R. Wagner (New York, 1942; 1969); and by the same editor and translator, *The Discovery of New Spain in 1518 by Juan de Grijalva* (New York, 1942; 1969).

REFERENCES: Prescott on young Cortés's idleness: p. 128 of the Modern Library edition. Gómara on Cortés's amorous adventure is in the *Historia*, II, 10. Balboa's exclamation, "What is this Francisco?" is given, among other places, in the Hakluyt Society edition of the Andagoya *Narrative*, p. 21n. Bernal Díaz's "book of Amadis" passage is on p. 178 of the *Historia verdadera*. The remaining quotations are from Cortés's *Cartas*: "Montezuma came": p. 51b; "Long ago": p. 52a; "we have always believed": p. 52; "The gold and other things": p. 162b.

CHAPTER 14: Bartolomé de las Casas. There has yet to be a complete edition of Las Casas's multitudinous works, some of which are only just finding print in our own day. The five volumes of his *Obras escogidas* in the *BAE* (Vols. XCV, XCVI, CV, CVI, and CX) contain the *Historia de las Indias* — although I have used the more authoritative edition of this cited under Chapter 6 — the *Apologética historia*, the *Brevísima relación*, and numerous shorter writings. There also are Spanish translations in print of certain of his Latin works, such as *Del único modo de atraer a todos los pueblos a la verdadera religión*, translated by Atenogenes Santamaría (Madrid, 1958); and the *Apología* — Las Casas's defense of the Indians at the debate with Sepúlveda in 1550 — translated into Spanish by Ángel Losada (Madrid, 1968), and into English by Stafford Poole under the title *In Defense of the Indians* (De Kalb, Ill., 1974). A one-volume English translation and abridgement of the *History of the Indies* was put out by Andrée M. Collard (New York, 1971), with an interesting introduction and short bibliography.

Of the considerable literature on Las Casas, I made special use of: Ángel Losada, *Fray Bartolomé de las Casas a la luz de la moderna crítica historica* (Madrid, 1970); Ramón Menéndez Pidal, *El Padre las Casas: Su doble personalidad* (Madrid, 1963), a demonstration of a forcefulness of personality on Las Casas's part so great that it can reach through the centuries and cause a great scholar to lose his objectivity in a fit of anger; Manuel Giménez Fernández, *Bartolomé de las Casas* (3 vols., Seville, 1949–1960), an unfinished work of staggering proportions; Henry R. Wagner (with Helen Rand Parish), *The Life and Writings of Bartolomé de las Casas* (Albuquerque, 1967); and Manuel José Quintana, *Fray Bartolomé de las Casas,* the classic nineteenth-century study. An indispensable monograph is Lewis Hanke's *Aristotle and the American Indians: A Study in Race Prejudice in the Modern World* (Bloomington, 1959), which is on the Sepúlveda disputation.

REFERENCES: The song "Mira Nero" appears in Las Casas, *Obras escogidas,* V, 148b; Prescott, p. 274n; and *Celestina,* 75. Las Casas's New Christian identity has been held by such scholars as Américo Castro and Manuel Giménez Fernández; the 1510 list of New Christians of Seville was discovered by Claudio Guillén and published in his article "Un padrón de conversos sevillanos (1510)," in *Bulletin Hispanique,* 65 (1963): 49–98. The quotations from Las Casas's *Historia de las Indias* are as follows: "We now have arrived": I, 27; "It is the custom of Divine Providence": I, 28–29; "It was customary": II, 536; Narváez–Las Casas exchange: II, 536; "began to ponder": III, 92–93. Cecil Roth on *casa* is in the preface to Madariaga, *Columbus* (1967 edition), p. xi. Las Casas's remark that "the same law" applies to Negro and Indian alike is quoted in Prescott, p. 204. The remarks on "Negroes or other slaves" and "Negro slaves" are in *Obras,* V, 9b and 34a, respectively. "The only way" is quoted in Losada, *Las Casas,* p. 167. The passage on Hatuey is in *Obras,* V, 142b. The Inquisition's condemnation of the *Brief Relation* is in Kamen, *Spanish Inquisition,* p. 108.

CHAPTER 15: *Estévanico's Revenge.*

There is a good account of Estévanico in Herbert Eugene Bolton, *Coronado, Knight of Pueblos and Plains* (Albuquerque, 1949; 1971). The best histories of the Negro in Spanish America are Rolando Mellafe, *Breve historia de la esclavitud en America Latina* (Mexico City, 1973); and Leslie B. Rout, Jr., *The African Experience in Spanish America, 1502 to the Present Day* (Cambridge, England, 1976). The source materials for this chapter were Frederic W. Hodge, editor, *Spanish Explorers in the Southern United States, 1528–1543* (ON, 1907; 1965); and F. R. and A. F. Bandelier, *The Journey of Álvar Núñez Cabeza de Vaca* (New York, 1905), which contains, in the appendix, Richard Hakluyt's translation of the Fray Marcos narrative.

REFERENCES: The passage from *El Conde Lucanor* is on p. 46 of the Colección Austral edition (Buenos Aires, 1966); and the Mandeville passage is on pp. 113–114 of the Dover edition cited under Chapter 3. Zorita's references to Black slaves harassing Indians are found, for example, on pp. 248 and 257 of his *The Lords of New Spain,* translated by

Benjamin Keen (London, 1965). The quotations from Cabeza de Vaca's narrative are all from Hodge: "We possessed great influence": p. 107; "we passed through": p. 107; "They were willing": p. 114; "Even to the last": p. 115; "Among other things": p. 95. The Fray Marcos quotes are all from the appendix to the Bandelier volume: "I, Fray Marcos": p. 203; "I commanded . . . a great cross": pp. 207–208; "a great cross high as a man . . . these seven cities": pp. 208–209; "in like sort": p. 222; "Here met us . . . meat or drink": pp. 223–224; "bloody . . . lamentation": p. 225; "when the sun": pp. 225–226. The quotes from Castañeda are in Hodge: "For three days": p. 289; "Besides these other reasons": pp. 289–290.

CHAPTER 16: Friars and Lost Tribes. The best modern work on the friars in sixteenth-century Mexico is Robert Ricard, *The Spiritual Conquest of Mexico*, translated from the French by Lesley Byrd Simpson (Berkeley, 1966); another indispensable work on the subject is John Leddy Phelan, *The Millennial Kingdom of the Franciscans in the New World* (second edition, revised, Berkeley, 1970), which, though primarily an account of the life and writings of Fray Gerónimo de Mendieta (1525–1604), deals with much of the spiritual history of the Mexican mission in that epoch. Useful for the general Spanish history of the period is R. Trevor Davies, *The Golden Century of Spain, 1501–1621* (London, 1937; New York, 1961); and for the general religious history, A. G. Dickens, *The Counter Reformation* (New York, 1969).

The literary sources for the chapter were: Motolinia, *Memoriales* and *Historia de los Indios de la Nueva España* (*BAE*, CCXL); Diego de Landa, *Relación de las cosas de Yucatán*, edited and with an introduction by Ángel M. Garibay K. (Biblioteca Porrúa, 13; Mexico City, 1973); Bernardino de Sahagún, *Historia general de las cosas de Nueva España*, edited and with an introduction by Ángel M. Garibay K. (4 vols., Biblioteca Porrúa, 8–11; Mexico City, 1969); and Diego Durán, *Historia de las Indias de Nueva España e Islas de la Tierra Firme*, edited and with an introduction by Ángel M. Garibay K. (2 vols., Biblioteca Porrúa, 36–37; Mexico City, 1967).

REFERENCES: I owe the felicitous phrase "spiritual conquest of Mexico" to the title of Ricard's book, as translated by Simpson. Motolinia's letter is in the appendix to the *BAE* edition of his works, pp. 335–345. On the possible New Christian origins of both Sahagún and Durán, see Garibay's introductions to his editions of their works: Sahagún, I, 21; and Durán, I, xv. Durán's story of the Indian and the *tiánguiz* is in Vol. I of the cited edition of his writings, pp. 179–180.

CHAPTER 17: The Passion of Luis de Carvajal. Useful for the general background of this chapter were Boleslao Lewin, *La Inquisición en Hispanoamerica* (Buenos Aires, 1967); and Jacob R. Marcus, *The Colonial American Jew, 1492–1776* (3 vols., Detroit, 1970). On Luis de Carvajal, the biography to consult is Martin A. Cohen, *The Martyr* (Philadelphia, 1973); and the source collection I used is *The Enlightened: The Writings of Luis de Carvajal, El Mozo,* edited and translated by Seymour B. Liebman (Coral Gables, 1967).

REFERENCES: All quotes are from *The Enlightened:* "The Winds": p. 56; "it must have been": p. 56; "to the house": p. 56; "I came to know": p. 57; "I watched her": p. 68; "Upon arriving": p. 118; "You have shown me": p. 119; "I asked in my poor manner": pp. 89–90.

CHAPTER 18: France Discovers the Noble Savage. On the general background, I used the classic work, James Westfall Thompson, *The Wars of Religion in France* (Chicago, 1909); as well as Ralph Roeder, *Catherine de' Medici and the Lost Revolution* (second edition, abridged, New York, 1964). On the French discovery and colonization of the Americas, I used another classic work, Francis Parkman, *Pioneers of France in the New World* (Williamstown, 1970); as well as W. J. Eccles, *France in America* (New York, 1972). For the early exploration of North America, a very important collection of studies is David Beers Quinn, *England and the Discovery of America, 1481–1620* (New York, 1974).

Source volumes used were Henry S. Burrage, editor, *Early English and French Voyages (Chiefly from Hakluyt), 1534–1608 (ON,* 1906; 1967); and Stefan Lorant, *The New World: The First Pictures of America* (New York, 1946; 1965); as well as the original volumes of André Thevet, *Les Singularitéz de la France antarctique* (Paris, 1558), and Jean de Léry, *Histoire d'un voyage faict en la terre du Brésil* (Geneva, 1577). Literary sources for the chapter were François Rabelais, *Gargantua and Pantagruel,* translated by Jacques Le Clercq (New York, 1944); and Michel de Montaigne, *Oeuvres complètes,* in *Bibliothèque de la Pléiade* (Paris, 1962), though for the quotations in this chapter I have used John Florio's translation of the *Essays,* taken in this case from the *Portable Elizabethan Reader,* edited by Hiram Haydn (New York, 1946).

REFERENCES: The quotation from the Spanish world-map of 1544 is on p. 207 of *The Cabot Voyages and Bristol Discovery under Henry VII,* edited by J. A. Williamson (*HS,* 1962). The Celtic cradle song is in Nora Chadwick, *The Celts* (Baltimore, 1970), p. 123. The Cartier quotes are in Burrage: "If the soil": pp. 9–10; "There are men": p. 10; "and all the way we went": pp. 57–58. The le Moyne passage is in Lorant, p. 36. The two Montaigne passages, appearing in the *Pléiade* edition on pp. 212–213 and 888 respectively, are quoted from the Florio translation in the *Elizabethan Reader*, pp. 92–94 and 96 respectively.

CHAPTER 19: *England Takes on the Ocean Sea.* On the general background, I used the two volumes of the *Oxford History of England* that covers this period: J. D. Mackie, *The Earlier Tudors, 1485–1558* (1952; 1966), and J. B. Black, *The Reign of Elizabeth, 1558–1603* (1936; 1965); as well as J. E. Neale, *Queen Elizabeth I* (London, 1934; New York, 1957), and A. L. Rowse's prolific writings on the epoch, especially *The Expansion of Elizabethan England* (New York, 1955), and *The Elizabethans and America* (New York, 1959). On English geography and voyages in this period, I used E. G. R. Taylor, *Tudor Geography, 1485–1583* (London, 1930; New York, 1968); George Bruner Parks, *Richard Hakluyt and the English Voyages* (New York, 1928; 1961); J. A. Williamson, *Hawkins of Plymouth* (London, 1949; 1969); the same author's *Age of Drake* (London, 1938), in the Pioneer Histories series; and George Malcolm Thomson, *Sir Francis Drake* (New York, 1972).

The source collections used were all reprints of Richard Hakluyt's writings: *Divers Voyages Touching the Discovery of America* (London, 1582; Readex Microprint, 1966); *The Original Writings and Correspondence of the Two Richard Hakluyts*, edited by E. G. R. Taylor (2 vols., HS, 1935; 2 vols. in 1, Liechtenstein, 1967); and *The Principall Navigations, Voiages, and Discoveries of the English Nation, made by Sea or over Land to the most remote and farthest distant quarters of the earth . . .*, of which the definitive modern edition is the one published by James MacLehose and Sons (12 vols., Glasgow, 1903–1905), reprinted in a slightly abridged form by Everyman's Library (8 vols., London and New York, 1907; 1962) — I used the latter.

REFERENCES: The passages on Saint Brendan are in *Lives of the Saints*, translated and edited by J. F. Webb (Baltimore, 1965), pp. 38–39. The Dunbar poem is in *The Poems of William Dunbar*, edited by W. Mackay Mackenzie (London, 1932; 1970), pp. 66–67. The Richard Eden and William Hawkins passages are in Blake, *Europeans in West Africa*, pp. 338 and 299–300, respectively. All the remaining quotations are from the Everyman edition of Hakluyt's *Voyages:* "that Negroes were very good merchandise": VII, 5; "where he received . . . that country yieldeth": VII, 5–6; "with this prey": VII, 6; "These people": VII, 11–12; Miles Philips: VI, 307; George Best on "Their sullen and desperate nature": V, 272; "They are very shamefast": V, 272; "with a suckling child": V, 217; "for so much as we could perceive": V, 218; "These people I judge": V, 270–271; "They are of the color": V, 271; "I myself . . . nature of the clime": V, 180; "none but a father": V, 181–182; "our people of Meta Incognita": V, 180; "a cursed, dry": V, 182.

CHAPTER 20: Roanoke. In addition to works cited under the previous chapter, I consulted: Máire and Conor Cruise O'Brien, *A Concise History of Ireland* (New York, 1972); and Muriel Rukeyser, *The Traces of Thomas Hariot* (New York, 1971). The major source collection for this chapter is David Beers Quinn, editor, *The Roanoke Voyages, 1584–1590* (2 vols., HS, 1955; 2 vols. in 1, Liechtenstein, 1967); but I also used Louis B. Wright and Elaine W. Fowler, editors, *West and by North: North America Seen through the Eyes of Its Seafaring Discoverers* (New York, 1971); and, for the John White drawings, Stefan Lorant's *The New World,* cited under Chapter 18 (Lorant's reproductions are complete, but for truer renderings one should look at Paul Hulton and D. B. Quinn, *The American Drawings of John White, 1577–1590,* published by the British Museum and the University of North Carolina in 1964).

REFERENCES: The quotations from Edmund Spenser's *View of the Present State of Ireland* are from the edition of his works published in New York in 1903 by T. Y. Crowell: "reducing of that savage nation" is on p. 758a, "Out of every corner" is on p. 804b; the Camden passage on Shan O'Neal is quoted in Taylor, *Two Hakluyts,* p. 71. David Ingram's narrative is in Wright and Fowler, pp. 138–146. The quotations from Edward Hayes are in Hakluyt's *Voyages,* VI, 3–4. Hakluyt's *Discourse of Western Planting* is in Taylor, *Two Hakluyts:* "Now if we" is on p. 241. All but one of the remaining quotes are from Quinn, *Roanoke Voyages:* "there came to us . . . as any of Europe": pp. 98–99; "When he came to the place": p. 99; "a village of nine houses": p. 107; "We found the people": p. 108; the killing of Pemisapan: pp. 287–288; on Joachim Ganz: p. 196n; Hariot's "The werowance with whom we dwelt": p. 377; "Most things": pp. 375–376; "some of our company": p. 381; "The cause of their ignorance": p. 323; "alteration . . . justly deserved": p. 381; John White's "I greatly joyed": p. 616. The van Meteren quote on the Armada is in Hakluyt's *Voyages,* II, 401.

CHAPTER 21: Dramatic Interlude. The whole bibliography is in the references. From *Tamburlaine the Great,* Part I: "Of Tamburlaine": I, i,

36–38; "With milk-white harts": I, ii, 98–101; and from Part II: "And I have marched": I, iii, 186–202; "We have revolted": I, i, 61–64; "And with an host": I, iii, 141–147. From *The Jew of Malta:* "As for myself": II, iii, 179–200; "Where wast thou born": II, iii, 132–134; "Why, this is something": II, iii, 218–220; "Welcome . . . jeers at him!": V, vi, 55–56; "thy inherent sin . . . for their transgressions?": I, ii, 110–116; "It's no sin": II, iii, 314–317. From *Titus Andronicus:* "Believe me, Queen": II, iii, 72–79; "Let fools do good": III, i, 205–206: "To mount aloft": II, i, 13; "Well, God give her": IV, ii, 63–71; "Coal-black is better": IV, ii, 99–103. From *The Merchant of Venice:* "Mislike me not": II, i, 1–12; "the condition of a saint": I, ii, 144–145; "Let all of his complexion": II, vii, 79; "my daughter is my flesh . . . red wine and Rhenish": III, i, 40–44; "tells me flatly": III, v, 34–35; "Hath not a Jew eyes?": III, i, 61–69. From *Othello:* "I have done the state": V, ii, 339; "that in Aleppo once": V, ii, 352–356; "my wits": I, iii, 363–364; "the souls of all my tribe": III, iii, 175; "She is abus'd": I, iii, 60–64; "the thick-lips": I, i, 66; "the gross clasps": I, i, 127; "Even now": I, i, 88–89; "Not to affect": III, iii, 229–233. The varied quotes are from Jonson, Marston, and Chapman, *Eastward Ho,* III, iii, 20–26; Shakespeare's *Twelfth Night,* III, ii, 83–85; *The Merry Wives of Windsor,* I, iii, 76; and *Othello,* I, iii, 143–145. From *The Tempest:* "still-vexed Bermoothes": I, ii, 229; "I' the commonwealth": II, i, 147–156; "to excel the Golden Age": II, i, 168; "We cannot miss him": I, ii, 311–313; "Thou poisonous slave": I, ii, 319–320; "Thou strokedst me": I, ii, 333–338; "You taught me language": I, ii, 363–365; "For I am all": I, ii, 341–342; "retire me": V, i, 310–311. The Michael Drayton quote is from the "Ode to the Virginian Voyage," stanza 4.

CHAPTER 22: L'Acadie. The best recent biography of Champlain is Samuel Eliot Morison, *Samuel de Champlain: Father of New France* (Boston, 1972). A good recent work on the general background is Roland Mousnier, *The Assassination of Henry IV* (New York, 1973). On the French in Canada, I used the works cited under Chapter 18, as well as John Fiske's classic, *New France and New England* (Boston, 1902). The source works used were W. L. Grant, editor, *Voyages of Samuel de Champlain, 1604–1618* (ON, 1907, 1967); H. P. Biggar, editor, *The Works of Samuel de Champlain* (6 vols., Toronto, 1922–1936); and Marc Lescarbot, *Histoire de la Nouvelle France* (3 vols., Toronto, 1907–1914).

REFERENCES: Champlain's "They are for the most part" is in *Works,* I, 111–112, translated by H. H. Langton. Lescarbot's "those men are indeed to be pitied" and his Masque are in his *Histoire,* I, 13, and III, 463ff. Champlain's fight with the Iroquois is in Grant, pp. 164–165.

CHAPTER 23: The Adventures of Captain John Smith. On English history in this period, I was greatly helped by Godfrey Davies, *The Early Stuarts, 1603–1660* (Oxford, 1959; 1967), which is Vol. IX in the *Oxford History of England;* Wallace Notestein, *The English People on the Eve of Colonization, 1603–1630* (New York, 1954; 1962), which is the second volume in the *New American Nation Series;* Carl Bridenbaugh, *Vexed and Troubled Englishmen, 1590–1642* (New York, 1968), which is Vol. I of his *The Beginnings of the American People;* and David Beers Quinn, *Raleigh and the British Empire* (London, 1947; New York, 1962). On Virginia in this period, I used two indispensable works: Charles M. Andrews, *The Colonial Period of American History* (4 vols., New Haven, 1934; 1967), especially, for this chapter, Vol. I; and Wesley Frank Craven, *The Southern Colonies in the Seventeenth Century, 1607–1689* (Baton Rouge, 1949; 1970).

Almost every American generation has produced its books on Captain John Smith, but the beginning point for our own must be Philip L. Barbour, *The Three Worlds of Captain John Smith* (Boston, 1964), an exhaustive, thoughtful study, which I greatly admire even though I thoroughly disagree with its basic positions. A good shorter work, which demonstrates what the position on Smith has become for many academic historians largely owing to Barbour, is Alden T. Vaughan, *American Genesis: Captain John Smith and the Founding of Virginia* (Boston, 1975). Skepticism about Smith has all but vanished, even though there was a time when scholars were more inclined to go along with the kind of demolition job performed on the Pocahontas rescue story by Henry Adams in "Captaine John Smith, Sometime Governour in Virginia, and Admiral of New England," reprinted in Henry Adams, *The Great Secession Winter of 1860–61, and Other Essays,* edited by George E. Hochfield (New York, 1958; 1963).

The source volumes used for this chapter were Captain John Smith, *Works,* edited by Edward Arber (2 vols., Westminster, 1895), which contains other source materials in addition to Smith's writings; Philip L. Barbour, editor, *The Jamestown Voyages under the First Charter, 1606–1609* (2 vols., HS, 1969); Lyon Gardiner Tyler, *Narratives of Early Virginia, 1606–1625* (ON, 1907; 1966); and Samuel M. Bemiss, editor, *The Three Charters of the Virginia Company of London, with Seven Related Documents, 1606–1621* (Williamsburg, Va., 1957).

REFERENCES: In the opening section on Smith, all the quotations are from the Arber edition of his *Works:* "At his entrance before the King": II, 400; "Yet my comfort is": I, 276–277; the autobiography: II, 821–880; "Bashaw Bogall" and his "fair mistress": II, 853; "Bashaw of Nalbrits": II, 854; "Lady Callamata": II, 867; Purchas on Ferneza: II, 852. The Purchas note reads: "Extracted out of a Booke intituled, The warres of *Hungary, Wallachia,* and *Moldavia,* written by *Francisco Ferneza,* a learned Italian, the Princes Secretarie, and translated by Master *Purchas.*" The London Company instructions, containing the warning "not to offend the naturals," is in Barbour, *Jamestown Voyages,* I, 51. So also is the statement that Smith was "suspected for a supposed mutiny": I, 129; the phrase is used by Samuel Purchas, in a note alongside a passage in George Percy's narrative (see below), from which he has obviously made a deletion. Wingfield's haughty remarks about Smith are in his later deposition before the London Company, which is reprinted by Arber among the prefatory material in his edition of Smith's *Works:* I, lxxxix. The changing author's credit on *A true relation* is reprinted in Barbour, *Jamestown Voyages,* I, 166n. Smith's *A true relation* can be found in its entirety in the source collections of Arber, Barbour, and Tyler, with slight textual variations; I have used Tyler: "Arriving at Weramocomoco": p. 48; the preface by "I. H.": p. 31; "I presented him with a compass dial": p. 44; and farther on, "That night passing by Weanock": pp. 34–35.

The two Percy texts are located as follows: "The next day": Barbour, I, 137, and Tyler, pp. 13–14; "Wednesday we went ashore": Barbour, I, 94–95, and Smith, *Works,* Arber ed., I, lii. But they require some bibliographical comment. The first text is from Purchas's edition of the "Observations gathered out of a *Discourse of the Plantation of the Southerne Colonie in Virginia by the English, 1606.* Written by that Honorable Gentleman Master George Percy." This is merely a set of extracts, and is the sole published version of the manuscript of Percy's journal of the expedition, which has all but completely disappeared. The sole surviving portion of the manuscript is the fragment from which the second Percy text was taken — but this, I hasten to add, is my own firm conviction against the consensus of scholars so far. The fragment is an unsigned manuscript that was found in the nineteenth century among the British Colonial State Papers, and which bears the title "A relatyon of the Discovery of our River, from *Iames Forte* into the Maine: made by Captaine *Christofer Newport:* and sincerely written and observed by a gent: of ye Colony." On the basis of a tenuous piece of internal evidence, Arber guessed that the author was Gabriel Archer (Smith, *Works,* I, xl); he assumed it was not Percy, who was present on this expedition upriver, because we already have Percy's *Discourse* covering this period. But a close look at Purchas's edition of the *Discourse* shows a distinct gap for precisely the duration of this expedition, filled in rather incoherently with other material, some of which may also have come from Percy's papers. There are minor stylistic differences between the *Discourse* and this unsigned manuscript, but it is known that Purchas often played free with the texts that he reproduced. If we have here the sole surviving fragment of the Percy manuscript, then, the two essential facts of its history — that Purchas did not use it, and that it has survived — are surely not just coincidental. Purchas let it get out of his hands for some reason, and so it found a safe refuge from the disaster met by all the other Percy material that Purchas had come to possess.

CHAPTER 24: The Adventures of Captain John Smith, Continued.
A useful secondary source for this chapter, in addition to those cited under the previous one, was Philip L. Barbour, *Pocahontas and Her World* (Boston, 1970). Source materials used for this chapter, in addition to those cited under the last, were William Strachey, *The Historie of Travell into Virginia Britania*, edited by Louis B. Wright and Virginia Freund (*HS*, 1953); Samuel Purchas, *Purchas his Pilgrimage* (London, 1613; 1614; 1617), his first geographical compilation, not to be confused with his *Hakluytus Posthumus, or Purchas his Pilgrims* (London, 1625; reprinted in 20 vols. for the Hakluyt Society by James MacLehose and Sons, Glasgow, 1905–1907); Alexander Brown, *The Genesis of the United States* (2 vols., Boston, 1890); Raphe [Ralph] Hamor, *A true discourse of the present estate of Virginia* (London, 1615: reprinted by the Virginia State Library, Richmond, 1957); and George Percy, "A True Relation of the proceedings of moment which have happened in Virginia from . . . 1609 until . . . 1612" (reproduced in *Tyler's Quarterly Historical and Genealogical Magazine*, 3 [1922]:259–282), an undated letter from Percy to his brother the Earl of Northumberland, with an accompanying fragmentary account of events at Jamestown between Smith's departure in 1609 and Percy's in 1612.

REFERENCES: Strachey's kind remark on Smith, "Sure I am," etc., is on pp. 49–50 of his *Historie*. His account of Smith's eyewitness observation is on pp. 96–97, and the corresponding passage in Smith is in Barbour, *Jamestown Voyages*, II, 366–367. For the prefaces to the first three editions of *Purchas his Pilgrimage*, I consulted the originals in the case of the first two; but my quote from the third, "Although in this third edition," is taken from George B. Parks, *Hakluyt*, pp. 225–226. The sources for Smith and Strachey on the young Pocahontas are as follows: "a child of ten": Tyler, *Narratives*, p. 69; "a well-featured": Strachey, *Historie*, p. 72. The sermon by the Reverend William Symonds is quoted from in Brown, *Genesis*, p. 284. John Rolfe's letter, originally appended to Hamor's *A true discourse*, is reproduced in Tyler, *Narratives*, pp. 239–244. The remark about Pocahontas's "tricking up" in London is quoted in Barbour, *Pocahontas*, p. 179, from *The Letters of John Chamberlain*, edited by Norman Egbert McClure (Philadelphia, 1939), II, 56–57. Rolfe's famous sentence, "About the last of August," is in Smith, *Works* (Arber ed.), II, 541; so are the long passage, "Thus have you heard the particulars" (II, 578–579), and Purchas's dedicatory verses (I, 283). Purchas's statement that he obtained the Hakluyt collection "not without hard conditions" is quoted in Parks, *Hakluyt*, p. 226. The prefatory and marginal comments from *Purchas his Pilgrims* are all taken from the MacLehose edition: "Divine things": I, xxxix; "These Savages": XVIII, 413; "How to deal": XVIII, 485; "Civility is not the way": XVIII, 494; "Opechancanough": XVIII, 514; "His Majesty": XVIII, 528; "As for gentlemen": I, xliv; "He was a made man": XVIII, 419; "The rest is omitted": XVIII, 419. Percy's complaint, "that many untruths," etc., is in "A True Relation," *Tyler's . . . Magazine*, 3:259. Purchas's "I rejoice" is in Vol. XX of *Pilgrims*. The passage from Smith's *Advertisements* is in *Works*, II, 955–956, as is Pocahontas's entertainment, II, 436; Purchas's comment on the latter is in *Pilgrims*, XVIII, 426.

CHAPTER 25: Squanto: The Story of a Pilgrim Father. On early New England history, the works consulted were John Gorham Palfrey, *History of New England* (5 vols., Boston, 1865–1890); John Fiske, *The Beginnings of New England* (Boston, 1898); James Truslow Adams, *The Founding of New England* (Boston, 1921; 1949); and Charles Francis Adams, Jr., *Three Episodes in Massachusetts History* (2 vols., Boston, 1896), which contains an excellent chapter on Squanto. Specifically on the Pilgrims, the modern work I used was George F. Willison, *Saints and Strangers* (New York, 1945). And on Anglo-Indian relations in early New England, a fine scholarly work is Alden T. Vaughan, *New England Frontier: Puritans and Indians, 1620–1675* (Boston, 1965).

The source volumes for the chapter were William Bradford, *Of Plymouth Plantation*, edited by William T. Davis (*ON*, 1908; 1952); Dwight B. Heath, editor, *A Journal of the Pilgrims at Plymouth, 1622* (New York, 1969), which is a reprint of *Mourt's Relation*, the collection of anonymous narratives of Plymouth sent back to England for publication in 1622, with a preface signed "G. Mourt." (possibly George Morton); and Edward Arber, editor, *The Story of the Pilgrim Fathers, 1606–1623* (London and Boston, 1897; New York, 1969).

REFERENCES: Smith's passage on Hunt's perfidy is in *Works* (Arber ed.), II, 699. Sir Ferdinando Gorges's remarks on the three Indians are quoted in Rowse, *The Elizabethans and America*, p. 96. The remarks that Samoset "spoke to them in broken English" and that he told them of "another Indian whose name was Squanto" on the afternoon of his first appearance to the English are by Bradford, on p. 110 of his history *Of Plymouth Planta-*

tion; otherwise, the rest of the story down to Squanto's remaining at Plymouth after the signing of the treaty with Massasoit is quoted from *Mourt's Relation,* pp. 50–59 of the Heath edition. Bradford's remarks that Squanto "began to plant their corn" and "continued with them" are on pp. 115–116 and 111 of his history, respectively. The story of the journey to Sowams (also called Pokanoket) by Winslow, Hopkins, and Squanto forms another unsigned narrative in *Mourt's Relation,* pp. 60–68 in the Heath edition, and all the quotes on it are from there; likewise the story of the journey to Nauset to reclaim John Billington (Heath, pp. 69–72), and that of Corbitant's revolt (Heath, pp. 73–76). Bradford's description of Hobomock as "a proper lusty man," and of the scuffle in which Corbitant "offered to stab" him is on p. 119 of his history. The remaining history, of Squanto's suspect behavior and his demise, is primarily from Edward Winslow's *Good News from New England,* published in 1624 and reprinted in Arber's *Story of the Pilgrim Fathers,* as follows: "signified to the governor": p. 519; "which, at our pleasure": p. 528; "the God of the English": p. 528; "But we had no sooner": pp. 523–524; "Thus, by degrees": p. 525; "cut off . . . according as he thought meet": p. 527; "at the instant when our governor": p. 527; "yet their joy was mixed": p. 536; God "had otherwise disposed": p. 536. Bradford's contributions to the story are that Squanto "sought his own ends": p. 128; "All things being provided" for Squanto's final expedition: p. 141; and his description of Squanto's death: p. 141.

CHAPTER 26: *Light and Vain Persons.* In addition to works listed for the previous chapter I used these source volumes: William Wood, *New England's Prospect* (Boston: Prince Society, 1865; New York, 1967); and Thomas Morton, *New English Canaan* (Boston: Prince Society, 1883; New York, 1967).

REFERENCES: The prefatory remarks by Winslow in his *Good News from New England* are in Arber as follows: "upright life and conversation": pp. 515–516; "light and vain persons": p. 512; "what great offense": p. 516. The story of Weston's colony comes from Winslow's *Good News* and Bradford's history *Of Plymouth Plantation,* as follows. Bradford: "rude fellows": p. 134; "It may be thought strange": p. 142; "In the end": p. 142. And Winslow: "one of Master Weston's company": pp. 563–564; the trip to the ailing Massasoit: pp. 549–550; "Tell him we know it": p. 568; "where they would whet": p. 568; "bragged of the excellency of his knife . . . for the present": p. 568; the fight in Standish's room: p. 569. My account of Morton comes entirely from Bradford: "there came over one Captain Wollaston": p. 236; "not finding things to answer": p. 237; "this Morton abovesaid": p. 237; "had little respect among them": p. 237; "fell to a great licentiousness": pp. 237–238; "to maintain this riotous prodigality": pp. 238–239; "the king was dead": pp. 241–242; "resolved to proceed": p. 242; "caused that Maypole to be cut down": p. 238. Morton's passage on the beaver tail is in *New English Canaan*, p. 162; the two remarks on the Indians, pp. 256, 270.

CHAPTER 27: The Massacre of the Pequots. The modern studies consulted, in addition to those cited for Chapter 25, were: Samuel Eliot Morison, *Builders of the Bay Colony* (Boston, 1930; 1958); and Perry Miller, *The New England Mind: The Seventeenth Century* (New York, 1939; Boston, 1961). Source volumes for the chapter were: *Winthrop's Journal: "History of New England," 1630–1649*, edited by James Kendall Hosmer (2 vols., ON, 1908; 1966); Alexander Young, editor, *Chronicles of the First Planters of the Colony of Massachusetts Bay* (Boston, 1846; New York, 1970); *Johnson's Wonder-working Providence*, edited by J. Franklin Jameson (ON, 1910; 1952); Edward Winslow, *Hypocrisie Unmasked* (New York, 1916; 1968); Charles Orr, *History of the Pequot War* (Cleveland, 1897), containing the Mason, Underhill, Vincent, and Gardiner narratives; and *The Complete Writings of Roger Williams* (7 vols., New York, 1973).

REFERENCES: The Thomas More quote is from *The Essential Thomas More*, edited and translated by James J. Greene and John P. Dolan (New York, 1967), p. 61. Higginson's remarks on the Massachusetts Indians are in Young, *Chronicles*, p. 257; Wood's remarks on them and the Pequots are in *New England's Prospect*, pp. 82 and 69 respectively. The Oldham incident is in Winthrop (I, 183–184), as are the first two quotations on the Endicott expedition, "The governor and council" (I, 186) and "When they had spent two days" (I, 188). Gardiner's angry remarks are in the narrative reprinted in Orr, pp. 126 and 122 respectively. Underhill's description of the rest of the Endicott expedition is in his narrative in Orr, pp. 55–60. Gardiner's remark, "and thus began the war," is on p. 127 of Orr, and his story of the taunt, "We are Pequots," is on p. 132. The John Tilley incident is in Winthrop, I, 194, and Roger Williams's mission in his *Complete Writings*, VI, 231–232. Winthrop (I, 193) describes Miantanomo's delegation, and the grisly gift that arrived in February (I, 212); he also tells us of the "general fast" in the churches (I, 208), and of the fact that the two girls kidnapped by the Pequots "had been well used" (I, 219). Mason's remark on the Pequots as "a great people" is in his narrative in Orr, p. 19. The description of Pequots at Saybrook putting on English clothes and jeering is Underhill's, in Orr, p. 60.

The description of the attack upon Mystic Fort is provided by its two commanders, Mason and Underhill, in their accounts reprinted in Orr. Mason's description of the Narragansetts' taunt is on p. 25, and the attempt to persuade them to stand by and watch is on p. 27. Underhill's description of the assault and his comments on Pequot courage are on p. 80, his horror at seeing "so many souls lie gasping on the ground" on p. 81. Mason's comment that it was "the just judgment of God" is on p. 30. Bradford's secondhand observations about the scene are in his *Plymouth*, p. 339.

Of the postmortem remarks about the slaughter, Underhill's are in Orr, pp. 80–81, and Mason's in the same volume, pp. 35 and 44. Bradford's remark that "the victory seemed a sweet sacrifice" is on pp. 339–340 of his book, Winslow's pronouncement of "God's just judgment" is on p. 72 of his *Hypocrisie Unmasked,* Philip Vincent's remarks are on p. 103 in Orr, and Johnson's feelings are expressed on pp. 170 and 182 of his *Wonderworking Providence.* Roger Williams's objection is in his *Complete Writings,* VI, 47. Winthrop's story of Captain Pierce's return is in his *Journal,* I, 260.

CHAPTER 28: *Islands of the Sable Venus.* Some useful modern works were Carl and Roberta Bridenbaugh, *No Peace Beyond the Line: The English in the Caribbean, 1624–1690* (New York, 1972), which is Vol. II of their *Beginnings of the American People;* Charles R. Boxer, *The Dutch Seaborne Empire* (New York, 1965); Charles Verlinden, *The Beginnings of Modern Colonization,* translated by Yvonne Freccero (Ithaca, 1970), a splendid collection of essays; K. G. Davies, *The Royal African Company* (New York, 1970); and two works already cited that must be mentioned again here — A. P. Newton, *The European Nations in the West Indies,* and Winthrop D. Jordan, *White Over Black: American Attitudes toward the Negro, 1550–1812.*

Source volumes consulted were Richard Jobson, *The Golden Trade* (Teignemouth, 1904); A. O. Exquemelin, *The Buccaneers of America,* translated by Alexis Brown (Baltimore, 1969); Samuel Sewall, *The Selling of Joseph: A Memorial,* included in the complete edition of *The Diary of Samuel Sewall,* edited by M. Halsey Thomas (2 vols., New York, 1973); and Bryan Edwards, *The History, Civil and Commercial, of the British Colonies in the West Indies* (2 vols. in 1, New York, 1972), which, since Edwards was a West Indian planter himself, can be considered a source for our purposes, even though it was published in 1793, somewhat after our period.

REFERENCES: From Jobson, *Golden Trade:* "We were a people": p. 112; Fulbies: p. 46; Gambians and music: p. 133; "For undoubtedly": pp. 65–

66. From Edwards, *West Indies:* "The accusation most generally brought": II, 21–22; "deceased friend . . . genuine poetry": II, 26; "The Sable Venus": II, 27–32. Sewall's "extravasate blood": *The Selling of Joseph,* in Thomas, ed., *Diary,* p. 1118. The Luis Brandão letter is in Elizabeth Donnan, *Documents* (cited under Chapter 4), I, 123. The Barbados statute of 1636 is quoted in Jordan, *White Over Black,* p. 64.

CHAPTER 29: Slavery Comes to North America. On the general background of this period, in addition to works cited in previous chapters, I used Sir George Clark, *The Later Stuarts, 1660–1714* (Oxford, 1934; 1965), which is Vol. X of the *Oxford History of England;* and two classic works by Philip A. Bruce, *Social Life in Virginia in the Seventeenth Century* (New York, 1907; Williamstown, 1968) and the *Economic History of Virginia in the Seventeenth Century* (2 vols., New York, 1895). On white servitude in the colonial period, the standard work is Abbot Emerson Smith, *Colonists in Bondage: White Servitude and Convict Labor in America, 1607–1776* (Chapel Hill, 1947; New York, 1971); and on Indian slavery, Almon Wheeler Lauber, *Indian Slavery in Colonial Times Within the Present Limits of the United States* (New York, 1913; 1969). On Black slavery, some of the standard works for this period are Ulrich B. Phillips, *American Negro Slavery* (New York, 1918; Baton Rouge, 1969), as well as his *Life and Labor in the Old South* (Boston, 1929; 1963); James Curtis Ballagh, *A History of Slavery in Virginia* (Baltimore, 1902; New York, 1968); G. H. Moore, *Notes on the History of Slavery in Massachusetts* (New York, 1866); and Lorenzo Johnston Greene, *The Negro in Colonial New England* (New York, 1942; 1968), which deals with the free Negro as well as the slave. On the free Negro in the South in this period, the classic work is John H. Russell, *The Free Negro in Virginia, 1619–1865* (Baltimore, 1913; New York, 1969). On the general history of Blacks in this and subsequent periods, the most distinguished work is John Hope Franklin, *From Slavery to Freedom: A History of Black Americans* (New York, 1947, and subsequent editions). On the comparison between the slave systems of the United States and Latin America, the two outstanding studies are Frank Tannenbaum, *Slave and Citizen: The Negro in the Americas* (New York, 1946), and Herbert S. Klein, *Slavery in the Americas: A Comparative Study of Virginia and Cuba* (Chicago, 1967; New York, 1971).

Source volumes used were Robert Beverley, *The History and Present State of Virginia,* edited by Louis B. Wright (Chapel Hill, 1947); Clayton Colman Hall, editor, *Narratives of Early Maryland, 1633–1684* (*ON,* 1910; 1953); Alexander S. Salley, Jr., editor, *Narratives of Early Carolina,*

1650–1708 (*ON,* 1911; 1953); Leslie H. Fishel, Jr., and Benjamin Quarles, *The Negro American: A Documentary History* (New York, 1967); Louis Ruchames, editor, *Racial Thought in America: From the Puritans to Abraham Lincoln* (Amherst, 1969); and Stanley Feldstein, editor, *The Poisoned Tongue: A Documentary History of American Racism and Prejudice* (New York, 1972).

REFERENCES: On the John Rolfe sentence, see the notes for Chapter 24. William Wood's story about a "Black-moor" is in *New England's Prospect,* p. 86. Downing's letter to Winthrop is in Donnan, *Documents,* III, 8. The view of Indians "as being of the cursed race of Ham" is in Winthrop's *Journal,* II, 18. For Samuel Sewall's "extravasate blood," see notes to the previous chapter; Saffin's reply is in Ruchames, *Racial Thought,* p. 55. The Massachusetts law of 1641 is quoted in Jordan, *White Over Black,* p. 67, as are the Rhode Island law of 1652, p. 70, and the Hugh Davis sentence, p. 78. Beverley's remark that "Slaves are the Negroes" is in his *History,* p. 271. The John Punch decision is reprinted in Fishe and Quarles, p. 19. The Virginia law of 1662 is reprinted in Feldstein, p. 26. The passage from Spenser's *Faerie Queene* is in Book I, Canto I, stanzas xxi–xxii. The clause on Negro slaves from "The Fundamental Constitutions of Carolina" is quoted by David Brion Davis in his *Problem of Slavery,* p. 118.

CHAPTER 30: A Lost Tribe Discovered in New York. On Montezinos and Manasseh ben Israel, the works used were Manasseh's own *Esperanza de Israel* (Madrid, 1881), and Cecil Roth, *Manasseh ben Israel* (Philadelphia, 1934). On the apocalyptic mood of the era, I consulted William Haller, *The Rise of Puritanism* (New York, 1938; 1957); and Gershom Scholem, *Sabbatai Sevi, The Mystical Messiah,* translated by R. J. Zwi Werblowsky (Princeton, 1973), as well as the seventeenth-century Thomas Thorowgood, *Jews in America, or, Probabilities that those Indians Are Judaical* (London, 1650; 1660). On John Eliot, I used Cotton Mather, *The Life and Death of the Reverend Mr. John Eliot* (2nd edition, London, 1691); *Tracts Relating to Attempts to Convert the Indians of New England* (Massachusetts Historical Society Collections, Third Series, Vol. IV, Cambridge, Mass., 1834); and Samuel Eliot Morison, "John Eliot, Apostle to the Indians," in *Builders of the Bay Colony,* pp. 289–319. On the Jews in the New World in this era, the works used were Jacob Rader Marcus, *The Colonial American Jew,* cited under Chapter 17; and Morris U. Schappes, editor, *A Documentary History of the Jews in the United States, 1654–1875* (New York, 1950; 1971). The most useful books on New Netherland were John Fiske, *The Dutch and Quaker Colonies in America* (2 vols., Boston, 1903); Edgar J. McManus, *A History of Negro Slavery in New York* (Syracuse, 1966); and J. Franklin Jameson, editor, *Narratives of New Netherland, 1609–1664* (*ON*, 1909; 1967).

REFERENCES: Montezinos's narrative, the "Relación de Aharon Levi, alias, Antonio de Montezinos," is the preface to Manasseh ben Israel, *Esperanza de Israel,* pp. 1–13. Cotton Mather's remarks are on pp. 75–76 of his *John Eliot.* Winslow's remarks are on pp. 72–74 of his pamphlet, "The Glorious Progress of the Gospel Amongst the Indians in New England," reprinted in *Tracts,* Massachusetts Historical Society; "J. D.'s" expectation appears on p. 93 of the same book. Manasseh's own *Esperanza* tells us of "a white people, with beards," on p. 40, "a white people, tall in stature," on pp. 34–35, and the Fleming who died, on p. 41. The outraged letter by the Dominie Megapolensis is reprinted in *Narratives of New Netherland,* pp. 392–393. The West India Company's permission for the Jews to remain in New Netherland is reprinted in Schappes, *Documentary History,* p. 5.

Index

Jacome of Majorca) 29 (*see also* Cresques, Jafuda [Yehuda])

Málaga, 85, 86, 297, 298

Malay Peninsula, 8

Mali, kingdom of, 6, 57, 64

Malleus Maleficarum ("Hammer of Witches"), 105, 106

Malocello, Lancelote, 35

Manamoyack, 314, 315

Manasseh ben Israel (rabbi), 365–371, 375; his *The Conciliator,* 366; *Hope of Israel,* 369

Mandeville, Sir John: his *Travels,* 166, (quoted) 167

"man from the sea." *See* Esdras (apocryphal prophet)

Manichaeism, 107, 123, 127

manifest destiny: Spanish, 125, 127, 146, 148, 188, 229, 327; English, 229–230, 285, 327

Manteo (Roanoke Indian), 232, 233, 236, 238–239

Manuel, emperor of Byzantium, 40

Manuel I, king of Portugal, 113–114, 115

map-making, 76; Majorcan school of, 3–4, 9, 29, (and Catalan Atlas) 4–16; monarchy as motif in, 4–7, 14; Ptolemaic concept of, 8–9, 97, (latitude and longitude) 8; and portolan charts, 8–9; introduction of compass and, 8; religious symbolism in, 9–16; and location of terrestrial paradise, *see* Eden; and Mediterranean as center of the world, 10–11; and Ebstorf map, 10–11; Portuguese, 29; and Spanish world map (1544), 201; by John White, of Roanoke country, 235; Hakluyt and, 252 (*see also* Hakluyt, Richard [the younger]); John Smith and, 300n. *See also* Catalan Atlas; Cresques, Jafuda (Yehuda); geography

Map of Virginia, A ('Smith), 281, 282, 283, 284

Marco Polo. *See* Polo, Marco

Marcos (of Nice), Fray, 245; quoted, 173, 174, 175–176, 177

Marina, Doña, 146, 149n, 263, 296

Maritime Provinces. *See* Norumbega

Marlowe, Christopher: quoted, 241–243, 244, 245; his *Tamburlaine the Great,* 242; *The Jew of Malta,* 243, 245; and Marlovian viewpoint, 249, 254, 325

Maroons. *See* cimarrones

Marranos, 66, 70, 71, 370; and "Marranism" among Indians, 163, 182, 187; emigration and Judaizing of, 189–

190, 192, 363–364, 372; Amsterdam community of, 363, 365. *See also* anti-Semitism; Christianity; messianism

marriage, interracial. *See* racism

Marston, John: (co-author) *Eastward Ho,* 252

Martha's Vineyard, 303

Martin, John, 270, 271

Marx, Karl, 15, 160, 161, 163–164

Mary I, queen of England, 219, 227

Maryland, 197, 355–359 (passim), 362, 373

Mason, John, 335; quoted, 336, 337, 338

Massachuset Indians. *See* Indian tribes

Massachusetts: Puritan commonwealth in, 206, 230, 293, 326, 327, 347 (*see also* Plymouth, Massachusetts, and Plymouth colony); General Court, and slavery, 356

Massachusetts Bay colony, 326–328, 329, 330, 341, 346, 347, 367, 368n; and Indian troubles, 330–335, 336, 339, 351; enslaves Indians, 339–340, 354

Massacre of St. Bartholomew. *See* Huguenots, the

Massasoit (Wampanoag chief), 303, 309, 310, 311; and treaty with Plymouth colony, 304–305, 306–308, 312–314; reports plot against Weston's colony, 318–319, 320

Mather, Cotton: quoted, 368

Matthew, St., 42n

Mauretania, "men of," 58n. *See also* Moors, the; Morocco, kingdom of

Maverick, Samuel, 354

Mayan civilization, 144, 146, 184; and destruction of antiquities, 181, 182

"Mayflower Compact," 300

Mecca, 5, 6, 115. *See also* Islam

Mediterranean, the: early commerce on, 3, 9, 76 (*see also* trade); in early map-making and navigation, 7, 8–9, (as "center" of the world) 10–11; English access to, 31; slavery in Christian countries of, 55; ideal of beauty, 56 (*see also* color); and rejection of Mediterranean classicism, 202; and westward expansion, 342. *See also* Middle East; *individual countries*

Megapolensis, Reverend Johannes: quoted, 374

Melville, Herman: his *Benito Cereno,* 175

Mendieta, Gerónimo de, 188

Mendoza, Don Antonio de, 173

Mendoza, Don Diego Hurtado de: quoted, 83

INDEX 441

352, (Hispaniola) 96, 99, 127, 128–
132, 145, 153, (Caribbean) 130,
142–143, 144n, 347, 352, (and
Mexican Conquest) 132, 145, 146–
151, (Chesapeake Bay) 158, (Venezuelan attempt fails) 160–161,
(Florida) 205–206, 229, 231, 238,
(vs. England) 233, 345, 346–347,
352; and manifest destiny, see
manifest destiny; relationship of,
with Indians, see Indians, the; and
search for gold, 128–132, 143, 144,
151, 167–168, 172–175, 177, 200,
341; and slave-raiding, 131, 145,
171 (see also slavery and slave
trade); of Middle Ages, 136, 187n,
(struggle for) 18–19, (as "America,"
"end of the West") 23; and search
for northwest passage, 167–168 (see
also northwest passage); and cultural
conquest, 183, 184n, 185n, 186, 258;
England and, 188, 207, 216, 226,
(war with) 218–220, 238, 239, 266,
267, 268, (and Ireland) 227, 230–
231, (and colonies) 233, 345, 346–
347, 352, (and "Western Design")
352, (and empire) 371; Portugal
unites with, 189, 345, (breaks away
from) 352; and Spanish world map
(1544), 201; and anti-Spanish attitudes, 207, 209, 210, 219–220, 226,
229, 230–231; Netherlands vs., 207n,
293, 345, 351, ("Eighty Years'
War") 365; and the Armada, 209,
239 (see also England and, above);
and sugar trade, 342. See also
Iberian Peninsula
Spenser, Edmund, 229; quoted, 227, 228,
361; his The Faerie Queene, 361
Spinoza, Baruch (or Benedict), 15
Squanto (Indian), 302, 316, 336; kidnapped by British whaler, 297–298,
(returns) 299; as guide, emissary
and interpreter, 303–310, 314; discredited, 308, 311–315, 317
Stadaconé (later Québec), 204, 260, 261
Standish, Miles, 301, 303, 305, 310–314
(passim), 319–320, 328; and
Thomas Morton, 323–324, 325
Stone, John, 329, 330, 331
Strachey, William, 253, 280, 283; his
History of Travel into Virginia Brit-
annia, 281, (quoted) 282, 286
Stuart monarchy. See monarchy
Stuyvesant, Peter, 374
sugar cultivation and trade, 128, 341,
342, 361, 372. See also trade
Summa Theologica (Aquinas), 11

Surinam, 345
Switzerland: pro-Indian sentiments in,
207
symbolism: religious, on early maps, 9–
16; "Christ-killing" and, 26; of
Prester John, 46; Columbus and, 80;
of arrival of "Gaspar da Gama," 117,
118; of Black captives, 118; "New
Christian," 138, 195
Symonds, Reverend William, 283, 286;
quoted, 287
Syria, 45

Tainos, the, 124, 129. See also Hispaniola
Talavera, Fray (later Bishop) Hernando
de, 81, 84, 126
Talmud, the, 66, 68, 185, 366
Tamburlaine the Great (Marlowe), 242
Taprobana/"Trapobana," 7, 108
Tarshish, 15n, 20, 21n
Tartars, the: as "Gog and Magog," 13; as
Lost Tribes of Israel, 14, 40, 44, 370;
as "Samoeds," 222; as ancestors of
American Indians, 269–270
Tartessus, 20, 21n
Tempest, The (Shakespeare), 253–254,
255, 280
Temple(s) of Jerusalem. See Jerusalem
Tendilla, Count of, 82, 126
Tenerife. See Canary Island(s)
Ten Lost Tribes. See Israel, Lost Tribes
of
Tenochtitlán, 146, 147, 150
Teresa of Ávila, St., 76, 191, 195
Texas, 170
Thevet, André: his Singularitéz de la
France antarctique, 206
Thirty Years' War, 367
Thomas, St., 41, 42, 144; and Acts of
Thomas, 42n, (quoted) 107
Thorowgood, Thomas, 367, 368; his Jews
in America . . . , 369
Thorpe, George, 289
"Three Indias." See India
Throckmorton, Elizabeth, 266n
Tigris River, 40, 98
Tilley, John, 333
Timbuktu, 6
Tisquantum. See Squanto (Indian)
Titus (Roman emperor), 147, 155
Titus Andronicus (Shakespeare), 243,
246, 344
tobacco: cultivation of, (in Virginia)
289, 345, 353, 356, 361, (in Carib-
bean) 346. See also trade
Tobias (son of apocryphal prophet), 192
Tokamahamon (Indian interpreter), 308,
309, 310–311, 312